MAHLER AND HIS WORLD

MAHLER

AND HIS WORLD

PART I

CONTEXT AND IDEOLOGIES

Whose Gustav Mahler?

Reception, Interpretation, and History

Leon Botstein

If it is true that Mahler's music is worthless, as I believe to be the case, then the question is what I think he ought to have done with his talent. For quite obviously it took a *set of very rare talents* to produce this bad music. Should he, say, have written his symphonies and then burnt them? Or should he have done violence to himself and not written them? Should he have written them and realized that they were worthless? But how could he have realized that? I can see it, because I can compare his music with what the great composers wrote. But *he* could not, because though perhaps someone to whom such a comparison has occurred may have *misgivings* about the value of his work through seeing, as it were, that his nature is not that of the other great composers,—that still does not mean that he will recognize its worthlessness; because he can always tell himself that though he is certainly *different* from the rest (whom he nevertheless admires), his work has a different kind of value.

—*Ludwig Wittgenstein,* Culture and Value *(1948)*

Mahler and the Twentieth Century

The popularity of the music of Gustav Mahler, on concert stages and in recordings, particularly during the last forty years, has been so commanding and widespread that it itself has become the subject of commentary and scholarship.[1] This Mahler phenomenon is characterized no longer merely by the revival that began in earnest in the mid-1960s, spearheaded in performance by Leonard Bernstein and defended brilliantly by Theodor W. Adorno's remarkable monograph *Mahler: A Musical Physiognomy.*[2] In the 1970s an explosion of serious research and publication occurred whose preeminent protagonists were Donald Mitchell and Henry-Louis de La Grange. Mahler's reputation benefited as well from the wide-ranging reexamination of the art and culture of fin-de-siècle Vienna (and consequently the Viennese contribution to modernism), a trend in the 1970s and early 1980s that coincided with a shift in culture and politics especially in the United States.[3] In retrospect, however, the fascination with Mahler the man and his music after 1960 took on its own trajectory, as the sheer volume and variety of recordings, performances, research, critical attention, and other forms of Mahleriana suggest. In an age when so-called "classical" music is understood as losing its audience, the popular attachment to Mahler, including the burgeoning scholarly industry, is a striking exception.[4]

By the end of the twentieth century Mahler had become the most visible figure from the high-art classical music tradition since Mozart.[5] The massive Mozart celebrations of 1991, the popular play and film *Amadeus*, and the enduring image of Mozart as childhood genius par excellence have resulted in permanent iconic status within popular culture. Mozart's music typifies the quaint, pleasing, unproblematic beauty of an antiquated form of music. At the same time, his legendary skills have sustained the notion that the traditional canon of music is educationally useful as a source of high levels of cognitive achievement in children. Mahler, on the other hand, still commands interest for having written music that sounds as if it possessed a contemporary, direct, and emotionally accessible meaning for today's listeners. The power of the symphonic music's expressive range and sonority, the humanity of the lieder texts and their settings, all remain undiminished, despite their roots in a distant culture. Mahler seems as adequate to the moment and the age (if not, superficially, more so) nearly a century after his death as he was a century after his birth. Mahler not only exerts an overwhelming if not oppressive presence in orchestral concert life, but his music has become the defining example of symphonic music. His music constitutes a paradigm for listening to instrumental music, of the attributes such music might possess, and of the meanings long-form music without words can convey.

No doubt conductors have wanted to program Mahler since Bernstein's success in part because his work is now seen as an essential test of a conductor's capacity as an interpreter and shaper of sound and drama—much the way Beethoven functioned as an obligatory vehicle in the repertoire before 1950. Conductors are drawn to Bruckner for similar reasons. Yet concert promoters and orchestra managers all over Europe and America will testify to the radical difference in audience response. Mahler plays to packed houses; outside of Germany and Austria, halls are far less easily filled when Bruckner is performed.

But the Mahler that has emerged victorious at the end of the twentieth century is not quite the Mahler put forth by Adorno in 1960. The Mahler that outraged his most discerning contemporary critics (Wittgenstein among them) and attracted, during his career, many supporters—particularly younger musicians like Alban Berg and Anton von Webern—has vanished. The aspects of negativity, rebellion, innovation, and resistance Adorno located in Mahler's music are neither heard by the audience nor communicated from the stage.[6]

The rise to popularity and prominence has made it increasingly difficult to disentangle the historical Mahler from the massive overlay of posthumous reception. This itself is a symptom of the role Mahler has come to play not only in musical life, but in the late twentieth century as a facet of cultural iconography. As the primary protagonist with an accessible core of musical works from within the traditions of high culture, the Mahler of the late twentieth century has its closest historical analogue in the role played by Beethoven during the late nineteenth century. Even Adorno's small book can be set side by side with Richard Wagner's seminal 1870 essay "Beethoven," although Wagner's Beethoven had a more lasting effect on the reception of Beethoven than Adorno's has had in the case of Mahler. In terms of scholarship, de La Grange's biography can be compared to Alexander Wheelock Thayer's pathbreaking and precisely chronologically ordered life of Beethoven that was published, after Thayer's death, in partial form from 1866 to 1879. These detailed, devotional, and definitive biographies each appeared more than four decades after their subjects' respective deaths; they exerted a lasting influence on readers in more than one language.[7] Beethoven and Mahler both entered fiction and, ultimately, the movies.[8] The visual images of these composers became emblematic of aesthetic inspiration and genius as contingent on the struggles and self-critical habits of adulthood (in contrast to Mozart, the naïve, inspired, childlike figure). Mahler, as one recent novel and movie suggest, now rivals Beethoven, not only in the repertoire, but as the stuff of pseudohistorical legend and biographical fantasy—perhaps because he was one of the few great composers with a notorious and beautiful wife.[9]

Beethoven's nineteenth-century popularity was intertwined dialectically with divergent responses to late romanticism: its radical expansion under the aegis of Wagner, and an antiromanticism of the sort pioneered by Debussy, whose antipathy to Beethoven was pronounced.[10] At the fin de siècle, Beethoven's work became a battleground in which Mahler, Heinrich Schenker, and Arnold Schoenberg all played particular roles.[11] The post-Debussy anti-Beethoven sensibility became cloaked in an antiromantic aesthetic skepticism and, after Debussy's death, in a novel neoclassicism (particularly through Stravinsky). However, the antiromantic trajectory within Second Viennese School modernism also owed something to Beethoven; a revisionist view of the Beethoven of the late quartets functioned as a legitimating precedent. Even the reactionary and conservative Viennese musical factions from the early decades of the century focused on Beethoven. In their fight against a perceived decline in cultural standards and taste, an obsession with Beethoven persisted, as Schenker's lifelong project to rescue Beethoven from misreading and popular bowdlerization attests.

From the start of his revival in the 1960s, Mahler took on a pivotal, Janus-like function in musical culture, comparable to Beethoven's a century earlier. On the one hand, Mahler continued to be appropriated as a prophet of modernism and model of progressive innovation, as Adorno suggested, albeit with decreasing plausibility. As modernism in music came under attack beginning in the 1970s, however, Mahler became utilized as a precursor and model of the postmodern, a source of inspiration for the restored viability of tonality, narrative, and traditional expressiveness in music. At the beginning of the twenty-first century, Mahler has become entirely emblematic of the emancipation from modernism. His music is understood as evocative of a path in twentieth-century music different from Stravinsky's or Schoenberg's and suggestive of a potential rapprochement between popular and concert music. His popularity led ultimately to the rediscovery of the substantial antimodernist orchestral repertoire composed between 1890 and 1960.[12]

Although Mahler has become the twentieth century's Beethoven, the contrasts are as instructive as the surface similarities. The Beethoven idealized and popularized initially in the mid-nineteenth century by the generation of Liszt and Schumann was a heroic figure. By the fin de siècle and well into the early twentieth century, the incarnation of Beethoven as hero had shifted away from the image of the romantic hero as artist to that of defiant egalitarian revolutionary hero, a trajectory sustained by the increasing popularity of the middle-period works and the revival of his late quartets and last piano sonatas. Beethoven's music, as Paul Bekker's enormously successful 1911 volume on the composer suggested, was deemed one of ideas, accessible to a wide audience and suffused with meaning beyond the strictly musical. It conveyed politics and philosophy. Although he was understood as a forlorn, isolated, temperamental, and romantic idealist, on the eve of World War I Beethoven persisted as a heroic larger-than-life figure, an antibourgeois revolutionary hero: the genius as aesthetic original who helped identify and promulgate conceptions of freedom, resistance to convention, and individuality.[13]

These residues of the heroic ideal lost their allure in the wake of fascism and the carnage of World War II. In the early 1970s, Beethoven was becoming subsumed within the early music revival in terms of performance practice. Interpretive revisionism with and without period instruments distanced him from his romantic legacy. By the start of the Mahler revival, the last great exponents of the late-romantic heroic approach to Beethoven on the concert stage had either died or were on the brink of retirement. However, the failure of the period-instrument movement to dominate the performance of Beethoven reveals how difficult it remains to reinvent Beethoven without invoking residues of nineteenth-century images of the heroic.

In this context Mahler's life and work seemed a perfect foil and alternative. Mahler's role as a symbolic successor of and surrogate for Beethoven possesses its own ironic overtones, given Mahler's obsession with and debt to Beethoven. Nonetheless, after 1960 Mahler was gradually transfigured and elevated into the exemplar of the artist as anti-aristocratic antihero, inclined toward democracy if not socialism. Here was the artist as vulnerable individual, struggling internally with conflict and alienation. Mahler was decidedly not heroic in the manner of Beethoven, in part because his life possessed familiar bourgeois attributes including social position, public office, marriage, and family. Cast into a pattern of life and career with which the audience could identify, Mahler, insofar as he transcended the ordinary, was deemed either martyr, saint, or prophet.

The antiheroic aspect of Mahler's reputation coincides with the impression that his music, even the later symphonies that have no texts or overt programs, possesses meaning beyond music alone. Mahler has succeeded in reducing the distance between composer and listener. Despite the massive scale of the music and its overpowering sonorities, all reminiscent of Beethovenian ambitions, Mahler's music seems nonetheless to communicate the personal and the intimate. His music implies a universal message that is neither dramatic nor didactic in the sense of the Third, Fifth, and Ninth Symphonies of Beethoven. Mahler's music appears to mirror the complexities, layers, and chaos associated with everyday life, rendering, for the larger public, the narrow debate about the role of secret or overt programs in his symphonies a purely scholarly question. Much like mid-twentieth-century popular accounts of Freud's theories, Mahler's music came to reveal in a normative way a temporal geography of the psyche; it offered a metaphor for the process by which the soul is tormented by modernity.[14] Mahler's life, replete with an actual encounter with Freud, a difficult marriage, the loss of a child, career setbacks, and a personal affinity for the way dreams mirror revelatory interactions between fantasy and reality, contributed to the image of the composer as confessional artist and quintessentially sensitive modern individual. He was, after all, in manner, gait, and habits appropriately intense and neurotic. Neither his music nor his personality qualified him for a romantic, larger-than-life, triumphant, or defiant hero status. The legend of Beethoven's death included a final shaking of his fist against the heavens; Mahler's passing was seen as that of a forlorn and isolated invalid.

This image of Mahler as the emblematic artist of modernity (uncannily compatible with the characterizations of aesthetic creativity found in Thomas Mann's prose, from *Buddenbrooks* to *Doktor Faustus*) also coincided with a post–World War II romanticization of the acculturated European Jewish cosmopolitan intellectual and artist. This subset within the pre-1945 European Jewish community (much of it centered in the German-speaking regions of Europe) had been a particular object of fear and derision on the part of the Nazis. Assimilated Jews with prominent roles in culture were highlighted in Nazi propaganda as the most dangerous and pernicious variety. They were seen as having infiltrated Aryan society. They exerted, invisibly, power and a corrupting influence.

As political anti-Semitism became a dominant factor in Central European interwar politics, the assumptions and trajectory mirrored by Mahler's life and career toward the Jewish question came under scrutiny, particularly within the Jewish community. The premodern shtetl Jew of Eastern Europe emerged as the object of idealization, an ironic reversal of the contempt German Jewry had for traditional Eastern European Jews. In lieu of the ideal of the Jew as good European and cosmopolitan world citizen,[15] German-speaking Jewish writers of the 1920s as diverse as Martin Buber, Alfred Döblin, Arnold Zweig, and Joseph Roth held up the traditional *Ostjude*, steeped in religion and proud to stand apart from the Gentile world, as a moral object lesson.[16] The life and career of Franz Kafka (with whom Adorno repeatedly compared Mahler) reveal similar doubts about the viability and stability of modernization and acculturation for European Jewry in the light of modern nationalism, anti-Semitism, and Zionism.[17] This interwar revisionist critique of the assumptions of upwardly mobile Jews in Central Europe after 1867 within the German-speaking Jewish community may have helped retard the appeal of Mahler in the 1920s and 1930s. As the Nazi critics liked to note, Mahler and his supporters seemed all too intent on achieving a place for him in the Germanic musical pantheon.

More significant in the respectful but mild reception of Mahler between 1918 and the mid-1950s was the connection between radical aesthetics and progressive antifascist politics. To many anti-Nazi critics, particularly in Germany, a modernism overtly at odds with Mahler's project—if only in terms of monumentality—seemed vital and necessary.[18] Mahler's life and aesthetic agenda were easily construed as mirroring the qualities of an epigone, a late exemplar of an antiquated neo-Wagnerian Germanic romanticism whose grandiosity and emotionalism sounded dated. Adorno's 1960 analysis was driven precisely by a need to defend Mahler against such views, ones with which Adorno was intimately familiar and which persisted well into the 1950s.

Yet that which may have made Mahler seem backward-looking or regressive during the 1920s and 1930s in the context of the Jewish question and the need to resist mass dictatorship led to nostalgia after 1960, particularly in Europe. With few exceptions, European Jewry had been obliterated in the years between 1933 and 1945. It is no accident that the Mahler revival occurred alongside the explosion of scholarly and popular attention to the Holocaust after the 1961 Eichmann trial. For a new generation of Americans and Europeans, Mahler took on an aspect evocative of a class of subsequent stellar victims unique to modernity: those who perished and those who emigrated. Innocence and injustice were underscored by the greatness of the aesthetic and intellectual contribution of those whom Mahler came to symbolize. His career was celebrated as a struggle against persecution and for acceptance within a resistant conservative and racist cultural milieu.[19] He and his music took on a significance in Europe in the later decades of the twentieth century not dissimilar in substance and dynamics to the elevation of historic Native American figures, artifacts, and spirituality in the United States, a revival that likewise came in the wake of a history in which entire peoples and civilizations were persecuted and nearly exterminated.

Mahler's posthumous status as antiheroic martyr gained momentum from the account of his own struggle as a Jew in European culture and society.[20] This post-1960 image of Mahler as prototypical modern artist became entirely compatible with, if not contingent on, his role as the representative of a laudatory, albeit failed, struggle to overcome prejudice and marginal status. Mahler's image was that of an endangered species, a Jew from the past, the Jew in search of acceptance and assimilation through cultural achievement, the Jew who, despite all obstacles, had actually helped define the dominant culture of the excluding majority.

By the mid-1970s, what was left in the United States of this dynamic between the Jewish artist and the majority culture was the reductive and embarrassing American popular version exploited by Woody Allen. By the 1960s, when the Mahler revival began in earnest, American Jewish acculturation and assimilation into white middle-class society appeared irreversibly and uniquely successful.[21] Thus the nostalgia and compassion for Mahler's plight in the era of Leonard Bernstein were timely. Bernstein was Mahler's most prodigious advocate in the seminal 1960s (and perhaps America's closest parallel to Mahler in terms of success as a composer and conductor, as well as desire for acceptance). For Bernstein, Mahler was a prophet for the twentieth century.[22] Bernstein implicitly set Mahler's ambivalence to his fate as a Jew alongside his own proud assertion of Jewish identity and faith (e.g., the 1963 Third Symphony, "Kaddish"). The story of Mahler's formal conversion in 1897 and his complex engagement with dimensions of Christian theology, audible in the Second and Eighth Symphonies, could be measured against the facile and all-embracing cultural eclecticism of Bernstein's 1971 *Mass*. For Bernstein, Mahler had pioneered a vision of a diaspora for Jews that, after defeat and tragedy, had ultimately found fulfillment in post-1960 America. The main difference was, of course, that being a creative and powerful part of a mainstream culture and society in America was not only truly possible, but it did not require the sacrifice of Jewish identity and traditions.

Not surprisingly, in the scholarly literature after the mid-1960s, Jewish identity and anti-Semitism, which occupied a subsidiary role in Adorno's monograph (particularly its closing sections),[23] came to be regarded increasingly as central to understanding Mahler's work and life. It was within this complex process of coming to terms with the brutal history of mid-century Europe that Mahler's music initially took on its role as a vehicle of nostalgia and personal identification. The historical and biographical sources of Mahler's status as a victim striving for acceptance and deformed by his environment were rendered most visible and ludicrous in *Mahler*, the 1974 film by Ken Russell. The film includes scenes that interpreted Mahler's attachment as a composer to rural life and nature in terms of a how a young "sensitive" Jew internalized the anti-Semite's view of the Jew as incapable of excelling at sports or possessing an authentic connection to the land and to nature.

In the context of successful postwar Jewish assimilation, to a new generation of listeners Mahler's fate as an exceptional and obsessive, nearly manic but tragic isolated figure, as the artist as antihero (for whom success in career or the surface of social acceptance through marriage failed to secure personal happiness) possessed relevance for all, not only for Jews. Mahler's music seemed to mirror generalized patterns of life and their attendant feelings and experiences; he and his work became germane to the ordinary, educated middle-class person. His existential struggle and its aesthetic expression seemed not merely the province of the exceptional individual. Mahler's political plight as a Jew in fin-de-siècle Europe became reformulated. It was dehistoricized and depoliticized into a template for understanding the generic psychological and personal alienation of the modern individual. Mahler's music became the voice of the individual per se as suffering outcast and victim.

Mahler was a "saint," as Schoenberg put it more than once.[24] His psychic pain, fear of death, childhood trauma, memories, and inner turmoil were reflected in his music, for all to grasp and empathetically appropriate. The specific historical details of the composer's travails in childhood, career, and marriage became irrelevant. Despite an increase in popular fascination with Mahler's biography, to the post-1960 audience the music successfully overwhelmed historical specificity without losing its relevance as psychological mirror. An unproblematic identification with his existential plight and an embrace of the music as personally meaningful overwhelmed any sense of historical distance.

The political conditions surrounding Mahler in terms of anti-Semitism and Jewish identity in the mid-1960s encouraged Bernstein's personal identification and an interpretive strategy that veered away from the political and the historical and toward the normative realm of the intimate, psychological, and personal. Mahler's music projected interiority, emotion, and subjectivity, a movement toward personal identification and emotional resignation, not a complex engagement with history and politics. Adorno's brief on behalf of Mahler's music as immanently radical and critical of the social order by virtue of its musical materials and procedures was designed to locate in Mahler a connection to a progressive agenda and a vision of music as a social activity capable of engendering critical resistance. But his argument was framed explicitly by an awareness of how easily the interpretation of Mahler could be dominated by an apolitical aesthetic and "kitsch" psychology. Adorno did not entirely anticipate, however, the extent to which the process of separating the political from the aesthetic would lead, initially through nostalgia and guilt, to the reinvention of Mahler as the consoling, accessible voice of confrontation with the contradictions of life, and a legitimate resultant turn inward.

The divergence from the posthumous influence of Beethoven is stark. As a symphonist Beethoven contributed to the nineteenth century's construct of art, drama, philosophical idealism, and the direct intersection between the aesthetic and political. No doubt his legacy was claimed by advocates of a view of music as above politics, abstract and absolute. But it was also the source for those, particularly Liszt and Wagner, for whom music was narrative, dramatic, and significant for politics. In contrast, in the late twentieth century, outside the Soviet Union, Mahler's symphonies attained widespread acceptance as essentially apolitical transcripts of the soul, intimate accounts of the psychological and the existential, bereft of engagement with the public sphere.[25] The post-1960s Mahler, in the United States, lacked an overt political significance beyond the vaguely philosophical; it never rivaled the political valence achieved by popular music already in the 1950s. Any political overtones were metaphoric and distanced. In the United States, the rise to popularity of Mahler's music, despite its apolitical content, coincided with the civil rights movement, the rise of feminism, and the celebration of the "other." As music that reveals the intimate, Mahler's works spoke to an audience eager not so much to redress the exclusion of divergent voices from the cultural canon, but to identify with the status of the victim. Mahler seemed to speak for everyone by articulating the experience of the unjustly marginalized.

The oft-repeated phrase attributed to Mahler concerning his "homelessness" mirrored the accepted reading of the composer as the quintessential outsider, the artist in modernity who mirrors an angst, loneliness, and nostalgia shared by all.[26] Yet the post-1960 Mahler emerged as an enabler for individuals to come to terms, as passive listeners, with despair, joy, incomplete happiness, and pain. It was precisely the fragments and evocations of what Adorno termed "exhausted" musical conventions, not the modernist aspects of Mahler's music, that were highlighted and reconfigured in performance to generate a consoling aural synthesis, marked by an unproblematic presentation of sensual beauty, monumentality, lyricism, and spectacular effects. These attributes informed Mahler's popularity. Mahler had become not confrontational, but therapeutic.

Efforts to invest Mahler with political significance, if not content, particularly in post-1968 West Germany, based in part on Adorno's interpretive stance, failed as counterattacks against the success of the psychologized reading of Mahler's music as ideal, spiritual, and subjective.[27] Mahler's depoliticized popularity gained, ironically, through the imposition of the generically biographical on the musical form, even that of the Seventh and Ninth Symphonies.[28] All the symphonies could be heard as chapters of an ongoing autobiography. This construct of Mahler's music as autobiography was achieved at the expense of the location of any articulated politics within Mahler's musical aesthetic, particularly of innovation and negation. Whatever political meaning remained had been refracted. Even Mahler's non-text-based music could be understood as a relevant mirror of the personal existential struggle characteristic of the atomic age and the Cold War. The ordinary individual could feel as powerless, as consumed by fear and doubt and as excluded from a significant role in politics, as Mahler undoubtedly was in fin-de-siècle Vienna. This identification with a constructed world of interior despair was one to which the ordinary listener had access. The massive exterior sonorities and wide if not harsh sound palette of Mahler's oeuvre came to communicate quite commonplace private sensibilities (the sufferings and travails of intimacy) and, above all, the capacity to adjust by retreating into privacy within a dehumanizing modernity.

Mahler's music functions in this manner because of one overriding quality that Adorno himself highlighted: the absence of a persistent and overwhelming self-referential and traditional formalism.[29] Listeners allergic to stylized romantic constructs of heroism can locate in Mahler's sprawling, episodic, multilayered textures a sense of duration, space, and collage that seems to approximate, realistically, the experience of life. In Mahler one could find many loci of affinity that parallel and ennoble one's quotidian experiences of loss, remembrance, fear, hope, joy, and mortality. The aspiration to the heroic within the listening public associated with Beethoven and the theatrical delusions of grandiosity of Wagner have given way. The vacuum left by the demise of modernism after 1975 has been filled by a widespread egalitarian discovery of Mahler. He provides a democratically accessible expanse of sound experience, eventually filled, over years of repetition, with pop-psychological echoes, facile profundities, affirmations, and consolations: a mirror of experience that offers reassurance concerning one's normalcy in situations of distress, rage, and anxiety—one's capacity for emotion.

By 2000 few traces were left of the edge of negativity and resistance, of opposition, breakthrough, and musical innovation so elegantly argued by Adorno.[30] Particularly since the end of the Cold War, the rage for Mahler has become so unproblematic and broad that even in contemporary scholarship an uncritical, hagiographical tone of awe and adulation predominates, reminiscent of a consumer mania. The residues of the thoughtful anti-Mahlerian criticism of pre-1933 Europe have been either suppressed or dismissed as philistine. Serious traditions of skepticism and doubt articulated by Mahler's contemporaries (for example, Wittgenstein's 1948 musings) have been swept away, in part because they possess a bad odor owing to some presumed guilt by association with pre-1933 anti-Semitism and the Nazi attack on Mahler's music. The sanctification and canonization of Mahler since the end of World War II have assumed characteristics compatible with the ideology of reparations. His music and reputation have benefited from a form of cultural *Wiedergutmachung*, particularly in Germany, vis-à-vis the historical role of Jews in pre-1933 German-speaking cultural and musical life. Neither Mendelssohn nor Meyerbeer, whose reputations were irreparably damaged by a mix of Wagnerian and post-Wagnerian aesthetic and anti-Semitic criticism, could be revived after 1945 sufficiently to serve as public expiation for the racism of Nazi and European cultural politics.[31] But Mahler could be.

From Politics to Therapy

The legitimacy of these characterizations of the post-1960 Mahler reception is underscored by two notable readings of Mahler by distinguished commentators outside of the field of music. The eminent philosopher Martha Nussbaum, in a major treatise on the philosophy of emotion, published in 2001, writes (after a close reading of the Second Symphony that follows an earlier analysis of *Kindertotenlieder*):

> Mahler achieves, then, a triumphant fusion of the Christian ascent with the Romantic emphasis on striving and imagination. He does this in the context of a Jewish emphasis on this-worldly justice and the this-worldly body. . . . This work, while claiming to solve the problem of our own all-too-human self-repudiation, is itself filled with disgust and repudiation: at everyday life, at its shortcomings and half-heartedness, at the very existence of fixed social forms. Acceptance of all humanity is achieved musically, but at a considerable distance from real human beings, who continue to be condemned from the viewpoint of authentic creativity. We wonder what this visionary perspective has to say about real people with their real and everyday shortcomings. . . . Nonetheless . . . we are left with a remarkable claim, the claim that love, while remaining human and embodied, can overcome hatred, exclusion, and resentment. Brontë expressed pessimism about the victory of love over hate. . . . Mahler, at least here, is an optimist. He does not exactly propose a therapeutic solution to Brontë's problem. He just expresses the thought that one may simply overcome primitive shame and stand forth in one's own being, without disgust, without envy. . . . [F]ollowing the movements of this music is a way of accepting love.[32]

Nussbaum is no ordinary listener. Aided by the advice of the brilliant theorist Edward T. Cone, she offers a careful description of the sequence of musical events. But she ably demonstrates the ease and facility with which Mahler's music is understood and invested by contemporary listeners with extramusical significance. Mahler is helpful as a guide to the subjective process of reflection about life. Beyond Mahler's power as offering a vehicle of self-awareness, the ideology she suggests is, if not affirmative, certainly sentimental. It offers an emotional coming to terms with the problematic and the contradictory in the human condition overtly described in and communicated by the music. The impact is not the least bit unsettling, but rather is reassuring.

Her mode of appropriation of Mahler had one highly visible American precedent: Lewis Thomas, the distinguished medical researcher and public intellectual. In the 1980s, during the last phase of the Cold War, Thomas echoed the use of Mahler as a confessional mirror of internalized feelings and the widespread perception of his music as concretizing personal psychological states of mind. Thomas expressed his relationship to the Mahler Ninth Symphony this way:

> I cannot listen to Mahler's Ninth Symphony with anything like the old melancholy mixed with the high pleasure I used to take from this music. There was a time, not long ago, when what I heard, especially in the final movement, was an open acknowledgment of death and at the same time a quiet celebration of the tranquillity connected to the process. . . . Now . . . I cannot listen to the last movement of the Mahler Ninth without the door-smashing intrusion of a huge new thought: death everywhere, the dying of everything, the end of humanity. . . . The thought that keeps grinding its way into my mind, making the Mahler into a hideous noise close to killing me, is what it would be like to be young. . . . There is a short passage near the very end of the Mahler. . . . I used to hear this as a wonderful few seconds of encouragement: we'll be back, we're still here, keep going, keep going. . . . I cannot hear the same Mahler. Now, those cellos sound in my mind like the opening of all the hatches and the instant before ignition.[33]

Thomas's conclusion, in terms of emotion, was the reverse of Nussbaum's, a fact that the geopolitical contrasts between early 2001 and the late 1970s help explain. Yet Thomas revealed that he, despite the resultant pessimism, reacted along lines Nussbaum later would, in 2001. The very same music permitted an interpretation of contradictory responses to death. Mahler's music had come to be shorn of particular

referents. The erasure of memory among listeners caused by discontinuities in history and the shifting manner in which musical traditions
were transmitted from one generation to the next permitted Mahler to
function as a powerful normative expressive medium devoid of stable
meaning. The music was heard through the imposition of an interpretation relevant to a subjective narrator; a narrative's aptness for
the music derived only from a sense of gravity, depth, adequacy, and
severity in the experience and feeling generated by Mahler. As for
Nussbaum, Mahler's music in Thomas's case seemed uniquely to present a flexible, adaptable medium of normative emotional expression,
identification, and self-recognition.

What, if anything, in the music of Mahler has lent itself so successfully to this kind of response, one that signifies shifting concrete
metaphors of the anxieties associated with negotiating life? How is it
that this composer's music satisfies, without embarrassment or restraint,
the need of the contemporary listener to recognize through empathy
in a musical narrative a confirmation of the universality of individual
human agency? Listeners regularly find deep and divergent spiritual
meanings, overarching claims beyond the musical, detailed specific
metaphors, a morality tale and unrestrained sentimentality, even in the
Fifth Symphony.

The assumption that Mahler's music is profound, universal, and
adequate to the inner experience of life, if not the confrontation with
love and death in the everyday—that his music is some sort of mirror
of life—would not have surprised some of his most loyal friends and
followers. After all, Mahler himself confessed to Sibelius in 1907 that
he sought to write symphonies that were "like the world . . . all embracing."[34] But the music's wide acceptance as such was never anticipated;
it is an example of the cunning of history. No doubt the success of
Mahler's music as a text for the eclectic reading or derivation of complex personal meanings owes something to late twentieth-century
expectations about musical interpretation and sound. Mahler's sound
world has the surface characteristics of movie soundtracks. It shares a
familiar veneer and superficial rhetoric that prevent the music from
sounding archaic. Furthermore, in an age when reading and writing
are construed as finding and uncovering webs of entanglements and
locating processes of transference well beyond literal meanings and
authorial intentions, Mahler's musical texts, through heterophony,
extreme contrasts, and episodic surface structure, offer an open-ended
and nearly inexhaustible source.[35] They are perhaps uniquely accessible
to the lay listener, in part because Mahler resisted defining the listener's
access to the application or perception of meaning as the recognition

of formal markers within a dominant self-referential, self-contained compositional technique of musical transformation.[36]

These attributes protected Mahler from the collapse after 1970 of a particular species of modernist musical aesthetics focused on the autonomy of musical materials, and the parallel disappearance of older forms of musical literacy within the public. These developments assisted Mahler's emergence as a central figure in the late twentieth century. Luchino Visconti's 1971 success in adapting the Adagietto from the Mahler Fifth for a film version of Mann's *Death in Venice* could not as easily have been accomplished using Strauss's *Metamorphosen*, for precisely the reason Adorno used to disparage Strauss and set him apart from Mahler: Strauss's rigorous adherence to traditional strategies of composition and counterpoint. Strauss in his later years assumed expertise and musical culture on the part of listeners, in the sense that he hoped they would hear within the music the references to and commentary on a musical past as well as the ironic habit of self-quotation.[37] The *Metamorphosen* resist the facile transfer of extramusical significance by the listener, whereas Mahler's music seems to invite it.

Furthermore, as Hermann Danuser and Kurt Blaukopf have suggested, the proliferation of high-fidelity recorded accounts on long-playing vinyl records and CDs has been particularly advantageous to Mahler's posthumous career. High-fidelity Mahler offers the lone listener a vast-sounding narrative in a private, domestic space that can be replayed, selected, interrupted, and repeated at will, the way a book can be read, reread, selected from, jumped around in, and skimmed. Emancipated from the need to share the experience in a public space, the individual can control the encounter with a massive, episodic, discursive expanse of sound, filled with clearly delineated and recognizable elements. The need for musical memory or informed recognition in terms of compositional precedents and traditions is supplanted. An intimate, private narrative experience, analogous to reading prose (complete with the potential of open-ended selection, restarting, and repetition) is made widely possible.[38] Private listening facilitates a form of absorption we associate with reading, at the expense of the sense of acoustic space, scale, and depth created in a live performance—the circumstance for which the music was written.

Leaving aside whether recordings or current live performances approximate the intentionality of the composer or adequately transmit some construct of what Mahler's music "is," the reality of and sources behind Mahler's late twentieth-century popularity have triggered a thoroughgoing reconsideration of the character of twentieth-century music. This shift in the relative historical significance of early twentieth-century composers, for both musicians and the public, comes at the expense of an earlier account (prevalent between 1920 and 1960) that privileged an overtly abstract and recalcitrant modernism, particularly that of Webern and Schoenberg, that is not susceptible to "easy listening" (as Adorno understood it). As early as 1969 Hans Werner Henze remarked, "I think that the most significant composer of this century was not Webern, but Mahler." Although Mahler did little to "free music from its grammatical difficulties," Mahler, for Henze, made music in a way that made him "a witness of his era." He possessed a truth factor; he was a composer who "represented frustration and suffering in an unambiguous and direct musical language." Mahler was "unaristocratic," whereas the members of the Second Viennese School placed "much value on the aristocratic element in their artistic endeavors."[39] In 1975 Henze underscored what Nussbaum later found in Mahler: a democratic, nearly populist, accessibility and a clear didactic aspect. Henze noted the music's "realism," its truth telling, its tragic universality, its mourning for that which has been lost, its pleas on behalf of the future of the human race, particularly hope and love.[40] So, too, did Nussbaum and Thomas. Henze became one of the first late twentieth-century witnesses to Mahler as a vehicle of nostalgia.

Insofar as there was a period at midcentury when the trajectory of twentieth-century music was centered on Schoenberg, it was not Mahler, but Brahms and the procedures of developing variation—a neoclassical argument on behalf of the self-referential coherence and sufficiency of musical language and logic—that defined modernism.[41] In turn modernism sought to continue to innovate in terms of what Henze called "the grammatical difficulties."[42] Schoenberg's ambivalence toward the musical procedures of Mahler, and the suspicion that the sonorities, the diatonicism, and the rhetoric were perhaps dated, were shared by those who, after 1911, looked to Debussy, Bartók, and Stravinsky as guides to the future of music. Schoenberg's praise of Mahler, even as early as 1904, rested more on the kind of reading of the music's moral and philosophical meanings later echoed by Nussbaum than on its technical innovations.[43] Writing to Mahler after a rehearsal of the Third Symphony, Schoenberg said, "I believe I responded truly to your symphony. I felt a struggle with illusions; I felt the pain of the disillusioned; I saw good and evil forces surrounding one another; I saw the individual human caught in anguished motion searching for inner harmony; I felt a human being, a drama, *truth*, uncompromising truth!"[44]

The irony lurking within the Mahler who has emerged victorious over the last forty years of persistent performance and recording is the fact that his music suggests, precisely as an integral dimension of its materiality, what otherwise might be construed as extramusical meaning. By 1960, as Adorno realized, Stravinsky's cold neoclassical virtuosity no longer possessed the sort of authentic, antiromantic radical construct of meaning as exclusively embedded in musical procedures. Mahler's music met the audience's need for the seemingly extramusical to be returned to music's substance and its sounding presence. The extramusical now came to be seen as inseparable from the definition of musical space and time.[45] Bernstein's Mahler advocacy tended toward the maudlin, but in the 1960s it coincided with his increasing resentment at the rise of radical modernism and his return to blatant sentimentality in his own music.[46] As Mahler's significance grew, that of both Stravinsky and Schoenberg—the central figures in Adorno's 1949 analysis of new music, *The Philosophy of Modern Music*—began to recede. This might have been predicted. After all, Bruno Walter, Bernstein's predecessor as the leading Mahler advocate, was well-known as a skeptic regarding post-tonal modernism. Following the midcentury, Mahler advocacy and the rise of conservative musical tastes went hand in hand; a perception of a need to free music from "grammatical difficulties" was replaced by an embrace of Mahler as a model in the use of premodernist musical means and time. Adorno's 1960 essay on Mahler was a defensive effort to secure Mahler for the future of modernism. He worked assiduously to disassociate him from Bruckner, in terms of compositional technique and procedure, and to interpret his music as a radical break with late romantic traditions. In Adorno's eyes Mahler emerges as an indispensable precursor of Berg, a composer who integrated an expressive but critical meaning with resistant innovative musical procedures based on the perception that indeed, music in the twentieth century was faced with a need to transfigure if not transcend inherited practice.[47]

In what now seems a wishful but thinly argued effort at optimism, in 1972 Carl Dahlhaus predicted that the Mahler revival might help bridge the gulf between the public and the avant-garde, thereby redeeming the possibilities and prospects of musical modernism.[48] However, the apex of Mahler's significance to the public and to contemporary music composition at the end of the twentieth century has coincided with the revisionism of that century's history and the collapse of the importance of modernism, the revival of neoromanticism, and the resurgence of minimalism and tonality in new music. Ironically, it has been Strauss—Mahler's closest rival and the bête noire of Adorno's defense of Mahler, the composer whom Adorno derided as the "model music student as genius"—who has emerged as a defining figure for twentieth-century music.[49] Twentieth-century modernism is being redefined in a manner that renders Strauss central, even innovative, in terms of modernism itself;[50] he is no longer the anachronistic figure whose moment in history passed in 1911, with *Der Rosenkavalier*. His music after 1912, much of it focused on explorations of marriage and love quite in contrast to the theatrical dramatic scale of *Elektra* and *Salome,* has found new advocates.[51]

The post-1975 historical revisionism that has catapulted Mahler to the center has appointed not Schoenberg or Berg, but Shostakovich, as the dominant successor to Mahler in terms of concert life. He is now considered the most important heir to the Mahlerian tradition. Shostakovich's music has moved from the place it occupied on the periphery between 1945 and 1965. The view of Mahler that survived Stalinist scrutiny during the 1930s and permitted Shostakovich to use him openly as model and inspiration deserves attention. Ironically, the construct of Mahler articulated by Ivan Sollertinsky was one that characterized the composer as a radical critic of bourgeois civilization. His music was a "protest" against impressionistic aestheticism, aristocratic individualism, degraded late romanticism. Mahler democratized musical speech. As the "last great symphonist" in the tradition of Beethoven, Mahler used the residues of the heroic style against itself, demonstrating the "impossibility" of a genuine symphonic expression within capitalism. The "bourgeois" symphony of the West died; but in that process "the clearest, greatest and most unhappy protagonist of the Beethovenian tradition" demonstrated dialectically the terms of a new aesthetic. Mahler's music expressed the alienation of capitalist society ("the scream into the void"), the sufferings of a transitional generation, and thereby pointed the way in an "artistic-ideological" manner to a new symphonic model that was adequate to socialist society.[52] Sollertinsky was right to predict Mahler's success, although the analysis and explanation did not actually reflect the reasons or the cultural content behind Mahler's emergence as a dominant figure in the history of music. Shostakovich, like Mahler, has been the object of revisionism and reversal. Shostakovich is now heard as critical of socialist Soviet society, much as Adorno and Sollertinsky wished Mahler to be heard as critical of the culture of late capitalism.

The persistent and radical fluidity in the response listeners have regarding the truth content of Mahler's works (even those with texts and the early symphonies with programs)—their possession not of a specific program in the sense of Berlioz, Liszt, or Strauss's tone poems, but of some narrative less artificial and more open-ended and adequate to external reality and our subjective sensibilities—partially vindicates Adorno's highlighting of Mahler's achievement as central to modernity. What has vanished from Adorno's apology for Mahler as a revolutionary and a critic of modernity is the perception of criticism and resistance. Adorno, in part owing to his proximity to the authorial moment and the historical context of Mahler's life and the attendant contemporary aesthetic debate, focused on Mahler's radical qualities and defiance of the conventions and compositional procedures associated with late romanticism. Mahler created a novel musical dialectic of negative critique at odds with the affirmative social rituals of post-Wagnerian musical culture and early twentieth-century neoclassicism. Inauthenticity, oppression, alienation, and false consciousness were unmasked, particularly by the unique use of sound, time, and space in the Ninth Symphony and *Das Lied von der Erde*.[53]

Yet the Mahler to which audiences and performers have become attached has, primarily through performance traditions, regressed into a species of neoromanticism. Mahler, as Nussbaum's reading attests, has been praised as the carrier of a metaphysics of emotionalism, bereft of the edge, harshness, and unsettling meaning Adorno believed was integral to the truth content of the music. The sound of today's performances has diminished the heterophony, the discontinuities, the brutalities, the angularity, and the long arc of negation and critique. A homogenized lush sound is favored, as are the obvious elements of affirmation, triumph, spectacle, and drama—the rhetoric and gesture of the grandiose. Mahler's ties to Schoenberg and modernism have been severed, as has his immanent critique of conventional culture and civilization. The teeth, so to speak, have been extracted, leaving a body of work favored for its richness of sound; its lyrical, albeit sad, accessibility; and its stirring monumentality.

We now face a post-twentieth-century Mahler wrapped, metaphorically speaking, in layers of appropriation that demand a skeptical unmasking. That process requires the posthumous assistance of Mahler's fiercest critics during his lifetime and before World War II. With their help, one might be able to explain the divergence between the readings of Adorno and those of Bernstein, Thomas, and Nussbaum. Why is it that Mahler fails to engender even faint echoes of resistance, as does, for example, the music of Charles Ives, with whom Mahler has been justly compared?[54] Adorno, writing in 1960, began his book with a direct reference to the Nazi critique of Mahler and the prior history of anti-Mahler criticism. Much of his monograph reads as a reply to a tradition of doubt about the qualities and character of Mahler's music and his aesthetic ambitions. Adorno sought to separate Mahler from the fin-de-siècle, late-romantic German tradition of lied and orchestral music, particularly Strauss. Adorno inverted the very shortcomings attributed to Mahler by his pre-1933 critics (augmented by Nazified criticism) into visionary breakthroughs central to the future of an authentic music of modernity.[55] In the wake of postmodernism and the attendant restoration of Mahler not as incipient modernist, but as fin-de-siècle protagonist and therefore a backward-looking figure suggestive of nostalgia, a sympathetic reconsideration of the pre-World War II critique of Mahler's music is timely.

As Adorno observed, Mahler's achievement can be compared to that of prose and the novel. He referenced Flaubert, Dostoyevsky, and Kafka.[56] Today's listeners, nurtured in their affection for Mahler by recordings, have chosen to listen to Mahler as if they were reading. They have been able to impose on the music their subjectivity, their intimate psychic dialogue, and to appropriate the music as providing a vantage point by which to read the external world and construct personal meaning. Mahler as author has ceded his intentionality to his readers in a way unanticipated by Adorno. The task then is to recover or reconstruct the historical Mahler. The way around the past forty years can begin with a serious reappraisal of witnesses for whom Mahler's music failed. The tendency in contemporary scholarship has been to dismiss Mahler's contemporary critics as biased, philistine, or crude. But one needs to overcome one's disgust of overt prejudice, particularly that articulated after 1933. In the denial of Mahler's greatness, even by the Nazis, clues to aspects of the music's character and power, now buried, can be found.[57]

Critical Skepticism as Insight: Mahler's Enemies Revisited

Despite the commonplace impression left by the controversy surrounding Mahler's resignation from the Court Opera in Vienna in 1907 and his move to New York, Mahler was neither neglected nor unsuccessful as a composer during his lifetime.[58] The notion that he was unfairly treated, misunderstood, and victimized is a historical distortion not dissimilar in its sources and currency from the familiar pseudo-historical assertions that shaped posthumous nineteenth-century legends about the lives and careers of Mozart and Schubert. The lingering impression that Mahler composed without sufficient acclaim and support is attributable to the triumph of Nazism and its destruction of European Jewry.[59] Mahler's music was performed and praised, even in Vienna before 1911, and was regarded seriously despite the doubts shared by established critics (e.g., Robert Hirschfeld) whose aesthetic prejudices Mahler offended. There were certainly anti-Semites who, following Wagner's construct of a Jewish incapacity for creativity, disparaged Mahler as a composer for no other reason than his Jewishness. Yet in his mature years Mahler experienced far more triumph than defeat and more enthusiasm than rejection by audiences. In comparison to Schoenberg or Stravinsky, or to Bruckner in an earlier era, Mahler experienced critical success in his lifetime. A case in point is the premiere of the Eighth Symphony in Munich in 1910, which was hailed as a major European cultural event.

That said, from the beginning of Mahler's career a sustained, nontrivial critique of his music existed. As Adorno himself astutely recognized, informed hostility can reveal more acutely than deferential praise the character and virtues of the music.[60] Mahler once quipped, at the end of his tenure at the Vienna Opera, "It's a funny thing . . . but it seems to me that the anti-Semitic papers are the only ones who still have any respect for me."[61] Consider, for example, the judgments of Otto Schumann, one of the leading guides to concert music, who wrote in the late 1930s, well into the Nazi era. After dispensing with the obligatory racist preamble, Schumann concedes the enormous influence Mahler exerted. Mahler created a *musikalisches Weltgefühl* (musical sensibility of the world), a description not too far from Mahler's own legendary and oft-quoted self-assessment, as reported by Natalie Bauer-Lechner.[62] Schumann distinguished between the impressive sensation that Mahler's sound world made and Schumann's normative ideal of a true musical *Erlebnis* (experience). Conceding that Mahler's ambition was a musical representation of the "truth," Schumann focused on the notion that Mahler was conveying the truth of a disturbed individual within a corrupt, conflict-ridden, fragmented world. Mahler indeed succeeded in mirroring modernity, construed by Schumann as reflective of social disintegration. Mahler did so, according to Schumann, with a "penetrating eye and an acute ear"; Mahler bore witness to the dissolution of European culture. Mahler revealed the "bursting superficiality of the world as barely any other musician had."

The difficulty, according to Schumann, was that his success was neither ironic nor intentional. As a rootless Jew, excluded from an organic relationship with an authentic national culture, Mahler was unable to penetrate to a deeper coherence in the world, a coherence that modernism had succeeded in suppressing.[63] Schumann's reading of Mahler is negative, however, only in terms of the ideology Schumann supports; given Schumann's premise that a coherent, healthy organic culture actually existed or could be nurtured, Mahler was found lacking. But if one replaces Schumann's politics with Adorno's, Schumann's analysis and description of Mahler hold up and assume a different valence.

Schumann concedes that Mahler's command of instrumentation was unparalleled. He prefigures Adorno's view that in Mahler, instrumentation was integral to musical thought and not a matter of decoration or ornamentation. The modernist prejudice shared by Berg (perhaps derived from Adolf Loos) that color and sonority were distinct and subordinate to musical ideas, and perhaps even deleterious distractions, was not applied by Schumann or Adorno to Mahler.[64] The view that Mahler was a pioneer in the use of color and sonority as fundamental elements of composition reflects a tradition in Mahler criticism dating back as far as Max Graf, who made this point eloquently around 1900.[65] Furthermore, Schumann acknowledges a dimension characteristic of the positive reaction to Mahler, the notion that he wrote "music as experience," as Graf put it. Mahler's music, with its appropriation of marches, folk songs, and hymns, is for Schumann a mirror of suffering and the expression of "intense desire."[66]

The shortcomings cited by Schumann in Mahler's music are predictable: the failure to generate convincing original thematic material and the inability to command large-scale symphonic form. Nonetheless, Mahler emerges as a figure not unlike the one celebrated by Henze as representing the "tragic *Weltgefühl*" of his era.[67] In Schumann's view, Mahler sought to promote philosophical reflection, but actually communicated disintegration. What is striking about Schumann's assessment is that his account of the music is uncannily in accord with Adorno's. The difference, of course, is that for Adorno the evident engagement with recognizable traditional formal procedures was a sign of a deep critical intuition and an innovative and more profound formal concept. The absence, for the listener, of obvious and unproblematic thematic subject matter in the sense of Bruckner becomes for Adorno a compositional breakthrough. Adorno's notion of resistance, negativity, and intensity in the music—its mirroring of contradiction—is, however, acknowledged by Schumann. The divergence rests not in the account or description of the music, but in the ideological evaluation. There was for Schumann an underlying authentic community, a *Volk*, susceptible to affirmation through music. Not so for Adorno. Rather, Mahler exposed the contradictions and hypocrisy of late nineteenth-century bourgeois culture precisely in the terms heard and described by Schumann.

Karl Blessinger was the most notorious and oft-cited Nazi-era critic for whom the ideology of anti-Semitism was pivotal. Although Blessinger's analysis is far more extensive than Schumann's and suffused with reductive claims about Jews and the social pathology of their effort to assimilate into German culture, he, too, hears, in the sense of Adorno's reading, qualities in Mahler that are susceptible to inversion. Blessinger recognizes the uniqueness of Mahler's attraction to the *Wunderhorn* texts as musical material; to most German composers, in Blessinger's view, the collection was hardly musical. This point—Mahler's special sense of the musical possibilities of those texts—was made as well by Adorno.

As a thought experiment, one might foreground positively the role of the Jew as the outsider, possessed by a "deep spiritual rootlessness" (as Blessinger termed it). As a witness, then, he would be adequate to mirror the process of exclusion in art. He would be emblematic of the dilemmas of modernity (thereby following, albeit perversely, the example of Karl Marx's 1844 essay "On the Jewish Question," in which the Jew becomes the exemplar of capitalism)[68] in a constructive sense. The assimilated Jew in European culture projects as prototypical the dehumanizing alienation of high capitalism and its social rituals and norms. By following this experiment, one discovers that Blessinger, like Adorno, understands Mahler well.[69] Mahler is explicitly unwilling to succumb to facile affirmation in compositional strategies; even in the Eighth Symphony his moments of triumph and closure ring hollow. Blessinger's critique of Mahler's approach to monumentality mirrors Adorno's defense of the Eighth. Adorno, despite his misgivings about the work, highlighted Mahler's problematizing of the notion of an affirmative finale in symphonic form, as Mahler did more powerfully in both the Fifth and Sixth Symphonies.[70] Ultimately for Adorno, apart from the Ninth and *Das Lied*, the Sixth and Seventh Symphonies (except for the last movement) best represented Mahler's modernism and critical engagement with tradition.

Blessinger's conclusion is a mirror image of Adorno's analysis. Mahler represents for both observers the harbinger of a modernist critique. In Blessinger, Mahler becomes the proponent of a progressive innovation that explodes the self-satisfied and formal self-containment of musical traditions. The radical and revolutionary in Mahler are acknowledged, but placed in opposition to an affirmative ideal of cultural community and aesthetic health. Mahler's heterophony is singled out by Blessinger and Adorno. His appropriation of folk and popular music, gestures from operetta, and inclusion of the exotic and the orientalist is not only acknowledged, but, as in Adorno, elevated in Blessinger's account as a hallmark of Mahler's originality. Blessinger understands the extent of Mahler's careful distortion of and commentary on the ideal of folk authenticity and the exotic. Blessinger realizes the extent to which Mahler prefigured the dissolution of tonality and experimented with tonal ambiguity. It is not in the description itself, but in the ideological evaluation, that Blessinger diverges. The "long gaze" that Adorno finds in late Mahler becomes in Blessinger the "never before realized extent of uninterrupted highest concentration of expression."[71]

The key point is that Blessinger, like Schumann, heard Mahler in a manner that bizarrely anticipates Adorno. The threat that Mahler represented was, ironically (in terms of the traditions of anti-Semitic criticism), not one of mediocrity or insufficiency, the sort so seemingly easily attributed to Mendelssohn and Meyerbeer.[72] For Blessinger the danger of Mahler's music did not derive from its superficiality, but rather from the evident appeal and plausibility of its claim to novelty. Nor did Blessinger view Mahler's fame and reputation as primarily a manipulation of the philistine and corrupt Jewish press. Mahler threatened the very basis of the Nazi aesthetic project of an antimodern renewal and the effort to construct an antimodern regressive cultural synthesis.

The leading Nazi-era critics were more than mere racists. They were not oblivious to the unique character and impact of Mahler's work. They may have responded to him more pointedly and profoundly than have his postmodern, late twentieth-century advocates. Adorno would have been gratified to read Blessinger's view that it was "almost impossible for the listener to find on his own a path to a work of art music."[73] It is precisely the reified, closed, aestheticized notion of the musical artwork favored by fascist ideology that Mahler deconstructed and exploded in his forays into symphonic form. Blessinger's attack represents a substantive vindication of Adorno's interpretation.

The point of divergence between the reception of Mahler by Nazi-era critics and by Adorno rests precisely in opposing objectives regarding the social and political function of the public making of music. The normative obligation of the composer vis-à-vis how listeners can and might respond to music is construed quite similarly, but the ideals diverge. Blessinger and Schumann sought the formation of a spiritual community through music-making of a sort that required comprehensibility and solidarity, including the propagation of new music susceptible to amateur performance.[74] Adorno recognized in Mahler the power of instrumental music to advance through its own material the cause of resistance to oppression, of freedom and justice; Mahler realized this power by foregrounding radical discontinuities, aborted expectations, and formal innovations. Art music could help alert the conscience and critical consciousness of the public to reach for a better world, one that might emerge from the negation of a corrupt consensus sustained by superficial cultural constructs of aesthetic standards and traditions. Adorno highlighted the fact that Mahler avoided or abandoned both excessive chromaticism and the kind of counterpoint at which Max

Reger and Strauss excelled.[75] The abandonment in Mahler of such evident, traditional signs of compositional virtuosity and a predictable sequence of musical events created for Adorno a novel ongoing exploration of musical space and time, all within an overarching diatonic framework. Yet Adorno, in the case of Mahler, applied an ideal that Blessinger shared: constant clarity and comprehensibility from the vantage point of the listener.[76] Blessinger in this sense heard Mahler's project accurately.

In the Mahlerian sound world there is a persistent and unrelenting transparency, despite the many layers of disparate-sounding events. A terrifying and unrelenting surface and the transparent and alluring sequence of events are what made his music so dangerous for the Nazis. Schoenberg was far less threatening because the surface of his modernist experiments was complex and off-putting.[77] Mahler's music was the aesthetic analogue of the assimilated Jew: the danger was successfully camouflaged, cloaked in a cultural language quite familiar to the unsuspecting audience and therefore pernicious and subtle. The music sounded almost affirmatively German, if only at first. Yet, as it moved from point to point, both the expert and the lay listener would fail to find in it a satisfying homage to the formal traditional expectations associated with sonata form and symphonic structure and, therefore, the attendant extramusical implications. For Adorno the lack of such confirmation was one of Mahler's virtues. Mahler fashioned works of purely musical materiality that carried within their structure critical cultural arguments about the way art confirmed ideology, without descending to the conventions of program music. The episodic long arch of the Mahler Ninth Symphony becomes an ironic commentary on formal closure and, therefore, on the culture beyond music that seeks it and is easily satisfied with it. Blessinger hears these distinctions but construes them differently. Yet the discomfort created by the evident gap between form and content that he derides is audible and real. What Adorno saw as intentional was dismissed disingenuously by the Nazis, who used a rhetoric of insufficiency and lack of capacity.

Richard Strauss, Mahler's antipode for both Adorno and the Nazis, commanded all the power and techniques of instrumental musical composition from within the historically inherited rituals of so-called art music. His consummate skill included the habits of classicism and those of Wagnerian and post-Wagnerian practice. His music did not seek to break the tacit, affirmative, accumulated consensus between composer and listener. Strauss appeared not to seek truth through negation. He avoided sparking critical resistance beyond a surface level of shock located in the novel orchestral effects he actually enjoyed exploiting before 1912.[78] In contrast, in the eyes of his critics Mahler distanced himself from the conservative narrative trajectory of post-Wagnerian romanticism. Particularly after 1900, he deviated from the contemporary engagement with realist program music best exemplified by the Straussian tone poems. Yet he also seemed to evoke, in an idiosyncratic manner, the classical symphonic form. In contrast, critics understood the skill with which Strauss integrated sonata procedures with literary narrative frameworks.

For Adorno, Strauss's synthesis of traditions of compositional procedure permitted the musical work of art to remain contained. As a part of culture, it was subtly delineated by craftsmanship. It was not threatening for the audience. The musical work of art failed to penetrate beyond the boundaries of innocence and entertainment associated with the aesthetic. Even when Strauss, in direct response to Mahler (and indeed in response to Mahler's death) sought to embody a Nietzschean critique of Christianity within a symphony about nature (which contains direct allusions to Mahler), the result was aestheticized into a balanced, worked-out, self-contained formal exercise.[79] In contrast, the realist narratives embedded in symphonic form in Mahler's first three symphonies, when they contained direct references to nature, were, as his Nazi-era critics recognized, unstable and complex; they suggested fragmentation and rebellion. In contrast to Strauss's *Alpine Symphony*, doubt, instability, and critique could be located in the evocation of nature and resurrection in the Second and Third Symphonies.

Clearly, the unique source of Mahler's music lay in his status as the excluded "other." Therefore Nazi-era critics implicitly conceded Mahler's capacity to expose the collusion between constructs of musical aesthetics, ideologies of tradition, and the political agenda of fascism, replete with its desire for cultural and political hegemony. Mahler, for Adorno, had the capacity to realize a "romanticism of disillusionment" as his "mediations of folk elements from a distance" revealed. This capacity in turn depended on the fundamentally alienated status so derided by the Nazis. Mahler redeemed music as a language of truth (in this Adorno followed Schoenberg) by revealing the extent to which the world was broken. As a "foreigner" Mahler exposes the "euphemism of foreignness," by which Adorno means the attempts by Jews to come to stable affirmative terms through assimilation and nationalism (i.e., Zionism), with which the "outsider seeks to appease the shadow of terror." Mahler's "homecoming" could only be into an "alien" world, which is why he was able to open up expressive potentials beyond the bounds of formalist traditions.[80] Schoenberg would retreat from a Mahlerian trajectory in his own music by inventing a system of musical grammar superficially remote from and resistant to conventional associations with nonmusical meanings and narratives.

Mahler's contemporary defenders (including the eminent scholar and writer Hermann Kretzschmar), not his critics, resisted the notion of Mahler's radicalism, as defined, retrospectively, by Schoenberg's rejection of tonality in the 1920s. As the Nazis knew, the distinguished non-Jewish defenders of Mahler struggled to downplay Mahler's critique of tradition and his challenge to the listener. Mahler's advocates before 1911 defended him as comprehensible in conventional terms, either as a formalist or as a composer of program music. Kretzschmar praised Mahler's "high and noble ideas," the extraordinary complexity of the materials and the unique sound world he generated. But Kretzschmar argued that Mahler in the Second Symphony only seemed more difficult than he really was. The appearance of difficulty was merely superficial. Mahler's music was actually quite easy to grasp, and with it, therefore, its signature: irony and the juxtaposition of "superlative humor" and "seriousness."[81] Mahler's expressive power and range was within the expected.

It was against the grain of this effort to praise Mahler as a great, distinctive, and nonthreatening exponent of German music, and to render his irony palatable, that both Nazi critics and Adorno rebelled. Precisely because Mahler's radical innovativeness and his critique of a superficial construct of compositional norms (and their attendant political and cultural implications) were minimized in a Kretzschmar-like reading (a fact that his Nazi critics realized), he was feared sufficiently to merit closely argued derision. The Nazi critics knew that Mahler had a significant following and could be linked with Bruckner and placed alongside Strauss and other neo-Wagnerians of his generation. It was against this categorization that both Adorno and the Nazi-era critics argued.

In this sense the Nazi critics and Adorno followed the pattern of reception succinctly expressed as early as 1909 by Max Burckhardt, who, unlike Kretzschmar, could not defend Mahler from within the tradition. "A totally unique phenomenon," Burckhardt wrote in a guidebook that was thinner than Kretzschmar's but equally popular, "in some instances a writer of program music, who then rejects that description, but with whose unprecedented works without a program one finds oneself entirely helpless, in that one's purely musical sensibilities are not always entirely satisfied."[82] From the perspective of Adorno, Mahler, as characterized by Burckhardt, was properly understood. The complacent construct of fin-de-siècle musical culture, described in terms of "pure musical sensibility"—inherited patterns of hearing and ascribing meaning to the listening of symphonic music, and their connections to reflection and the experience of life—was precisely what Mahler sought to challenge. Mahler's overt references to rural life and nature within the symphonic context, particularly that of the Sixth and Seventh Symphonies, reveal what for Adorno is Mahler's ironic reversal of conventional expectations of beauty and completeness. Using fragmentation, interruption, and extremes of orchestration, Mahler highlighted the corruption or "exhaustion" of constructs of musical beauty and form. He reconfigured the listener's self-reflection, not only on music as "pure"—absolute and pleasing in some deracinated sense—but, by extension, on the perception of the world.[83]

Burckhardt, Blessinger, and Schumann got the point, so to speak, when, as contemporaries or near-contemporaries, they expressed doubts about either Mahler's grasp of the connection between musical convention and nature or his sense of form and beauty. This becomes apparent in their references to Mahler's "banality" and his appropriation of fragments from the acoustic environment. In the postwar interpretive revisionism, the Nazi construct of the weakness of the Jewish composer as cut off from the genuine sources of aesthetic inspiration, became, ironically, a virtue. The consequences were the precise opposite of what Nazis wished to claim. Mahler's nonbelonging, his rootlessness, provided him with the critical distance to fashion a revolutionary reordering of the relationship between art and life, through a deconstruction of compositional traditions, sonorities, and narrative realism in music, in a manner that was more adequate to modernity, true and suggestive of the possibilities of cultural renewal.[84]

The notion that Mahler might be best understood through the lens of his most dedicated critics can be tested in a far less ideologically repugnant context.[85] Within the Viennese critical community before 1911, Robert Hirschfeld (born in 1858) assumed the mantle of the most determined enemy of Mahler. An eloquent and relentless critic of Mahler as a composer, opera director, and conductor, Hirschfeld, like Mahler, was a Jew who was a newcomer to Vienna (Hirschfeld came from Moravia). He rose rapidly in the cultural world of Vienna as an acculturated and sophisticated participant, not only as a music critic, but as a theater critic, editor, writer, and teacher. One can no doubt apply crude analytic approaches to his views and behavior as a Jew—his father was a rabbi, but he himself was eager for assimilation—that suggest self-hatred and other psychological attributes (e.g., envy of Mahler derived from too close an intra-ethnic identification). But the fact remains that Hirschfeld was deeply admired by a strikingly diverse and distinguished group of individuals, ranging from Karl Kraus to Max von Morold.[86]

Hirschfeld was not a rigid conservative; he was one of the earliest defenders of Frank Wedekind. He earned Kraus's respect by his relentless exposure of the pretense of modernism among writers in the Young Vienna circle and the extent to which style, personality, and fashion masqueraded in fin-de-siècle Vienna, in the name of modernism, as surrogates for originality and art. Hirschfeld shared with Kraus a conviction that the aesthetic and the ethical were intertwined. Although far less original than Kraus, his views tended in the direction of the radical conservatism shared by Kraus and Loos. These Viennese radical conservatives attacked the Secession, Hofmannsthal, Schnitzler, Bahr, and many of the aesthetic innovations of fin-de-siècle Vienna, including Mahler's music, opera productions, and conducting and the cult of personality surrounding him. Ludwig Wittgenstein's dismissal of the worth of Mahler's music, nearly forty years after the composer's death, can be understood in this context. For him, as for Hirschfeld, Mahler's music lacked the integrity and discipline of aesthetic greatness, despite the not inconsiderable talent and ambition of the composer.[87]

The connection between Kraus and Hirschfeld is significant for the case of Mahler. Adorno explicitly lamented that Kraus said so little in defense of Mahler. Kraus, whose status as a seer and whose influence on Schoenberg and Berg and their contemporaries was significant, should have been an outspoken defender, given Adorno's view of Mahler. Adorno's explanation of Kraus's silence was his admittedly weak interest in music per se.[88] But the explanation does not suffice. Kraus was skeptical of Mahler and the circle around him. His praise was limited to Mahler's role as an interpreter. He was critical of Mahler as the director of the Court Opera and, like his friend Loos, not quite enthusiastic about the Mahler-Roller collaborations. When in 1909 Paul Stauber published his pamphlet *Das wahre Erbe Mahlers*—a defense of Mahler's tenure at the Opera, subtitled *Dokumente zum Fall Hirschfeld*—Kraus did not join in the chorus of outrage against the critic. For years after Hirschfeld's untimely death in 1914, Kraus continued to remember him in the pages of *Die Fackel* with respect and affection.[89]

The depth of Hirschfeld's negative reaction stemmed from his own project with respect to the function of the aesthetic. Insofar as Jewish identity can be brought to bear as illuminating Mahler's music, it is plausible to view critical assumptions and compositional innovations as stemming partly from the inevitable sorting-out of the dynamics between cultural traditions and assimilation and acceptance in the Viennese milieu between the mid-1870s and the First World War. Mahler and Hirschfeld represent two related but antithetical responses to this sorting-out. Hirschfeld, like Kraus, fought to rescue the aesthetic from its adherents and defenders within the elaborate cultural infrastructure of Vienna. The culprits included the performing institutions, the journalists, and commercial enterprises within music, art, and literature. The debasement of taste, the collapse of the standards of high art in the face of fashion-mongering, the abuse of culture for social advancement, the loss of normative values that transcended time (the unique elevated province of the aesthetic), needed to be stopped. Hirschfeld was committed to reinvigorating the stability of aesthetic norms and the legitimacy of the notion of classicism against the fragmenting and corrupt pressures of modernity. He wished aesthetic taste to be democratized properly and not reduced to mere style. Early on in Mahler's career in Vienna, in 1899, he complained that as a conductor Mahler was too obsessed with "feelings of the moment . . . change in color and shadows," thereby subordinating the underlying logic of musical form.[90] Hirschfeld was a fanatical admirer of Bruckner. In Bruckner's music the innovative, in the sense of post-Wagnerian musical language, had been integrated properly into music. Bruckner highlighted not only a formalism, but a spiritual aesthetic that was at once accessible and affirmative of nobility and above all ethical attributes. Bruckner reconciled originiality with respect for the history of music and culture.[91]

Bruckner's art was seen as a universal discourse, comprehensible, novel, and impervious to passing fashion and trends. Protecting that discourse from appropriation by those who would seek to break its claims to universalism (e.g., nationalists), permanence (modernists), or accessibility (snobs) became Hirschfeld's life's work. The utility of this conception of high culture, particularly music, as a field for participation that secured the integration of the outsider within Viennese society—the notion that musical culture was, owing to its claims to autonomy and abstraction, a unique vehicle of acculturation for Jews in particular—was never explicitly articulated. But that function was legitimated by Hirschfeld's and Kraus's notion that art possessed not only universal aesthetic attributes, but truth and ethical validity. The defense of aesthetic norms and classical ideals was no superficial expression of tradition. For Hirschfeld and Kraus, the virulence of their critical language mirrored the depth of their attachment to the possibilities of aesthetics and language to realize a world in which truth and justice triumphed over a closed oppressive social order dominated by corruption, disregard, complacency, venality, prejudice, and violence. These aspirations defined whether Hirschfeld and Kraus identified artists as enemies or allies. The symptoms of inadequacy and inauthenticity rested not in the overt claims of a work of art, but in the uses of the languages of art.

They agreed therefore in the case of Wedekind, whose theater and language were radical and honest. Wedekind challenged the smug fashions of theatrical naturalism and an aestheticized symbolism. Likewise, Hirschfeld praised Max Klinger's famous 1902 Beethoven statue as a rare event in modern art, a sign of how a sense of form and of technique permitted the artist to integrate the true details of Beethoven's historical personage with originality and fantasy. Klinger communicated, through art, not platitudes, vacuous idealism, or unbridled subjectivity, but truth. In Klinger's hands "a beautiful, elegant split second" could be experienced that broke the bounds of space and time, as in a "realized dream." The polar opposite to Klinger, in Hirschfeld's view, was the work of Gustav Klimt, the exemplar of the undisciplined, arbitrary display of personality and decorative style at the expense of any deeper connection to truth or human insight that ultimately constituted the province of art.[92]

For Hirschfeld, Mahler's faults as a composer and conductor derived from a diagnosis that Mahler had developed his considerable talents into a caricature of precisely what was wrong with contemporary cultural life. Mahler was seen as the quintessential artist of the modern moment, concerned with his own passing emotions and his self-image as a personality. Mahler exaggerated the modern habit of asserting one's individuality arbitrarily, thereby undercutting the stability of cultural norms and a continuing stable discourse with the public, whose access to culture and civilization needed to be expanded. Just at the moment when high-cultural traditions could be democratized, in terms not only of ethnicity but of social class, a fashionable set of self-appointed modernists, intent on asserting their own subjectivity and surface originality at the expense of valid norms, undercut the use of culture as an instrument of social stability, if not of reform.[93]

Hirschfeld also had little use for Richard Strauss, whose penchant for reducing the autonomy and abstract character of musical discourse into parodies of program music and mock illustrations with brilliant effects revealed a cynical attitude toward his own facility and virtuosity. The cultural philosophy espoused by Hirschfeld during the first decades of the twentieth century approximated, ironically, that of the aging Strauss.[94] In the music after 1945, Strauss openly asserted his allegiance to the traditions and norms of high culture exclusively through closed, if not austere, self-referential instrumental musical textures bereft of the benefit of variety in color or literary program.

Hirschfeld owed a debt to the aesthetic philosophy of Friedrich von Schiller. His objective was to resist the ethical disintegration and fragmentation evident not only in modernity, but in aesthetic modernism. Music's role in this struggle was unique, owing to its nondescriptive and non-naturalistic character. Its dependence on formal traditions and an artificial grammar were its virtues. Mahler's music was therefore little more than a sequence of self-indulgent sound effects, bereft of form. Writing in 1907, Hirschfeld declared Mahler's Second Symphony a "farewell" to art. "The art of the symphony is gradually taking leave of music," he wrote. "Since the time when music achieved its independence, the pinnacle of architectural completion in a piece of music has been understood to be synonymous with a high standard of motivic use. This is itself no longer separable from the concept of music. One therefore is forced to strike centuries-old or older, unforgettable masterpieces from history. An expansion in length and breadth, however, in the sense of laying out the canvas of a musical work and sprinkling the surface, albeit with the most endearing, delightful colors, is not based in the nature of music. Rather, these are much more essential and helpful means designed to camouflage the inadequate inspiration and formal capacity through decorative elements." For Hirschfeld, not only Mahler but Debussy as well were "distancing" themselves "from musical principles" through the use of sound effects in defiance of the inherent autonomy of the musical subject (which justified a norm of thematic completeness and coherence) and form.[95] His analysis ran parallel to a familiar modernist prejudice articulated in Loos's distinction between ornament and structure, Schenker's notion of musical logic, and, ironically, Schoenberg's dichotomy of style and idea.

No doubt Hirschfeld's animus toward Mahler was deepened by the extent to which Mahler was lionized in Vienna and connected to the fashionable literary and artistic circles for which Hirschfeld and Kraus had contempt. The irony in the Hirschfeld critique is that he shared with Mahler the sense of the historical moment as one of crisis. Both sought to rescue the aesthetic as an instrument of progress and truth. Both sought to challenge the nature of the transaction of meaning created by the act of listening. Both sought to reconfigure the notion of tradition and rescue the valid practices of musical culture from their presumed defenders. Mahler's reforms in the Court Opera and his rejection of the inherited performance conventions associated with Hans Richter (e.g., cuts in Wagner) had their parallel in Hirschfeld's critique of standards in the Society of the Friends of Music, Richard von Perger's musicianship, Hanslick's views on music history, and the leadership of the Burgtheater.

Despite the virulence of Hirschfeld's attacks, he correctly characterized the radicalism of Mahler's project, the extent to which Mahler had distanced himself from Bruckner and Wagner and rethought the symphonic form and musical communication. Hirschfeld's view of Mahler suggests the evident affinity between his radical conservatism and the views of Heinrich Schenker, whose respect for Mahler was extremely limited.[96] What distinguished Hirschfeld from Schenker was not only the former's capacity to admire both Brahms and Bruckner, but also his wider and more optimistic confidence in the need and possibility of new music, theater, and art. Consequently, from the perspective of the view that Mahler innovated—in the sense that he intentionally used traditions against themselves and invested what Adorno termed "exhausted" practices with new meaning by audible strategies of appropriation, including distortion, interruption, combination, surprise, exaggeration, and fragmentation—Hirschfeld, as a contemporary listener, responded to Mahler with more clarity of understanding (including his sense of rage) than did many of Mahler's fawning admirers. In one sense Hirschfeld spoke for a conservative fin-de-siècle Viennese audience with complacent habits of listening and philistine attachments to tradition that realized that its tastes and capacities for judgment were being assaulted by Mahler's music. At the same time, Hirschfeld was as critical of reigning fashions as was Mahler. The fundamental difference rested in their aesthetic and political strategies. Hirschfeld idealized tradition and hoped for its renewal in modernity. Mahler sought to transcend tradition through a mode of critical exposure and innovation in which tradition was used against itself.

Listening as Reading: Mahler and the Late Nineteenth-Century Novel

The clarity and transparency that Mahler succeeded in creating amid complexity and variety, particularly in his large-scale works after the Fourth Symphony, as witnessed by Kretzschmar and other contemporary critics, remain hallmarks of his music. These attributes were keys to the powerful reaction the music elicited and to its ease of appropriation. As Adorno observed, density never obscured the capacity of the listener to follow the course of events at first hearing. In Mahler's use of counterpoint, orchestration, and multiplicity of events, surface comprehensibility was not sacrificed. The grammatical references to form were present, even if thwarted. No extent of thematic alteration obscured recognition. Repetition and restatement were utilized against a tonal backdrop that made following the elapse of time and responding to the spatiality of the music overtly unproblematic. Even when forms were aborted, expected symmetries distorted, or, in the late work, episodes elongated, the distinction between Mahler and the subsequent generation of modernists remained clear. It was Mahler who utilized largeness of scale to generate a detailed canvas providing multiple recognizable points of entry and connection to the music. This included the implication of a narrative structure even when there was no program. While Strauss appealed (if only on the surface) to the mythical average listener through his brilliant surfaces, illustrative gestures, and memorable colors, Strauss's conversation as a composer was also with his fellow musicians. On this level a non-Mahlerian covert sense of irony emerges, as Strauss offers variations of formal precedents, clever subtleties, private jokes, tricks, and veiled references to the history of music.

Mahler's conversation remained exclusively with the larger public. He sought no dialogue dependent on expertise. Rather, the intended hearer represented the widest range of listeners. He explicitly avoided a transaction of meaning confined to an elite or the musically initiated. The ideal of a Verein für musikalische Privataufführungen (Society for Private Musical Performances) would have been alien to him. As his relationship to sympathetic critics indicated, Mahler did not share Schoenberg's aversion to journalists. The multilayered design and intent of Mahler's music was a response to the composer's intention to write music for the broad public. Therefore he crafted works on a grand scale that burst the assumptions bred by musical education and challenged the accumulation of cultural recognition as either a necessary or sufficient basis for response. The effect of many of his most remarkable moments of originality, as in the outer movements of the Sixth Symphony or the Scherzo of the Seventh, was certainly enhanced by an audience's awareness of precedent and the composer's manipulation of expectancies created by form. But Mahler did not depend entirely on the kind of listener one encounters in Adorno himself. The elements of surprise, engagement, attraction, and astonishment remained audible to a wide public precisely because Mahler wrote music to generate a response beyond the terms of the self-referential autopoetic dynamics of music history.

The range of responses that Mahler sought and encountered in his contemporary audiences—from enthusiasm to bewilderment and rejection—and the ease with which listeners assigned disparate meanings to the music from the start, as they became absorbed and found resonances within it, suggest the utility of a strategy of interpretation that links Mahler to reading prose and the nineteenth-century novel. The novel was emblematic of an art form unique to the existence of a wide reading public in modernity. Danuser pursued this line of thought, deriving his starting point with Schlegel and the early nineteenth-century novel.[97] Adorno, in contrast, makes several passing references to Kafka and one intriguing mention of *Madame Bovary*.

The appeal that Mahler has sustained may actually be explained by the extent to which his construction of musical time is defined by and adaptable to the habits of the late nineteenth-century reading public. Not only is a comparison of Mahler as composer to the role of the novelist apt, but so too is the comparison between the novelist's relationship to the reader and Mahler's relationship to the listener. The way Mahler's symphonies were structured, even in the cases of the First and Third Symphonies, can imply the model of the novel.

Mahler's symphonies, as opposed to the orchestral songs, can be construed as placing the listener not only in the role of reader, but also in the role of a protagonist within the work, who, as in some notable examples of late nineteenth-century prose realism, is forced out of a passive, dependent posture as reader/observer. The listener in Mahler's case, like the reader of a third-person realist narrative, has the sense of direct confrontation with a musical mirror of the chaos and ambiguities of the external world and subjectivity, and seems to circumvent the mediation of a narrator. Therefore, he or she must actively impose meaning and use memory, observation and recognition—crucial elements in the encounter with advanced techniques of prose realism—to complete the work. The listener is asked not so much to succumb to the evident artificiality and intentionality of the composer's technique and invention, but to engage a more aggressively realistic and less one-dimensional construct of events. The listener as reader is drawn into the fabric of musical time and forced to generate meaning and a narrative response. The listener approximates the role of the composer, since the multivalent realist illusion Mahler generates succeeds in suppressing the awareness of a dominant narrator or a protagonist. The listener thereby creates his or her own novelistic frame over the course of the music's duration. The reality—or, as he put it, the "world"—Mahler presents in his works, without any hint of program beyond the implication of the autobiographical (Symphonies nos. 5, 6, 7, and 9), suggests an inherent instability of meaning quite different from that suggested by a formalist view of music as abstract and autonomous. The ambiguity created is in fact a mark of the sophistication and power of Mahler's success in using musical means and symphonic structure to generate a convincing but complex verisimilitude of real time and space.[98]

In order to probe the idea of Mahler as a novelist whose use of musical materials does not approximate a mere story line or plot, it is necessary to explain how the music permits the listener to realize that there are layers of meaning and perception in the world that can be rendered coherent in ways that may in fact have nothing to do with any authorial intention. Adorno's contention that Berg's 1925 Chamber Concerto bears some relationship to Mahler may be more telling than he realized.[99] We know that in addition to a musical structure based on variation form and rhythmic interrelationships (including a palindrome), there are also a host of extramusical connotations of a biographical and narrative sort. Unlike the programs of Strauss's *Death and Transfiguration* or the *Symphonia domestica*, these are nonessential, not predictive, and not contingent on the musical form, and not entirely discoverable from within the music itself. Berg's assignment of meaning is nevertheless real. It was, as in Mahler, essential to the generation of the work. The realist and narrative intent is not a superimposition. The dedicatees of each variation, the evocation of Mathilde Schoenberg's death, the quotes and spellings of names, and the presentation of "friendship, love and the world" are actual dimensions of realism, but their particulars are not imposed on the listener, as, for example, is the plot of *Till Eulenspiegel*. The musical structure in the experience of listening suggests the presence of narratives, descriptions, evocations, and stories about life and the world that need not parallel Berg's intent, in the way Strauss's music at a minimum calls for some sort of story line comparable to *Till*.[100] The music, however, invites the listener to generate his or her own equivalents. So, too, in Mahler, even though a particular narrative seems more present, especially in the first three symphonies. Yet a program never functions like a plot or sounds necessary or discoverable. At the same time, all the symphonies seem replete with meaning about life and the world that from the perspective of the listener, in response to the formal musical procedures, requires a novelistic extrapolation.

Mahler's novelistic strategy can be best explored by using three examples from the late nineteenth-century novelistic canon to show how the listener is placed in the position of the reader of a novel. If Mahler's intent was to communicate beyond the range of well-educated cultural taste in music (much the way Debussy felt oppressed by the learned expectations of the cultured audiences of Paris), he did so by making symphonic music accessible to an audience accustomed to reading complex narratives in literature. The prose narratives with which Mahler associated himself were, apart from the works of Dostoyevsky (whom he read), those of the generation of novelists who rendered the early nineteenth-century strategy of realism problematic.

The first example comes from the indisputable master of complex realism, Flaubert. The most Mahlerian moment in *Madame Bovary* (first published in serial form in 1856) is the scene in part two that describes the agricultural fair. The novelist not only describes a scene depicting external reality in this remarkable section. Flaubert achieves a heterophony, including several clocks of time. There are two basic events, the fair that proceeds as an external framework and the encounter between Emma and Rodolphe. The reader, without confusion, encounters always discernible but disconnected narratives inside and outside contiguous spaces. Flaubert achieves a nearly symphonic simultaneity that was possible after the acceptance of earlier conventions of narrative realism. The reader's attention is arrested, interrupted, and the vantage point of the reader is thrown back and forth, from that of an observer of objective reality to that of a confidant of the differentiated subjectivity of the characters. The reader not only observes the interaction of the two characters, but perceives each individual's divergent construct of the course of events. The reader must ultimately reflect on the uncertainty of meaning that the jumble of detail and the fragments of perception located in discontinuity generate. The reader is forced to forge a sense of connection between the competing subjectivities and events. Flaubert demonstrates a technical virtuosity that adds multiple dimensions of space and time to the routine techniques of the realist novel and alters the experience of the reader by forcing her or him to grapple with the ambiguities and uncertainties. The reader must generate hypotheses of meaning, as if what was encountered in reading had been real in the sense of its confusing juxtapositions.

Flaubert's achievement as a novelist offers the reader not only the illusion of descriptive realism through narration, but the opportunity to see the external world through the eyes of Emma Bovary. The reader experiences space and time through subjective consciousness in a manner that highlights not the notion of reality, but the significance of the perspective from which it is viewed. The interpretation of the world becomes unstable, as fragments of external reality, like dishes and minor objects of detail, assume meaning only as a result of a "deliberate confusion between the subjective and the objective."[101] While the reader retains some independence, the allure of Emma's consciousness is such that the recognizable elements of the world we experience in the everyday change their meaning.

Georges Poulet has identified the notion of a circularity in Flaubert's representation of reality.[102] That, itself, can be understood as parallel to the framework of a Mahler symphony. Using simultaneity, a Mahler symphony turns on itself, yet never loses the connection to the world outside the artifice of a performed piece of music. Whether it is the post horn, offstage trumpets, fragments of a waltz, folk tunes, cowbells, or snow bells, the tension between subjectivity and objectivity is never reconciled. The listener is left in the uncomfortable position of having to assign meaning in the absence of a circumscribed narrative that purports to represent a closed, realistic story line. Many disparate yet seemingly valid and relevant interpretations can be constructed as readily by listeners to Mahler as by readers of Flaubert.

The second example comes from a novelist whom, one can surmise, Mahler himself read: Theodor Fontane. The relationship of Fontane to Brahms has been explored.[103] This master of German realism (profoundly underrated for most of the twentieth century) has been compared to the great German realist painter Adolph Menzel.[104] The view of Fontane as a conservative realist is unwarranted, as his great novel *Der Stechlin* (1897) makes most evident. The strategies upon which that novel is dependent were already present in his most famous work, *Effi Briest* (the German successor to *Madame Bovary*), published in 1895. Two scenes merit attention. One is the scene in chapter 13 in which Effi looks at a funeral procession through a window. In the process, she not only observes alongside the reader, but drifts away from the reader as external reality triggers an entirely divergent process of self-reflection.[105] The second passage, in chapter 22, again presents Effi as a perceiver of reality.[106] Here Fontane generates not a Flaubert-like multiplicity, but forces the reader to follow the process of fragmentary memory and recollection on the part of the protagonist. The improbable connections, as well as shifts in meaning triggered in a single moment by the encounter with the trivial details of external reality, become the defining material of Fontane's realist technique. The reader is forced not only to remember alongside Effi, but also to reflect on his or her own memory of having read the novel up to that point. The artificiality of the reader's position as witness to reality, of having the illusion of observing another person's life, is upended by Fontane as the reader is forced to confront his or her own act of reading and its inadequacies. The reader's encounter with Effi's conclusions creates surprise and detours from anticipated outcomes.

The reader, like a listener to a Mahler symphony, is invited to juxtapose three conflicting parallel dynamics of perception, memory, and reflection. First is the individual reader/listener's own subjective response to recognizable elements that the composer or novelist places before him or her. The associations that are generated challenge, particularly in their fragmentary use, the author's authority or the composer's command over the listening experience. Mahler's habit of borrowing materials from everyday life or inventing themes and mottoes that possess the aspect of ordinariness or familiarity is intentional. These fragments function like the details in Effi's perception. Their meaning is detached from their origins and becomes open to counterintuitive resolutions. Second, the reader confronts his or her own need to empathetically follow the development of the leading character. This is much like the need to understand what the composer wishes to communicate. But the musical surface, as in Fontane's prose, complicates the effort to follow the path of motives and themes and their development. This second dynamic is deepened by Fontane and by Mahler in a third way. They each challenge the reader/listener's assumptions about reading/listening by distracting, surprising, and defying within the work's construct of time the reader/listener's own capacity to remember, follow, and anticipate.

The last and most speculative suggestive novelistic parallel can be found in Henry James's *The Ambassadors*. First published in 1903, it reveals James's singular mastery at illuminating and destabilizing internal psychological processes by the way references from objective external reality are framed. Although it is unlikely that Mahler ever read James, the comparison is justified not only by the contemporaneity of the two artists, but also by James's place in the evolution of the modern novel. His work bridges the generation of realists, including Flaubert and Fontane, and the work of modernists such as Joyce and Musil. This parallels Mahler's place between the late nineteenth-century symphonic tradition of Brahms and Bruckner and the modernism of Webern. James's particular skill rests in the use of time as perceived by the reader and as the instrument by which interiority is delineated. James slows time down, as if to generate the real-time experience of subjectivity. He then varies the elapse of time as an instrument of narration and description. In contrasting temporal frames, the perception of detail changes, and, with it, the interaction of the subjective with the objective. This offers a suggestive parallel to Mahler's control of duration. Both artists force the reader—or, in Mahler's case, the listener who acts as reader—to relinquish the expectation of a stable pace of narration. This occurs in the Ninth Symphony and in the last movement of *Das Lied von der Erde*. James's and Mahler's strategies lend their late works of prose and music a sense of extension and duration that heightens the contrasts in scale between memory and experience in the present.

Mahler's references to natural sounds or passing events (funeral processions, marches, herds) function differently within his symphonic structures, as a result of the way time is controlled as a descriptive instrument and not as mere background. This can be heard when the Third Symphony is contrasted to the Seventh. James lends plausibility to the idea that Mahler's innovativeness and strategy as a composer had the effect of forcing listeners to respond as if they were readers grappling with a distortion of the temporal expectations of a narrative. In literature those expectations derived from inherited techniques of prose realism of the sort pioneered by Balzac. The example of James supports the idea of Mahler as writing novelistic prose in a manner that pierced an earlier tradition of musical realism. It is in James that the expectations placed on the reader, in terms of the interaction of time observed, time elapsed, and time experienced in reading, can be understood as most comparable to the parallel demands Mahler's music places on the listener.

Mahler intensified the realist illusion, pioneered by Wagner. Mahler's discontinuities within shifting uses of time underscore the function of the listener as creator of coherence. In Mahler there is more than one defining temporal logic. Yet the listener, like the reader, is helpless unless he or she actively pieces together meaning from simultaneous events that move at different rates. The author as controlling intermediary appears to vanish. Reality in Mahler's Seventh Symphony, like reality in James's *Ambassadors*, can then be understood in terms of the multiplicity of temporal processes of comprehension and interpretation asked of the reader/listener. The real is no longer found in the text as a single frame, described as if it were just there, or as multiple fragments rendered whole. This helps explain Mahler's wide appeal to listeners without the capacities to follow or identify technically the composer's engagement with practices and strategies that refer directly to traditions of instrumental and symphonic composition. Mahler uses inherited musical techniques by extracting them from their past practice in music history. He makes them function as novelistic episodes of detail, placed in sequences of sound that, as the opening of the third movement of the Seventh Symphony suggests, appear fragmentary. Yet they are not obscure. They evoke associations but are left unresolved, except for the integration into a complex, multilayered whole. These resolutions are seemingly accomplished by the act of listening and not controlled by the composer.

In the second chapter of the eleventh book of *The Ambassadors*, toward the end of the novel, the reader's access to the internal consciousness of the protagonist Strether Lambert is rendered extensive. The realistic sense of the subjective internal dialogue in relationship to lived experience is plausible in its detail and content. James uses language to augment the moment in time and place experienced by the reader. This chapter functionally resembles the frequent long lyrical episodes in Mahler, even in the last movement of the First Symphony, that verge on the sentimental and seem at first convincingly self-contained. However, the appearance of a fragment of objective reality in the subsequent chapter of the James novel—"a boat advancing around the bend and containing a man who held the paddles and a lady at the stern with a pink parasol"—interrupts the reader and the protagonist alike within the frame of the novel. By so doing, it forces both to invert the very complex subjective musings, meanings, and conclusions achieved and explored so painstakingly in the prior extended sequence. James uses the interruptive appearance of a fragment external to the subject to trigger a self-critical awareness in both reader and protagonist about the validity of one's subjective procedure of constructing truth.[107]

Like James, Mahler confronts the listener by forcing him to question the basis of one's response to events and the psychological process of lending meaning to the experience of the everyday world. The confidence in subjectivity itself is undermined. A process of negation is at work in James that parallels Mahler's procedure of dirtying lyricism with extreme shifts in instrumental balances and the displacement of accents and stresses. By interrupting lyricism and the calm surface of soothing sonorities with extraneous or distantly connected interventions, Mahler suggests the contradictory, incomplete, and multifaceted faces of realism. Interventions that the listener can recognize, much like a boat on the river, emerging from the world external to the viewer, function less to confirm externality or locate the individual in space and time than to undercut a facile subjective synthesis.

Mahler's endings, like James's, reveal that the work of art is not structured to legitimate or celebrate mere subjectivity. Rather, the work forces both performer and listener to engage the dialectic of interpretation that depends on the interplay between the fragmentary experience of the external world and the self-conscious internal reflection about how meaning is constructed. The dialectic between instability and reliability that Strether experiences alongside the reader is precisely parallel to that which a listener, by the use of memory, seeks to construct retrospectively as the first and final movements reach their close, as in Mahler's Symphonies nos. 5, 6, and 7. The extended expositions, the use of repetition and the failure to adhere to expectations of recapitulation and closure, including use of the *morendo* ending, can be compared to the linguistic uses and formal strategies in late Henry James. Mahler, like his contemporary German-language writers, including Hermann Bahr and the brothers Mann, sought a way out of the conceits of realism and naturalism. In music, that exit led to a rejection of Wagnerian techniques of realism and toward symbolism and an obsession with subjective consciousness. This can explain in part Mahler's failure to write opera and his commitment to the possibilities of pure instrumental forms.

Listeners to Mahler's symphonies, much like readers of the late nineteenth-century generation of realist prose, are forced to come to terms with the instability and incompleteness of the imagination and any construction of meaning or the assignment of truth. This extends beyond the artificial temporal space of an artwork such as the novel or the symphony. It applies also to the constructs of external reality we call politics and culture. The accumulated meaning experienced through the act of listening and reading can illuminate that which lies beneath the surface of our experience of the passage of real time. The Mahler symphony becomes like the world. It does not contain it, but it forces the listener by its expanse and detail to be self-aware about the inadequacy of the fixed norms and forced coherences and resolutions with which we judge the world. The experience of listening to Mahler is intended to be unsettling because it defies more than the expectations of what listening to symphonic music ought to have been about; it seeks to defy the logic by which daily experience is justified. In this sense, music approximates philosophical criticism.

By the same token, the complexity, difficulty, and shock have worn off since Mahler's lifetime and the era when the novels of Flaubert, Fontane, and James were new. What is left are an immanent complexity and a diversified surface that seem compatible with the most banal of narratives. As Mahler became a model for composers after the mid-1970s, the radicalism of his formal strategies in the use of musical materials themselves took on the aspect of conventions. This development had the effect of inspiring new music and performances that flattened out both Mahler's negativity and his complexity, just as the novels of James and Flaubert have become sentimentalized through movie and television treatments. In its postmodern incarnation, Mahler's use of so-called "exhausted" musical rhetoric has lent the composer merely the aura of synthetic nostalgia.

In Mahler's lifetime and shortly thereafter, his music was understood as an overt challenge to a species of nostalgia about traditions of culture and the relation of art to society, human consciousness, and truth telling. Yet nearly a century after his death, Mahler's music has itself become emblematic of the very affirmative sense of meaning he sought to challenge. The facile appropriation of Mahler as offering a mirror of psychological struggle has become its own reductive cliché. Mahler's standing outside and apart from the illusion of a cultural synthesis and center, as well as his aura as critic, have become idealized through simplification and distance. This has succeeded in upending the negativity in Mahler into a routine cry of anguish and a sentimental attachment to the difficulties each listener encounters in negotiating life with its ordinary failures and aspirations: a colorful soundtrack for the journey of the soul. Perhaps a more careful and harsher reading of his music, adequate to the composer's vision, can challenge this bland, narcotic effect.

One consequence of the taming of Mahler's project has been the reconsideration of the utility of traditional and even conservative materials and forms of music to inspire criticism and resistance. Strauss, for example, buried the ironic and the problematic beneath a surface of virtuosity in the handling of musical logic. It may be that in his late works more negation than affirmation and easy listening can be located, alongside the implicit demand that the listener question the facile closure of the work of art he presents to us. Strauss continued to resist the temptation of the Mahlerian absence. Without seeking to innovate or use tradition against itself, the mature Strauss—after Mahler's death, through distance, self-criticism, and commentary on the past in music— sought to pursue an agenda responsive to Mahler. He uses formalism to come to terms with the world and to deepen self-recognition within our subjective encounters with the everyday.

The irony of the shifting posthumous evaluations of Mahler's and Strauss's music can be evoked in terms of *Don Quixote*. Strauss completed an instrumental *Don Quixote* in 1897, the year Mahler returned to Vienna. *Don Quixote* offers a resplendent and subtle musical account and response to Cervantes, demonstrating Strauss's command of musical traditions that could match the unique narrative framework of the first modern novel. Yet it was Mahler who demanded through his music that listeners engage the essence of the protagonist of Cervantes's masterpiece. Mahler asked listeners to rethink their lives through the prism of his startling and unsettling musical formulations of the world. He became to his public a figure akin to Cervantes's hero. Mahler sought to remake the world as it ought to be, not as a result of reading chivalric romance, but on account of his capacity to construct reality through music. Mahler the protagonist-composer, like Don Quixote, has been vindicated by posterity for seeing the world through the accounts of the imagination. He has not been punished like Flaubert's Emma (who dreams of the world as it appears in novels of romance). After all, the world Quixote and Mahler imagined for us is perhaps as it ought to be. Their worlds were far better places than the one Strauss knew existed and which he, through music, suffused with self-deprecatory candor and described with bittersweet affection and regret.

NOTES

The translation of the essay epigraph from Wittgenstein's *Culture and Value* is by Peter Winch (Chicago, 1980), p. 67. I want to thank Christopher Gibbs, Bryan Gilliam, Lynne Meloccaro, Karen Painter, Michael P. Steinberg, and Irene Zedlacher for their suggestions and criticisms. The critical apparatus is not intended to adequately reflect the massive literature on Mahler and fin-de-siècle Vienna.

1. The year 1960 marked the centennial of Mahler's birth. See Christoph Metzger, *Mahler-Rezeption: Perspektiven der Rezeption Gustav Mahlers* (Wilhelmshaven, 2000). I wish to draw the reader's attention not only to Metzger's extremely useful summary and analysis, but to the enormously helpful statistical material at the end. One needs to look at the performance history to realize that in point of fact, the explosion in Mahler performances begins only in a dramatic fashion during the late 1970s. However, one can begin to see a revival around 1960 in the United States. As the argument that follows points out, there was a low even in the United States throughout the 1920s. There was a flurry of interest, particularly during the 1940s (in the United States), a low in the 1950s, and then the revival spearheaded by the 1960 centennial (see Metzger, pp. 243–49). See also the special volume *Gustav Mahler* in the Musik-Konzepte series, eds. Heinz-Klaus Metzger and Rainer Riehn (Munich, 1989), and *Gustav Mahler: Durchgesetzt?* (Munich, 1999) from the same series; Georg Borchardt, Constantin Floros, et al. *Gustav Mahler: "Meine Zeit wird kommen": Aspekte der Mahler Rezeption* (Hamburg, 1996); and Hermann Danuser, *Gustav Mahler und seine Zeit* (Laaber, 1991), where the impact of the Mahler revival is discussed. The Danuser volume is especially recommended.

2. Theodor W. Adorno, *Mahler: A Physical Physiognomy*, trans. Edmund Jephcott (Chicago, 1992). All quotes are from the English edition. See also his essay "Mahler" in the volume *Quasi una Fantasia: Musikalische Schriften II* (Frankfurt/Main, 1963), pp. 115–54. The Mahler monograph was first published in German as *Mahler: Eine musikalische Physiognomik*, in 1960. Adorno, in response to the intense interest in Mahler, produced a second edition in 1963. By the early 1970s it had been republished numerous times and finally appeared in English in 1992.

3. See Carl Schorske, *Fin-de-Siècle Vienna: Politics and Culture* (New York, 1980); and Leon Botstein, "The Viennese Connection," *Partisan Review* 49, no. 2 (1982): 262–73.

4. It should be noted that Mitchell's volume 1 (*Gustav Mahler: The Early Years*) appeared first in 1958.

5. See, for example, the account of Mahler's rise to canonic status and popularity in Peter Franklin's *Life of Mahler* (Cambridge, 1997), particularly his citation of a quote from a 1983 film, *Educating Rita* (p. 5). The irony in Franklin's citation is that the character referred to tries to commit suicide because being consoled by listening was not quite enough. It can be said that after all Mahler predicted his own success when he reputedly said "my time will come." But he was not the only composer, after Wagner, to assert this rhetorical gesture of self-defense against criticism.

6. On Adorno's view of Mahler, see Max Paddison, *Adorno's Aesthetics of Music* (Cambridge, 1993), pp. 174–75 and 256–62; Robert W. Witkin, *Adorno on Music* (London, 1998), pp. 113–20; and Peter Franklin, " ' . . . his fractures are the script of truth.'— Adorno's Mahler," in *Mahler Studies*, ed. Stephen E. Hefling (Cambridge, 1997), pp. 271–94.

7. The parallels are indeed uncanny. Henry-Louis de La Grange wrote in French. The first volume, still awaiting a revised English version, first appeared in English in 1973. The author has updated his massive work at least once. Ironically, the influence of Thayer's volume was greatest in its German version, portions of which first appeared between 1866 and 1879. It was completed by Hermann Deiters and Hugo Riemann in 1908. The English translation by H. E. Krehbiel was published in 1921. It remains an indispensable document, owing to the fine and thoroughgoing revision prepared by Elliot Forbes in 1964. See Forbes, ed., *Thayer's Life of Beethoven*, 2 vols. (Princeton, 1967). The same long-lasting history and utility will befall de La Grange's biography. See Henry-Louis de La Grange, *Gustav Mahler: Chronique d'une vie*, 3 vols. (Paris, 1973–84); the first volume of the English version was published by Doubleday, volumes 2 and 3 by Oxford. I wish also to underscore the importance of Donald Mitchell's three-volume opus, *Gustav Mahler: The Early Years,* rev. and ed. Paul Banks and David Matthews; *Gustav Mahler: The Wunderhorn Years*; and *Gustav Mahler: Songs and Symphonies of Life and Death* (Berkeley, 1980–85).

8. There are too many examples to mention. Notable in the case of Beethoven was Romain Rolland's *Jean Christophe*. In the case of Mahler, there is of course Thomas Mann's *Death in Venice*. As for movies, there has been everything from Abel Gance's *Un grand amour de Beethoven* (1936) to Ken Russell's *Mahler* (1974). See Philip Reed, "Aschenbach becomes Mahler: Thomas Mann as Film," in *Benjamin Britten, 'Death in Venice,'* ed. Donald Mitchell (Cambridge, Eng., 1987), pp. 178–83.

9. See the 2001 film *Bride of the Wind*, directed by Bruce Beresford and based on Susan Keegan's 1991 biography of Alma Mahler of the same title, and the novel by Max Phillips, *The Artist's Wife* (New York, 2001).

10. On Debussy and Beethoven, see Edward Lockspeiser, *Debussy: His Life and Mind* (Cambridge, 1978), vol. 2, pp. 65–66.

11. See the introduction to Heinrich Schenker's monograph *Beethoven's Ninth Symphony: A Portrayal of Its Musical Content, with Running Commentary on Performance and Literature As Well*, ed. and trans. John Rothgeb (New Haven and London, 1992), pp. 3–27.

12. See a similar argument, but with a divergent conclusion, about the place of Mahler in a revised account of twentieth-century music in Christopher Hailey, "Franz Schreker and the Pluralities of Modernism," *Tempo* 219 (January 2002): 2–7.

13. See Paul Bekker, *Beethoven* (Berlin, 1912). It is important to note that Bekker went on to write the first serious analysis of all of the Mahler symphonies. See Bekker, *Gustav Mahler's Sinfonien* (1921; repr. Tutzing, 1969). I do not wish to imply that there have not been efforts to characterize Mahler in the image of the heroic. See the reference to such attempts in Franklin, *The Life of Mahler*, pp. 4–5. Wittgenstein noted (*Culture and Value*, p. 20) that Mahler's music, if it is a "work of art," is "totally different" from the "heroic" symphony.

14. It is important to note that Mahler's rise to popularity coincided with the height of currency enjoyed by psychoanalysis and Freudianism. Two figures now largely forgotten exemplify this parallel phenomenon in psychology. The first is Erich Fromm (1900–1980), whose book *The Art of Loving* (1956) remained a bestseller well into the 1960s. The other example is Erik Erikson (1902–1994), whose popularization of the identity crisis had its moment in the late 1960s and early 1970s. For Erikson, see Lawrence J. Friedman, *Identity's Architect: A Biography of Erik Erikson* (Cambridge, Mass., 2000).

15. I wish to draw attention to the image of the cosmopolitan Jew depicted in Stefan Zweig's autobiography *Die Welt von Gestern: Erinnerungen eines Europäers* (Frankfurt/Main, 1953). See also Leon Botstein, "Stefan Zweig and the Illusion of the Jewish European," in

The World of Yesterday's Humanist Today, ed. Marion Sonnenfeld (Albany, 1983), pp. 82–110. See also Hannah Arendt's scathing review of Zweig's autobiography, "The Jew as Pariah: The Hidden Tradition," reprinted in *The Jew as Pariah*, ed. Ron H. Feldman (New York, 1978), pp. 67–91. It is ironic but important to note that nostalgia for the assimilated Jew and the Jew as the good European can be discerned in Franz Werfel's "An Essay Upon the Meaning of Imperial Austria," in his *Twilight of a World*, trans. H. T. Lowe-Porter (New York, 1937), pp. 3–42. Werfel was of course Mahler's widow's last husband.

16. Americans will know Martin Buber, *Tales of the Hasidim*, trans. Olga Marx, 2 vols. (New York, 1947–48). But his first forays into the world of the Eastern European Jew date from at least 1916. Buber completed the main work in the 1920s and 1930s; see Martin Buber, "Vorbemerkung" in *Deutung des Chassidismus* (Berlin, 1935), p. 6; Alfred Döblin, "Reise in Polen" (1925) in *Schriften zu jüdischen Fragen*, ed. Hans Otto Horch and Till Schicketanz (Munich, 1997); Arnold Zweig, *Das ostjüdische Antlitz* (Berlin, 1920); Joseph Roth, *Juden auf Wanderschaft* (Cologne, 1937, rpt. 1985). See also Leon Botstein, *Judentum und Modernität: Essays zur Rolle der Juden in der deutschen und österreichischen Kultur, 1848–1938* (Vienna, 1991), pp. 149–70, 194–207.

17. See Hillel J. Kieval's extremely subtle and differentiated analysis of these issues, particularly as they apply to Bohemia, Moravia, and the Jewish community caught between German culture and the rise of modern Czech nationalism: Kieval, *Languages of Community: The Jewish Experience in the Czech Lands* (Berkeley, 2000). I wish to direct the reader to pp. 217–29. Also see the classic statement on the issue of German-Jewish identity published in 1921, Jakob Wassermann's *Mein Weg als Deutscher und Jude* (Berlin, 1987). There is an immense literature on Kafka's relationship to Judaism; see, for example, Ritchie Robertson, *Kafka: Judaism, Literature, and Politics* (Oxford, 1985). For a fine general account of these issues, see Steven E. Aschheim, *Brothers and Strangers: The East European Jew in German and German Jewish Consciousness, 1800–1923* (Madison, Wis., 1982), pp. 185–214.

18. See Metzger, *Mahler-Rezeption*, pp. 184–202. Debussy's antipathy to Mahler, succinctly expressed by his walking out of a performance of the Second Symphony, has exercised an enormous influence, reversed symbolically by Pierre Boulez's return to Mahler at the end of the century.

19. Within the nostalgia for the loss of European Jewry, he even could be construed as a figure whose past spanned the traditional gap between Eastern European and German Jewry. This idea seemed justified by the presence in his music of presumed evocations of the typically Eastern, exotic Jewish references. There is an extensive literature that discusses the exotic or oriental influences, including presumably Jewish liturgical and folk influences on Mahler. See, for example, Vladimir Karbusicky, *Gustav Mahler und seine Umwelt* (Darmstadt, 1978).

20. De La Grange in particular has stressed Mahler's status as martyr. See Henry Louis de La Grange, *Mahler*, vol. 1 (Paris, 1979), p. 9.

21. A useful analysis of the perception of the place of Jews in America that corresponds to the time frame under discussion is Charles E. Silberman, *A Certain People: American Jews and Their Lives Today* (New York, 1985). It is ironic that in the March 4, 2002, issue of *The New Yorker*, Woody Allen published a vignette entitled "Sing, You Sacher Tortes," in which Mahler is described as a "fragile tunesmith" who speaks of his "quotidian preoccupation with mortality" (pp. 34–36).

22. See Leonard Bernstein, "Mahler: His Time Has Come," in *Findings* (New York, 1982), pp. 255–64; this is a reprint of a 1967 essay written for *High Fidelity*. For Bernstein to have stressed the idea of Mahler as a prophet who predicted that his "time would come" does not suggest that Mahler himself predicted or wished for his music to be understood the way it has come to be seen, partly under the aegis of Bernstein's readings.

23. See Adorno, *Mahler,* pp. 17, 149–50. It is crucial to recall that Adorno's view of Mahler's Jewish identity was influenced by Adorno's ambivalence about his own identity. Adorno was brought up a Catholic. Only one of his grandparents had been Jewish, and had converted. The rise of the Nazis forced Adorno reluctantly from the center, in which he thought he belonged, to the periphery, into the role of an emigré tied to the Jews. Adorno's career was in this sense an inversion of Mahler's and led to some discomfort and distance with respect to a closer analysis of Mahler's career as a Jew and a convert.

24. Schoenberg made this point in his memorial address of 1912, "Gustav Mahler: In Memoriam." See his *Style and Idea: Selected Writings*, ed. Leonard Stein, trans. Leo Black (London, 1975), pp. 447–48. He did so also in the dedication to the 1911 *Harmonielehre*.

25. See, for example, the complex and fascinating confrontation with this development articulated by Pierre Boulez in 1979. Interestingly, within performance practice, Boulez's readings avoid the sentimentality of Bernstein. See "Mahler: Our Contemporary?" in *Orientations* (Cambridge, Mass., 1986), p. 295.

26. See Mitchell, *Gustav Mahler: The Early Years,* pp. 2–3.

27. Indeed, significant post-1960 German scholarship on Mahler does not highlight the political. See the three-volume study by Constantin Floros, *Gustav Mahler* (Wiesbaden, 1977–85); Hans Heinrich Eggebrecht, *Die Musik Gustav Mahlers* (Munich, 1982); and an exception, Bernd Sponheuer, *Logik des Zerfalls: Untersuchungen zum Finalproblem in den Symphonien Gustav Mahlers* (Tutzing, 1978). Mahler studies have also resurrected Mahler's school colleague Hans Rott as part of an effort to develop fresh perspectives on Mahler. See *Gustav Mahler: Der unbekannte Bekannte*, eds. Heinz-Klaus Metzger and Rainer Riehn, Musik Konzepte 91 (Munich, 1996), and Uwe Harten, ed., *Hans Rott, 1858–1884* (Vienna, 2000).

28. See Pierre Boulez, "Gustav Mahler: Why Biography?" first published in 1979, in *Orientations*, pp. 292–94. On the Seventh Symphony, see the essays in James L. Zychowicz, ed., *The Seventh Symphony of Gustav Mahler: A Symposium* (Cincinnati, 1990); and on the Ninth, see Peter Revers, *Gustav Mahler: Untersuchungen zu den späten Sinfonien* (Hamburg, 1985), pp. 79–160.

29. Adorno, *Mahler*. See, for example, pp. 26–39, 83–104.

30. In terms of performance practice, with the exception of early accounts by Georg Solti, Jascha Hornstein, Harold Farberman, and Lorin Maazel, the trend in the late twentieth century, as witnessed even by Klaus Tennstedt, Claudio Abbado, and a host of younger gifted conductors, is to underscore the continuities, lyricism, and sensuality—a late-romantic aural coherence—in Mahler.

31. The contrast between the post–World War II reputations of the three Jewish composers most virulently attacked by the Nazis—Mendelssohn, Meyerbeer, and Mahler—is indeed instructive. The problems associated with repeated efforts to revive wide interest in Mendelssohn have been explored. More interesting, however, is the case of Meyerbeer and his ironic use of the evident artificiality of the theatrical and virtuosity in producing a spectacle. Meyerbeer conveys more than a sense of elegance and of the entertaining and the lyrical (as well as a contempt for and resistance to the Wagnerian manipulation of the spectacle as part dream, fantasy, and mythic surrogate for narrative realism). Meyerbeer's rehabilitation in terms of criticism and performance may be harder to achieve, but it is timely. See, for example, the essays in Carl Dahlhaus, ed., *Das Problem Mendelssohn* (Regensburg, 1974); Leon Botstein, "The Aesthetics of Assimilation and Affirmation: Reconstructing the Career of Felix Mendelssohn," in *Felix Mendelssohn and His World*, ed. R. Larry Todd (Princeton, 1991), pp. 5–42. The question of Meyerbeer is still unresolved, despite the efforts of Heinz Becker. See the Festschrift for Becker, *Giacomo Meyerbeer: Musik als Welterfahrung*, eds. Sieghart Döhring and Jürgen Schläder (Munich, 1995); see also the catalogue for the 1992 exhibition in Berlin, *Giacomo Meyerbeer: Weltbürger der Musik*, ed.

Heinz Becker and Gudrun Becker (Wiesbaden, 1991); and Heinz Becker and Gudrun Becker, *Giacomo Meyerbeer: Ein Leben in Briefen* (Wilhelmshaven, 1983).

32. Martha C. Nussbaum, *Upheavals of Thought: The Intelligence of Emotions* (Cambridge, Eng., 2001), pp. 642–44.

33. Lewis Thomas, *Late Night Thoughts on Listening to Mahler's Ninth Symphony* (Toronto, 1984), pp. 164–66.

34. Quoted in Paul Hamburger, "Mahler and *Des Knaben Wunderhorn*," in *The Mahler Companion*, ed. Donald Mitchell and Andrew Nicholson (Oxford, 1999), p. 62.

35. See Susan Robin Suleiman, *Subversive Intent* (Cambridge, Mass., 1990), p. 89.

36. Adorno, *Mahler*, pp. 16–17, 41–49.

37. Timothy L. Jackson has explored thoroughly the program, or rather the meanings of the secret programs, in *Metamorphosen*. His argument, however, only strengthens the difficulty one would encounter in trying to adapt that work in a manner directly opposed to its implied programmatic intent. See Jackson, "The Metamorphosis of the *Metamorphosen*: New Analytical and Source-Critical Discoveries," in *Richard Strauss: New Perspectives on the Composer and His Work*, ed. Bryan Gilliam (Durham, 1992), pp. 193–242. The Adagietto is about love, but it is used, often slowed down to intolerable lengths, to stand for death and loss. Even if one sped up or slowed down the *Metamorphosen*, one could not achieve such an inversion; it could not suffice as coronation music. However, when Haitink, for example, performs the Adagietto in 1988 in nearly 14 minutes, it can be deadly or represent death. At the roughly 7 minutes used by Mengelberg, or the 9 minutes Mahler is reputed to have played it in, it could be about love. I want to thank Christopher Gibbs for the Mengelberg and Haitink timings. The Mahler timing is in Karl Heinz Füssl, "Vorwort," in Gustav Mahler, *Symphony No. 5* (London, 1992), p. xxiii.

38. Danuser, *Gustav Mahler und seine Welt*, pp. 288–89.

39. Hans Werner Henze, *Musik und Politik: Schriften und Gespräche 1955–1984*, rev. ed. (Munich, 1984), pp. 141–42.

40. Henze, *Musik und Politik*, pp. 254–55.

41. See Schoenberg, "Brahms the Progressive (1947)," in *Style and Idea*, pp. 398–441; and Walter Frisch, *Brahms and the Principle of Developing Variations* (Berkeley, 1984). Perhaps the most compelling analysis of the relationship between Schoenberg and Mahler as seen through a close reading of Schoenberg's op. 9, all accomplished within the context of a subtle command of the historical context, is Reinhold Brinkmann's "Die gepreßte Sinfonie: Zum geschichtlichen Gehalt von Schönbergs Opus 9," in *Gustav Mahler: Sinfonie und Wirklichkeit*, ed. Otto Kolleritsch (Graz, 1977), pp. 133–56. (See translation, "The Compressed Symphony: On the Historical Content of Schoenberg's Op. 9," in *Schoenberg and His World*, ed. Walter Frisch [Princeton, 1999], pp. 141–61.)

42. Henze, *Musik und Politik*. It should be noted that Webern and Berg had no reservations in their admiration of Mahler and both credited his music, particular his later works, as having exerted a decisive influence on their own music. My reading of Schoenberg's ambivalence is based on his longer 1912 essay on Mahler, revised in 1948, in *Style and Idea*, pp. 449–71. See also Dieter Rexroth, "Mahler und Schönberg," in *Sinfonie und Wirklichkeit*, pp. 68–80.

43. See Danuser, *Gustav Mahler und seine Zeit*, pp. 256–62. See also Gereon Diepgen, *Innovation oder Rückgriff: Studien zur Begriffsgeschichte des musikalischen Neoklassizismus* (Frankfurt/Main, 1997), pp. 119–38, 219–49, 336–44.

44. Schoenberg to Mahler, 12 December 1904; quoted in Renate Ulm, ed., *Gustav Mahlers Symphonien: Entstehung, Deutung, Wirkung* (Munich and Kassel, 2001), p. 117.

45. Adorno, *Mahler*, pp. 144–67.

46. See Joseph N. Straus, "The Myth of Serial 'Tyranny' in the 1950s and 1960s," *Musical Quarterly* 85, no. 3 (1999): pp. 301–43.

47. See Theodor W. Adorno, *Alban Berg: Master of the Smallest Link*, trans. Juliane Brand and Christopher Hailey (Cambridge, Eng., 1991); "Bergs kompositiontechnische Funde," in *Quasi una Fantasia*, pp. 245–73; and his 1949 *Philosophie der neuen Musik* (Frankfurt/Main, 1978).

48. See Carl Dahlhaus, "Die rätselhafte Popularität Gustav Mahlers: Zuflucht vor der Moderne oder der Anfang der Neuen Musik?," in *Gustav Mahler: Durchgesetzt?*, pp. 3–7.

49. Adorno, *Mahler*, p. 83

50. See Leon Botstein, "Strauss and Twentieth-Century Modernity: A Reassessment of the Man and His Work," in *Richard Strauss und die Moderne*, eds. Bernd Edelmann, Birgit Lodes, and Reinhold Schlötterer (Berlin, 2001), pp. 113–38.

51. See Bryan Gilliam, *The Life of Richard Strauss* (Cambridge, 1999); and essays in *Richard Strauss and His World*, ed. Bryan Gilliam (Princeton, 1992).

52. See Ivan Sollertinsky, *Gustav Mahler—Der Schrei ins Leere*, ed. Günter Wolter, trans. Reimar Westendorf (Berlin, 1996) passim. See also Krzysztof Meyer, "Mahler und Schostakowitsch," in *Sinfonie und Wirklichkeit*, pp. 118–32.

53. Adorno, *Mahler*, pp. 145–56.

54. See Robert P. Morgan, "Ives and Mahler: Mutual Responses at the End of an Era," *Nineteenth-Century Music* 2, no. 1 (July 1978): 72–81; and Leon Botstein, "Innovation and Nostalgia: Ives, Mahler, and the Origins of Twentieth-Century Modernism," in *Charles Ives and His World*, ed. J. Peter Burkholder (Princeton, 1996), pp. 35–74; Danuser, *Gustav Mahler und seine Zeit*, pp. 299–301; and Stuart Feder, *The Life of Charles Ives* (Cambridge, Eng., 1999).

55. Adorno, *Mahler*, pp. 3–39.

56. Adorno, *Mahler*, pp. 61–80.

57. See Pamela M. Potter, *Most German of the Arts: Musicology and Society from the Weimar Republic to the End of Hitler's Reich* (New Haven, 1998), esp. pp. 189–90 on Blessinger. The account that follows is confirmed in brief and reductive sources from the Nazi era. See the articles on Mahler in Hans Brückner, *Judentum und Musik mit dem ABC jüdischer und nichtarischer Musikbeflissener*, 3d ed. (Munich, 1938); Theo Stengel and Herbert Gerigk, *Lexikon der Juden in der Musik* (Berlin, 1941), pp. 168–72; and Ernst Bücken, *Wörterbuch der Musik* (Leipzig, 1940), p. 261.

58. See Leon Botstein, "Gustav Mahler's Vienna," in *The Mahler Companion*, pp. 6–38. Another source that underscores Mahler's success is the short résumé of his career placed at the end of Richard Specht, *Gustav Mahler's VIII Symphonie* (Vienna, 1912), pp. 46–48. The standard account of Mahler's tenure at the Court Opera is Franz Willnauer, *Gustav Mahler und die Wiener Oper*, 2d ed. (Vienna, 1993). For a fine, useful, and carefully delineated introduction to the critical context into which Mahler arrived in Vienna in 1897, see Sandra McColl's monograph *Music Criticism in Vienna 1896–1897: Critically Moving Forms* (Oxford, 1996). Readers may wish also to consult the proceedings of a conference on the year 1897 published in the volume *Wien 1897: Kulturgeschichtliches Profil eines Epochaljahres*, ed. Christian Glanz (Frankfurt/Main, 1999). The literature on turn-of-the-century Vienna is, as everyone knows, immense. Readers seeking a useful jumping-off point will find it in Jürgen Nautz and Richard Vahrenkamp, eds., *Die Wiener Jahrhundertwende: Einflüsse, Umwelt, Wirkungen* (Vienna, 1993).

59. The extent and intensity of the controversy that accompanied Mahler's career in Vienna between 1897 and 1907 had many parallels in contemporary Vienna, where virulently articulated partisanship in cultural matters was unexceptional. Examples contemporaneous to Mahler include the Klimt murals for the University, entitled

Philosophy, Jurisprudence, and *Medicine* (1899–1907), the construction of Adolf Loos's Goldman & Salatsch building on the Michaelerplatz in 1910–11, and the ongoing debate over the direction and repertoire of the Burgtheater. Yet, in the light of their posthumous successful reputations, the memory of the controversies in the cases of Klimt and Loos has receded. They have not lasted as defining elements in the reception of these artists' life and work. For the Klimt murals, see, for example, Peter Vergo's essay "Between Modernism and Tradition: The Importance of Klimt's Murals and Figure Paintings," in *Gustav Klimt: Modernism in the Making*, ed. Colin B. Bailey (New York and Ottawa, 2001), pp. 19–40. See also Schorske, *Fin-de-Siècle Vienna*, pp. 225–43. For a detailed history of the construction and the controversy regarding the house on the Michaelerplatz, see, among others, Hermann Czech and Wolfgang Mistelbauer, *Das Looshaus* (Vienna, 1984).

60. This essay uses newspaper reviews (e.g., the writings of Robert Hirschfeld), periodicals, and guidebooks. Journalistic criticism is, in the construction of music history, a complex source. It is difficult to sort out levels of meaning, given the ephemeral and shifting character of daily issues, personal agendas, and passing political and cultural trends of a local nature associated with newspaper criticism.

61. This quote comes from Alfred Roller, *Die Bildnisse von Gustav Mahler* (Leipzig and Vienna, 1922), quoted in Norman Lebrecht, *Mahler Remembered* (New York, 1987), pp. 163–64.

62. A great deal of Mahler commentary has been based on Bauer-Lechner's recollection (*Recollections of Gustav Mahler*, ed. Peter Franklin, trans. Dika Newlin [Cambridge, 1980]), whose richness of material and veracity have never been seriously contested. Given the relative insecurity one necessarily has about the memoirs of Alma Mahler from a later period, one should retain some skepticism. There is an inherent limitation in this material, as there is even in Mahler's own correspondence. One always has to have some hesitation about too facile an acceptance of a composer's verbal assertions. Authorial intentions as articulated in music may not correspond with the composer's confessional musings, conversations, or written statements. However obvious this may be, it is significantly more so in the case of the recollections of an individual whose relationship with her subject has to have been more complicated than we might wish. Nonetheless, Bauer-Lechner remains a primary source not only for Mahler's self-professed ambitions, but also his views on Bach and Beethoven (see pp. 139–43 and 165–70). Perhaps the most frequently quoted statement is the following from 1895: "But, to me, 'symphony' means constructing a world with all the technical means at one's disposal. The eternally new and changing content determines its own form" (p. 40).

63. Otto Schumann, *Meyers Konzertführer: Orchestermusik und Instrumentalkonzerte*, 2d ed. (Leipzig, 1938), pp. 384–86.

64. See Alban Berg's manifesto on the Verein für musikalische Privataufführungen, reprinted in Willi Reich, *Alban Berg* (New York, 1974), pp. 46–49; Loos, "Ornament und Verbrechen (1908)," in *Trotzdem, 1900–1930* (1931; repr. Vienna, 1982), pp. 78–88.

65. See Max Graf, *Wagner-Probleme* (Vienna, 1900), pp. 131–34; and Graf, "Über Gustav Mahler," *Wiener Rundschau* 13 (1899), pp. 315–18.

66. Schumann, *Meyers Konzertführer*, p. 386.

67. Henze, *Musik und Politik*, p. 254.

68. See Karl Marx, "On the Jewish Question," in *Early Writings*, ed. and trans. T. B. Bottomore (New York, 1963), pp. 1–40; and Botstein, *Judentum und Modernität*, pp. 30–43.

69. See Karl Blessinger, *Mendelssohn, Meyerbeer, Mahler: Drei Kapitel Judentum in der Musik als Schlüssel zur Musikgeschichte des 19. Jahrhunderts*, Kulturpolitische Reihe, vol. 9 (Berlin, 1939). A revised and expanded version of the volume was published in 1944 under the title *Judentum und Musik: Ein Beitrag zur Kultur- und Rassenpolitik*.

70. Adorno, *Mahler*, pp. 92–97, 135–42.

71. Blessinger, "Mahler," in *Drei Kapitel Judentum*, pp. 74–90, quote on p. 84.

72. Blessinger, *Drei Kapitel Judentum*, pp. 13–42 and 43–73; also Bücken, *Wörterbuch der Musik*, pp. 272–73 and 277; Brückner, *Judentum und Musik*, pp. 194 and 28; and Stengel/Gerigk, *Lexikon der Juden*, pp. 180–84 and 186–94. See also Thomas Mathieu, *Kunstauffassungen und Kulturpolitik im Nationalsozialismus* (Saarbrücken, 1997), pp. 154–56.

73. Blessinger, *Drei Kapitel Judentum*, p. 89.

74. Eberhard Preussner, *Die Bürgerliche Musikkultur* (Hamburg, 1935), pp. 199–210; see also Fabian R. Lovisa, *Musikkritik im Nationalsozialismus* (Laaber, 1993); and Fred K. Prieberg, *Musik im NS-Staat* (Cologne, 2000).

75. See a different reading of Mahler's approach to counterpoint and historical models, based on Mahler's attachment and debt to Johann Sebastian Bach in Philipp Otto Naegele, *Gustav Mahler and Johann Sebastian Bach* (Northampton, Mass., 1983). It is ironic that the anti-Semitic strategy by which Mahler was criticized for lacking "musical" skills echoed Nietzsche's last comments on Wagner. Wagner innovated with "dramatic" music because he was simply not musical enough or well-trained. See Richard Weltrich, *Wagners Tristan und Isolde als Dichtung* (Berlin, 1904), p. 171.

76. Adorno, *Mahler*, p. 113.

77. See also the statements on Schoenberg in Brückner, *Judentum und Musik*, p. 253; Stengel/Gerigk, *Lexikon der Juden*, pp. 245–49; Bücken, *Wörterbuch der Musik*, pp. 389–90.

78. See the selection "Strauss and the Viennese Critics (1896–1924): Reviews by Gustav Schoenaich, Robert Hirschfeld, Guido Adler, Max Kalbeck, Julius Korngold, and Karl Kraus," in *Richard Strauss and His World*, pp. 311–71.

79. Strauss completed his Alpine Symphony explicitly in reaction to Mahler's death, which he regarded as a "grave loss." See Stephan Kohler, "Vorwort" in Richard Strauss, *Eine Alpensinfonie, Op. 64* (London, 1996), pp. iii–xi.

80. Adorno, *Mahler*, pp. 148–150. Wittgenstein once noted (*Culture and Value*, p. 13) that theater with masks, something akin to music, "will attract only Jews."

81. See Hermann Kretzschmar, *Führer durch den Konzertsaal*, vol. 1: *Sinfonie und Suite*, 5th ed. (Leipzig, 1919), pp. 793–814.

82. See Max Burkhardt, *Führer durch die Konzertmusik* (Berlin, 1918), p. 175; see also pp. 176–78.

83. It is for this reason that Adorno, and others, have found fault with the last movement of the Seventh Symphony and contrast it unfavorably to the last movement of the Sixth. The evocation of *Die Meistersinger*, replete with the use of C major, suggested a more regressive effort at old-fashioned triumphalism. This reader does not share this interpretation of that movement. Adorno, *Mahler*, p. 136. See also the essays in Zychowicz, *The Seventh Symphony*; and Norman Del Mar, *Mahler's Sixth Symphony: A Study* (London, 1980).

84. Mahler's utilization of folk material and his explicit references to urban popular music became hallmarks of the divergent readings of Mahler's project and intentions. See the essays by Tibor Kneif, "Das triviale Bewusstsein in der Musik," and Lars Ulrich Abraham, "Über Trivialität in protestantischen Kirchenmelodien des 19. Jahrhunderts," in *Studien zu Trivialmusik im 19. Jahrhundert*, ed. Carl Dahlhaus (Regensburg, 1967), pp. 29–52 and 83–96.

85. Other possible cases of serious important critics of Mahler whose views deserve closer scrutiny might be Richard Wallaschek, in Vienna, the critic of *Die Zeit*, and Carl Krebs, the critic of the *Deutsche Rundschau*, whose dismissive views cannot be ascribed to philistinism, envy, or ignorance. See, for example, Wallascheck (April 15, 1899), *Die Zeit* 237, pp. 44–45 (a review of the Second Symphony), and Krebs, "Aus dem Berliner Musikleben," *Deutsche Rundschau* 88 (1896), pp. 137–38.

86. On Max von Millenkovich Morold, a Bruckner advocate, see Botstein, "Music and Its Public: Habits of Listening and the Crisis of Musical Modernism in Vienna, 1870–1914," Chapter 4 (Ph.D. diss., Harvard University, 1985). See also *Hugo Riemanns Musiklexikon*, 11th ed., rev. Alfred Einstein (Berlin, 1929), p. 1209.

87. Wittgenstein was himself a great admirer of Kraus (see *Culture and Value*, pp. 19, 65, 67). On Loos and Mahler, see Botstein, "Music and Its Public," pp. 1159–73; see also Edward Timms, *Karl Kraus: Apocalyptic Satirist* (New Haven, 1986); and Botstein, "Gustav Mahler's Vienna."

88. Adorno, *Mahler*, p. 127.

89. Kraus, *Die Fackel*, April 1914, 17; December 1902, 23–26; December 1904, 9; June 1903, 16–17; December 1907, 27–28. See also Paul Stauber, *Vom Kriegsschauplatz der Wiener Oper: Das wahre Erbe Gustav Mahlers* (Vienna, 1909).

90. See Botstein, "Music and Its Public," pp. 1018–56; on Hirschfeld see Elisabeth Riz, "Robert Hirschfeld: Leben–Wirken–Bedeutung," in *Biographische Beiträge zum Musikleben Wiens im 19. und frühen 20. Jahrhundert*, ed. Friedrich C. Heller (Vienna, 1992), pp. 1–80.

91. Hirschfeld on Bruckner, see *Wiener Abendpost*, 14 February 1903.

92. On Klinger and Klimt, see Robert Hirschfeld, "Feuilleton: Konzerte," *Wiener Abendpost*, 17 December 1907.

93. Hirschfeld on art and social reform: see Botstein, *Music and Its Public*, pp. 1018–75.

94. See Robert Hirschfeld, "Wien," *Frankfurter Zeitung*, 22 November 1903, p. 2.

95. Hirschfeld on Debussy and Mahler: *Wiener Abendpost*, 17 December 1907. Also, Botstein, "Music and Its Public," on Hirschfeld's views on Perger et al.

96. See Helmut Federhofer, *Heinrich Schenker: Nach Tagebüchern und Briefen in der Oswald Jonas Memorial Collection* (Hildesheim, 1985), pp. 62, 238–39. However, it is important to note that Schenker did not wish to be associated with Hirschfeld, even though he acknowledged that they shared similar points of view. Schenker's view of Mahler's music was dismissive.

97. See Danuser, *Gustav Mahler und seine Zeit*, pp. 152–84. I do not directly pursue the utility of Georg Lukács's view of the novel vis-à-vis Mahler as well as its connection to Adorno, in part because of the extent to which that view itself is so deeply located in the political and historical context from which Adorno's theory of art and politics stems.

98. On Mahler and realism in music, see, for example, Martin Geck's brief summary of Mahler's relationship to the midcentury evolution of musical realism in *Zwischen Romantik und Restauration: Musik im Realismus Diskurs* (Vienna, 2001), pp. 194–97.

99. See Brenda Dalen, "'Freundschaft, Liebe und Welt': The Secret Programme of the Chamber Concerto," in *The Berg Companion*, ed. Douglas Jarman (Boston, 1990), pp. 141–80.

100. See Adorno, *Mahler*, pp. 69, 132–33.

101. Flaubert, *Madame Bovary* (New York, 1964), pp. 137–57. On Flaubert and realism, see Erich Auerbach, *Mimesis: Dargestellte Wirklichkeit in der abendländischen Literatur* (Bern, 1946), pp. 449–52.

102. Georges Poulet, "The Circle and the Center. Reality and *Madame Bovary*," *Western Review* 19 (summer 1955): 245–60.

103. See Reinhold Brinkmann, *Late Idyll: The Second Symphony of Johannes Brahms*, trans. Peter Palmer (Cambridge, Mass., 1995), pp. 1–4.

104. See Helmut Nürnberger, *Fontanes Welt* (Berlin, 1997).

105. Theodor Fontane, *Effi Briest. Die Poggenpuhls. Mathilde Möhring* (Berlin, 1993), pp. 108–10.

106. Fontane, *Effi Briest*, pp. 191–92.

107. Henry James, *The Ambassadors* (New York, 1986), pp. 341–56. See also Theodor Schmitt, *Der langsame Symphoniesatz Gustav Mahlers* (Munich, 1983); and Rüdiger Schenck, "Zur Neunten Symphonie Gustav Mahlers" and Burkhard Spinnler, "Zur Angemessenheit traditioneller Formbegriffe in der Analyse Mahlerscher Symphonik: Eine Untersuchung des ersten Satzes der Neunten Symphonie," both in *Form & Idee in Gustav Mahlers Instrumentalmusik*, ed. Klaus Hinrich Stahmer (Wilhelmshaven, 1980), pp. 165–222 and 223–76. The distinctions made at the end of this essay between Strauss and Mahler are in part derived from Adorno's reading of Mahler's attitude to formal conventions and techniques associated with compositional practice and symphonic music. However, it must be remembered that Mahler had little use for mere innovation detached from norms of craftsmanship that derive from tradition. Natalie Bauer-Lechner reported that in 1896 Mahler said, "The 'modernist' twaddle that art can dispense with the highest artistry in every detail, is just nonsense. On the contrary, such a tremendous amount of artistic technique is needed to perfect a work of art, from its first conception to its final detailed realization. . . . Whatever is not imbued through and through with this highest artistic mastery is doomed to die even before it is born" (*Recollections of Gustav Mahler*, p. 68). This needs to be set side by side with the facile misreading of Mahler's oft-quoted attack on the appeal to tradition as a justification for sloppy habits.

Mahler's Theater:

The Performative and the Political in

Central Europe, 1890–1910

CHARLES S. MAIER

Introduction: A Performative Culture

"Born in Bohemia 7 July 1860. Moved to Vienna at the age of fifteen. . . . I am now thirty-five years old, scarcely known and scarcely *performed*," Gustav Mahler wrote a Hamburg correspondent in March 1896.[1] But if not performed, certainly performing at a prodigious pace, and making his way as a conductor from marginal orchestras in Central Europe, from Hall to Laibach (Ljubljana), Olmütz (Olmouc), and Kassel, cajoling from them musicianship beyond their previous capacity, then to major responsibilities as musical director in Prague and Budapest, finally to the prize he admitted he always sought, Vienna, and thereafter as a sort of epilogue to New York. From his post in Prague, midway through this life-long trajectory, the busy director wrote his previous supervisor in Kassel, "So far I have conducted new productions of *Don Giovanni*, *Les Deux Journées*, *Fidelio*, *Tannhäuser,* and *Meistersinger;* the first performances here of *Trompeter, Rheingold,* and *Valkyrie,* and am busy preparing a new *Tristan* and a Mozart cycle. So I have [had] plenty to do for five months."[2] And so it was, indeed, for about three decades.

Listeners and critics followed this sustained achievement as musical director and conductor—what Mahler occasionally described as his "theater hell"—as attentively as they did his own compositional output. Even those hostile realized they were in the presence of a great director. What gripped them, I believe, was not just an abundant musical

talent. Contemporary descriptions of Mahler's "performative" achievement, in fact, disclose fundamental stances toward what was understood
to be "modernity," political and social and not just aesthetic, at the
threshold of the twentieth century.

Granted that as an artist Mahler compelled attention in his own
right. Testimonies abound to his unceasing demands at rehearsal, his
"severe and domineering 'will to power,'" his "tyranny," his obsession
with staging, "the perfect execution of the slightest detail," but also to
his leadership in transforming the theatrical experience, and his "salvation" of the Court Opera.[3] "How we were all borne away by his spirit,
transported by this temperament," recalled the Berlin cantor and opera
singer Magnus Davidson from the perspective of restricted Jewish cultural life in the 1930s.[4] When the performances went well, according
to the vocal coach from the Court Opera, Fritz Stiedry, they conveyed
"an artistic magic without equal," transforming his players, captivating
his listeners, and fulfilling the claims for music, drama, and theater of
both masters of his youth, Wagner and Nietzsche. "His ecstasies had a
hypnotic effect. Vienna was in a state of Mahlerian delirium."[5] The
writer Felix Salten (who founded the Jung-Wiener Theater zum Lieben
Augustin cabaret with Hermann Bahr), reported that during a Munich
visit "the intensity of his being seemed to have filled the entire city."[6]
Alma Mahler recalled performances where "no one in the audience
dared to breathe" and the conductor was pursued afterward by
"Bacchic maniacs."[7]

These observations, I would propose, responded to more than just
the charisma of Mahler the performer. The conductor's successes
reflected an entire generation's appetite for the dramaturgic and the
theatrical in all areas of life. Mahler's talent made its mark as part of
the avid reception for performative eminence in modern culture and
public life in general; this essay explores that interaction.

The concept of performance at the center of this investigation
deserves scrutiny. It calls attention to the fact that the presentation of
ideas or images, written text or musical notation, bodily gestures or display to a public depends upon the qualities and choices made by the
intermediary, and that the success of this presentation is judged in its
own right and not just according to whatever content resides in the text
or work and images "before" presentation. "Performative" has become
a common term in cultural studies, and now in feminist theory is often
associated with the public role of the body.[8] Recent usage, however,
derives from speech-act theory according to which an utterance "does"
something as well as describes something.[9] Performance is designed not
only to communicate intentions scripted by a playwright or composer,

but to impress an audience with the capacities and persona of the performer and/or director: "all live performance involves both spontaneous action and the playing of a role," Simon Frith reminds us.[10] And although it is not the ordinary use of the word, when the focus of musical creation becomes the composer himself, composition itself takes on a performative aspect. "The life, as it was represented through his creativity," as Paul Bekker concluded his 1921 book on Mahler's symphonies, "was Mahler's greatest work of art. . . . The consciousness of the artistic disappears, only the power of artistic revelation remains to move us."[11]

The "us" is crucial: performance implies, in addition to an artist, the existence of an audience and a bounded space—arena, theater, or city square—where their interaction takes place. "The advent of an audience is, on the visible surface of the normal course of things, a ratification of the social," writes one of its principal theorists, Herbert Blau. It "is not so much a mere congregation of people as a body of thought and desire . . . a consciousness constructed."[12] Performance, as Frith puts it, is less "a means by which a text is represented, 'licensed,' or made 'excessive' than . . . an experience . . . of sociability." He is speaking about modern popular music but believes his concepts are valid for classical performances as well. The audience, he suggests, is created by the performer, who fuses disparate individuals into a common public.[13] On the other hand, listeners must be ready to coalesce; they bring to the artist's presentation a prior potential sociability and, in Victor Turner's quasi-theological language, "communitas." It is further understood that while performances can be repeated, they are never exactly replicable; thus each conveys a particular aura as a one-time event. For the duration of the music or the play or the acting-out, people come together and share a common exhilaration, which must then dissolve. The experience constitutes what Turner called a liminal moment—an interval that is "framed," as Frith describes it—that is, separated from the quotidian life of "structures" and institutions before and after, but one that makes transformation of those constraints appear possible at least for a brief period.[14]

The theoretical issues surrounding performance, such as the degree of independence of the work from its rendition, or the scope sanctioned for improvisation, remain lively debates. To draw a crude distinction, the aesthetic "Left" tends to critique the idea of the work in itself as an artifact of bourgeois culture.[15] Stan Godlovitch, for example, insists that performance is "a way of communicating, not especially a work or a composer's notions, but a person, the performer, through music." Aesthetic conservatives, on the other hand, reaffirm the autonomy of the artwork in the tradition of Leonard B. Meyer, who envisaged performance as an "expressive deviation" from the normative work. For Roger Scruton the performer's contribution is hardly greater than "the awed silence of the audience," which itself becomes, in effect, a part of the score: composer and hushed public together merely make use of the performers. "In the symphonies of Mahler we find silence shaped by the surrounding tones and placed before us like a mirror, in which we find our own astonished faces."[16]

Less important for the historian than the abstract debate is the fact that some milieus—call them performative cultures—attribute more or less importance to the mediating experience, to the performance, in its own right than do others. Members of a performative culture are particularly sensitized to the issue of presentation: the medium becomes crucial to the message. The Greek city state, the Baroque court and theater, and the advent of modern political societies have all been sites where performance counts for a lot—and not only in the theater, but for the ordering of public life in general. The line between theater as such and the organization of urban interactions that define social classes, establish group claims to public space, and bring political conflicts into staged confrontation becomes more blurred and tenuous than in less performative societies.

Cultures that prize performance in one sphere are likely to encourage it in others. The society in which Mahler developed his career was a highly performative one and his talent resonated—if it did not directly develop—as a response to these wider societal expectations. By the late nineteenth century, political theater, including the resort to highly charged and accusatory rhetoric, public demonstrations, and campaigns against internal and external enemies were becoming a continuing mode for regulating collective issues. Revolutionary uprisings had traditionally been occasions for oratory, public protest, and political violence, but they had been episodic. By the final third of the century, theatrical politics was becoming a frequent recourse, at least in urban arenas. The migration of an industrial working class to Europe's growing metropolises and the growing stridency of national rivalries encouraged a new populism. Physical clashes in parliaments, riveting political trials, a sensationalist penny press, and street demonstrations became continuing modes for political rivalry. This was true where parliamentary politics would earlier have safely contained party struggles, as in Britain, and it was equally the case where legislatures still seemed feeble and constrained by bureaucrats and dynasties as in Central Europe. Thus even the mixed political systems of imperial Germany and Austria, in which democratic and so-called feudal elements coexisted, mobilized a high degree of performative politics. Indeed, it might be argued that performative politics thrives all the more, either as a governing tactic or a strategy of resistance, when regimes appeal to the masses but hesitate to entrust them with effective power.

Two Models of Modernity

This last observation points to a fundamental ambiguity underlying notions of performance, be they applied to art or to politics. Does the theatrical experience—whether spoken or musical and visual—serve to undermine human autonomy and the capacity for social action; that is, does it reduce the audience to mere passivity and the collective isolation of the "lonely crowd?" Or do music and the performative provide the basis, not merely for the suggestibility of the crowd (recall Thomas Mann's "Mario and the Magician")—a softening up for fascism as theorists on the Left have tended to suggest—but for a reconstitution of the public, in effect, so it can undertake rational collective action and advance its capacity for autonomy and democracy? The problem has long been posed for Wagner's musical drama: was it an effort through music and art to reweld a public, or just to provide a bourgeois "phantasmagoria" (Adorno's term) through artistic tricks?[17] Hugo von Hofmannsthal praised the capacity of stagecraft to create "dream imagery" and to open a vision of the irrational, whether love or terror.[18] Theorists on the Left remain uncomfortable with such a mission, although they will endorse the artwork's exposure of ideological mystification. Historians of the visual arts have similarly celebrated modernist paintings, which, even when they cannot construct new civic communities (read implicitly: socialist or social democratic), at least testify to the subversion of bourgeois solidarity, as recently suggested for the work of Georges Seurat, himself an attentive student of Wagner's theater.[19]

This question is part of the larger debate about the political valence of modernity—progressive and liberating or technocratic and repressive—that has engaged so many social theorists since members of the Frankfurt School framed it in neo-Marxian terms. By interpreting Mahler's music against the backdrop of this issue, Adorno ensured that no matter how inspired by the vicissitudes of personal life, the works must be taken seriously for their politically progressive role. My intention here is not to attempt to ratify or dissent from a political evaluation of the music. Instead, from the perspective of performance, I would propose a different framework for the alternatives in which contemporaries were likely to evaluate Mahler's achievement. Early twentieth-century observers tended to describe the conditions of modern society, above all the contemporary metropolis, which seemed to epitomize all its problematic and exciting trends, in terms of two contrasting interpretive models or perspectives. The first perspective tended to emphasize urban anonymity and its potential for spectatorship, leisure, and consumption; envisaging, in effect, what we might term a postmodern devaluation of collective or utopian politics. Social theorists through the 1960s emphasized the potential for fascism inherent in this development, although some celebrated its possibilities for personal liberation. In contrast, adherents of the second model emphasized new possibilities for social solidarity, political organization, and mass activism, whether these resulted in victories for the Right or, as often hoped, for the Left. Mahler as performer, I propose, played an emblematic role within the framework of this second perspective.[20] Whether critics approved or not of the implications of his performances tended to depend on their political perspective.

Over the last two decades cultural historians have increasingly drawn on those social thinkers who took the first approach and cited depersonalization, detachment, and even anomie as hallmarks of the modern. They "read" the rise of the metropolis through the eyes of Georg Simmel circa 1910 or Walter Benjamin a quarter century later. For them, the modern metropolis dissolved traditional sources of personal identity—family, workplace loyalty, church, fixity of abode—thus undermining the individual's capacity as a civic actor, but bestowing in return a new freedom as spectator and consumer. While the exhilarating fluidity of the modern city allowed modern subjectivity and freedom, it allegedly reduced the scope for individual or collective political activity and thus for meaningful historical agency. The metropolis isolated the individual from his primary groups even as it washed away the human interior, placed everything into flux, overwhelmed consciousness with traffic, crowds, and commodities. For Simmel, the essence of modern urban life lay not in the social actors themselves, whether individuals or institutions, but arose from their reciprocal relationships or from interactions in a ceaseless dialectic of integration and individuation. The activity of the individual—whether in love, politics, or fashion—centered on a continual effort at differentiation from the group to whose unity he was nonetheless indispensable. The stranger was the prototypical economic actor, relating to the group by assets brought from elsewhere, outside and inside simultaneously.[21] Insofar as collective identity is forged, it was created by withdrawal into a nonpolitical enclave—one that might secure "distinction" but not power, and attained through the social club more than the political association.

Robert Musil provided a literary analogue of Simmel's city; his *Man without Qualities* and his Austrian aristocratic milieu tended to drift through life, their one common project, the Parallel Campaign to celebrate the dynasty's long service and "the Austrian idea," oriented toward the past and never quite taking cohesive shape. (By contrast, when Thomas Mann created characters most akin to Musil's feckless protagonists he placed them in an Engadine tuberculosis sanatorium, not in any urban center.) For Musil and Simmel alike, urban relationships were erotic and personal and adventitious (Simmel terms them "adventures"); they coexist with technological modernity but provide no human resources for a dramaturgy of urban politics and collective action.[22] Indeed, there was the danger that authoritarian leaders could exploit this unmoored individualism to manipulate politics—i.e., in Benjamin's terms, to impose fascism by aestheticizing politics.

But certainly through the 1960s, the alternative model of urban modernity that had emerged alongside the sociology of the flaneur and consumer remained just as influential. It envisaged the city as the site for enhanced political and economic action on the part of individuals and social groups, and it suggested that the urban dweller was a continuing participant in the dramatization of modern public life. This second model often envisioned a continuing political mobilization of society, whether one that resulted in victories for the Right or for the Left. Max Weber theorized the city as a chapter in the emergence of the modernizing class par excellence—the bourgeoisie. Among the German liberal circles he frequented, the city was an arena for *Sozialpolitik*—active intervention to ameliorate urban distress, whether on the part of religious activists or political and social reformers. It remained the crucible of mass movements, including socialism and later fascism. The physical planning of the city should itself reflect the will of strong authority, political and architectural—Baron Haussmann in Paris a generation earlier, the Viennese Liberals who built the Ringstrasse in alliance with the Monarchy in the 1860s and 1870s, or the urban theorist and designer Otto Wagner among Mahler's Viennese contemporaries. Within this worldview, the theater—earlier a privileged arena for Baroque and Rococo allegories of power—came to serve as a critical site for asserting bourgeois social and cultural ascendancy. Dramas of class power and national pride were staged as much on the staircases and in the lobbies as on the deep new stages of the Palais Garnier, the Vienna Court Opera or Burgtheater, the Czech National Theater or the Budapest Opera, and many others such as the Massimo in Palermo. By the twentieth century, theater (though not these particular theaters) would be ascribed a working-class agenda, and even more broadly, the dramatic struggles over politics—access to the vote, control of the economy, choices for war and peace—moved to the public squares of Europe's cities, which became continuing theaters for struggle.

Two visions of the modern thus contended, separated less by specific ideologies than by the scope they afforded for politics and collective action.[23] But they were separated as well by their different reliance on urban space and theater. The changes in relationships that Simmel and Musil described were associated with the rise of the metropolis, but without specific reference to its spatial resources, which remained a homogenous backdrop to the corrosion of solidarities. But theorists of the theater and performance, along with such sociologists as Durkheim and Weber, saw urban space not just as a historical backdrop but as the arena for forces of change and resistance, which remained locked in dramatic confrontation.

In his role as musical director, Mahler implicitly took up the second vision of modern urban life, with its emphasis on active civic and cultural participation. The cities where he took up posts were sites of performance, contention, and historical agency, not settings for the "blasé" (Simmel's characterization) spectatorship of the urban crowd.[24] As a musician so skilled at performance, Mahler had the resources to control the theater's public space. "Yesterday evening," Gerhard Hauptmann, celebrated as a dramatist of social protest, raved about Mahler's performance of *Fidelio* in his journal, "The immaterial stands almost materially before one's soul. It is present from the first tone until the last note has died away. No one but Mahler today can achieve this."[25] Theater, wrote Mahler's gifted stage designer, Alfred Roller, provides a "view into another world that excites, stirs, uplifts, unnerves, diverts, in any case engages." But to make theater work, he cautioned, required powerful personalities, citing Mahler's "extraordinary strength imposed quite against the tendency of his organization."[26] Still, this talent could be deployed for different political agendas. Ever since the Greeks, dramatic performance might suggest different ideological options. Drama might stress the role of recurring ritual and timeless fate; it could emphasize the chorus as a source of conservative admonitions against innovation—ultimately a summons to unchanging community cohesion and, in the twentieth-century context, to conservative or even fascist politics. Conversely, it might emphasize individual choice and a narrative of progress and change—ultimately an exemplification of liberal or socialist transformation. The first interpretation privileged structure and permanence over narrative, the second proposed history and temporal linearity. Not by chance, Mahler's champions and critics heard the second approach in his music.

His liberal advocates celebrated the sense of development and unfolding they heard; his conservative adversaries contrasted it unfavorably with the symphonic tradition they understood, sometimes in favor of the Brucknerian alternative.[27] So too they denigrated his conducting for its alleged jerky gesticulations, chin jutting, arm waving, describing its style as a "St. Vitus dance," allegedly Semitic in its excitability. Certainly he was easy to caricature. Nonetheless, his supporters and those who sang under his direction praised his discipline, the authority he evidently radiated, and the capacity to elicit the best they had. As a Dutch critic said: "Calm, exactness, fiery temperament, and an infallible ear, are the great properties of this special man."[28] (See Figure 1 for another contemporary impression of Mahler's conducting.) So too was his unremitting dedication to performance. Mahler paid a wistful tribute to his lifelong commitment to the theater in the last letter he wrote to Guido Adler from New York, four months before his death: "I absolutely require a practical exercise of my musical abilities as a counterpoise to the enormous inner happiness in creating. . . . " But how happy he now claimed to be, finally to have a concert orchestra, and not the theater with its "entirely different acoustical conditions," to allow him that outlet.[29]

Theater, Politics, and Pluralism in Central Europe

The theater was central to Mahler's artistic working life. But the idea of the theater as a political arena, open to the public and enclosed not by walls but by a national frontier, is also useful for understanding his political world in Central Europe The theater serves many functions. By establishing a perimeter it keeps performative energies from indefinitely dissipating in time and space. It sets up a place of heightened expectations where it is anticipated that performers and publics are to interact. Like churches for religious rites or museums for exhibitions, it allows for practices that represent and reinforce relations of domination and subordination, but also contests them.[30] More specifically, by applying the analogy of the theater to politics and culture, we can see how Mahler's career so appropriately unfolded in turn-of-the-century Austria.

The idea of the theater offers a revealing alternative to the tropes usually invoked to analyze Austrian politics and culture. Most frequently these have centered on the conflict between allegedly modern and archaic constitutional elements, or on the linguistic disputes of a multinational empire that supposedly encouraged a fascination with language in general on the part of so many brilliant writers and philosophers.[31] Precisely these ethnic quarrels made it difficult to move beyond what progressive liberals believed to be the archaism of Austria-Hungary, assuming as they did that cohesive national states should form the basis of modern politics. As Robert Musil understood, given a more imaginative political leadership, Habsburg multinationalism might conceivably have foreshadowed a multicultural future, and not just seemed the her-

Figure 1. Otto Böhler, *Gustav Mahler as Conductor*

itage of an anachronistic prenational past. Musil also suggested—though less convincingly in light of the military rivalries that were becoming so threatening—that ritual and theater might conceivably have served as a substitute for political modernization. As he wrote about the ritualized national conflicts that paralyzed liberal politics: they had merely crystallized earlier than anywhere else, "assuming the form of a sublimated ceremonial that might have become of great importance if its evolution had not been prematurely cut short by a catastrophe."[32] In effect, Musil suggested that the Habsburg Empire had become what Clifford Geertz calls a "theater state"—a regime that existed not for utilitarian ends of the general welfare or to expand, or even any longer to support a dynastic family—but just to be theatrical, to stage ceremony, to affirm itself and the role of its elites through a dramaturgic politics.[33] As both the novelist and the anthropologist indirectly conceded, however, these theater states could not survive military confrontations. Nonetheless, for as long as they survived, they revealed the integral connection of performance and politics.

If Austria-Hungary seemed Europe's theater-state par excellence, the other countries, democracies and empires alike, were also becoming arenas for the ritualized conflict of politics. Increasingly throughout Europe, public space was theatricalized—or more precisely retheatricalized—from the 1890s to the eve of World War I. Consider the historical succession of such well-staged public manifestations as the 1894 degradation of Dreyfus; the 1897 German-Czech clashes in Prague and the Imperial Reichsrat after Prime Minister Badenyi sought to cede linguistic equality to the Czechs; the Milan urban riots of 1898 followed by the imposition of martial law in Italy; the Russian Revolution of 1905 and the mass strikes in Central Europe in the same period; thereafter, from 1910 to 1913, demonstrations in Germany and Scandinavia to broaden the suffrage and in Vienna to end the paralysis of the Austrian Parliament by the Czech parties; finally, the demonstrations of militant suffragettes and major industrial unions in the very stronghold of social stability, Great Britain! Throughout this period, Vienna—the sixth largest city of the world by 1908—did not lag in public confrontational politics. The inauguration of Karl Lueger's Christian Socials and the continued progress of the Marxian Socialists set the stage for episodic confrontations that would finally culminate in civil war by 1934.

Mahler arrived at the Court Opera in time for Lueger's installation and the Badenyi riots—a series of German nationalist demonstrations that may have led him to produce Smetana's *Dalibor* on the Emperor's name day as a show of support for the government's pro-Czech policies.[34] Mahler would witness the struggle over the planned torchlight celebrations for Lueger's sixtieth birthday in 1904, which had to be canceled because of Socialist counterdemonstrations; in November 1905, he could witness 200,000 Socialist sympathizers occupy the Ringstrasse to call for equal male suffrage. Until 1907, suffrage for the parliament of the Austrian half of the Empire (so-called Cisleithania) was based on electoral colleges or curiae weighted by voters' wealth. Hungarian agitation against renewing the decennial joint military budget had led the crown to threaten reforming the gerrymandered electoral system that maintained Magyar control of the parliament in Budapest. The measure was finally withdrawn, but not before general and equal male suffrage was enacted for the Austrian legislature in 1906–1907. Nonetheless, the democratically elected parliament of May 1907, and its successor elected in June 1911, could not overcome long periods of ethnic and class stalemate, with filibusters by aggrieved minority representatives, and the government's recourse to rule by decree.[35] As Musil later wrote, "There was a parliament which made such vigorous use of its liberty that it was usually kept shut; but there was also an emergency powers act by means of which it was possible to manage without parliament, and every time when everyone was just beginning to rejoice in absolutism, the Crown decreed that there must now again be a return to parliamentary government."[36] In fact, decisive confrontations took place increasingly in the streets and public squares. Political analysts on the Left, such as Rosa Luxemburg, who claimed the virtues of the mass strike, and on the Right, such as Georges Sorel and Vilfredo Pareto, understood that political movements were created through demonstrations and even clashes. This sort of politics was particularly urban not because it could not take place outside the city but because, as Richard Sennett has argued, "a code of interpreting appearances which arose among strangers in the city came to influence general political language."[37] This intense dramaturgy was certainly noted by one aspiring artist-politician in Vienna, Adolf Hitler.

No one active in public life—whether in the arts or politics or the economy—could have ignored the basic trends of politics after 1890, as the multinational life of the Empire grew ever more brittle. From the financial crash of the mid-1870s until the outbreak of World War I, cosmopolitanism came under attack and anti-Semitism rose in the Empire, as elsewhere in Europe and North America. The assault on pluralism was a general trend but particularly acute in Middle Europe. The Habsburg realms were in fact becoming less cosmopolitan as multilingual towns were settled by peasant workers from the Slavic hinterlands who pressed for greater use of their respective languages: by Slovenes migrating into Marburg an der Drau, or Czechs into Budweis, for example.[38] Imagine a Canada composed of half a dozen Quebecs, and one might have some sense of the evolution. Among the "historic" or dominant peoples of the Empire, Germans became less patient with non-Germans, Magyars sought a greater domination of their half of the monarchy. The national minorities who had ethnic kin living in neighboring states—Italy, Serbia, Romania, and more problematically Russian Poland or the German Empire—added centrifugal pressure to their national demands.

Mahler did not live long enough to witness the final crises of the multinational Empire. Nonetheless, as did every artist and intellectual of the ramshackle empire, he had to cope with the centrifugal impulses as a backdrop to his own career. As a musical director, seeking to develop talent among diverse provincial orchestras, ethnic tolerance and cosmopolitanism made sense. For a young man of provincial Bohemian-Jewish origin transplanted to the capital, the commitment to supranationalism was all the more urgent. Mahler made his career against this backdrop of ethnic mobilization, sensing it (as did his contemporary composers and architects) perhaps less as a threat than as a potential for artistic vitality. From his first appointments in Bad Hall and Laibach he migrated to Olmütz in Moravia, then briefly to Kassel in Germany. He then departed for Prague, where he took up the mission of trying to help recuperate the German theater (i.e., the eighteenth-century Estates or Tyl theater) from its declining fortunes vis-à-vis the new Czech National Theater (the city was three-fifths Czech and two-fifths German, although almost seventy percent spoke Czech and only a shade more than a quarter German as their everyday language). Thence to Leipzig, as an impatient second choice to Arthur Nikisch, then to Budapest, where the mandate was to help the Hungarians elevate their new opera into an imperial institution coequal with the Vienna Court Opera. "I have the honor," he addressed the orchestra members, "to step to the head of an institution that has been summoned in every respect to be the home and hearth of the national art of this land."[39] He demanded works sung in Magyar; he would tolerate no bilingual performances; and he rejected performers unable to sing in the national language.[40]

Mahler was nonetheless criticized for not programming enough Hungarian operas and music; how long he could have withstood the currents of Magyar nationalism (even without its being augmented by anti-Semitic accents) was uncertain. His intense activism, in fact, should have been congenial to the Budapest middle classes with their program for redeeming national backwardness, if not to the magnates' disdain for labor and productivity.[41] Ultimately, however, he would have remained an outsider in Hungary—even more than among Austrians and Germans, as depicted in his famous self-description of alienation as Jew and Bohemian.[42] Accepting a generous severance package after two years and a change to a temperamental and anti-Semitic court theater commissioner, he took over in Hamburg. It was the call to the Vienna Court Opera, however, to which he had aspired for over a decade; he lobbied for it and underwent baptism for it on February 23, 1897. Having climbed to the top of the greasy pole, to cite Disraeli, another Jew who stormed the summit of a gentile society, he helped to transform it, musically and theatrically.

In Disraeli's Britain, of course, anti-Semitism did not emerge as the basis for a political movement at the turn of the twentieth century, whereas it played a significant, if not constant, role in Central Europe, allowing unscrupulous politicians on the Right to assemble powerful electoral movements among peasants and the new urban middle classes. Resentment at the Jews' allegedly encroaching if not conspiratorial influence was especially easy to fan when, as second generation residents of one of the capital cities, they claimed a place in journalism and the arts or finance and industry and identified with German or Magyar culture. In an age of ethnic nationalism, conversion hardly removed the taint of their origins. Mahler took up his position at the Court Opera in the same year that Emperor Franz Joseph finally allowed Lueger, who had mobilized an anti-Semitic Christian Social electoral coalition, to take office as Mayor. Despite the conductor's nominal conversion to Catholicism, the City Council declined to accept a concert by the Opera orchestra if Mahler insisted on conducting it.[43] The Jews of the dual monarchy had a vested interest in a tolerant pluralism. This they saw best preserved by either a *k. und k.* liberalism that supported the dynasty or later by for a multinational Austromarxism.[44] To be sure, not all nationalist trends appeared menacing. Cultural nationalism and ethnic diversity could appear as progressive forces, especially when they inspired artistic innovation. By the new century, a young generation of creative intellectuals cultivated national expression in art, music (including the operetta and folk music), theater, and architecture. Nonetheless, such nationalism with a human face or incipient multiculturalism remained a precarious and vulnerable cultural stance.[45]

Public life in Central Europe in the decade before World War I was thus beset by contradictions. Despite increasing anti-Semitism, Jews played an ever more influential role in cultural, political, and commercial life. Liberalism survived in Austria although the legislature hardly functioned and censorship persisted; a democracy for the Magyar half of the kingdom was sustained by virtue of a gerrymandered suffrage in Hungary; universal male suffrage returned a large Social Democratic delegation to the German Reichstag but could exert only a limited influence over policy choices; and in all three states there were overpowerful bureaucracies and aristocracies. Nonetheless, city politics remained vibrant throughout, and for all the limits on its efficacy, the dramatic confrontations of political life were staged as vigorously as anywhere else. The issue was whether they counted for more than theater. Or whether (as Geertz might have asked) performance might not really matter more than politics: As Max Burckhard wrote in the liberal *Neue Freie Presse,* "We have after all been finished as a Great Power politically for quite a while. . . . Once upon a time we were something like a State. Now what we have is something like two halves of something which has not even a proper name. . . . But we do have something! We do still have something in which we really and truly are something. . . . We have our Opera."[46] Ironically, the occasion for writing was precisely that for political reasons Mahler was being pressured to resign as director of the Court Opera.

Mahler, Alfred Roller, and Max Reinhardt: Opera Renewal and Total Theater

Mahler came to the opera with a reputation as a vigorous conductor, a slight aura of mystery about the exact role he had been designated to play (other more senior musical directors were still present), and high hopes that he might rescue the institution from the lifeless routine into which performances had degenerated. Mahler's genius as a conductor was frequently conceded even by the adversaries of his compositions. Once he had established a record at the Court Opera, friendly commentators singled out for praise his capacity to penetrate works of vastly different character. Max Graf cited his ability to conduct both a *Tristan* "with an intense and impassioned exaltation which lashes all the fervour of the work from its utmost depths," and direct *Figaro* "with a delicate and witty serenity." That he was director of the Court Opera meant in fact a revolution—"think of it: an artist, not a bureaucrat, a strong human temperament with sympathies, dislikes, enthusiasms, depressions, moods, opinions, enthusiasms, passions: no paper-pusher or director-official."[47] Mahler was credited with powerful productions of Wagner, introducing new works, and resurrecting Mozart from lifeless repetition. Important as these achievements were, more was at stake, in fact, than even a wide-ranging genius for musical interpretation. Opera direction, as Mahler so tirelessly engaged with it, required a more encompassing effort. The term that kept emerging in so much of the theater criticism was "synthesis," whether for plays or opera—bringing to the stage a work with visual impact, dance, and drama—an organic fusion or smelting, as the impresario for the premiere of his Symphony of a Thousand emphasized.[48]

Mahler in fact participated in a remarkable era of theater renewal in Europe; he shared its ideology and its achievements. At a moment when European politics and culture were becoming more performative in general, theatrical performance itself entered a period of lively discussion and experiment. New drama, whether naturalist or symbolist, a generation of celebrated performers, the development of cabaret and new theaters, innovative set design, journals devoted to music and theater, manifestos about theater reform, all testified to an extraordinary ferment.

Underlying all these ventures was the effort to overcome traditional divisions of the theater arts, to fuse dance and music and spoken drama, and to unite performers and public, to a degree that earlier productions, so it was felt, had not achieved. A generation previously Wagner had similarly envisaged his musical dramas as integral artistic experiences or Gesamtkunstwerke, and although the innovators of the new century shared this goal, their approaches and emphases evolved. The term total theater (borrowed by analogy from World War I's notion of a total war that mobilized society as a whole) might best convey their updated vision. First of all, the visual element of the theatrical synthesis emerged out of a critique of Bayreuth scenic literalism: it was intended to second the dominant mood of the drama, not provide just a painted backdrop. The Geneva director Adolphe Appia took Bayreuth stage design to task in his writings from the mid 1890s, which he continued to elaborate into the 1920s. Wagner had reformed the theater but not the stage setting, "which presented nothing comparable to the marvelous score." Light, not stage painting was the appropriate accompaniment for music; simplicity was crucial for focusing on the performer, whom Appia envisioned as a musical gymnast or dancer representing the body in space. Appealing to the fusion of the arts, Appia wanted the theater to serve as a locus for all sorts of public commemorations and festivals: "Yes—it is the cathedral of the future that we are invoking with all our heart. We want a place where our new-born community can affirm itself clearly in space: a space supple enough to help bring to reality all our desires for an integral life."[49] Such concepts for staging and theater reform had a major impact on many of the German-language stages. The Scottish producer Gordon Craig conveyed similar notions from London to Weimar; the important modernist architect Peter Behrens, who would design the celebrated machine assembly plant for German General Electric in 1912, planned the Darmstadt Theater as a "holy shrine for all art." In 1909, Wassily Kandinsky's experimental "Yellow Sound" was set to music and conceived of as a virtual light drama, a dramatization of Goethe's *Farbenlehre* that associated color harmonies and dissonances analogous to musical chords with specific emotions.

In total theater, the social setting for performance was just as important as what occurred onstage. The revitalized theater was to be sited in the midst of the city; it was integrally woven into the life of the metropolis and was to speak to the social, political and sexual or gender issues of modernity. Although the privileged apartness of the music festival still beckoned impresarios, the vitality of performance had to prove itself in the urban center—against all the impediments imposed by repertory routines, as Mahler's set designer, Secession artist Alfred Roller, lamented.[50] The modern city, after all, was itself an arena. This concept entailed the idea of an active audience drawn into a performative transaction by means of dance and color and light as well as words. By the first decade of the twentieth century the challenges of total theater recruited not just the isolated visionary, but theater producers and designers throughout Europe, including such impresarios as Max Reinhardt and Sergei Diaghilev, Mahler's collaborator Roller, and, I would propose, Mahler himself.

Less of a theorist than Wagner, Mahler nonetheless shared a commitment to enhancing opera as a visual experience. The collaboration with Roller began in February 1903 with a *Tristan* based on color backdrops that changed with the emotional course of the work. The critic Max Graf described a "nervous color romanticism," of "light and air that make music."[51] Roller's sets became laboratories for the innovative use of color and light and the articulation of the stage into architectonic masses, not the conventional and fussy realism for which Bayreuth mises-en-scène had set the tone.

Although the settings generally won enthusiastic support, they provoked serious questions. Historical appropriateness was one. Julius Korngold, Hanslick's successor as music critic at the *Neue Freie Presse*, was reserved at first about the *Fidelio* of October 1904. He showed his familiarity with the history of "stage reform" since Appia, but feared that the production offered an "excess of scenic ambiance [*Stimmung*] for an old-style opera."[52] Bruno Walter similarly worried that Roller's use of color was too overwhelming for Mozart's subtleties.[53] Just as problematic was the moral effect of the new stage aesthetics. Was it not possible that the idea of liberation from narrow-minded representation which they supposedly stood for might not degenerate into mere prettiness? Committed to the socially pedagogic value of serious music, David Josef Bach could still rhapsodize over Roller's settings for *The Magic Flute*, as a "concordance of colors that creates the most wonderful of images."[54] But precisely such aesthetic delight presented a danger, at least according to rationalist critics: might not the light and colors undermine the moral content of the music? Robert Hirschfeld felt that Mahler had become so preoccupied by visual art in *Tristan* and *Aida,* that it led "to the indulgence and gratuitous charming of the public and the suppression of those more noble musical impulses which Mahler as director had known how to awaken with incomparable subtlety at the beginning of his regime."[55] In this respect critiques sometimes paralleled the criticism of Mahler's luxuriant timbres and orchestral coloration.[56]

Did color and light merely lead to enchantment and beauty—or did they contribute, as Roller and others implied, to a redemptive or emancipatory theater? Marxist postwar producers such as Erwin Piscator and his designer implicitly sided with the more didactic judgments and would mount productions with austere constructivist concepts. But the justification for Roller's settings and other synesthetic designs—its invocation of unity and totality—was in fact a moral and not merely an aesthetic one. Hermann Bahr cited Appia, Gordon Craig, Josef Olbrich (who had designed the Secession building), and Peter Behrens, along with Roller, for understanding that staging must "create, not imitate," must be "suggestion, not reality," and must synthesize, as Mahler also insisted, the real and the ideal.[57] By the time that *Don Giovanni* was presented at the end of 1905 Korngold, who had been critical a year earlier, praised the visual experience as a great success for Mahler and Roller. Stage lighting endowed the setting with its life and its poetry. "For the first time the illusions of music and dramatic action are fused into an inseparable unity."[58]

Unity of the theatrical experience—the performer's synthesis of prose, body movement, and song, when the genre called for it; the designer's placement of the performer in a visual context that was emotionally suggestive rather than merely representational; the audience's collaboration in the liminal drama—seemed to justify itself. The goal raised some key issues: to what extent must total theater be based on illusion, and to what degree could an illusionistic experience really be morally uplifting? But the premise of a performative culture was that there was no conflict between the culture of aesthetics and morals. Strauss and Hofmannsthal self-consciously tested the premise even if they ultimately reaffirmed it; Mahler and Roller largely accepted it. For Roller, Mahler earned the status of a theatrical producer in the broadest sense, and he compared him with the preeminent theater impresario of the day, Max Reinhardt. In one interview, protesting against the effort to compartmentalize different aspects of the theater, Roller argued "one can't simply cordon off areas and say, here the musician begins and the painter stops. . . . [Theater] has to involve the development of the whole, and Reinhardt's merit is simply to have accelerated the course of this development through honest experiments and thus to have brought us closer to a possible new shaping of the stage." Only working under Mahler's direction, Roller said, had provided a more passionate and exciting experience than working with Reinhardt.[59]

The comparison of Reinhardt and Mahler was apt, and not merely because the set designer worked for both. Mahler's directorship in Vienna coincided with the rapid rise to prominence of the impressario, originally Viennese, in the Berlin theater world. (Reinhardt in fact employed Roller in 1901 to stage *Faust* Part I in Vienna, then engaged him in late 1905 to design Hofmannsthal's *Oedipus and the Sphinx* at the Deutsches Theater, and sought unsuccessfully to woo him permanently from the Vienna Court Opera a year later.[60] Progressing beyond cabaret productions, Reinhardt opened two theaters in 1902–03, then took over the Deutsches Theater, employing such artists as Lovis Corinth and Max Slevogt, and exploiting the latest lighting and machinery, staging Wedekind's *Erdgeist*, Strindberg's dramas, Maeterlinck's *Pelléas and Mélisande*, Wilde's *Salome*, and Hofmannsthal's *Elektra*. (See figure 2.) Reinhardt would present *Oedipus Rex* in the three-thousand-seat Munich Musikhalle in the same year and city that Mahler finally staged his massive Eighth Symphony; he also sent huge arena productions to London, St. Petersburg, and Moscow.[61] He and Hofmannsthal envisioned building a vast theater complex outside Salzburg (a concept to be inaugurated after the war with the Salzburg festival) to be designed by Hans Poelzig, who never got to construct the festival theater but planned the expressionist Grosses Schauspielhaus, resembling a vast cave of stalactites, for Reinhardt in Berlin in 1920. For all of Reinhardt's support of the new and avant-garde, he never abandoned his instinct for showmanship, a search for profitable middle-class entertainment that would later play a role in the Salzburg festival's presentation of Hofmannsthal's popular reworking of the drama *Everyman* and the virtual marketing of Mozart.

The key to Reinhardt's genius, argued Richard Specht, an enthusiast of both Reinhardt and Mahler, was his talent for grasping the central point of every drama: "He feels with the utmost sensitivity the spiritual and sensuous atmosphere of every dramatic representation, its rhythm and its inner music. . . . The word music needs to be repeated: therein rests perhaps the strongest aspect of Reinhardt's talent, one in which the poetic, the mimetic, the painterly and the musical merge into each other in so rare a unity."[62] Reinhardt was for spoken drama what Mahler was for music drama: "the artist who creates a living, i.e., a presented drama by means of words, body, voice, gesture, tone, and color." Mahler and Reinhardt met only once and enthusiastically shared their views of theater—so "representative of their era and inner needs," as Bruno

Figure 2. W. A. Wellner, *Large Autumn Parade for the Opening of the Theater Season* (1911). The picture includes among others Franz Léhar, Richard Strauss, Maurice Maeterlinck, Hugo von Hofmannsthal, and Gerhard Hauptmann. The rich tradition of theater caricature in the press of Central Europe, as elsewhere, testified to the continuing importance of performative culture in the public sphere.

Walter recalled.[63] Mahler in Vienna, Reinhardt, the Austrian, in Berlin—each raised their theater to unprecedented attainments in the half decade after 1905, revived the classics and welcomed the modern (unless censorship intervened), experimenting to a degree with the avant-garde, exacting the highest demands on quality, yet sometimes settling for a theatrical vocation that mobilized huge performance resources, and in the case of the composer, works of unprecedented length.

Looking ahead to the interwar years, we might wonder whether the transition that Central European composers and directors—including Reinhardt and later Erich Wolfgang Korngold—eventually made to a larger public in America had not been prepared by the expansiveness of these prewar urban performances with their deployment of massed performers and lavish settings in huge auditoriums. While the Central European metropolis certainly nurtured experimental music and theater, it would do so after the war in smaller and more dedicated conventicles or on the sparser stages of Brecht and Piscator. Total theater, with its synthesthetic aspirations, emerged at the turn of the century as in part a reformist political project, but it could not sustain its ideological thrust, which passed instead to a far more astringent dramaturgy. Mahler and Reinhardt certainly encouraged avant-garde efforts, but their commitment to performance posited a public that yearned for the familiar even if it might accept the innovative, and sought reaffirmation of a performative tradition as well as its renovation. Could these differing objectives be satisfied in the long run through staging and bold theatricality? Mahler would not live long enough to answer. Reinhardt and Hofmannsthal's Salzburg festival suggested that ritual or even revival placed in the service of rehabilitating a national identity shattered by World War I would prevail over innovation.[64]

Music as Theater, Music as Politics

The issue of theatricality carries this inquiry finally from conducting to composition, and from the politics of performance to the politics of musical interpretation. Throughout Mahler's career critics separated the conductor from the composer, and even those who condemned his compositions recognized his gifts in evoking a superb performance from an orchestra. When commentators sought to assess both sides of the career, however, ideas of theatricality allowed them to connect composition and interpretation. Theatricality by name was by no means a compliment. Culminating an unremittingly hostile critique of the Berlin premiere of the Third Symphony, Paul Moos wrote that the Adagio's evocation of divine love "must appear as blasphemous: it is so wordy, so external, so theatrical, so untrue," and that Mahler without realizing it was "a musical comedian, a farceur, an imitator of the worst sort."[65] For appreciative listeners, however, the power and originality of the music lay precisely in the characteristics attributed to theatricality, that is its bold or exaggerated contrasts of tonality, rhythms, and dynamics. As Ludwig Schiedemair explained, "we are struck in Mahler's symphonies by the penchant for sharp contrasts and popular melodies, . . . the sharp contrast of powerful fortes and scarcely audible pianos," the unequal divisions of light and shade, the deployment of a small and distant brass section, of bells and multiplied horns—devices that were all the more moving in that they were evidently rooted in the composer's own experience of pain, sadness, joy, and desire.[66] Richard Specht's Mahler obituary cited his effort as conductor to achieve "the purely drawn line, the division of light and shadow, the differentiation of polyphonic tissue, the carefully equilibrated dynamics, as unique for their ascent to dizzying peaks climaxed by ecstatic force as for their pianissimi hovering at the point of dematerialization." Specht praised the symphonies for their "boldness and often unchecked violence of the most extreme expression," and as well for their evocation "of those secrets and questions that are most consoling and threatening for every existence."[67]

Theatricality, after all, is a venerable strategy for performance that deliberately intensifies or stylizes mood and emotive stance. It involves a conscious taking on by the artist of the emotional depths being plumbed or heights ascended, the wracking sense of abandonment, or the conviction of redemption. The author, composer, or performer becomes a vicar or surrogate for the audience, whether authentically or spuriously; indeed the charge of theatricality was sometimes invoked to imply that the stance was spurious. Reliance on the personal perception or experience of the creator was squarely in the tradition of the performative—"subjectifying the artist as the site of the narrative" (to cite Frith again), that is, experiencing the otherwise unimaginable through the artist's retrieval of beauty from despair and exaltation.[68] Bekker's exposition of the symphonies a decade after Mahler's death asked the reader in effect to repeat a journey through spiritual realms in the company of the composer as once Dante accompanied Virgil.

Theatricality, however, necessarily raises problems of aesthetic coherence. Deployment of theatrical modes, with their intensification of alternating emotions, strains the cohesion of a work. Contemporary critics as well as subsequent analysts have returned continually to the relation of part to whole, whether the resolution of conflicting voices, the role of disruptions and fractures, songs to symphonies, the commonplace themes to the exalted synthesis, outer to inner movements, or programs to music, in the search for the logic that unifies the works.

Critical commentary has tended to focus on three sources of unity or cohesion in Mahler's massive works. The most prevalent interpretations have repeatedly emphasized the composer's unceasing search for religious salvation and individual redemption—his openness to transcendent impulses from the Second Symphony to the intense lyrics of the *Kindertotenlieder.* The other traditional answer has invoked the artist's own personality and creativity. Edward Stein felt that Mahler's approach to thematic development was crucial, as his variations never really departed from the exposition, but instead became more and more inclusive and self-referential, and thus pulled the work together from his own successive insights and creative power.[69] The composer in effect guaranteed by his own identity and virtuosity an inner coherence to the profusion of themes and developments. Richard Specht likewise believed that Mahler's own creativity ensured his musical achievement. As he wrote about the Seventh Symphony: "What his admirers love and what his enemies object to is articulated with clarity: Unless we are totally deceived the struggle that the singular nature of the composer has aroused through every one of his expressions will . . . be decided by this work."[70]

For one hostile critic the respectful treatment of Mahler as "hero of the modern symphony" amounted to a "cult of personality," when in fact he lacked artistic discipline and his endless formless movements were better seen as "kilometer music."[71] Robert Hirschfeld felt that Mahler enthusiasts were seduced by the cliché of personality: "Personality—certainly! Only one must be sure that this personality possesses inner strength and composure; continuity in progress on a straight course, following a line; and the immense spiritual calm of shaping, in order to produce symphonic structure."[72] This skepticism raises the same question for the composer as for the performer, namely: Can the artist guarantee the validity of his creation by virtue of his own personal authenticity or aesthetic charisma? Does the artist's personal experience validate his art?

Interpretations since Adorno have debated a third source of artistic cohesion, namely the composer's capacity for musical dialectic, such that, on the one hand, he could sustain a convincing sense of symphonic unity across every disruption, yet, on the other, endow each of his "characters," as Adorno put it, with their own dramatic autonomy.[73] It is easier to accept his argument that Mahler's "characters" retained their identity and were not merely subsumed into the whole than his defense of them as virtual peasant-revolutionary harbingers of the future war that the composer allegedly intuited must culminate the imperialist era. Adorno has Mahler make of the "Wunderhorn" crew who appear in the Fourth Symphony the same sort of characters that Brecht was later to take from Grimmelshausen for *Mother Courage*; it is not the most convincing part of the defense, although it remains consistent with his view of the Mahler symphony as a picaresque.[74]

Each of these interpretations has entailed political implications, though often indirectly. To focus on the religious settings did not mean renouncing a secular and reformist reception of the music. But it led those interpreters who wanted to celebrate the music's potential for individual or collective change to stress the conditions of performance itself, to seek social value in its properties as public theater. On the other hand, to celebrate the musical achievement in terms of the composer's genius or personality could ultimately, and doubtless against the intentions of Mahler's advocates, provide the basis for a reactionary or even fascistic aesthetic. Finally, Adorno's effort to interpret Mahler in terms of musical dialectics faced still another difficulty: the very musical excesses that the philosopher claimed were the bases of Mahler's radical vitality. The autonomous "characters" embodied in dances and marches that Adorno saw as so central to Mahler's exposition threatened to escape the sovereign control of the composer.

No artist can risk theatricality without occasionally falling over the line into kitsch or banality. Given the infatuation with Wagner and the exalted Nietzschean rhetoric that Mahler inherited from his late adolescent fling with the Pernerstorfer circle—the coterie of the early 1880s that included the young Mahler, Victor Adler, the future pan-German leader Georg von Schönerer, and his long-term friend Siegfried Lipiner—there was always the danger of excess. Modern critics, embarrassed about the inevitable lapses, suggest that irony must be at stake. The composer himself, after all, left instructions for parody. For Adorno, the composer is redeemed by his utopianism and his recognition in the final works, not just of his own grief, but that of all the downtrodden. Adorno was willing to confront the charge of banality and kitsch occasionally by apparently defending kitsch itself. "Kitsch hoaxes with what, at the same time, it has that art lacks."[75] Pierre Boulez, in contrast, dissents from Adorno's defense and contests the effort to make Mahler a quasi-radical precursor of the Second Vienna School: there is "too much nostalgia, too much attachment to the past."[76]

When Octavian presents the silver rose or Ariadne and Bacchus fall so gorgeously for each other after the witty and brittle introduction, the listener senses that Strauss and Hofmannsthal are playing on multiple levels of emotional response; and Zerbinetta brings us down to earth.

But how can the contemporary audience be certain that in fact Mahler did not just become indiscriminately populist and self-indulgent with his massive scoring and timbre, as his harsher critics suggested? Theatrical contrasts rendered by the empathetic performer risk becoming just a meretricious device for representing a succession of mental states. For the generation after Mahler, such a performative strategy was likely to be distrusted, which is why, after the collapse of the empires that still, precariously, seemed to sustain Mahler's world, Brecht believed that the playwright and director must shatter the stage's illusion of empathy. In its stead, the producer was to present a so-called epic theater, which intellectually compelled the audience to deconstruct bourgeois human- istic values.[77] Besides suspecting the techniques of empathy by which theater supposedly represented conflicts of values, Marxian analysts rejected the liberal ideals that were offered. The conflicts that bourgeois drama and musical programs supposedly represented were hardly "timeless" in Marxist eyes, but supposedly artifacts of bourgeois cultural hegemony. Was not Mahler's dramaturgy hopelessly passé?

Mahler was willing to run the risk of empathy in his deployment of theatricality. Sympathetic listeners understood he trod a fine line but generally responded positively; they eventually ratified his theatricality in part by changing the literary metaphor from drama to novel, the metaphor that one early critic, Hermann Kipper, borrowed from Charpentier's operatic subtitle for *Louise* when he reviewed the premiere of the Fifth Symphony in Cologne.[78] Since Adorno it has become com- mon to analyze Mahler's work as "novelistic." Can ideas of performance and theatricality as an interpretive category be squared with the novel- istic concept? The theatrical or dramatic narrative, after all, is not just a picaresque succession of episodes, but a story hinged around a profound crisis: Adorno distinguished Beethoven's symphonies as dramas, in which the musical climax is prefigured from the outset, from Mahler's as nov- els that had no equivalent teleological momentum. There is a further challenge. Even if we allow that narrative and dramatic development need not be fundamentally opposed, narrative and performance are hardly identical. Narrative implies some sort of linear development, whether direct or meandering, whereas the idea of performance merely signals the decisive charismatic presence of the artist.[79]

In fact, the distinction matters little. Whether conceived in terms of its narrative concept or as the basis for performance, Mahler's art had an activist orientation. It was created to be interventionist, to change the world as well as interpret it. The music exploited familiar themes and rhythms, constructed a narrative whether "historical" or novelistic, was presented in a highly charged encounter between audience and players, and in so doing presupposed the possibility of taking a musical audience beyond music to constituting itself as a spiritual or perhaps civic public. Even when his songs and symphonies seem most personal they endeavor to make sense not just of the great metaphysical issues of death and redemption, but to do so on behalf of a broader community. The artist performs on behalf of his audience; each needs the other and presupposes that their interdependence enhances collective life. Recall the two images social commentators had posited for modernity. The first image—the modernity depicted by Simmel and Musil—was certainly the product of history, but its participants hardly acted as participants in history. Instead the acceleration of capitalist consumption increasingly dislocated those caught within its web of relationships, depriving them of historical agency, undermining their capacity for political intervention and even for authentic artistic or performative art. But the second image of the modern, which Mahler shared with so many historical contemporaries, sociologists and social reformers, with progressive journalists and political party leaders, such as Victor Adler, with the artists of the Secession ("To every age its art"), justified unceasing historical action and activist intervention as intellectual, political leader or artist. Modern society as a site for political contention, and for performative intervention that would help constitute a responsive public—whether as audience or as citizenry—had to have a historical or temporal dimension. The commitment of the artist, performer, novelist presupposed the stance not of the flaneur, but of the reformer. Both as conductor and composer Mahler's musical dramaturgy is intensely personal, but it is precisely its performative characteristics that make possible the creation of modern collective life. No matter how personal the music, no matter how concerned with issues of death or redemption, the activity of composition and conducting had a social dimension. The performances and the music amounted to a statement on behalf of a modern and often urban world that escapes the merely anomic or relational and admits the progressive.

In their interventionist implications, some of the compositions—not the later songs or the Ninth perhaps—may risk too easy a historical and musical reassurance. They suggest that the mass deployment of human and instrumental energies can overcome the destructive tendencies of twentieth-century political communities. The line between the rousing march, even the rousing funeral march, and the simplistic assurances of mass nationalism or a conformist proletcult that would follow a generation later, is a fragile one. Was there an alternative musical program that reflected the other vision of modernity—one that corresponded musically, say, to Simmel's world of sophisticated and complex reciprocities—

rather than attempting a vision of mass redemption? In very different ways Strauss and Hofmannsthal or perhaps Debussy and Schoenberg suggested alternatives.[80] And Berg would insist on an approach that paralleled Brecht's call for epic theater. No Dionysiacally inspired audiences allow for historical progress in these works. In the end, to transcend the historical cul de sac of bourgeois romanticism Adorno wished to grant Mahler the subtlety of dialectic. But the bourgeois qualities that Mahler encompassed, if the application of such class terms still makes sense at all, were not negative or escapist, but in line with what Marx himself had identified as the great transformative and modernizing program of the bourgeoisie. They moved history forward, but perhaps at some points with misleading confidence, as if choral masses or brass scoring might overcome the historical dangers that lay ahead. The issue we face with Mahler is whether we can still let ourselves listen to his metanarrative of modern performativity on his own terms, or whether the century's subsequent politics and music does not suggest he attempted too easy a resolution, even with the most capacious of talents.

NOTES

I wish to thank the staff at the Bibliothèque Gustav Mahler in Paris, especially Aline Partonnaud. Without this collection, and the documentary guidance provided by Henry-Louis de la Grange's vast biography of Mahler for which it was partly assembled, this essay would not have been possible. I am grateful also to Andrea Maier, who helped me gather Paris documentation, and to Karen Painter, who provided copies of some reception sources.

1. Mahler's letter to Annie Mincieux, 2 March 1896, in *Mahler's Unknown Letters*, ed. Herta Blaukopf, trans. Richard Stokes (Boston, 1987), p. 119, translation adapted.

2. Mahler's letter to Baron von Gilsa, 29 December 1885, from the archive of the Kassel theater, trans. in *Mahler, His Life, Work and World*, ed. Kurt Blaukopf and Herta Blaukopf (New York, 2000), p. 65.

3. Arthur Seidl described the "will to power" and "salvation" of the Opera in *Moderne Dirigenten* (Berlin, 1902), pp. 44–45; this and other descriptions of his directorship are cited in Henry-Louis de La Grange, *Gustav Mahler*, vol. 3, *Vienna: Triumph and Disillusion (1904–1907)* (Oxford, 1999), pp. 351–90.

4. Magnus Davidson, report on a Prague concert of June 4, 1899, in *C.V.-Zeitung* [paper of the Central-Verein of German Jews], 14, no. 2 (1935), supplement.

5. Fritz Stiedry, "Der Operndirektor Mahler," *Melos* 2 (1920): 135; cited by de La Grange, *Mahler*, vol. 3, *Triumph and Disillusion*, pp. 387, 390.

6. Felix Salten, "Mahler," *Die Zeit*, 18 December 1904.

7. Alma Mahler, *Gustav Mahler: Memories and Letters*, trans. Basil Creighton, ed. Donald Mitchell and Knud Martner, 4th edn. (Seattle and London, 1990), pp. 87–88, 113.

8. For the connections of performance and feminist theory, see Judith Butler, "Performative Acts and Gender Constitution: An Essay in Phenomenology and Feminist Theory," in *Performing Feminisms: Feminist Critical Theory and Theatre*, ed. Sue-Ellen Case (Baltimore, 1990), pp. 270–82.

9. On speech-act theory, see J. L. Austin, *How to Do Things with Words* (Oxford, 1962), and John R. Searle, *Speech Acts: An Essay in the Philosophy of Language* (Cambridge, Eng. 1969).

10. Simon Frith, *Performing Rites: On the Value of Popular Music* (Cambridge, Mass., 1996), p. 207. Frith stresses that in popular art, at least, there must be a sense of "risk, danger, triumph, virtuousity"; but this applies to classical performance as well.

11. Paul Bekker, *Gustav Mahlers Sinfonien* (Berlin, 1921; rpt. Tutzing, 1969), pp. 355–56.

12. Herbert Blau, *The Audience* (Baltimore and London, 1990), pp. 9, 25.

13. Frith, *Performing Rites*, p. 204.

14. Victor Turner, *The Ritual Process: Structure and Anti-Structure* (Chicago, 1969). On social drama, ritual and stage drama, see his *From Ritual to Theater* (New York, 1982), pp. 72–78; and for the conditions in which social drama occurs, see his *The Anthropology of Performance* (New York, 1982), pp. 72–99.

15. This controversy overlaps with, but is somewhat different from the argument surrounding the "work concept," in which the discrete product of the composer or writer with respect to her or his continuing productivity was, according to its critics, virtually fetishized. See Lydia Goehr, *The Imaginary Museum of Musical Works* (New York, 1992).

16. Stan Godlovitch, *Musical Performance: A Philosophical Study* (London and New York, 1998), pp. 81–96, 144. Leonard B. Meyer, *Emotion and Meaning in Music* (Chicago and London, 1956). Roger Scruton, *The Aesthetics of Music* (Oxford, 1997), p. 440. Nicholas Cook argues for suspending the argument for the sake of concrete musical analysis, in his "Analyzing Performance and Performing Analysis," in *Rethinking Music*, ed. Cook and Mark Everist, (Oxford, 1999), pp. 239–61.

17. Theodor W. Adorno, *In Search of Wagner*, trans. Rodney Livingstone (London, 1981), pp. 85–96.

18. Hugo von Hofmannsthal, "Die Bühne als Traumbild," in *Das Theater* 1, no. 1 (1 October 1903): 4–9; fac. ed. (Emsdetten, 1981).

19. Jonathan Crary, *Suspensions of Perception: Attention, Spectacle, and Modern Culture* (Cambridge, Mass., 1999), pp. 247–360.

20. For consideration of Mahler against the backdrop of these issues, see Thomas Peattie, *The Fin-de-siècle Metropolis: Time, Memory, and the Music of Gustav Mahler*, Ph.D. diss., Harvard University, in progress.

21. Georg Simmel, *Über soziale Differenzierung. Sociologische und psychologische Untersuchungen* (Leipzig, 1890); and "The Metropolis and Mental Life" (1903), "Fashion" (1904), "Group Expansion and the Development of Individuality" (1908), and "The Stranger" (1908), in Simmel, *On Individuality and Social Forms*, ed. Donald N. Levine (Chicago, 1971), pp. 251–339, 143–49.

22. On Musil's dissolution of agency, see Stefan Jonsson, *Subject without Identity: Robert Musil and the History of Modern Identity* (Durham, N.C., 2000).

23. Admittedly, these alternatives can be interpreted as different sides of a common social theory in which the myth of impersonality leads to a reactionary effort to create communal politics. The more persuasive the myth of impersonality, Richard Sennett has

written, the more men seek out community "in terms of a created common self." See his *The Fall of Public Man* (New York and London, 1976), p. 255.

24. On "the blasé outlook" as the psychic phenomenon reserved to the city, see Simmel, "The Metropolis," in *On Individuality*, p. 329.

25. Diary entry of 26 March 1905, in Gerhart Hauptmann, *Tagebücher 1897 bis 1905*, ed. Martin Machatzke (Berlin, 1987), pp. 416–17.

26. Alfred Roller, "Bühnenreform," *Der Merker: Österreichische Zeitschrift für Musik und Theater* 1, no. 5 (10 December 1909): 193–97 (quotation from p. 194).

27. See Karen Painter, "Symphonic Ambitions, Operatic Redemption: *Mathis der Maler* and *Palestrina* in the Third Reich," *Musical Quarterly* 85, no. 1 (2001): 135–36.

28. Daniel de Lange in *Het Nieuws van der Dag*, 24 October 1903.

29. Mahler's letter of 1 January 1910 to Guido Adler; in *Gustav Mahler and Guido Adler: Records of a Friendship*, trans. Edward R. Reilly (Cambridge, Eng., and New York, 1982), p. 110.

30. For suggestive analogies with respect to the hierarchies created by artistic institutions, see Tony Bennett, *The Birth of the Museum: History, Theory, Politics* (London and New York, 1995).

31. For the centrality of language concerns in Austrian cultural history, see Allan Janik and Stephen Toulmin, *Wittgenstein's Vienna* (New York, 1973). Moritz Csáky, however, depicts Austrian history as a multicultural experiment, of which operetta was the integrating art form, in *Ideologie der Operette und Wiener Moderne* (Vienna, Cologne, Weimar, 1996).

32. Robert Musil, *The Man without Qualities*, trans. Eithne Wilkins and Ernst Kaiser (New York, 1965), vol. 1, p. 33.

33. Clifford Geertz, *Negara: The Theater State in Nineteenth-Century Bali* (Princeton, 1980). On the 1879 *Festzug*, see Leon Botstein, "Gustav Mahler's Vienna," in *The Mahler Companion*, ed. Donald Mitchell and Andrew Nicholson (Oxford, 1999), p. 29.

34. Peter Franklin, "A Stranger's Story: Programmes, Politics, and Mahler's Third Symphony," *The Mahler Companion*, ed. Mitchell and Nicholson, pp. 171–86. Franklin further suggests, more problematically I believe, that the Nietzschean references in the Third Symphony, completed the preceding year, reveal that Mahler's political stance had already started to become more cautious as he set his eyes on a call to Vienna. William J. McGrath, by contrast, interprets the Third as an allegory of *völkisch* synthesis in his *Dionysian Art and Populist Politics in Austria* (New Haven, 1974), pp. 156–61.

35. William A. Jenks, *The Austrian Electoral Reform of 1907* (New York, 1950); and John W. Boyer, *Culture and Political Crisis in Vienna: Christian Socialism in Power, 1897–1918* (Chicago, 1995), pp. 16–17, 55–57, 80–81, 88–90, 111–63, 268–97.

36. Musil, *Man without Qualities*, vol. 1, p. 33.

37. Sennett, *Public Man*, p. 239.

38. Jeremy King, *Budweisers into Czechs and Germans: A Local History of Bohemian Politics, 1848–1948* (Princeton, forthcoming in 2002).

39. Mahler, "An die Mitglieder der Budapester Oper" (from before October 10, 1888), in *Gustav Mahler Briefe*, ed. Herta Blaukopf (Vienna and Hamburg, 1982), pp. 73–74.

40. Interview in *Budapesti Hirlap*, 7 October 1888; cited in Blaukopf and Blaukopf, *Mahler, His Life*, p. 78.

41. For a suggestive evocation of the difference between Austrian and Hungarian liberal and national cultures, including attitudes toward work, death, and ethnic outsiders see Peter Hanak, *The Garden and the Workshop: Essays on the Cultural History of Vienna and Budapest* (Princeton, 1998).

42. Mahler's remark is from Alma Mahler, *Gustav Mahler,* p. 109.

43. Reported in *Deutsche Zeitung,* 17 January 1899.

44. "K. und k.": "*kaiserlich und königlich,*" "imperial and royal"—referring to the constitutional role of the Habsburg dynast as Emperor of the whole monarchy, as Emperor in Austria (Cisleithania), and as King of Hungary. German-speaking liberals in Austria (in contrast to the Pan-Germans or German Nationalists), the Dual Monarchy's Jews, and even the Socialists committed to the national pluralism of Austro-Marxism, tended to support the monarchical institution precisely for its supranational function despite its simultaneous role as the bulwark of conservative traditionalism. Musil coined the acronym *Kakania* for the vanished, pre-1914 Austria-Hungary; the closeness to the universal European baby term *kaka* (shit) was no accident.

45. On the promise of the national cultural trends see among other sources, Moritz Csáky, "Multicultural Communities: Tensions and Qualities, the Example of Central Europe," in *Shaping the Great City: Modern Architecture in Central Europe 1890–1937,* ed. Eve Blau and Monika Platzer (Munich, London, and New York, 1999), pp. 43–54; also on nationalist trends in architecture, Ákos Moravánsky, *Competing Visions: Aesthetic Invention and Social Imagination in Central European Architecture, 1867–1918* (Cambridge, Mass., 1998).

46. Max Burckhard, *Neue Freie Presse,* 16 June 1907; trans. from Blaukopf and Blaukopf, *Mahler, His Life,* p. 203.

47. Max Graf, *Wagner-Probleme und andere Studien* (Vienna, 1900), pp. 124–26.

48. Emil Gutmann, "Gustav Mahler als Organisator" in *Die Musik,* 10, no. 18 (June issue 2, 1911, entitled *Gustav Mahler*): 364–65. This document is translated in Part IV of this book.

49. Adolphe Appia, *L'oeuvre d'art vivant* (Paris, 1921), p. 101. This volume recapitulated many of the earlier ideas and reproduced Appia's designs for Wagner's *Ring* and *Parsifal,* which had been published as a French pamphlet in 1895 and as a two-part treatise in German translation (Munich, 1899). Both parts appeared in the original French as *La musique et la mise en scène* (Bern, 1963), and in an English version as *Music and the Art of the Theatre,* ed. Bernard Hewitt (Coral Gables, 1962). See John Willett, *The Theatre of the Weimar Republic* (New York, 1988), pp. 26–27.

50. Roller, "Buhnenreform": 193–94.

51. Max Graf, *Hamburger Nachrichten,* 15 March, 1903; cited in Norbert Tschulik, *Musiktheater in Österreich: Die Oper im 20. Jahrhundert* (Vienna, 1984), p. 34.

52. Julius Korngold, *Neue Freie Presse,* 8 October 1904.

53. Bruno Walter, *Theme and Variations, an Autobiography,* trans. James A. Galston (New York, 1946), pp. 171–72.

54. David Josef Bach, *Arbeiter-Zeitung,* 23 October 1906; cited from Tschulik, *Musiktheater,* pp. 43–44.

55. Robert Hirschfeld [signed R.H.], *Wiener Abendpost,* 13 May 1903.

56. Karen Painter, "The Sensuality of Timbre: Responses to Mahler and Modernity at the Fin de Siècle," *Nineteenth-Century Music* 18, no. 3 (1995): 236–56.

57. Hermann Bahr, "*Fidelio,*" (review of December 1904), in *Buch der Jugend* (Vienna and Leipzig, 1908), pp. 21–23.

58. Julius Korngold, review of *Don Giovanni,* in *Neue Freie Presse,* 22 December 1905.

59. Hugo von Hofmannsthal, Alfred Roller, and Bruno Walter, "Gespräch über Reinhardt mit Hugo von Hofmannsthal, Alfred Roller und Bruno Walter," in *Der Merker* 1, no. 17 (10 June 1910): 699.

60. De La Grange, *Mahler,* vol. 3, p. 172 n. 87.

61. Willett, *Theater of the Weimar Republic*, pp. 34–51; Peter Jelavich, *Berlin Cabaret* (Cambridge, Mass., 1993), pp. 80–84.

62. Richard Specht, "Reinhardt," *Der Merker* 1, no. 17 (10 June 1910): 702–03.

63. Walter, *Theme and Variations*, p. 243.

64. On the political and cultural impulses behind the festival, see Michael Steinberg, *Austria as Theater and Ideology: The Meaning of the Salzburg Festival*, 2d ed. (Ithaca, 2000).

65. Paul Moos, *Berliner Neueste Nachrichten*, 11 March 1897.

66. Ludwig Schiedermair, "Tonsetzer der Gegenwart VIII. Gustav Mahler," *Neue Zeitschrift für Musik* 101, no. 20 (10 May 1905): 422.

67. Richard Specht, "Gustav Mahler," *Die Musik* 10, no. 18 (June issue no. 2, 1911, entitled *Gustav Mahler*): 338–39.

68. Frith, *Performing Rites*, p. 205.

69. Erwin Stein, "Mahlers Sachlichkeit," *Musikblätter des Anbruchs* (March 1930): 99–103; trans. in *On Mahler and Britten: Essays in Honour of Donald Mitchell on His Seventieth Birthday*, ed. Philip Reed (Woodbridge, UK, and Rochester, N.Y., 1996), pp. 115–18.

70. Richard Specht, *Neue Freie Presse*, 20 September 1908.

71. Gustav Altmann, "Tonkünstlerfest in Essen," review of Mahler's Sixth Symphony, *Die Musik* 5, no. 19 (June issue no. 1, 1906): 49–50.

72. See Robert Hirschfeld's review of Mahler's Third and Seventh Symphonies in the *Wiener Abendpost*, 5 November 1909; cited from Painter, "Symphonic Ambitions": 135–36.

73. Theodor W. Adorno, *Mahler: A Musical Physiognomy*, trans. Edmund Jephcott, (Chicago, 1992), p. 50.

74. Adorno, *Mahler: A Musical Physiognomy*, pp. 46–47. See Donald Mitchell's respectful but extended dissent from Adorno: "'Swallowing the Programme': Mahler's Fourth Symphony," in *The Mahler Companion*, pp. 187–216.

75. Adorno, *Mahler*, pp. 145, 166–67, 44.

76. Pierre Boulez, "Gustav Mahler. Why Biography?" rpt. in *Orientations* (Cambridge, 1985), p. 303.

77. For Brecht's important theoretical statements, see *Brecht on Theatre: The Development of an Aesthetic,* ed. John Willett (New York, 1964), pp. 22–25, 33–47, 69–81, 84–103, 130–47.

78. Hermann Kipper, *Kölner Volkszeitung*, 17 October 1904.

79. Two contributors to *Music and Meaning*, ed. Jenefer Robinson (Ithaca, 1980), maintain the compatibility of novelistic and dramatic metaphors. See Leo Treitler, "Language and the Interpretation of Music," pp. 49–55, and Fred Everett Maus, "Music as Drama," pp. 127–30.

80. Gérard Pesson relies heavily on abstract attributes—a common search for fragmentation, shared sense of loss, and anticipation of modernism—to claim similarities between Debussy and Mahler. See his "Mahler and Debussy," in *The Mahler Companion*, pp. 153–70.

Mahler's Jewish Parable

Talia Pecker Berio

This essay is dedicated to Henry-Louis de La Grange

The meaning of a word is perhaps only its openness to meaning. The word God has no meaning. Not several either. It is meaning: the adventure and ruin of meaning.

—*Edmond Jabès*

Music and religion: the subject becomes tricky as soon as we turn away from strictly functional music, created within a religious context or for liturgical purposes. At the peak of the classical style, the production of church music was conceived of as a natural activity, even for those composers who had severed their ties with the court and with the ecclesiastical authorities. Well into the nineteenth century a composer could still gain recognition and prestige with masses composed for special occasions. Nonetheless the masterpieces produced in this genre by Mozart and the Haydns (Joseph and his younger brother Michael) have little to do with the Catholic liturgy, and the question of whether and to what extent they reflect the religious faith of their authors remains unanswered. Beethoven's *Missa solemnis* can be taken as an emblem of individual faith; it is the proclamation by a modern, free man of his right to relate to a canonic religious text and to comment upon it independently from any institutional framework. Along with the Ninth Symphony and the late quartets, this monumental work celebrates the power of music to convey *ideas,* to raise questions, to sound its voice in the ethics and social debate of its epoch. As in all genres and forms of musical expression, here too we are confronted with a line of division: there will always be a "before Beethoven" and an "after Beethoven." With Schubert, Liszt, Wagner, Bruckner, Mahler, and Schoenberg, the encounter between musical creativity and religious faith belongs to the

domain of the individual—an interior dimension that escapes definition and imposes on the critic the utmost caution and respect.

All the more so when the composer belongs to a religious minority
that for centuries had lived confined under strict limitations of movement and activity, without access to the cultural and artistic life of the
surrounding community. Religion, under such circumstances, survived
on the strength of personal faith, common fate, and collective memory
rather than as a powerful social and cultural structure. The very notion
of religion is insufficient, if not inadequate, to embrace the complex
and manifold issue of Jewish tradition and identity in the European
diaspora. A question then arises: Given the climate of emancipation
and tolerance in which Mahler grew up, given the Romantic ideal of
music as a divine art (and in the perspective created by Beethoven and
Wagner, a possible substitute for religion) upon which his musicianship
was shaped, and the nonreligious character of his social and professional circles—is it necessary or even justifiable to inquire about his
Jewish roots in order to gain a better insight into his music? Rather than
an answer, the following essay will ultimately suggest a reformulation
of the question.

Hermeneutic Biases

Any attempt to deal with Mahler's Judaism cannot possibly avoid biographical issues such as his family background and the cultural and
political context in the historic lands of Bohemia and Moravia in the
late nineteenth century and that of early twentieth-century Vienna. His
conversion to Catholicism in 1897, the vicious anti-Semitic attacks
directed at him during his years at the Court Opera, his own remarks
concerning his Jewish background, and Alma Mahler's comments on
it in her memoirs—all can and must be taken into consideration in the
appraisal of the weight of Jewish heritage in Mahler's life and work.[1]
However, none of these elements or their simple sum can adequately
answer yet another question: How Jewish is Mahler's music? (Or else,
in a playful inversion: How is Mahler's music Jewish?)

Theodor W. Adorno's remarks on the "Jewish element" in Mahler's
music are worth quoting: "One can no more put one's finger on this
element than in any other work of art: it shrinks from identification yet
to the whole remains indispensable. . . . What is Jewish in Mahler does
not participate directly in the folk element, but speaks through all its
mediations as an intellectual voice, something non-sensuous yet
perceptible in the totality."[2] This zone of indeterminacy has attracted

conflicting interpretations from the extremes of the cross-cultural area that Mahler's music actually represents. Adorno speaks of an attempt to deny the Jewish element "in order to reclaim Mahler for a conception of German music infected by National Socialism," which is "as aberrant as his appropriation as a Jewish nationalist composer."[3] This is an emphatic and partially exaggerated judgment that reflects both Adorno's own painful elaboration of the postwar trauma and the general tendency to emotional extremes in the reception of Mahler's work during those years, especially in Jewish and German environments. Such extremes can only be understood when viewed against the background of earlier Mahler criticism.

The history of the anti-Semitic campaign against Mahler and of the few philo-Semitic voices in his favor during the 1920s and 1930s is well-known.[4] More than the specific argumentation on both sides, the similarity of the evidence they bring to reinforce their arguments is striking (and in some cases embarrassing). Echoes of East European folklore and urban music, the exasperation at expressive extremes, the mixture of the trivial and the sublime, the intellectual complexity and the play of irony and "double meaning." All these features are recognized as "Jewish" and judged as virtues by one party and as faults by the other. Beyond such essential factors as the tragic historical consequences and the obvious racism of the anti-Semitic criticism, we have here an extreme case of hermeneutic bias—manipulating certain biographical and historical facts in order to ground one's interpretive inclinations.

The grounds for a clear-cut assertion of Mahler's Judaism are extremely fragile; to build on them an aesthetic evaluation of his music is ethically wrong. It wrongs the composer, who considered himself an emancipated (and for that matter privileged) citizen of European culture and had no intention and no desire to belong to one or another nation or ethnic group. (His famous remark on being "thrice homeless" seems to have the same ambiguous bent of some of his music: it is at once a matter of lament and of pride, an existential truth to be observed from a distance that evokes both acceptance and revolt.[5])

It wrongs Judaism, which does not lend itself to any such specification (one can barely suggest a definition of a Jew, let alone Judaism). It wrongs music, which is too complex a phenomenon to be reduced to a channel for the expression of ethnic and national sentiments and affiliations. From an aesthetic point of view such evaluations ignore an elementary hermeneutic rule: the study of single elements in form and style is a necessary step in a critical reading, but the findings remain meaningless unless they are put into a larger perspective. When the perspective itself is biased, the isolated constituents become mere labels that may be attached, removed, or substituted without revealing or affecting the content of the labeled element.

In his accusation of appropriation, Adorno might have had in mind Max Brod's *Israel's Music,* published in 1951 by the Zionist Educational Department in both German and English.[6] In a number of articles published in the twenties Brod had centered his argumentation of Mahler's Jewish roots mainly on melodic analogies with East European Hassidic music.[7] But now, after his emigration to Israel in 1939, Brod counterbalanced the insistent prewar and wartime anti-Semitic Mahler criticism in Austria and Germany with a proud claim of Mahler's Jewish identity and his contribution to the history of Jewish music. A decade later Brod summed up his view of Mahler's Judaism in a major book that treats the issue in the light of the complex and symbiotic dialectics of German-Jewish relationships in prewar Europe.[8]

The history of Mahler's reception in Israel is significant in this context, not only because of the homogeneity that is presumed of an all-Jewish audience, but also because of the extraordinary heterogeneity of its cultural background. Musical life in Palestine in the late thirties and forties was animated by immigrants from Central Europe. In a multiethnic and history-charged Jerusalem, and on the dunes of a rapidly expanding and very secular Tel Aviv, groups of intellectuals who had left Europe soon after Hitler rose to power and formed their "little Vienna," Prague, and Berlin, transplanting to the Middle East the cultural and artistic heritage to which they had contributed immensely as eminent and integrated Jews in their home countries. Music was the ideal bridge over linguistic and environmental barriers. Rehearsals of the Palestine Orchestra founded in 1936 by Bronislav Huberman (which became the Israel Philharmonic), were often conducted by such new immigrants, and led in a mixture of German, Yiddish, English, and Hebrew, with occasional Hungarian and Czech.

Reviews of Mahler's music performed in the late 1930s reveal the complex problems his figure presented to an educated audience that was at once Jewish and European, Zionist and German, and Viennese, proud of its newly acquired national identity but nostalgic for the old continent. Whether with sentimental pathos or with embarrassed, sometimes severe judgment of his conversion, Mahler's Jewishness was a central issue in the early years of the state of Israel. The First Symphony, which along with the Fifth was the most frequently performed, figured in the inaugural season of the Orchestra (1936–1937), and initiated a tradition of at least two Mahler performances per season. The Third, sung in Hebrew in 1939, disappeared from the repertory until 1962.

Also sprach Zarathustra, along with Jesus acquitting Peter of breaking the Ten Commandments, was more than the Israeli public could take in the postwar years; for those who survived the *Shoah*, the mere sound of the German language was intolerable. When in 1960 Sir John Barbirolli refused to conduct Mahler's Second Symphony sung in Hebrew, an odd compromise was reached: "Urlicht" was sung in German and the last movement in English!

It is interesting to note that the Mahler boom exploded in Israel later than in Europe and the United States. Its peak came only in July 1967 with the festive performance on Mount Scopus of the Second Symphony sung in Hebrew, conducted by Leonard Bernstein, to celebrate the victory of the Six Day War. The Jewish connection, which from the early 1960s on had become less and less insistent, is completely absent in the reviews of the event. The choice itself (of the composer, the work, the conductor, the language) is more eloquent than any apologia: Mahler, who by now was an international hero, is tacitly acclaimed a national asset. The disruptive issue of his Judaism ceases to be a subject of debate. Unresolved or irresolvable, it seems to be avoided for the sake of coherence: a composer born a Jew is a Jewish composer regardless of whether or not his music is Jewish.[9]

Jewish Elements

What makes music, any music, "Jewish"? The issue is complex both conceptually and empirically. At the conceptual level we may pose the question differently: Is there such a thing as Jewish aesthetics? Or, to what extent and by what means is it possible to trace Jewish roots, ideas, and idioms in the music of Jewish (and non-Jewish) composers, and what are the methodological and ideological limits of tracing them? When dealing with Mahler we can exclude a whole category of works that present themselves as Jewish by the use of distinct musical and textual materials; by subject (biblical, historical, or derived from traditional Jewish folklore); by context (liturgical or ritual), or by a declared poetic choice. The Jewish "intention" in those cases is *explicit* and its external manifestation (a title, a text, a descriptive program) does not always correspond to a distinctive musical content or style. How Jewish are Salomone Rossi's cantatas? Does the Jewish identity of their author make them more Jewish than Schubert's setting of Psalm 92? And on the other hand, would anybody object to the classification of Stravinsky's *Abraham and Isaac* or Shostakovitch's Yiddish songs as "Jewish music" just because their authors were not Jews?

Mahler obviously does not fit into this category, and his Jewish aesthetics are at most *implicit*, regardless of the few reminiscences of Hassidic tunes that occur in his music, conscious or not, and whatever the concrete circumstances of his acquaintance with them may have been.[10] I believe that the search for properly Jewish melodic elements in Mahler's music (even if occasionally they may indeed exist) does not offer new insight into his poetics. The same is true for matters of gesture and tone, which make a slippery hermeneutic terrain if examined from a nonmusical perspective.[11] The heartbreaking solos of the violin, the strident nasal tone of the woodwinds, the accordionlike alternation of expansion and contraction so frequent in Mahler's phrasing and dynamics may sound strikingly "Jewish" to many. But labeling them as such simplifies and renders banal the complex texture in which they invariably occur and opens the way to interpretive abuses of the kind we have condemned above. What, then, is left?

If we replace the term *element* with *matrix*, a considerable enrichment of the metaphoric field is gained. The notion of element remains but loses its specificity; it becomes "something (as a surrounding or pervading substance or element) within which something else originates or takes form or develops."[12] The archaic meaning of a uterus calls back the Latin root of the term, *mater* (mother). We have here a primary condition, a living cavity that absorbs and transforms the elements that flow into it. The family traits that such a process produces cannot be traced back to any single source or pattern. The flow and the transformation modify the origin, and the result is an individual whole that must be appraised on its own grounds and in relation to its context.

A quick comparison of Mahler with Mendelssohn and Schoenberg may prove useful to illustrate the general and musical historical context in the complex (and often enigmatic) interaction between the Jewish "matrix" and the individual artistic physiognomy of a composer. Felix Mendelssohn Bartholdy, grandson of the great Jewish philosopher and reformer Moses Mendelssohn, was baptized at the age of nine and grew up in the climate of economic comfort and social assimilation of the intellectual Jewish elite in northern Germany. Musically he was the ingenious and precocious product of the most articulate "linguistic" phase in the history of Western music. His transformation of the "classical style" maintains a delicate and spontaneous balance between tradition and the new spirit of the "Romantic generation."[13] A similar attitude of peaceful conciliation seems to underlie his relationship with religion. His oratorios, *Elijah* in particular, convey a profound faith in a sort of a new-age, nonpartisan religion that finds in music its truest and utmost expression. Indeed, there is nothing either Jewish or

Christian in Mendelssohn's religious music. His aesthetics is explicitly ecumenical: an unmistakable awareness of the nonconflictive plurality of his roots transmits itself through the music, the text, and the choice of subject and form. Mendelssohn revives and consciously transforms a genre of religious music establishing new grounds for the difficult dialogue between music and religion.

Unlike Mendelssohn, Schoenberg lived during one phase of a complex and general cultural crisis. Born to a modest, semiobservant family, he grew up to face the catastrophic end of the assimilation dream. His conversion to Protestantism in 1898 was part of that dream, and his reconversion to Judaism in 1933 was the proud and definite act of scission from a society that had turned the dream into a nightmare. His artistic development reflects a similar process: the early passionate search of continuity and renovation within a glorious musical tradition gives way to a radical break. He found himself at a crossroads facing a choice both as a musician and as a European of Jewish origins. From the early 1920s on, the consciousness and significance of these origins became ever more relevant in Schoenberg's intellectual life. The Jewish matrix is present in his musical *thinking:* through the need and quest for a new musical law, through his mystical approach to numbers, through the prophetic tone of his writings, and of course, in the frequent employment of biblical themes and texts in his works. The unfinished cantata *Jakobsleiter* (1917–1922) is emblematic from this point of view: it is the first time Schoenberg turns to a biblical subject, and it is one of the first works that contain specific seeds of the dodecaphonic technique that soon after was to become the commandment of his poetics. From there on, Schoenberg's aesthetics, or rather the ethical foundations of his art, become more and more pronouncedly Jewish. However, nothing similar can be said about his *music:* There is no voice in it that lends itself to be described as Jewish, or as more Jewish than that of his companions Alban Berg and Anton Webern. We daresay that Schoenberg's Jewish aesthetics are explicit as a founding *idea* but not as a component of *style* and sound.

Mahler's case stands apart from those of both Mendelssohn and Schoenberg. Unlike Mendelssohn, Mahler lived and acted in the twilight of an era both as a Jew and as a musician. Assimilation was at its peak but already threatened by strong anti-Semitic undercurrents from which, as we have seen, he suffered directly. His conversion to Catholicism did not assure him the hoped-for protection; his Judaism was too residual to offer him the comfort of belonging. Unlike Schoenberg, he was spared the racial ferocity of the Nazi regime, and with it the opportunity to assume a full consciousness of his origins and to face the necessity of making an uncompromising ideological and political choice. Mahler's musical background is substantially similar to Schoenberg's, but the historical weight of the fourteen years of age that lie between them is evident not only in retrospect. Mahler himself was conscious of it in his encounter with Schoenberg's music. His own music seems to become progressively aware of the twilight zone within which it was coming to life, and of the no-man's land into which it was heading. Mahler is immersed in the oceanic tradition of Western music; being aware of the storm that shakes it, yet unable to withdraw, he navigates vigorously along and against the stream. A constant dialectic current underlies Mahler's poetics: he is at once within and without. There is something profoundly Jewish in this existential attitude, something that translates itself into a whole world of sound. The feeling is that while Mahler's music cannot be described as properly Jewish, only an assimilated Jew of his time could have written it. But we'll never be able to say whether Mahler himself sensed it or thought of it deliberately. In his case we can speak of a *virtual* Jewish aesthetics: Whether it is conscious (and in that case entirely secret) or not, our discussion of it must remain essentially *metaphoric*.

Mahler and Judaism

An emphasis on metaphor allows us to avoid oversimplification. Neither Judaism nor Mahler's music can be reduced to the sum of the elements that compose them (which is precisely what happens in the biased readings examined above), yet they have a lot in common. All studies of Mahler's roots, including the most illuminating, invariably presume a universal acceptance of the terms Jew, Jewish, and Judaism. But the truth is that there are nearly as many ways of being Jewish as Jews who consider themselves so. Religious faith, ethics, thought, and concrete modalities of everyday life make up a polyphony of values and a counterpoint of events that cannot be pinned down to any central doctrine or set of canons. Jewish history is at once an ongoing manifestation of the divine presence, a well of collective ancestral memory, and a chain of fractures and dispersions. Remembrance for the Jew is a living process; there is no single narrative to retell, no hero or symbol to worship. Time is shaped by action: The day, the week, the year are regulated by a rhythmic sequence of deeds and duties, scripture and lecture, prayer and study that transform and actualize tradition. Jewish space is composite and mobile under the ancient token of perpetual exile. This complex reality, along with the traditions that it has generated through the centuries and throughout the diaspora, embraces the

Jew even when he or she does not consciously embrace it. The voices and echoes of this polyphony may take different shapes. In the context of Mahler's poetics I would like to concentrate on two of them: distance and commentary.

The notion of distance has deep roots in Judaism. It goes back to the Second Commandment: "Thou shall not make unto thee any graven image, or any likeness of any thing that is in heaven above, or that is in the earth beneath" (Exodus 20:4). This prohibition of any figurative representation and its absolute priority in the foundation of the creed (it is second only to the proclamation of the oneness of God) have had far-reaching consequences in the shaping of Jewish thought and life. The entire Hebrew Bible can be seen as the story of a tormented struggle to overcome the temptations of idolatry and to reconcile the abstract nature of the Jewish deity with the human need for concrete rituals and earthly *space* for religious worship. The temporary denial of a permanent holy place and land, and the perpetual threat of their destruction, are inherent to the founding history of the Jewish people. The prevalence of time over space in Judaism is a consequence of this ancient condition. The inclination (or readiness or intention) implied in the act of waiting (to reach the promised land, to win the distance that separates man from a nameless and faceless God) endows time with a quality of space. Time is filled with meaning and is inhabited as if it were a home.

Jewish memory is marked by this ancient prohibition of figuration. Judaism sublimates remembering through *evocation,* unlike the ancient Greek and Roman traditions, where the memory of a beloved person was immortalized in a portrait, and the craving for a faraway or destroyed homeland could find an outlet in a simulated double.[14] The *Mizrakh* (orient)—a small ornamented wooden plate that hangs on the eastern wall in the homes of observant Jews in the diaspora—has a non-figurative symbolic value. The memory of Jerusalem is kept alive not in a picture of its landscape or its holy sites but by the illuminated Hebrew letters of its name that is glorified daily in a prayer facing east. The voicing of a written word, the sound that evokes an image (and through it, an idea), is at once an act of sublimation of the distant land (and of a higher instance: an "elsewhere" that cannot be named), and a compensation for the forbidden icon.[15]

There has always been a "here" and an "elsewhere" in Jewish history. The condition of otherness, the nonbelonging or half-belonging to a place, a land, a nation, was imposed from without and cherished from within.[16] The suffering of nonacceptance by the surrounding environment was compensated by the reinforcement of a "mental homeland."

Restrictions and persecutions were countered by a growing degree of inner freedom. The cultural scene of central Europe in the course of the nineteenth century was marked by the intellectual and artistic work of Jews who were allowed to win their otherness. By the end of the century the process of assimilation seemed complete and profound, but the men and women who made it true did not lose the ancestral capacity of distancing themselves with a subtle and varying dose of caution, regret, and hidden contempt. Heinrich Heine, Karl Kraus, Franz Kafka, Sigmund Freud: Mahler belongs to the same line of Jewish minds whose work expresses something of the Jewish matrix of their condition, without however exposing its constituent elements. The work of writers and poets allows ample space for the illustration of such a hypothesis, either through explicit affirmations (Heine's Jewish poetry, Kafka's fragmentary references to his Judaism, Freud's essays on Jewish subjects, etc.) or through literary style and genre (Heine's irony, Kafka's surrealism, Kraus's pitiless sarcasm, Freud's sometimes talmudic style). Music rarely offers such direct evidence and Mahler's is hardly an exception. All we can do is once again turn to metaphor.

With respect to his Jewish roots, Mahler seems to me a man on the frontier between cultures and epochs, who observed the world and created his own metaphor for it.[17] I like to think of Mahler's universe as a huge sphere with a gate through which a multitude of creatures and experiences flows in from the outer world: nature and man, children and flowers, angels and beggars, choirs and klezmer and military bands, simple tunes and sophisticated masterpieces, popular proverbs, masters of thought, and ancient poets. A visual correlate for Mahler's engagement with the world might be the famous illustration of Psalm 24.1, reproduced as Figure 1, published by Israel Landau (1758–1829), who was one of the pioneers of *Haskalah,* the Jewish Enlightenment movement inaugurated by Moses Mendelssohn.[18]

The dialectic tension between the outside and the inside of the sphere is essential for the understanding of its poetic content. When the gate is shut the living mass that has gathered in the sphere takes on an autonomous life; its inhabitants are put into a new orbit and lose their original physiognomy. Figures are sublimated, amplified, and distorted in Mahler's hand, through prisms of dream and irony. Nature is never realistically depicted; folk tunes never appear undisguised; there is no portrait of a hero. This is a process of distancing, a way of commenting on reality while avoiding any form of representation. The composer's voice is absorbed and multiplied in a counterpoint of many voices. An authorial presence is thus established without appearing in the foreground, without ever using the first person. It is a play of masks

Figure 1. Psalm 24:1, "The earth is the Lord's, and all that is in it, the world and all who live in it."

that allows Mahler to be emphatic and reluctant, transgressing and defensive at the same time.

Every single Mahler work, be it a symphony or a song cycle, is a world of its own, but at the same time it represents the global sphere of the whole oeuvre, communicating with it and with each of the other single works through a complex net of cross-references and transformations.[19] Evolution and cyclic return, variation and repetition, reminiscence and expectation are tightly interwoven in Mahler's compositional technique, creating a unity that produces its own vocabulary, its own grammar, and its own codes for analysis and interpretation.

The exercise of commentary is as ancient as Judaism itself. As Kafka wrote to Franz Werfel in a letter perhaps never sent, "Judaism has always produced its pains and joys almost simultaneously with the Rashi comment that goes with it."[20] The Bible contains chapters and whole books (Deuteronomy and Chronicles) that resume and interpret earlier events and laws. The immense body of post-biblical scriptures that makes up the Talmud is a sum of many layers, genres, and methods of commentary. One of these genres is the parable (*mashal* in Hebrew), which, as David Stern has written, "suggests a set of parallels between an imagined fictional event and an immediate 'real' situation" and appears in the Rabbinical literature mostly in exegetical contexts (*Midrash*).[21]

The Midrashic reading of a given text (and through the text a reality) is a laborious hermeneutic process with endless ramifications and implications for each phrase, each concept, each nuance. The technique of quotation and repetition, while serving as a tool for logical and theological investigation, was developed into a real art in the hands of the masters of the Jewish wisdom, producing a distinct rhetorical style. The starting and crucial point of the whole procedure is always a *question*. A text or a small portion of it becomes the subject for an interrogation that can go on and on, sometimes without reaching a definite answer.[22]

I tend to hear in Mahler's sound world (and in the complexity of the scores that transmit it) an echo of this Jewish all-embracing vision of the text as reality and of reality as a hypertext to be interpreted in its most minute ingredients, with no distinction between the "high" and the "low," the holy and the profane, the past and the present. Mahler's parables invite interpretation. His many voices seem to *demand* to be recognized, at times even named; they ask to be related to their source and to one another. Their belonging to a larger meaningful whole makes itself sound, reaching far beyond the immanent structure of the work. This constant allusion to a virtual "elsewhere" requires a listening that is at once broad and acute; it requires an imagination that cannot afford distraction from the autonomous logic of the musical event. The process of elaboration of such a complex input and the questions that arise along the way are by far more significant than the answers. This is in my view the ultimate and truly indispensable Jewish element in Mahler's music. Like the Jewish parable, it "tends to imply the parallel rather than explicate it," it "actively elicits from its audience the solution of its meaning, or what we could call its interpretation."[23]

Adorno's Mahler and the Narrative Model

The narrative programs that accompany the genesis of the first four symphonies, the poetic texts, and the tight musical relation to the world of the *Des Knaben Wunderhorn* lieder, create a highly evocative context that sets the scene for figurative interpretations of Mahler's music beyond any considerations about his Jewish matrix. The sensation is that something is being constantly described, related, sometimes even *told*, that does not necessarily coincide with the vocal text or the narrative scheme. Hence the epoch-making metaphor of "novel" applied by Theodor Adorno to Mahler's symphonic form: "Like novels, each of his symphonies awakens the expectation of something special as a gift."[24] The comparison was not a new one for Mahler's symphonies—indeed, Adorno most likely knew Erwin Stein's analogy in an article from 1930: "It all sounded like an exciting novel which again and again took a new and unexpected and surprising turn."[25]

For Adorno, the "configuration of content and style" seems to compensate with a gesture that is at once "epic and naive" the void of meaning created in this musical form at the twilight of its evolution.[26] But his metaphor involves neither a proper narrative nor a specific musical parallel to narrational techniques. It is precisely the scope of the gesture, the images that inhabit it and their "intonation"—their tuning into the whole—that make up the analogy. The Jewish voice implied in Adorno's remark quoted earlier, is one of a multitude; sometimes these "unsung voices" become indeed quite tangible and sensuous, conveying breathing and body movement, figures and phantoms, cry and wonder, an ironic grimace and shrill mockery.[27] The nameless yet unmistakable physiognomy of such voices endows Mahler's music with a sense of collectivity, a breaking of barriers that allows Adorno to push quite far his social and ideological reading: "The parade-step of musical logic is disrupted by reflection on the social wrong that art-language irrevocably does to those denied the privilege to culture. The conflict between the higher and the lower music in which, since the industrial revolution, the objective social process . . . has been aesthetically reflected, . . . is renewed in Mahler's music. His integrity decided in favor of high art. But the breach between the two spheres had become his special tone, that of brokenness."[28] Such extreme statements brought Adorno much criticism and delayed the introduction of his essay to English speaking audiences.

Whether or not one endorses Adorno's sociological critique in general, the crucial point here is if and in what way it affects the reading of Mahler's *poetics*. In his essay Adorno never loses sight of the music; he penetrates its sounding reality with the skill and passion of the musician he was, inquiring step by step into the logic of its making. The single metaphors that constitute his inquiry (curtain and fanfare, tone, characters, novel, decay and affirmation, the long gaze) add up to a complex and illuminating vision of Mahler's world. The musical perspective thus obtained is of such pertinence and depth, that the nonmusical considerations become themselves a macrometaphor. They act as antidotes: They trigger a doubt, a shift in the hermeneutic process, obliging us to reflect upon the ethic and social role of the composer, and upon music's immanent capacity to become cultural critique. In his dialogue with Mahler's music Adorno claims its significance for the historical conscience (civil and social, intellectual and artistic) of its own time and for the following generations. The critic's own ideology (certainly the only form of faith for Adorno), rather than imposing itself on the analyzed object, becomes a *distinct* dialectic tool in the quest for comprehension. It is precisely this unique cohabiting (but never confounding) of cultural engagement and analytical rigor that makes Adorno's quest so intense, so insightful, and ultimately so completely *honest*. This is why it has not lost, and hopefully will never lose, its relevance for Mahler research, for musicology, and for the history of ideas in general.

All recent studies of musical narrative have paid the due debt to Adorno's metaphor of Mahler's music as a novel. Most of them, however, tend to avoid the ideological implications of his essay.[29] What usually passes unnoticed is the tight relationship in Adorno's essay between the "ideological" dimension and the musical content. Adorno hears a *message* in Mahler's music, and explains how it is conveyed to him in purely musical terms. The crucial point is not the specific nature of the idea but the music's capacity to convey ideas and the *technical* procedures through which it conveys them. In his discussion of the novel-like quality of the symphonies, Adorno points to the *Wunderhorn* songs which, "through their own symphonic element," act as "the link between the novelesque nature and the ductus of Mahler's music."[30] On the other hand, the romancelike quality of the *Wunderhorn* songs allows them to fit into the epic world of the symphony as reminiscences of another existence (tales and figures of old times, the innocence of a lost childhood, and so on).

The strophic form of the songs turns them into a disruptive agent that breaks into the large structure obliging it to integrate such elements that would be (and often were) considered nonsymphonic by all previous aesthetic standards. The overall result of such a procedure conveys a *vision* that bypasses the immediate musical and aesthetic domain. There is no need to express this sense of vision in specific social or political terms in order to grasp the composer's intention to make a strong statement on the status of the symphony, and to reshape its form and content in order to reflect the true spirit of his time.

In the chapter "Decay and Affirmation" Adorno speaks of the "irruption of the horrible" in the coda of the first movement of the Sixth Symphony: "To conventional thinking this seems literary and unmusical; no music ought to be able to say no to itself. But Mahler's music is receptive precisely through its stringent capacity to do so, . . . a content that is both non-conceptual and yet incapable of being misunderstood." One does not have to agree with Adorno's insistence on Mahler's *negativity* in order to appreciate the strength of this statement. It is that capacity to convey a message, whether "negative" or not, that becomes in Mahler's hands "a purely compositional category."[31] What is implied here is the noncontradiction between the autonomous nature of musical expression and its capacity to arise (and be understood in) nonmusical concepts. It is noteworthy that Adorno goes as far as defining the musical content as "non-conceptual" (*begriffsfernen*).[32] It would suffice to call it "non-literal" or "unnamable" in order to grasp the true scope of the idea of music being capable of "saying no to itself." Music can say a whole lot to itself; it can say no, and yes, and perhaps; it can question itself; it can *comment*—upon its own ideas and through them upon reality. Mahler's music does it in a way that is at once paradigmatic and unique. His choice to inject new life into the collapsing edifice of the Romantic symphony implied the necessity to deal with an excess of connotations both musically and socially. One could say that at that point of its history, music had accumulated enough subject matter to allow it to be self-referential without becoming hermetic. Yet Mahler's standpoint vis-à-vis tradition and his method of "constructing a world with all the technical means at one's disposal" are, in my view, unique.[33] The narrative readings obscure this uniqueness not so much by bringing Mahler's symphonies too near the tone poems of his contemporary Richard Strauss, or by claiming them to be a substitute (or a sublimation) of the opera he never wrote. What they obscure is exactly that nameless substratum within which Mahler enacts his musical and nonmusical exegesis.

Whether or not this exegetic quality of Mahler's music is related to his Jewish roots and to the sense of distance that—as I have claimed above—is inherent to them, I believe that introducing it into the hermeneutic debate can enhance the understanding of his poetics. Mahler interrogates and reinvents the materials deposited by the long tradition he inherited; through his reactivating of familiar musical ideas he removes them from their original context into a new perspective. The idea becomes one with its sound presentation, the musical discourse (the "saying" in sound) produces meaning (the "unsaid") without pronouncing it. The concept of music as exegesis does not exclude the notion of *voice;* rather, it renders it at once more specific and more open. The voices can be played or sung, narrated or narrating, allusive or explicit, but their recognition is exclusively *musical;* it takes shape in relation to other specifically musical elements. Once formulated, these elements are submitted to a purely musical logic that exceeds and transcends the idea or message that nevertheless it conveys.[34]

In her analysis of the *Tödtenfeier* movement of the Second Symphony as a "misreading" of Adam Mickiewicz's poem, Carolyn Abbate ignores philological, textual, and documentary evidence in forcing the music and its author to fit into her own fascinating narrative of the "deafness of operatic characters."[35] To begin with, strong evidence against Abbate's interpretation is found in Mahler's description of the process of invention in the Scherzo: "It's a strange process! Without knowing at first where it's leading, you find yourself pushed further and further beyond the bounds of the original form [the *Fischpredigt* song], whose potentialities lay hidden within it like the plant within the seed. In connection with this, it seems to me that only with difficulty could I conform to the limitations imposed by an opera libretto (unless I had written it myself), or even by composing an overture to somebody else's work."[36] The sense of otherness that Abbate rightly reads in the episode marked "music from a distance" in the *Tödtenfeier* movement is eloquently illustrated in Mahler's famous comment on the third movement: "if, at a distance, you watch a dance through a window, without being able to hear the music, then the turning and twisting movement of the couples seems senseless, because you are not catching the rhythm that is the key to it all. You must imagine that to one who has lost his identity and his happiness, the world looks like this—distorted and crazy, as if reflected in a concave mirror."[37] But Abbate's elaboration of the notion of otherness loses its effectiveness in the process of her attributing faces, actions, and proper names to musical characters.

The sense of space and distance, oscillation and collapse, which certain passages in Mahler's music evoke, is a result of musical gestures that may have well been triggered by a poetic or figurative idea. But these gestures acquire complete autonomy by means of specific procedures of elaboration and orchestration that have no parallel in, or relation to, the world of words and images. They set themselves free of their nonmusical background, substituting for it an autonomous musical logic that conditions and transforms their physiognomy. The isolation of such gestures from their larger musical context and their labeling as narrative events in order to fit them into a predisposed hermeneutic model overturn the very aesthetic principle that generated them. Mahler's music, as charged and allusive as it may be, does not intend to substitute or compensate the absence of plot and dramatic action. Rather, it explores and exploits to the utmost the potentialities of such absence. The process of signification in Mahler inverts the logic of Wagnerian musical drama. The *event* in Wagner takes shape through a dialectic process of rejection and reactivation of narrative elements.[38] The surface narrative (the "story" of each of his works from *Siegfried* and *Tristan* on) is nothing but a mere trace of that process, yet its presence is determinate as an active guide to the musical-dramatic complex that constitutes the event. The principal negation of narrative as mere plot allowed Wagner to employ its deeper layers, into which only music, his music, could penetrate. His music exhausts the possibilities of such penetration. Mahler assimilated and admired Wagner's art as few before or after him, but he could make no use of the master's dramatic conception.[39] His approach to narrative is exactly the opposite. He welcomes a story in its simplest and most essential form (a fairy tale, a ballad, a popular strophic song) and uses it as a departure point for a musical journey that, once embarked upon, swallows up its origin and cancels any specific trace of it. Mahler's symphonic parable absorbs and transforms its real parallel rather than explicating it. His invention flourishes precisely in the void created by this process of absorption and concealing of the initial element. To rename it and trace it back to that starting point is not only reductive in the face of the intentional ambiguity of the music; it is a form of tautology in the face of Mahler's explicit indication of his sources in his detailed description of the genesis of his early works, in the texts of the lieder, and in the quotations from them in the symphonies.

Anthony Newcomb's reading of the Ninth Symphony introduces the concept of narrative archetype as an essential element in Mahler's method of intersecting formal paradigm, thematic return, and transformation. His inquiry into the particular nature and significance of repetition in the outer movements of Mahler's Ninth leads to revealing observations about the *nature* of Mahler's procedures of repetition, in particular of transformed thematic rebeginnings rather than entire blocks.[40] Newcomb's reading transcends the textual inquiry by placing its findings in a larger ontological perspective of how experience is transformed into memory. But the *meaning* of the whole process remains open. As Newcomb himself admits: "The question as to whether the symphony presents the suspension of temporality or its triumph in death is left in a state of ambiguous uncertainty." Yet I disagree with his claim that music "as a narrative art . . . can embody such a question so concretely without having to imply an answer."[41] Music, for me, is *not* a narrative art even when it intends or appears to narrate; Mahler's music does indeed embody many existential questions, but none of them is concretely exposed in the music. The presence of the question in the text set to music (*Also sprach Zarathustra, Veni Creator Spiritus, Der Abschied*), or in the text *of* the music (the emphatic exclamations scattered in the manuscripts of the Ninth and the Tenth) provides us with a key—one of the many keys—to Mahler's immense universe. But once we cross the threshold, the key may remain in the keyhole. To use it to open each of the many doors we would find on our way may be an interesting and useful methodological experiment, but whether successful or not, it should not condition our evaluation of what we find behind the doors.

The Jewish Key

The keys a writer has at his disposal—a whole set of them—are those which let him enter his books.

Like the writer, the Jew expects his identity from the book. He owes his Jewishness less to the accident of his birth than to the future he strives to shape down to the smallest details.

In these aphorisms from Edmond Jabès's *The Key*, the "writer" can be seen either as the author of the work we are reading (or listening to) or as our own *persona* in the act of writing about the work. Jabès goes on and asks: "Which of all the keys spread out before me will I use?"[42] We have seen how Mahler's "otherness" (the element of distance I have pointed to) can be reached for with the key of a narrative strategy that contrasts the very principles of the composer's declared aesthetics. We have gained insight into his concrete strategies of elaborating musical memory (an aspect of musical commentary) through a reading of his work as a *Bildungsroman*, which in all likelihood he did not intend to write. Is the Jewish key I have ventured to propose in these pages more valid, safe, or illuminating than the narrative, ideological, or purely formalistic keys? Can it open more doors to Mahler's world? Did he ever use it himself to enter his "book"? Does it wrong our composer, who was notoriously reluctant to discuss his Jewish origins or heritage?

Having thus reformulated the questions posed at the beginning of this paper, I should withdraw now and leave the key in the hands of my readers. It is up to them, listening to Mahler's music, to formulate an answer and to pose new questions. Before doing so, I would like to let Mahler's own voices occupy, if only briefly, the final stage of my inquiry.

Where, in particular, do I hear his Jewish voice? In the faceless crowd that moves slowly forward toward an unknown destination to the sound of a popular song turned into a funeral march in the third movement of the First Symphony. In many of the scherzi, where Mahler's vocation for commentary comes forth most explicitly—commentary on his own music and on that of others, commentary on preexisting forms and on the commonplaces that populate them.[43] The evolution of the scherzi from one symphony to the next shows the increased distance between the composer and the materials of his invention. By the time of the phantomlike Scherzo of the Seventh, the process of interrogation and elaboration reaches a degree of detachment that makes of this musical tableau a hallucinating caricature of the very idea of a scherzo. The second movement of the Ninth and the *Purgatorio* movement of the Tenth are the extreme consequences of this process. In the Ninth's "Im Tempo eines gemächlichen Ländlers," as in the Scherzo of the Seventh (to which it bears some melodic reminiscences), three different themes, related to one another through common cells, are mixed and superimposed within a movement that departs far from the conventional scherzo form. Here, too, the metric skeleton is at once acknowledged and challenged. But the terminal imagery of the Ninth is at work here as elsewhere in the symphony; the "ruins" are composed with a grammar that is no longer alive, every gesture is a shrill parody of what it had once been, and the remaining life is governed by the law of nothingness.[44]

The *Purgatorio*—less dramatic and more detached—seems to condense and freeze certain traits of Mahler's language: The energetic propulsion of the scherzi; the repeated enunciation of the same statement with a minimal variation at the end—like a question that is answered by yet another question, which restates the previous one while pushing it forward. The typical Mahlerian *perpetuum mobile* (Adorno's *Weltlauf*) spins from one instrumental group to another like a yarn through the loom, with scattered fragments and halts, sharp angles and jumps that seem to stop the motion in a gesture of sarcasm and distancing. The sudden irruption of a voice from without (or within?) is as typical in its wild contrast to the apparently innocent melody in B-flat minor that precedes it. There is nothing specifically

Jewish in any of these traits. It is the picture in the whole, in its brevity and its mimic quality, that brings to mind the famous Jewish self-irony. The *Purgatorio* is a miniature and infernal self-portrait; it is a sketch drawn by an able and disenchanted hand; a rapid photograph taken from a distance, like Kafka's fragmentary contemplations (in the collection of short pieces titled *Betrachtung*).[45]

Irony—that ancient Jewish tool of distance and defense—is exercised in Mahler's early works on primary materials borrowed or invented in reference to recognizable sources and codes. Later in his compositional career, his materials become more abstract, and their elaboration more lucid and concise. All the more do they bear the distinct fingerprints of their author and of their own history as components of his language. Irony in the late Mahler is at once everywhere and nowhere. Everything in his music, from *Das Lied von der Erde* on, is filtered by the growing presence of memory. Mahler sets the stage for his long farewell, from the oboe's lament that opens *Der Abschied* with a melismatic liturgical arabesque, to the alto Qaddish-like recitative that unfolds above a twenty-six-measure C pedal and an endless fermata. From then on he allows his creations to lead an ever more autonomous, even rebellious, life. The voice of an Other, of an unnamable elsewhere, sounds with growing insistence in Mahler's late works. Schoenberg's remarks are revealing in this context: "His Ninth is most strange. In it, the author hardly speaks as an individual any longer. It almost seems as though this work must have a concealed author who used Mahler as his spokesman, as his mouthpiece."[46]

Mahler's own voice was cruelly broken by premature death, leaving posterity with the certainty of a turning point. The Adagio of the Tenth Symphony looks far ahead with unprecedented vital audacity (see Example 1). In its indefinable tonality and in the freedom of its rhythmic and melodic unfolding, the viola theme escapes precise historical or stylistic premises. Oscillating between a vague reminiscence of the English horn solo of *Tristan*'s Act III and the anticipation of a dodeca-

Example 1. Mahler, Tenth Symphony (Universal Edition), Adagio, mm. 1–15.

phonic idea, it stands out as an extraordinary moment of void and memory, of silence and *récit*, of departure and of no return. It is, indeed, as if he were striving to shape the future while conserving the past-ridden identity of his work. The Adagio confirms and exasperates the sense of estrangement that creeps through Mahler's work after the apotheosis of the Eighth. Under a similar light, the reappearance of fragments of the *Purgatorio* in the sketches for the highly experimental Finale of the Tenth could be interpreted as a signature: the author returns momentarily, wearing a mask, and observes the ever more complex vicissitudes of his music.

We have said that a voice of an "elsewhere" sounds in Mahler's mature world: It sounds without making itself directly heard. It is a masked voice, fatally drawn into silence. Mahler's Jewishness is silent, too; it makes itself sensed without producing a sound. Could they be one and the same voice? To return to my starting point: as Edmond Jabès suggests, "The meaning of the *question* is perhaps only its openness to meaning."

NOTES

I am deeply indebted to Henry-Louis de La Grange for the impulse he gave to my first venture into Mahler's Jewish roots and for his encouragement and priceless knowledge ever since.

1. One of the rare documents on Mahler's attitude to his Jewish origins is a revealing and moving testimony by Magnus Davidsohn (b. 1877), cantor at the Fasanenstrasse Synagogue in Berlin, who in the late 1890s was an opera singer in Prague. He sang the bass part of Beethoven's Ninth conducted by Mahler on June 4, 1899 and they had a drink together the day before. Davidsohn published his report of that meeting ("Begegnung mit Gustav Mahler") in the Jewish review *Centralverein Zeitung* in 1935, rpt. in Bernd Sponheuer, "Musik auf einer 'kulturellen und physischen Insel.' Musik als Überlebensmittel im jüdischen Kulturbund 1933–1941," in *Musik in der Emigration 1933–1945*, ed. Horst Weber (Stuttgart and Weimar, 1994), pp. 133–35. See also my "Mahler and Judaism," *Muziek & Wetenschap* 5 (1995/1996): 405–16.

2. Theodor W. Adorno, *Mahler: A Musical Physiognomy*, trans. Edmund Jephcott (Chicago, 1992), p. 149. The word *voice* is absent in the German: "Was jüdisch ist an Mahler, partizipiert nicht unmittelbar an Volkstümlichem, sondern spricht durch alle Vermittlungen hindurch als ein Geistiges, Unsinnliches, gleichwohl an der Totalität Fühlbares sich aus." (*Mahler: Eine musikalische Physiognomie*, in *Gesammelte Schriften: Die musikalischen Monographien*, vol. 13 [Frankfurt am Main, 1998], p. 291). One could translate "ein Geistiges, Unsinnliches" as "something intellectual (or spiritual), nonsensuous (or nonsensual)." The translator's choice is insightful and more than legitimate, given

the objective difficulty to render in English (or in any other language) all the hidden shades of Adorno's dialectical and highly metaphoric discourse.

3. Adorno, *Mahler: A Musical Physiognomy*, p. 149.

4. Susan M. Filler, "Mahler as a Jew in the Literature," in *Dika Caecilia: Essays for Dika Newlin,* ed. Theodor Albrecht (Kansas City, 1988), pp. 66–85.

5. The remark is from Alma Mahler, *Gustav Mahler: Memories and Letters*, trans. Basil Creighton, ed. Donald Mitchell and Knud Martner, 3d ed. (Seattle and London, 1975), p. 109.

6. Max Brod, *Die Musik Israels*, trans. by T. Volcani as *Israel's Music* (Tel Aviv, 1951). A revision appeared with additions by Y. W. Cohen (Basel and London, 1976).

7. Other studies by Brod include "Gustav Mahlers jüdische Melodien," *Musikblätter des Anbruch* 2 (1920): 378–79, and *Zionismus als Weltanschauung*, ed. Brod and Felix Weltsch (Mährisch-Ostrau [Ostrava], 1925); cited in Susan Filler, *Gustav and Alma Mahler: A Guide to Research* (New York, 1989), pp. 29–30.

8. Max Brod, *Gustav Mahler: Beispiel einer deutsch-jüdischen Symbiose* (Frankfurt am Main, 1961).

9. See my "Mahler and Judaism," 406–07.

10. André Hajdu, *Réflexion sur la judaïté de Gustav Mahler*, in *Colloque International Gustav Mahler,* ed. L'Association Gustav Mahler (Paris, 1985), pp. 101–07; and my "Radici ebraiche in Mahler," in *Musica senza aggettivi: Studi per Fedele d'Amico*, ed. Agostino Ziino (Florence, 1991), pp. 477–86.

11. See, for example, Rudolf Louis, *Die deutsche Musik der Gegenwart* (Munich, 1909), p. 182; quoted in Nicholas Slominsky's *Lexicon of Musical Invective: Critical Assaults on Composers Since Beethoven's Time,* 2d ed. (Seattle and London, 1987), p. 121.

12. *Webster's Third New International Dictionary.*

13. The reference to the title of Charles Rosen's book is not casual. The debate around Mendelssohn's "neoclassicism" benefits considerably from the fundamental distinction between style and generation, allowing Mendelssohn's originality to emerge on the merits of his own very personal Romantic style. See Charles Rosen, *The Romantic Generation* (Cambridge, Mass., 1995); Mendelssohn's religious music is discussed on pp. 569–98.

14. See Maurizio Bettini, "Ghosts of Exile: Doubles and Nostalgia in Virgil's *Parva Troia (Aeneid* 3:294ff.)," *Classical Antiquity* 16 (1997): 8–33; and his *The Portrait of a Lover,* trans. Laura Gibbs (Berkeley and Los Angeles, 1999).

15. *Ha-Maqom* (the place) is one of the Hebrew words with which Orthodox Jews refer to God; *ha-Shem* (the Name) is another.

16. See my "Ailleurs. Gustav Mahler et l'ironie de la Diaspora," in *Gustav Mahler et l'ironie dans la culture viennoise au tournant du siècle,* ed. André Castagné, Michel Chalon, Patrick Florençon (Castelnau-le-Lez, 2001), pp. 45–60.

17. There is a quality of affirmation and strength to Mahler's music (and personality) that contrasts with any idea of "marginality," which to my thinking invalidates the basic thesis and title of Henry Lea's *Gustav Mahler: Man on the Margin* (Bonn, 1968), pp. 11–18. See my "Radici ebraiche in Mahler" and "Mahler and Judaism."

18. The image first appeared in an edition of a famous Hebrew text by the fifteenth-century scholar Abraham Farissol; Landau published the image in Prague. See Ruth Kestenberg-Gladstein, *Neuere Geschichte der Juden in den böhmischen Ländern*, vol. 1, *Das Zeitalter der Aufklärung 1780–1830* (Tübingen, 1969), after p. 152.

19. Henry-Louis de La Grange, "Music about Music in Mahler," in *Mahler Studies,* ed. Stephen E. Hefling (Cambridge, Eng., 1997), pp. 122–68.

20. The letter, which was some time before a second letter Kafka wrote Werfel and likewise did not send (from December 1922), is not included in scholarly editions of the letters but is cited in David Meghnagi, "Freud e la coscienza ebraica contemporanea," in *Ebrei moderni: Identià e stereotipi culturali*, ed. David Bidussa (Turin, 1989), p. 96.

21. David Stern, *Parables in Midrash: Narrative and Exegesis in Rabbinic Literature* (Cambridge, Mass., 1991), p. 5.

22. On the possibility of applying the spirit and principles of Jewish textual interpretation to musical hermeneutics in general, see my *Dire la musica: Studi di ermeneutica musicale*, ch. 1, "*Dire la musica:* Ermeneutica musicale e *Midrash* ebraico," pp. 5–68.

23. Stern, *Parables in Midrash*, p. 5.

24. Adorno, *Mahler: A Musical Physiognomy*, p. 61.

25. Erwin Stein, "Mahlers Sachlichkeit," *Musikblätter des Anbruch* (March 1930): 99-103; trans. in *On Mahler and Britten. Essays in Honour of Donald Mitchell on His Seventieth Birthday*, ed. Philip Reed (Woodbridge, UK, and Rochester, N.Y., 1996), pp. 115-18. By contrast, Mahler's Viennese detractor, Robert Hirschfeld, argued that the composer's only originality lay in performance indications, "which make the Mahler score swell into a thick novel." The observation occurs in a review of the Viennese premiere of the Sixth Symphony, *Wiener Abendpost*, 10 January 1907. I am grateful to Karen Painter for drawing my attention to Hirschfeld's argument.

26. Adorno, *Mahler: A Musical Physiognomy*, p. 61.

27. We shall be forever grateful to Carolyn Abbate for her acute coinage "unsung voices" and for the insight her studies collected under this title have given us into musical narrative in nineteenth-century opera. See her *Unsung Voices: Opera and Musical Narrative in the Nineteenth Century* (Princeton, 1991). Whether the narrational criterion is indeed apt to unveil and comprehend the "voices" in Mahler's music remains an open question, as I address below and in my *Dire la musica*, pp. 46-54.

28. Adorno, *Mahler: A Musical Physiognomy*, p. 32.

29. Hermann Danuser's study of the Third Symphony is a significant exception. He situates a rigorous musical analysis in the aesthetics of the nineteenth-century novel and investigates the philosophical and sociological implications of the term "musical prose." The result is a balanced correspondence between the initial analogy and the analytical findings, which is rarely found in other "narrative" readings. See his *Gustav Mahler und seine Zeit* (Laaber, 1991), pp. 152–203.

30. Adorno, *Mahler: A Musical Physiognomy*, p. 32.

31. Ibid.

32. Ibid. Adorno's concept of "truth content" (*Wahrheitsgehalt*), developed in his *Aesthetic Theory*, trans. and ed. Robert Hullo-Kentor, *Theory and History of Literature*, vol. 88 (Minneapolis, 1997), derives, in my opinion, from the concrete discussion of Mahler's music (pp. 33–34, 123–29, 166–67, for example). Any discussion of Adorno's *Aesthetic Theory* that ignores the essay on Mahler is doomed to miss this concrete dimension, which can hardly be found in his other musical writings. There is no mention of Mahler's name in Lambert Zuidervaart, *Adorno's Aesthetic Theory: The Redemption of Illusion* (Cambridge, Mass., 1991).

33. Conversation from summer 1895, in Natalie Bauer-Lechner, *Recollections of Gustav Mahler*, ed. Peter Franklin, trans. Dika Newlin (Cambridge, Eng., 1980), p. 40.

34. See my *Dire la musica*, pp. 41–54.

35. For a critique of Abbate's "excessive use of Adam Mickiewicz's dramatic poem" and of the narrative model in general, see Gianmario Borio, "Le parole cancellate e le tracce. Sul primo movimento della Prima Sinfonia di Mahler," in *Scritti in memoria di Ugo Duse*, ed. Nino Albarosa and Roberto Calabretto (Udine, 2000), pp. 9–22.

36. Conversation from July/August 1893, Steinbach am Attersee, in Bauer-Lechner, *Recollections of Gustav Mahler*, p. 32.

37. Conversation from January 1896, Hamburg, in Bauer-Lechner, *Recollections of Gustav Mahler*, pp. 43–44.

38. Abbate, *Unsung Voices*, pp. 156–70.

39. *Das Klagende Lied* (1880) is a clear illustration of how soon in his career Mahler moved in his own direction. It is at once an homage and a farewell to Wagner. The homage is inherent to the musical language; the farewell is manifest in the choice of subject, the elaboration of the text and the ultimate conception of genre and form.

40. Anthony Newcomb, "Narrative Archetypes and Mahler's Ninth Symphony," in *Music and Text: Critical Studies*, ed. Steven Paul Scher (Cambridge, Eng., 1992), p. 132.

41. Newcomb, "Narrative Archetypes and Mahler's Ninth," p. 136.

42. Edmond Jabès, "The Key," in *Midrash and Literature*, ed. Geoffrey H. Hartman and Sanford Budick (New Haven and London, 1986), pp. 349, 353, 351. The epitaph to this essay is from p. 352.

43. A well-known case of a direct quotation is, of course, the Scherzo of the Second Symphony ("In ruhig fliessender Bewegung"), where Mahler quotes Bruckner (the trio of the Fourth Symphony). The entire movement, of course, is an adaptation of his own and himself (the song "Des Antonius von Padua Fisschpredigt"). For further echoes in the Scherzo, see David Osmond-Smith, *Playing on Words: A Guide to Luciano Berio's Sinfonia* (London, 1985), pp. 39–46. For other cases, see de La Grange, "Music about Music."

44. See my "Perspectives of a Scherzo," in *The Seventh Symphony of Gustav Mahler: A Symposium*, ed. James L. Zychowicz (Madison, 1990), pp. 74–88.

45. See my *"Ailleurs"* and the revision of that essay in *Dire la musica*, pp. 69–91.

46. Arnold Schoenberg, "Gustav Mahler" (1912, rev. 1948), in his *Style and Idea*, ed. Leonard Stein (New York, 1975), p. 470.

A Soldier's Sweetheart's Mother's Tale?

Mahler's Gendered Musical Discourse

PETER FRANKLIN

> Rather than protecting music as a sublimely meaningless activity that has managed to escape social signification, I insist on treating it as a medium that participates in social formations by influencing the ways we perceive our feelings, our bodies, our desires—our very subjectivities—even if it does so surreptitiously, without most of us knowing how.
>
> —*Susan McClary*

Gender-sensitive approaches to music have generally sought to reground and reembody what Romantic idealism sent into ethereal space with E. T. A. Hoffmann's transcendent-spiritual flashes of cosmic, Beethovenian lightning.[1] Given musicology's often idealizing appropriation of Mahler's now more or less canonical works, a more earth-bound historical reexamination of the cultural meanings of early twentieth-century musical modernism might be furthered by an examination of gendered discourse within them. Mahler, unlike Susan McClary's Franz Schubert and Johannes Brahms, unlike Pyotr Ilich Tchaikovsky, offers innumerable invitations to hear gendered manners and voices in his music.[2] Some of these suggest a startling awareness of the problem about his culture's conventional, patriarchal attitudes toward women, their role in society and their relations with men. At times his music appears more aware even than he himself seems to have been in his day-to-day life. The trouble *there* was documented in the notorious letter he wrote to Alma Schindler, telling her what her role in their marriage—which could support only *one* composer— should properly be, while seeking contradictorily to assure her that he did *not* hold "the bourgeois view of the relationship between husband

and wife . . . which regards the latter as a sort of plaything for her husband and, at the same time, as his housekeeper. Surely you would never suspect me of feeling and thinking that way, would you?"[3]

Nor were those mere words pragmatically echoing the modish conversation of Alma and her friends whom he secretly scorned. Questions about gender and power play a foregrounded role in many of his works; they had certainly underpinned the stylistically assured *Lieder eines fahrenden Gesellen* early in his adult career. These songs in the folk manner significantly evinced all the self-destructive masculine vulnerability of the protagonist of *Die Schöne Müllerin* at a time when the language and obsessions of fin-de-siècle misogyny were well-developed—although Mahler's hero, broken by the loss of his woman, no more seeks revenge than does Schubert's—just a way to cope with the psychological effects of his painful loss. Remembering that the dedicatee of Mahler's poems had been an actual woman who had rejected him, we might alternatively pull them back into the patriarchal frame by reinterpreting them as a male composer's self-regarding attempt to shame into pity the woman singer, Johanna Richter, he had both directed and loved in Kassel. Other works corroborate the underlying ambivalence of the gender polarities of the *Lieder eines fahrenden Gesellen* in ways that speak with eerie foresight to more recent students of narrative theory in relation to music.

The *Wunderhorn* song *Der Schildwache Nachtlied* is a famous enough example. It is one of Mahler's "soldier's tale" songs, but it is also the song of his sweetheart, who addresses the soldier's self-regarding heroism in music that is strikingly characterized as Other, as feminine in its dancelike reiterations, comforting as a lullaby. The text reads:

Ich kann und mag nicht fröhlich sein!
Wenn alle Leute schlafen,
so muss ich wachen, ja wachen!
Muss traurig sein!

I can and will not be cheerful!
When everyone else is asleep,
I have to stay awake!
Have to be sad!

Lieb' Knabe, du musst nicht traurig sein!
Will deiner warten, im Rosengarten!
Im grünen Klee!

Dear boy, you needn't be sad!
I'll wait for you, in the rose garden!
In the green clover!

Zum grünen Klee da geh'	No green clover for me!
ich nicht!	It's the field of shining arms
Zum Waffengarten! Voll	That I've been sent to!
Helleparten!	
Bin ich gestellt!	
Stehst du im Feld, so helf' dir	When you're in the field, may
Gott!	God be with you!
An Gottes segen ist alles gelegen!	God's blessing is meaningful for
Wer's glauben tut!	all!
	Whoever believes in it!
Wer's glauben tut ist weit davon!	Whoever believes in it is far away!
Er ist ein König! Er ist ein	He is a king! He's an emperor!
Kaiser!	He wages the war!
Er führt den Krieg!	Halt! Who goes there? Patrol!
Halt! Wer da? Rund!	Keep clear of me!
Bleib mir vom Leib!	
Wer sang es hier? Wer sang	Who sang that? Who sang just
zur Stund'?	now?
Verlor'ne Feldwacht sang es	A lost sentry sang it at midnight!
um Mitternacht!	Midnight! Sentry!
Mitternacht! Feldwacht!	

The sentinel's rejection of her words of spiritual comfort in the fourth stanza lead him to a blasphemous and implicitly treasonous outburst in the fifth, at which point he seems to catch himself in the act, suddenly turning in fear to ward off an approaching threat in the darkness. The poem ends with a three-line stanza in a surprise, metanarrative voice that asks, "Who sang it here? . . . A lost sentinel." Interestingly, Mahler sets that to the "girl's" music and even lets the whole song die away on her recurrent unresolved dominant seventh. Since it previously resolved back into the sentinel's song, a kind of misogyny nevertheless potentially emerges here as the girl's ostensible modernism in fact frames and quells the boy's bold rebelliousness.

We do not need strategic and arguably unhistorical recourse to A. B. Marx's gendered explication of contrast in sonata form to see that this is a musical structure, albeit with sung text, in which any distinction between the musical and the extramusical ceases to be helpful. Music and text *explain each other* here, and behind the explanation lies a threatening question, explicit in its gender concern, about music itself: who *does* sing it? From Mahler's cultural viewpoint, does the masculine composer's voice tend to assume a feminized *Muttersprache* in his compositions, when he begins to "sing"? Might this music in some way unseat, or does it rather appropriate the "master narrative" that would favor the iconoclastic sentinel over his conservative girlfriend with her sirenlike consolations?

Comparisons between earlier and later Mahler suggest conflicting answers to this possibly tendentious question. The *Wunderhorn* songs' masculine voice, focusing the passively broken and alienated one of the Romantic wayfarer in a more specifically historical and social context, is typically that of a soldier: the sentinel, the drummer boy, the ever-departing war-bound lover. His masculine assertiveness is always controlled and owned by others—by the kings and emperors whose guards seem suddenly to appear round the corner at that literally unguarded moment in *Der Schildwache Nachtlied*. We might compare and contrast the first movement of the Sixth Symphony, with its famous depiction of Alma. As so often in Mahler, the main "opposing" musical force is characterized from the outset as a march, although the masculinity of that stark, A-minor juggernaut is figured as a symbolic distillation of the coercive power that terrifies and oppresses the singer-sentinel in *Der Schildwache Nachtlied*. The semiotic practice on which Mahler seems to rely positions the march as antagonistic to the establishment of a secure subject-position; when one is established, it is celebrated with a veritable eruption of lyrical energy . . . precisely at the onset of the Alma theme. It therefore seems more convincingly not to depict her but to sing her praise in Mahler's own subjective voice, in a mode of release, of abandonment to and for the woman he loved. He would describe her not only as his muse or lyre but also in quasi-Wagnerian terms as his redeeming "port after storm"[4]

Here what is once more at issue, therefore, is a creative silencing or ventriloquizing of Alma's voice, replacing it with his own in music whose conventionally feminine lyrical qualities arguably reinscribe patriarchal power. This exposes the whole problematic of music's wider symbolic meaning within a culture predicated on the increasingly tense and threatened exercise of that power—as when he had demanded that she abandon thoughts of a composing career as a condition for marrying him. But he did come to see how wrong that was, prompted by Alma's long-feared rejection of him for a younger man. The evidence lies not only in his all-too-late move to reempower her creative, musical voice and publish her songs in 1910, but also in his dedication to her, on the eve of its first performance, of the Eighth Symphony. This most ostentatiously public of all his works—he even described it as his "gift to the nation"—takes the form of a two-movement symphonic cantata for the fullest and most extravagant forces available. Ever since Emil Gutmann's publicity campaign for the premiere, in Munich in 1910, it has been known as the "Symphony of a Thousand": a work designed for vast arenas, perhaps even the circus buildings (as some of his detractors noted) in which its early performances often took place.[5]

Invoking another kind of gendered discourse, Mahler himself affected to detest Gutmann's publicity, feeling that it put him in the position of a serious artist "prostituting himself" to the economically driven world of mass entertainment.[6] That tension between idealized benefaction and "Barnum and Bailey" spectacular (another association Mahler himself made) was, of course, inscribed in the Eighth Symphony on almost every level—as it was inscribed in the developing fin-de-siècle debate about art versus mass culture. The discursive gendering of these very terms, as masculine versus feminine, has been explored by many commentators on the period. As if responding to and even engaging with just such a discourse, the Eighth Symphony seems to celebrate the masculine teleology of power-driven, goal-directed aspiration in the first movement's dynamic hymn to the creator spirit (*Veni Creator Spiritus!*) but then, in the setting of the *Schlussszene* from Goethe's *Faust* Part II, it reinterprets that teleology as driven not by will but by Eros.

The masculine subject—symbolized by Goethe in Faust's now unvoiced "immortal part"—is passively drawn toward the "Eternal Feminine," symbolically defined in a series of epiphanic revelations as both idealized former lover (the penitent, interceding Gretchen) and distantly apprehended *Mater Gloriosa:* the transcendent mother who is clothed in an appropriately intertextual garment, woven from musical signs of pleasure, sensuality and angelic purity. Almost static E-major harmony supports an extended first-violin melody marked floating (schwebend) and vibrando; harp arpeggios are complemented by a halo of sustained harmonium chords, "Schwächstes Register" giving way to "Tremolo-Register," as a second harp joins a swelling force of wind instruments. Erotic, upward-gliding portamenti herald the entry of the worshiping male chorus—an added touch of gender differentiation engineered by Mahler, who replaced Goethe's originally responding chorus of *women* penitents.[7]

"Look up at the saving sight!" calls Dr. Marianus: "Virgin, Mother, Queen, Goddess, remain gracious!" The closing *Chorus Mysticus* leads us onward and upward toward a peroration of violent, phallocentric masculine power and wilfulness—the deus ex machina is a separately placed brass choir proclaiming the *Hauptmotiv* of the opening invocation to the creator spirit. This emphasizes the alternative significance of what it celebrates and ostensibly supercedes in its overdetermined volume and enacted unanimity. On this reading, Mahler's dedication of the Eighth to Alma might even have represented a final dialectical move to persuade himself that a utopian synthesis, the feminization of the masculine will, *was* what it was about, as a kind of summation of all transcendental symphonics.[8]

* * * *

Did a prototypical New Man lurk within Faust's immortal essence—or just the old one waiting for redemptive rebirth? Two things we can be certain about: that we can't be certain, and that the terms and issues of Mahler's multivoiced symphonic discourse were both defined by and projected into a wider one in which eros and gender are mediating terms between worries about a controlling creative power and the possibility of utopian conviction. The historical failure of that conviction for Mahler and his culture is surely what makes the Eighth Symphony so significant in its public aspect as a historical meeting place for all the disparate voices of a world whose center it aspired to hold. It seems by extension to symbolize music itself engaged in a reflexively, perhaps posthumously, troubled celebration of all it had hoped itself to be (transcendent, unifying, supranational). Mahler's dedication of it to Alma might even represent a kind of admission that the *Unbeschreibliche* had still really not been *getan;* that the *Ewig-Weibliche* was a construction marked by the ideological residue of *Alles Vergängliche;* that the *Ereignis* remained *unzulänglich*. I would further argue, however, that his ability to make that admission was conditioned by more than the marital infidelity that prompted it and that presaged the collapse of his private life. Its roots lay in something that had defined his artistic personality and the trajectory of his career—something that had been contingent upon the way it had begun and upon the way its unfolding had been marked by a peculiar tension between what I would call the immanent meaningfulness of his music as a multivoiced discourse of telling and contradicting, doing and undoing, and the ways in which he variously articulated, concealed, or camouflaged, that meaningfulness in public statements "about" his works.

This tension resonated with others embedded in the nineteenth-century discourse of Romantic idealism in its dealings with music. If music *were* secretly more than just music, then that secret was jealously protected by diversionary circumlocutions that insisted on ambivalence about the mysterious, supposedly private and purely personal some-

thing that lay beyond the barred gates of musical signification. Bruno
Walter's ghosted letter to Ludwig Schiedermair about Mahler's Fourth
Symphony, dangling clues about the private programmatic titles for the
movements and then dismissing them with a stern admonition about the
absoluteness of absolute music, represents a characteristic document of
this process.[9] Reading such material, one develops the suspicion that the
significant meaningfulness of music was indeed so revealing, so significant
that it *had* to be guarded with mythical beasts and philosophical-aesthetic
hocus-pocus. I am aware that I might almost be talking about nineteenth-century bourgeois attitudes toward sex and sexuality and its
public discussion—a correspondence that renders the discursive mut-
ing of music its own implicitly gendered and bodily connotations.
Spiritual or universalizing allegory and symbol in discourse *about* music
may conceal gendered subjects in situations and relations that project a
kind of three-dimensional personal and cultural history.

Much is worth exploring with respect to Mahler's slow movements,
which were often heard, not least by his detractors, as the ones in which
he most nearly attained the transcendent purity of German art music
at its most noble. In his first symphonic Adagio, the closing movement
of the Third Symphony, Mahler relevantly signaled its resolving, unifying and redeeming qualities by calling it "What Love tells me,"
deliberately distancing that higher form of love from an implicitly
lower" kind involved with physical sexuality (this in a letter to Anna
von Mildenburg).[10] In *Gustav Mahler and the Courage to Be*, David
Holbrook inadvertently proposed an intriguing alternative to Mahler's
suggestion that a patriarchally masculine musical voice of the spirit
might be asserting itself over a feminized music of the body. Reminding
us of the virgin/whore dichotomy that defined so much of the troubled
male discourse about women in the fin de siècle, he hints that the first
movement of the Ninth Symphony was dominated, in its D-major first
subject, by a feminine voice whose uneroticized qualities were associated with its character as a comforting and specifically maternal one.[11]
Another link to be made here would be with the parental lamentation
of the *Kindertotenlieder*, quoted at the very end of the Ninth Symphony.
To return to the Fourth Symphony, there is the specific instance of
Mahler's association of *its* Adagio with images of suffering spirituality
that he associated, in conversation with Natalie Bauer-Lechner, specifically with a memory of his own mother, "laughing, as if through
tears"—the mother who, in Mahler reported words, "suffered endlessly,
but had always resolved everything in love and forgiveness."[12]

All of this, as I have already hinted, richly supports Lawrence
Kramer's and Richard Taruskin's recent moves to deconstruct the

problematic category of the extramusical."[13] The very values that, at least in Mahler's culture, prompted people to seek more than just intellectual refuge in a purified, autonomous music were as contingent, historical, and cultural as their variously gendered implications reveal. But it is not enough simply to suggest that music's most sublime voice might have been constructed by Mahler as feminine or somehow androgynous (the utopian union of masculine and feminine). Such a suggestion would leave open important questions about the status of more forcefully masculine musical voices and dynamics in his works, viewed from a broader cultural-historical perspective—one that would include the process of assimilation into German culture that dominated much of Mahler's early career.

* * * *

The anxieties related to sexuality and gendered positions that the self-destructive narrative of the *Lieder eines fahrenden Gesellen* reflects take on a stronger coloration when mapped onto the dialectically opposing dynamics of either heroically conquering or being more submissively "given" to a dominant German culture that structured the possibilities of assimilation, success, and "mastery" in the Austro-German Empire and beyond its borders in Kassel, Leipzig, or Hamburg. To understand more about Mahler's conflicting investment in the alternative constructions of colonizer and colonized, active conqueror and more passively pragmatic immigrant, we must return to his treatment of gendered voices in works written when he was closer to the margin of German culture (in Henry Lea's term).[14] This might be the case even in his *Wunderhorn* settings, if they evince a deliberate attempt to assume or buy into the authentic German voice of a Romantically constructed folk tradition, distinct from the Moravian or Bohemian ones he would have encountered on the outskirts of Iglau (where the town gave way to the country, to nature).

The *Wunderhorn* Germanness was predicated upon hearth and home, the innocence of children, the truth of established religion . . . and the complementary but "naturally" different roles of men and women. Yet in keeping with the critical moment of Romanticism—in its regressive, anti-urban antimaterialism, that Germanness was also defined by the shadows that surrounded it in the dark forest and crossed its path on moonlit nights. The texts themselves, in Arnim and Brentano's versions, are therefore actively engaged in cultural-ideological work of a kind that Mahler, the Jewish outsider-insider, was able to heighten and articulate from a critical perspective born of personal sympathy. He certainly managed to highlight ambivalence about gendered roles and positions in some of the most striking and curious lyrics he chose to set—like *Der Schildwache Nachtlied*. An interesting comparison might be made with Eduard Lassen's 1903 arrangements of genuine folksong melodies for *Wunderhorn* poems. None of the texts deemed appropriate by Lassen or his editor, Arthur Smolian, had been set by Mahler. It is furthermore unlikely that Mahler's settings would have been found by them to serve the *alte gut-deutsche Volksseele*, which Smolian hoped would once again "be victorious in the world."[15]

Another relevant example might be the outwardly slight and more humorous "Trost im Unglück" (1892). Here a soldier, a rather self-satisfied hussar, bids farewell to his sweetheart, assuring her that their affair was good enough while it lasted but that he will easily live without her. To his rather bumptious martial music, the girl responds, giving as good as she'd got. At first her music sounds more like a trio to his march than anything radically different; but gradually it displays its femininity in almost parodistically winding chromaticism as she describes the flower in her father's garden whose full growth will mark the end of her love: "I can do just as well without you!" The implication of her stanza's ability to begin and end with music that quotes and seamlessly abuts onto "his" is stressed in the third and final stanza: rather graphically, if two singers perform it; more subtly and demandingly (also for the singer) if there is only one performer. Where the first and second stanzas are headed (as in Mahler's score) The Hussar and The Girl, the last is headed "Both." What sounds like a reprise of the boy's martial music ends with a mutually defiant version of the girl's concluding flourish as they sing (more or less): "See if I care—I'd be ashamed to be seen out with you anyway!" The joky little scene has curious implications. The literal union of the *two* voices, each defiant, suggests (particularly from the girl's point of view) that either voice might be a performative mask, a manner that can be assumed. Nervy questions are left about who wins; what happens; what they really feel; and *what do we make of a world in which male and female, soldier and sweetheart, can each assume the other's voice*? Such questions remain unanswered behind the arch smile that is no doubt intended to be triggered by the song's capriciously assertive conclusion, which figures not union but the hussar galloping away into the sunset.

Much more could be said about Mahler's elaborate, emphatically multivoiced and contradictorily meaningful *Wunderhorn* songs, whose protosymphonic symbolic arguments occasionally *became* symphonic movements, in which communication and noncommunication, hearing and not-hearing are mapped onto allegorically meaningful contrasts and oppositions that are frequently gendered. I will conclude here by pressing back even further than the *Lieder eines fahrenden Gesellen* in search of the roots of Mahler's musical engagement with the tropes of gender in a narrative piece that takes us still closer to the margins of his emergence as a creative voice—one constructed out of a multiplicity of voices, of which one is that of music itself.

I am referring to *Das klagende Lied*. Its earliest three-part version (performed complete for the first time in Manchester in 1997)[16] confirms what is already evident about Mahler's subsequently revised cantata, which he submitted unsuccessfully for the Vienna Beethoven Prize at a stage in his career when it might (as he later believed) have made all the difference.[17] The aspiring young composer, as yet with no clear position to defend (but everything to aim for), had produced a fairy-tale piece which thematizes the intervention in (and as) music of a justifiably subversive outsider; it also plays oddly with standard tropes of gender difference.[18] Cultural and sexual achievement linked to power are unequivocally at stake here.

We can read *Das klagende Lied* as a cultural document, however, only by abandoning trite psychologizing (what Dika Newlin once called "necropsychiatry")[19] about the work's supposedly symptomatic motivation by guilt feelings about the death of Mahler's brother Ernst. Instead, let us note initially how the narrative of "Waldmärchen" (the first part of the cantata) begins with hand-me-down misogyny, blaming everything on a proud queen who, *Turandot*-like, sends the two brothers up the proverbial garden path in search of the rare flower that will win one of them her hand (in the Grimms' version, the instigator of the quest was a king, anxious to rid his lands of a troublesome wild boar.) Although *Parsifal* had yet to be staged, one implication is that Mahler's boys might have avoided a good deal of trouble had they left her to her own devices and opted to become chaste Grail knights. Once upon a time . . . the old misogynistic story is told.

But Mahler was not only ahead of Wagner here, he was also alert to issues that have more recently provoked some of Carolyn Abbate's ideas about music and narrative and, indeed, her dispute with Lawrence Kramer about the closing scene of Richard Strauss's *Salome*, leading to the former's insistence that women singers' voices drown out and trump those of the male composers who always supposedly plot their swan song.[20] In order to appreciate the multilevel sexual politics of "Waldmärchen," we might initially note that a tenor both narrates the first stanza and assumes the metanarrative voice that admonishes the *wonnigliche Weib* in its last two lines, asking, "For whom *will* your sweet love blossom?" In the second stanza, where the beautiful red flower in the forest is described, the narrative is taken up by a baritone who is, however, denied access to the tenor's metanarrative voice; here the final two lines, addressing the queen ("Oh weh! Du stolze Königin!") are given to the chorus (altos, tenors, and basses) in the first of the choralelike refrains that seem symbolically to include the audience as like-minded inheritors of the implications of Bach cantata practice.

The third stanza serves to fix the voice-character typology of the two male soloists by linking the tenor with the "kind and gentle" brother, the baritone with the "evil knight . . . who could only curse." While the chorus takes over the narrative in the fourth stanza, this typology is reinforced in a striking way by Mahler's now giving the penultimate metanarrative line, addressing both brothers, to the baritone soloist (originally two bass soloists singing in octaves). His dark voice tone and winding chromatic line lend an evil quality to the words: "My knights, running so quickly, who will actually find the flower?" The burden of guilt seems lifted from the *stolze Königin* and placed onto one of the two male protagonists, thus divided conclusively into good and bad. Even more strikingly, the gentle younger brother is now claimed by a solo soprano, who enters for the first time, taking up the narrative with the chorus. She recounts his successful discovery of the flower and subsequent slumber. Apart from his brief participation, later in the stanza, in a generalized passage for solo quartet, the evil baritone has no further part to play in the work; in fact, the bulk of the solo narrative will henceforth be carried by women, the soprano giving way to a more maternal mezzo (*Alt* in Mahler's score) at the moment of the murder: she forbears to give an actual account of it, but describes the dead boy's smile "as if he were dreaming." The final stanza of the "Waldmärchen" finds her addressing the forest flowers and the sad breezes, establishing her link with the natural world as the narrating "mother" who will dominate the rest of the work, although the final two lines of "Waldmärchen," presented by Mahler in inverted commas, like the quoted beginning of another story ("In the forest . . . there stands an old willow"), are given to the male chorus.

The purpose of dwelling on the migration and gender instability of the narrating voice in "Waldmärchen" is to indicate above all how its ostensibly misogynistic tale becomes a tale of male rivalry told, in the end, *by* a woman who (unlike the male soloists) is directly associated with none of its protagonists. Beyond mimesis, music's true diegetic voice (Mahler seems to suggest) *is* indeed feminine, motherly, all-knowing, and understanding—where it is not that of the generalizing chorus that implicitly includes us in its collectivity. But that is not, as it were, the whole story. Abbate's more specific, and arguably problematic, notion (in *Unsung Voices*) of musical narration as a rare event of "disruption" is also corroborated here in a striking version of a symbolic reflexive performance within the work of the kind that interest her in opera (like Senta's ballad and Tannhäuser's "Rome" narration). In *Das klagende Lied*, this sets up an alternative image of music's voice as a male one that is explicitly performed, or ventriloquized, by a woman in a way that reflects, but without fully reinscribing, the usual patriarchal narrative of the active male hero opposed to the untransformable female principle of nature.

The occasion is striking. The only other significant solo role in "Der Spielmann" and "Hochzeitsstück," the second and third parts of *Das klagende Lied*, is for the tenor. These two movements, incidentally, became parts I and II of the abbreviated and revised version in which Mahler first performed the work in February 1901—a version that he may have considered more conventionally saleable in its structural economy and musical coherence, or indeed (to be tendentious again), more properly musical. Music is precisely the business of the genial minstrel who now replaces the murdered brother as the tenor role. The association is narratively stressed by his chance discovery of one of the latter's bones, from which he innocently fashions a flute (quite literally a *Wunderhorn* in the Grimms' original). The melody it magically plays is also a transparently meaningful discourse—a *klagende Lied* to which the metanarrating mezzo soprano (*Alt*) puts words that immediately identify its subject-position as that of the murdered brother. Only as a musician may the dispossessed outsider effectively address the world he had wanted to make his own—"Um ein schönfarbig Blümelein hat mich mein Bruder erschlagen." Originally Mahler had given all the utterances of the bone flute to two prepubertal boys' voices, emphasizing both the gender and the childlike innocence of the murder victim in a striking way. In one sense, however, it makes little difference to the flute's climactic intervention in the gaudily depicted public festivity of "Hochzeitsstück": the anachronistically delayed wedding celebration of the murderer to the "proud queen" whose hand he had so nefariously won. The repeated, framed performance by the minstrel of the mysteriously articulate flute melody emphasizes the metaphor of music as a solemn, sad, and indeed *shockingly* beautiful sounding from the bones and flesh of dead creatures, protesting the fate that has undone them. Here the protest is explicitly politicized: the adult world of power and sexuality is itself undone by musical intervention in a musical scenario that links the specific accusation of the bone flute with the seemingly threatened incursion of the rowdily autonomous off-stage band. Its marchlike carouseling extends the piece's carnival imagery into one that involves a double threat to the status quo by both music and musicians.

What we have here, then, is a youthful cantata whose narrative complexity, in terms of the strategic gendering (and regendering) of its many voices, positions music itself, at its most intense and literally significant, as ideally associated with the voices of an innocent boy on the one hand—whose cultural task is that of intervening and disruptive self-expression—and on the other the understanding voice of an Erda-like mother figure (compare the contralto who will articulate the voice of Man in the Third Symphony's Nietzsche setting). That voice bridges threatening cultural aspiration and art's beneficent role as the comforting *Muttersprache* that loves everything and threatens no one. In *Das klagende Lied* these cultural tropes and the constructed gender roles they utilize are presented dramatically in an oppositional relationship. It seems to suggest that the utopianism of a value-laden music, as constructed by German Romantic ideology, was quite literally impossible. There really was (in the words of *Das himmlische Leben*) no music like this on earth: in the real world, whose perceived constitution would be threatened by it. In this way Mahler incorporated the critical thrust of German Romantic philosophy, along with the internal contradiction of its problems with women, sexuality, and the body, into the very center of his creative work as a musician in a culture that was as much his as it was not his, where he was himself forced to confront the abyss that separated the ambitious boy from the all-affirming love of tradition as nature, as the desired mother resolving everything in love; in the end her tears prevail, her song is a lamentation.

The kaleidoscopic fragmentation and postponement of a secure subject position in Mahler's music is thus significantly, if not exclusively, evinced in its play of gendered voices. These often undermine, even as they highlight, the constructedness of the music that eludes them, save in the transitory moment of revelation or the humorously parodistic and thus implicitly tragic image of an art that was (as Theodor Adorno more or less put it)[21] the living testimony to its own impossibility. The constructedness, as we would now see it, of the image of the maternal voice as both sonorous envelope and entrapment has been explored by many feminist writers, including Kaja Silverman (drawing on Guy Rosolato, Michel Chion, and Julia Kristeva).[22] Mahler's famous national and ethnic designation of himself as "thrice homeless" has therefore another implication: the soldier, the sweetheart, *and* the mother are all, in some sense, masks or voices that he assumes. Mahler's specially reflexive, alienated, and yet manipulative relationship with the master narrative of the culture he appropriated, as an exoticized or even implicitly feminized outsider, gave rise to a musical project in which music seemed constantly to question and reconstruct itself as a phantasmagoria of voices. Beyond and behind it, that of the heroic male subject quite literally dies away in the hushed *morendo* that closes all the major movements of his last works.

NOTES

This essay began life as a paper delivered at the Royal Musical Association conference "Whose Voice Is It Anyway?" at City University, London, in November 1997.

1. E. T. A. Hoffmann, "Beethoven's Instrumental Music" (1813), trans. by Oliver Strunk in *Strunk's Source Readings in Music History,* vol. 6, *The Nineteenth Century,* ed. Ruth A. Solie (New York, 1998), pp. 151–56.

2. The epigraph to this essays is taken from Susan McClary, "Constructions of Subjectivity in Schubert's Music," in *Queering the Pitch: The New Gay and Lesbian Musicology,* ed. Philip Brett, Elizabeth Wood, and Gary C. Thomas (New York and London, 1994), pp. 211–12.

3. Mahler's undated letter (19 December 1901) to Alma, in *Ein Glück Ohne Ruh': Die Briefe Gustav Mahlers an Alma,* ed. Henry-Louis de La Grange and Günther Weiß (Berlin, 1995), p. 108; the letter is translated in de La Grange, *Gustav Mahler,* vol. 2, Vienna: *The Years of Challenge (1887–1904),* trans. Roy MacDonald Stock (Oxford, Eng., 1995), p. 451.

4. Letter to Alma of 14 December 1901, in Alma Mahler, *Gustav Mahler: Memories and Letters,* trans. Basil Creighton, ed. Donald Mitchell and Knud Martner, 4th ed. (Seattle and London, 1990), p. 211.

5. On the early performance history of the Eighth, particularly in Leipzig, see Steffen Lieberwirth, "Die 'Sinfonie der Tausend' oder Tausend für eine Sinfonie," in *A Mass for the Masses: Proceedings of the Mahler VIII Symposium Amsterdam 1988,* ed. Eveline Nikkels and Robert Becqué (Rijswijk, 1992), pp. 153–66.

6. Undated letter to Emil Gutmann from March 1910, in *Mahler's Unknown Letters,* ed. Herta Blaukopf, trans. Richard Stokes (London, 1986), p. 74. An influential example would be Andreas Huyssen, *After the Great Divide: Modernism, Mass Culture and Postmodernism* (London: 1988), ch. 3, "Mass Culture as Woman: Modernism's Other," pp. 44–62.

7. In Goethe's *Faust,* Part II, act 5, scene IV, the *Chor der Büsserinnen* (penitents) are explicitly gendered feminine.

8. Alma Mahler's account of the dedication, a decision at a time of intense crisis in their relationship, will be found in her *Gustav Mahler,* pp. 178–79.

9. Letter of 6 December 1901, in *Bruno Walter: Briefe 1894–1962,* ed. Lotte Walter Lindt (Frankfurt am Main, 1969), pp. 48–52. See my "A Stranger's Story: Programmes, Politics and Mahler's Third Symphony," in *The Mahler Companion,* ed. Donald Mitchell and Andrew Nicholson (London, 1999), pp. 173–74.

10. Letter of 1 July 1896, an edited version of which appears in *Selected Letters of Gustav Mahler,* ed. Knud Martner, trans. Eithne Wilkins, Ernst Kaiser, and Bill Hopkins (London, 1979), p. 169; a fuller text appears in *Gustav Mahler Briefe: Neuausgabe erweitert und revidiert,* ed. Herta Blaukopf, 2d ed. (Vienna, 1996), pp. 189–90.

11. David Holbrook, *Gustav Mahler and the Courage to Be* (London: 1975), pp. 123–25. No less relevant here is a wonderful sentence of Theodor Adorno: "Mahler's music passes

a maternal hand over the hair of those to whom it turns," from his *Mahler: A Musical Physiognomy*, trans. Edmund Jephcott (Chicago and London, 1992), p. 29.

12. Conversation from summer 1900 in Natalie Bauer-Lechner, *Recollections of Gustav Mahler*, ed. Peter Franklin, trans. Dika Newlin (Cambridge, Eng., 1980), pp. 152–53.

13. See Lawrence Kramer, *Classical Music and Postmodern Knowledge* (Berkeley and Los Angeles, 1995), p. 67; and Richard Taruskin, *Defining Russia Musically* (Princeton, 1997), pp. 372–73.

14. Henry Lea, *Gustav Mahler: Man on the Margin* (Bonn, 1985).

15. Arthur Smolian, "Zur Einleitung," in Eduard Lassen, *Aus den Knaben Wunderhorn: Alte Minneweisen und Volkslieder* (Leipzig, 1904[?]), p. vi. The book is undated, but the introduction is signed "Christmas, 1903."

16. Kent Nagano, conducting the Hallé Orchestra (7 October 1997); Nagano and the Hallé subsequently recorded the original version on Erato 3984-21664-2 (1998).

17. Conversation from April 1898 in Bauer-Lechner, *Recollections of Gustav Mahler*, p. 116.

18. While many early writers on Mahler cited Ludwig Bechstein (a compiler and re-presenter of popular stories) as the story's author, there is no clear evidence to indicate any primary source other than "The Singing Bone," from the *Kinder- und Hausmärchen* of the Brothers Grimm.

19. Dika Newlin, "The 'Mahler's Brother Syndrome': Necropsychiatry and the Artist," *Musical Quarterly* 66, no. 2 (1980): 296–304.

20. Lawrence Kramer, "Culture and Musical Hermeneutics: The Salome Complex," *Cambridge Opera Journal* 2, no. 3 (1990): 269–94; and Carolyn Abbate, "Opera, or the Envoicing of Women," in *Musicology and Difference: Gender and Sexuality in Music Scholarship*, ed. Ruth A. Solie (Berkeley and Los Angeles, 1993), pp. 225–58.

21. Two related passages in Adorno's Mahler book are relevant. In the first chapter, he proposes that "Mahler's primary experience, inimical to art, needs art in order to manifest itself," and in the final chapter (concerning *Das Lied von der Erde*), he suggests, "That metaphysics is no longer possible becomes the ultimate metaphysics" (*Mahler: A Musical Physiognomy*, pp. 6, 154).

22. Kaja Silverman, *The Acoustic Mirror: The Female Voice in Psychoanalysis and the Cinema* (Bloomington, Ind., 1988).

The Aesthetics of Mass Culture:

Mahler's Eighth Symphony and Its Legacy

KAREN PAINTER

Shortly before the Munich premiere of the Eighth Symphony, the inde-fatigable Mahler disciple Richard Specht published an article designed to show that the gigantic work was a musical and spiritual culmination of all the composer's previous symphonies. "Mahler's path resembles one of those dizzyingly high tower staircases whose spiral turns always lead the climber to view earth from the same point, except that having clambered another hundred steps up, he always looks down from an ever higher level." For Specht, the panorama was personal and reli-gious: looking back over the periods of Mahler's life and achievement, he beheld the composer's initial struggle with "the world and the ego, God and Nature," his transcendence of the everyday world, his ascent into the realm of spirit, and his sovereign mastery of polyphony beyond "mere" harmony, "until the mighty dome of the 'Eighth' vaults over the entire structure."[1] Certainly the vocal texts that compose its two halves confirm Specht's approach to the work as intensely personal and spiritual. Yet more than any other of Mahler's works, the Eighth Symphony had a political career in the first half of the twentieth cen-tury, which began with its premiere in 1910 and continued even after National Socialism silenced the composer's voice in 1933, until a final performance in Vienna in 1936 under Bruno Walter, the Jewish con-ductor who had been expelled from his position in Germany.

How could a symphony built around the "Veni Creator Spiritus" and the final texts of redemption from Goethe's *Faust* be construed as political? And what can "political" possibly mean in the context of Mahler's creative trajectory, first in 1906, when the Eighth Symphony virtually seized the composer, and in 1910, when he devoted such great effort to its premiere in Munich (the same city and year Max Reinhardt planned an *Oedipus Rex* in the 3,000-seat Musikhalle).[2] This essay proposes that in the context of Mahler's public world, the aspirations he held for the Eighth, through its premiere some months before his death, had important social and ideological dimensions. In particular, the work represented an engagement with the notion of "the masses," which became so crucial an interpretative term for understanding society and politics from the 1890s through the 1930s. What is more, the Austrian Social Democratic movement—which was the major force for Austrian democracy, both in the decade before the First World War and during the polarized First Republic—appropriated the legacy of this and other Mahler symphonies for its own collective vision. After Mahler's death, this work and his musical legacy continued to serve the artistic and pedagogic program of the Austrian socialists—less now by virtue of what it suggested about the genius of the composer than by the values it promised for a new, mass audience that was to be actively involved in the production and appreciation of art.

The Awareness of a Mass Society

The years 1905 to 1908 saw a decisive transformation in European and especially Central European history. This was the period during which significant breakthroughs of scientific and artistic modernism—recall the special theory of relativity and early quantum concepts, on the one hand, Picasso's *Démoiselles d'Avignon*, on the other—dramatically revealed the implications of accumulating innovation. International crises centering on Morocco and Bosnia raised the specter of possibly catastrophic armed conflict; and the Russian Revolution of 1905 brought Europe's first mass upheaval in two generations. Celebrations of a hygienic violence and cleansing social conflict spread among intellectuals left and right, whether Rosa Luxemburg's call for the mass strike, Georges Sorel's diatribes against bourgeois humanism, the French Right's impatience with the peaceful routines of the Third Republic, pan-German flirtations with preventive war, young Italians' yearning for imperialist adventure, or strident mutual denunciations of Habsburg hegemony. Each of these envisaged a society that for better or worse would mobilize its members in the great collective causes. All these expectations, as well as the growing strength and militancy of labor unions, made the diagnosis of so-called mass politics a major theme of public life. Mahler's Eighth emerged against this challenge of mass politics—so frightening and repugnant to some, but welcome and exciting to others.

"As the French Revolution was the prelude to the nineteenth century, so the Russian Revolution would be the prelude to the twentieth century," declared the venerated Austrian socialist leader, Victor Adler. Julius Braunthal, then a young editor at the Social Democratic *Arbeiter-Zeitung,* recalled: "The news from Russia overshadowed everything; it came as a great stimulus to heart and mind. It is now very difficult to convey the profound impression which the first Russian Revolution in 1905 made on its contemporaries . . . but to us in 1905 Russia's first revolution sparkled in the dew of a new dawn."[3] For German and Austrian leaders of the Left, the Russian Revolution was also a rebuke. Mass demonstrations had forced the most autocratic regime in Europe to concede a far more powerful parliament and a far wider suffrage than liberals and socialists had wrested in Austria or Prussia. This would now change; the years 1906–1907 brought a transformation of the suffrage in both halves of the Austro-Hungarian Empire, while Prussia resisted. However, neither Germany nor Austria would institute a prime minister responsible to parliament, even if it now seemed (prematurely) that the Russians had achieved this at a stroke. Nonetheless, the events of 1905–1906 aroused ebullience on the Left: a feeling of decisive, imminent transformation and the political promise of crowd action—sadly to fade within two years, as the Russian government rolled back some of the gains of the revolution, the German Chancellor engineered a nationalist electoral victory, and the Austrian parliaments elected under the new reformed suffrage remained stalemated by quarrels among national delegations, and successive crises increased international tension. These were precisely the years when Mahler completed the Seventh Symphony and composed the Eighth, works often seen as a decline—at least in the depth and complexity in expressive content, from a listener's perspective—though certainly not from the musicians' perspective, and especially not that of the choruses in the Eighth. However, after the formally demanding and tightly constructed Sixth Symphony, this music could seem facile and sometimes banal.

The ferment of the years 1905–1908 confirmed that the new century was initiated by the entry of the masses onto the political stage. The idea of the masses, mobilized at the polls or in the streets as a powerful collective political force, to be deployed for radical or national causes, had emerged as a major theme of political and cultural discourse in the 1890s. The "rise of the masses" was a challenge—whether promising or threatening; they loomed as inspiration to some, menace to others. For most commentators in the early twentieth century, the term referred to the labor unions and socialist parties that aspired to transform capitalist society. The working-class masses remained the preordained historical

protagonist of the Austrian Socialist Party, while the alleged revolutionary masses would be claimed by the interwar Communist parties.
Analysis on the Right, however, tended to apply the term "masses" to
the new middle classes, clerical workers, and sales personnel—the
anonymous crowds who went to offices in the morning and streamed
homeward at night. In his 1896 tract *Psychologie des Foules*, Gustave Le
Bon claimed that crowds believed as irrational collective units, not as
thinking individuals. And even analysts on the Left ascribed the new
enthusiasm for nationalism and imperialism not to factory workers but
to the lower middle classes, who could be manipulated by populist dem-
agogues. Karl Lueger, the populist mayor of Vienna, built his Christian
Social Party and the political machine that controlled the city on the basis
of these new, lower middle classes.

Perhaps the most trenchant analysis of this phenomenon was Roberto
Michels's extensive treatise, *The Social Psychology of the Anticapitalist Mass
Movements,* published in the great collaboration *Grundriss der Sozialökonomik* in the mid-twenties. For the Italian sociologist, trained in Germany
by Max Weber yet increasingly attracted to Mussolini during the 1920s,
socialism might represent the major anticapitalist movement, but nationalism and fascism formed right-wing variants. To be successful, each of
these movements had to rely not on a view of inevitable historical
transformation but on the active mobilization of their respective con-
stituencies. In Michels's analysis, symbols and music were critical to this
mobilization—he cited flags, flowers, symbolic clothing, and songs.
Socialist music "is lively, full of rhythm and energy. It is not, however,
autochthonous but rather the product of composers belonging to other
classes." The real resource of socialism was not its economic doctrines
or its faith in inevitable victory but its "ethical idealism," which, Michels
emphasized, was developed even through workers' songs (e.g. "Wir sind
ein ehrliches Geschlecht / Und kämpfen um ein ehrlich Recht").[4]

Ethical idealism played a key role in the Austrian socialist doctrines
known as Austromarxism. In the writings of some of its exponents,
notably Karl Renner and Otto Bauer, Austromarxism addressed the ethnic conflicts in the Habsburg Empire by combining plans for local
democracy with cultural autonomy for the diverse nationalities. The
Marxist philosopher Max Adler—like the German theorist of reformism,
Eduard Bernstein, but with greater intellectual sophistication—urged
that socialism be understood as a fulfillment of Kantian ethics. Socialism
finally made it possible to conceive that men and women could be treated,
as Kant had demanded, according to the categorical imperative. In the
Austromarxist intellectual framework, political emphasis shifted from
waiting for a social revolution to building a political movement that

sought to improve the condition of workers through social reform, education, and culture.[5] Musical performance and musical listening constituted major elements of that cultural heritage.

In the language of the Left, the Austrian socialists were reformists, not revolutionaries. The German Social Democrats remained sharply divided between orthodox Marxists, who wanted to reject all collaboration with progressive middle-class parties and remain committed to the ideal of revolution, and the reformists who looked to work with political allies on the Left. But the Austrian movement never split along these lines. It rejected the Leninist belief that a small authoritarian party must establish the dictatorship of the proletariat. What was important was democratic practice in the here and now—the continuing organization of youth movements and cultural institutions, including lending libraries, orchestras and choruses, and athletic teams, which along with the great public housing settlements would characterize Party activity before 1914 and then their policies in the city of Vienna after 1918. Michels warned (and he was not alone—Bernstein had said the same in 1900) that to the degree that anticapitalist mass movements functioned as parties, they must shed their base within just a single class and become broader and more inclusive. "Thus socialism," he wrote, "became again in the late nineteenth century a movement on behalf of humanity, not only in the Marxian teleological sense—that is, that the goal would be the happiness of humanity—but in the sense of the means as well. The appeal went back again to humanity: Humanity had to free humanity."[6]

The virtue of reformist socialism was that it might attract a significant number of intellectuals and idealists from middle-class milieus. Its defect, in the eyes of radical critics, was that it would lose its sense of revolutionary mission, making one compromise after another with those who wielded power or wealth, and become just another party seeking to hold on to a piece of power at the local level. It would settle for a do-good but ultimately hollow rhetoric, such that even the eloquence of the revered party leader Victor Adler became viewed as inauthentic and empty. This was much the same critique that later detractors would apply to Mahler's Eighth. The attacks on reformist Social Democracy were to become far harsher once an organized Communist movement formed to contest the political space on the Left in the 1920s. Given the nature of the emerging dictatorship in Soviet Russia, the growing stridency of Communist criticism can be condemned as brutal and prejudiced, but not without a harsh truth. What critics from the far Left were not prepared to set much store by the didactic thrust of the reformist program and language. Social Democratic doctrine and practice would be exemplified in the continuous efforts to organize workers and youth, above all between the wars, into musical societies, gymnastic associations and teams, excursions, lecture offerings. (On the other hand, the cultural arbiters of the Social Democrats could not come to terms with the new potential of spectator sports, radio, and cinema: light entertainment was an unworthy diversion.)[7] The masses in the social democratic vision were not just a term for the multitudes who were to be gathered to assemble at the polls or rally at Ringstrasse demonstrations. They were the collective potential of humanity as a whole, to be elevated in consciousness, bodily fitness, and mental awareness. The masses embodied a force that was greater than just the aggregation of individual participants, for both the Left and Right. For those willing cynically to manipulate them on the Right, and those yearning to believe in their emancipatory potential on the Left, the masses assumed an almost organic or integral status. From 1905 until fascist authoritarianism closed down over Central Europe in the 1930s, the masses loomed as a true collective historical protagonist.

A Symphony for the Masses

Why did the powerful inspiration for his Eighth Symphony strike Mahler in 1906? Biographers like to point to a personal agenda involving professional ambition and his marital problems. Mahler sought to outdo his earlier symphonies, claiming an interpretive power that surpassed Goethe, the great German cultural icon, and dedicated this symphony of extreme forces to his wife. Alma responded to the work at least as a demonstration of power if not as an invitation to intimacy. Her account of the premiere reads like those of German women overwhelmed by the mass choreographic propaganda of the Nazis:

> The whole of Munich as well as all who had come there for the occasion were wrought up to the highest pitch of suspense. The final rehearsal provoked rapturous enthusiasm, but it was nothing compared with the performance itself. The whole audience rose to their feet as soon as Mahler took his place on the podium, and the breathless silence that followed was the most impressive homage an artist could be paid. I sat in my box almost insensible from excitement.
>
> And then Mahler, god or demon, turned those tremendous volumes of sound into fountains of light. The experience was indescribable. Indescribable, too, the demonstration that followed. The whole audience surged towards the platform.[8]

It is not coincidental that the Eighth is the only symphony for which photographs were taken of the rehearsals—a visual memento to the detailed reports, during those same days, that Mahler sent to Alma, who was deciding between her husband and young Gropius. But the private biographical cues have distracted scholars from considering the symphony's public aesthetic agenda.

It made sense that Mahler should have the vision of a symphony for and by the masses in the historical moment of 1905–1906. From the accounts and testimonies available, however, it is difficult to separate the political from the religious dimensions of his inspiration. The composer was seized by texts, in this case by finding the "Veni creator spiritus" in an old hymnal, somewhat as he had been seized by the Klopstock ode at Hans von Bülow's funeral in 1894, which he incorporated into the Finale of the Second Symphony. "Try to imagine the whole universe beginning to ring and resound," he wrote Willem Mengelberg during the summer he composed the Eighth Symphony.[9] "Within the last three weeks," Mahler reported to his friend Specht, "I have completed the sketch for an entirely new symphony, something that makes all my other works seem like preparatory efforts."[10] The composer compared himself to the Creator of Heaven and Earth and quoted the Bible in a letter to Alma about a rehearsal of part two: "God (Mahler) saw it was good."[11] At the same time, the work was to be a conduit for humanity in its collective presence. The Eighth, dubbed the Symphony of a Thousand, was clearly to deploy an unprecedented mass of singers and musicians; it would vastly outdo the gigantism of earlier Mahler performances. *Vox dei*, in effect, *vox populi*. "In conceiving the work, Mahler undoubtedly thought in terms of the effect of masses. . . . He seeks to arouse in a violent manner, through ecstatic gestures," claimed Paul Bekker, upon hearing the work in 1912.[12]

The composer's ambitions only strengthen the association between his creative voice and mass forces. Mahler must have reflected on the significance and the possibilities for the promotion of his own work after witnessing the founding of the Viennese Symphony Workers' Concerts in 1905 by his friend David Josef Bach (in fact, the first work Mahler composed after this point was the Eighth Symphony). The concert series was inspired by a Schiller celebration of the Viennese Workers' Union on the traditional May Day holiday of the working classes. The *Arbeiter-Zeitung* reported: "In the masses of the *Volk* there is a deep desire for true art, and as soon as it is offered to them, they are thankful; indeed an enthusiastic receptivity is to be found. Unconsciously the idea emerges that it may be possible to meet this need and make a small but not unimportant contribution to the education and elevation of the working class."[13]

Several of Mahler's symphonies offered powerful analogues to the Social Democratic reformist vision. Think of their struggling heroes, deployment of massed human voices, their progression of marches and folk tunes, and perhaps above all their democratizing polyphony. Here the Eighth Symphony is exemplary. It is far from the vast spatial polyphony of his early symphonies, the austere interlacing in the songs on Rückert texts, and especially the tightly wrought motivic counterpoint of the Sixth and Seventh Symphonies. Like Hindemith and even Copland when they aspired to a broad public, Mahler simplified the interaction of voices, opting for a buildup of momentum more than any true simultaneity. The composer was preoccupied by the objective of strength, even for the passages of female redemption. He had hoped "to combine the hermit scene and the Finale with the Mater gloriosa quite differently from all the sugary and feeble ways it had been done."[14]

From its opening in E-flat major—the nature key and the harmony Wagner used to create the world at the opening of his Ring cycle—in the lower winds and strings, and organ bass, then confirmed with a full chord in the organ, the symphony suggested a synthesis of strength and transcendence. Perhaps alluding to Beethoven's "Eroica," Elsa Bienenfeld heard a "heroic E-flat major" and described the "marchlike, punctuated rhythm of 'Accendi lumen'" as "the central nerve of the entire symphony," emphasizing how, in the second part, "every movement, every intensification, becomes a visual image." There is an "enormous intensification of struggle [*Kampfsteigerung*]."[15]

Mahler's vocal writing was designed to augment the sense of massed energy. The significant process was the abandonment of a Beethovenian compression of time through motivic work and counterpoint in favor of what contemporaries called "linearity" and *Bildhaftigkeit*—a visual realization of music that replaced the logical models from the generation past. In effect, the legacy of counterpoint as tension between voices yields to the idea of music as a process of shaping. The best example is the celebrated "Accende sensibus," the climax of the symphony's first part. The punctuated, homophonic writing of the first line, "Ignite our senses with light" opens up fugally at "pour Thy love into our hearts." No single line, certainly not in the orchestra, proceeds as a veritable thematic unfolding, but each cuts across the sonic mass to great effect, so that the extension occurs horizontally, not vertically—over time, not across space. The effect (*Wirkung*) was a quality critical for mass reception when music must powerfully move a noncultivated audience. More explicitly than ever before, the evaluation of music now came to be associated with its effect.

The most obvious moment of "effect" is the double fugue concluding the first part. Unlike the fugal procedures in the Finale of Mozart's

"Jupiter" or Bruckner's Fifth Symphony, which inspired a sense of the sublime, in Mahler's Eighth the fugue produced an impression of power. For Specht, who experienced the music physically, rather than intellectually, the counterpoint in this work was not logical; nor was there a free polyphony that heightened the listener's consciousness—the two aesthetic traditions for contrapuntal writing. He admired the "most rigorous form" of the symphony's first part, with its gripping and powerful development section leading through a crushing and magnificent double fugue, in which the human voice is the decisive instrument."[16] The critic at the *Sächsische Volkszeitung* claimed that "of all Mahler's symphonies, the Eighth makes by far the deepest impression." The double fugue concluding the first part "is unmatched in the entire musical literature with regard to its magnificent invention and genius in technique." The critic continued, "An American millionaire apparently said to Mahler after the Munich premiere, adapting the famous phrase, 'to die like Molière': 'To die under the sounds of this fugue would bring one to heaven.' The man certainly had gall, but there is a kernel of truth in what he said."[17] By contrast, the Viennese critic Richard Robert reported that even with the best of intentions, he "could not identify the 'grand double fugue, which has already become famous,' according to the infatuated author of the thematic analysis, which is fraught with superlatives."[18]

Mahler's symphonic programs often introduced dimensions of religious salvation that secular socialism would not easily accommodate. Yet his contemporaries usually saw no conflict between ideas of religious and secular salvation. For Walter Schrenk, "Mahler has created a confessional work with this 'Eighth'—so to speak, philosophical music [*Weltanschauungsmusik*] in which the rigorously ethical tendency of his creative will penetrates an enormous, sounding cosmos with passionate force."[19] The struggle for salvation in the Eighth Symphony could also express the ethical vision of socialist reform—not excluding the high-toned banality that a second generation of more radical theorists and artists would criticize. Reformism presupposed that the highest cultural products of the bourgeoisie, including the symphony, could be appropriated for the socialist working class. Reformist socialism also argued that democracy was compatible with a peaceful transition to collectivism, that with enough voices or votes—the word *Stimme* serves both concepts in German—the political resistance to socialism would be overcome. Indeed the Austrian Socialist Party persisted in this vision, even as Christian Social and Fatherland Front political leaders progressively imposed a quasi-fascist regime from the end of the 1920s to the denouement of February 12, 1934, when the Karl-Marx Hof was shelled and the Party outlawed.

This is not to claim that Mahler's own political stance was consistent or deeply held. He occasionally went to a fashionable lunch or party with visiting French left-wing circles: the pro-Dreyfusard brother of Georges Clemenceau, and the courageous Georges Picquart—who had supported Dreyfus in the face of his peers' hostility and came to Vienna determined to hear Mahler conduct at the Opera. But the converted Catholic kept his distance from this Dreyfusard cause. We know that he happened to join a workers' parade on May Day 1905, but the adventure seems to have been spontaneous and brief.[20] This did not stop his gesture from being transformed after his death into an enthusiastic adulation in the pages of the socialists' arts periodical *Kunst und Volk: Mitteilungen des Vereines Sozialdemokratische Kunststelle.*

A famous composer, whose name shall remain unmentioned [Hans Pfitzner], was visiting Mahler's house. Both had walked through the inner city early in the morning. The guest appeared at midday, exclaiming, "How awful, these people on the street, these unintelligible and half animalistic faces, these fallen women, this pushing and shoving, this smell! I could hardly get through and therefore have come late." Somewhat later, Mahler appeared and said, "You must pardon me, but it was too magnificent. These determined and happy people, this joy, cheerfulness, this energy! It was so beautiful that I had to march with them for a while. Hence my tardiness."[21]

As with his religious feelings, Mahler's political commitments seem to have been emotional but episodic. His politics are well described as a specimen of what the acute right-wing critic of the Weimar Republic, Carl Schmitt, condemned as "Political Romanticism." The Romantic, Schmitt argued, was neither conservative nor radical per se; he was profoundly self-absorbed, caught up by the influence of the moment— using the landscape, the cause, the parade, and external stimuli in general as a backdrop to craft his own ego.[22] Although the temperament hardly allowed a deep political commitment, it meant that a "mass" work, precisely in those middle years of the first decade of the twentieth century, would seem appropriate and compelling.

But it is also worth reflecting on a further aspect of Mahler's reported inspiration: not just its occasional nature, but the sensuous quality and synesthetic aspiration of the Austrian Baroque and Rococo. In Europe this meant the effort to find physical representations of spirituality, whether grandiose and sublime or merely light and graceful. Intimations of a divine realm or even an overwhelming sense of historical time are not infrequent sources of architectonically massed works, whether intellectual or artistic. Such artists and writers tend to report their response either in terms of an austere and an abstract intellectual content, grand in lack of adornment—consider the "systems" of Calvin, Spinoza, Hegel, Marx—or in terms of a sensuous inspiration in which color, motion, sound, all merge (one might cite Bernini, Monteverdi, Mozart and Goethe). Mahler's works were a product of the latter sort of inspiration, but he was hardly alone in the early twentieth century. The emergence of the masses epitomized for the increasingly confident forces of the Social Democratic Party an almost cinematic image of history as it would progressively unfold, and not just the final decline of the bourgeois era. Their social drama in the palace square of St. Petersburg the year before, or on the streets of Vienna, endowed history with a palpable representational quality, advancing the unfolding European crises beyond the texts alone—whether those of Otto Bauer, or Karl Kautsky or Rosa Luxemburg, to cite just a few of the theorists productive at the time.

The nature of Mahler's Austrian inspiration is revealed as much by what remained excluded as by what was included. There is no serious reference to Faustian struggle in the second part of the symphony, except the explanation by the first (and less perfect) angel that "To whoever persists, active and striving / We can grant redemption" (Wer immer strebend sich bemüht / Den können wir erlösen). Granted the verse is musically highlighted when it borrows the theme of the "Accende" and the "Infirma," it remains overshadowed by the theme of redemption as a divine gift. Indeed, Goethe himself intended the final angelic choirs to signify the role of divine grace and not just human effort in salvation, but for the poet the final scene was just an epilogue to Faust's vast struggle.[23] More dramatically crucial was the Protestant theme of Faust's self-redemption by helping a courageous peasantry seize polder from the sea—"Only he is worthy of freedom and life, who conquers them each day anew": the dramatic climax to Faust's life that Schumann, to take another oratorio-like setting of the poem, emphasized with a lengthy vocal solo. Certainly there is no reason to expect Mahler to have been a committed political activist. Neither, despite his own intense work schedule, could he have had much understanding of how much a modern political movement consisted of patient and undramatic organization, recruitment, and meetings. For all his own labor—which in his own bifurcated life he associated with conducting and production—Mahler seemed to have responded to the political sphere as he did to the religious, as the source of epiphanies and redemption from the everyday. He beheld the masses as a grand parade, and the collective as mystical inspiration.

Contemporary Responses to the Eighth Symphony

In its dimensions and conditions of performance, Mahler's Eighth Symphony expressed some of the tensions inherent in European society that were acted out so publicly on the eve of World War I, above all the ominous gathering of collective forces, whether for internal transformation or for impending war. The mobilization of huge performance resources to confront a mass audience had a particular appeal. The very size of the audience was a source of pride. The poster for the 1910 Munich festival listed prominently, on the third line, that the new hall held 3,200 seats (Figure 1). Three days after the two performances of Mahler's Eighth in Leipzig, the same conductor, Georg Göhler, drew from the choral forces for a mass performance of Handel's *Messiah*. Citing the economic benefit of such programming, one reporter boasted that even the Handel concert and dress rehearsal drew a total of 4,000 to 5,000 listeners.[24]

The energy from a mass gathering, to which Alma and others responded so fervently, left others anxious. Even as reviewers attempted to interpret the work according to familiar landmarks and reassuring values, it raised powerful issues about the relationship of music to mass society. The requirement of a special performance site was itself a challenge to earlier, safe boundaries for musical listening. The musical work could no longer be confined to the concert hall's secure isolation, but was a vehicle for experiencing the social and urban context in which it was heard.

The location of the performance became important to musical listening in ways never mentioned in reviews of Mahler's earlier symphonies. The site now seemed critical to achieve the "effect" on listeners. For example, in the smaller Leipzig hall, apparently, "the total effect did not reach the intensity of the premiere in Munich."[25] From the new concert hall to the aggressive publicity, the premiere of the Eighth Symphony commanded attention for reasons beyond the music itself. Rehearsals and the two performances took place in the 1908 Munich exhibition hall. Noting its "sober, circuslike iron structure," the *Berliner Börsen-Courier* critic argued that the building "requires extraordinary effort from an artwork to make us forget where we are. A composition must be suitable for huge dimensions in order to produce a good relationship. Mahler's Eighth . . . is just such a work." The experience of the performance was, at least to this critic, integral to judging and comprehending the music. "An immeasurable mass of people—three to four thousand artists, Americans, tourists, Munich residents, these people and those people—sat there, expectantly, facing a musical corpus that was again

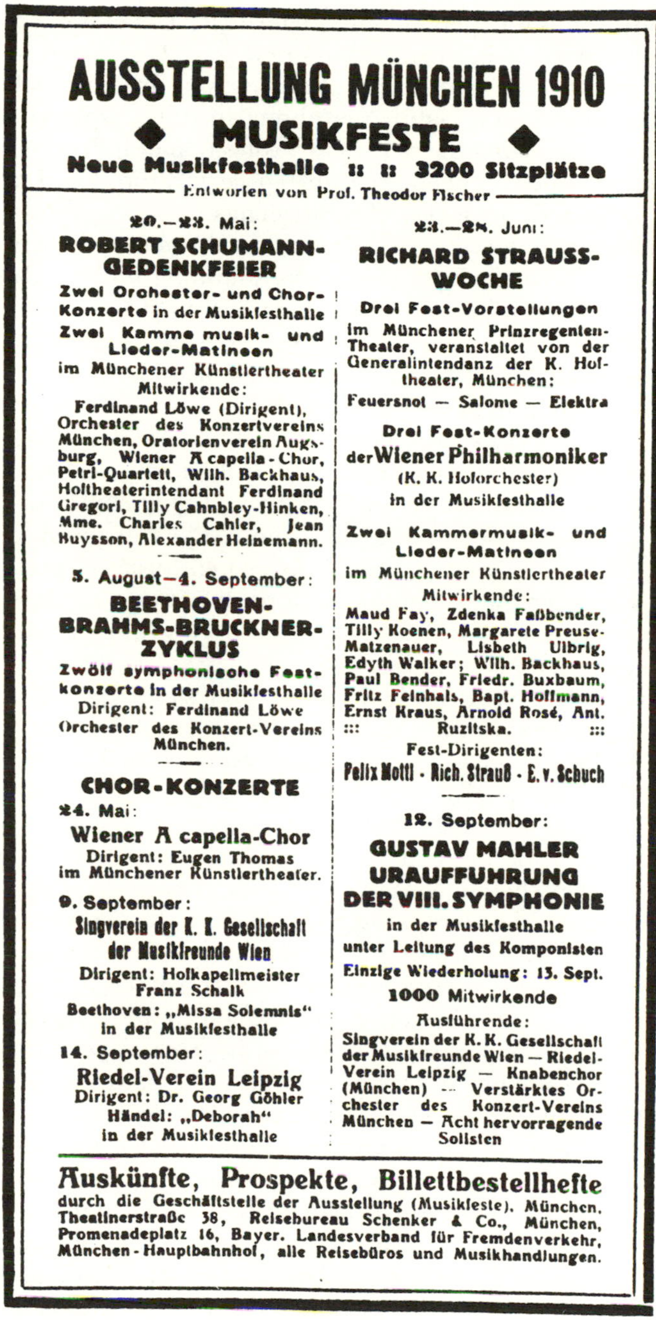
AUSSTELLUNG MÜNCHEN 1910

◆ MUSIKFESTE ◆

Neue Musikfesthalle :: :: 3200 Sitzplätze

Entworfen von Prof. Theodor Fischer

20.–23. Mai:

ROBERT SCHUMANN-GEDENKFEIER

Zwei Orchester- und Chor-Konzerte in der Musikfesthalle
Zwei Kammermusik- und Lieder-Matineen
im Münchener Künstlertheater
Mitwirkende:
Ferdinand Löwe (Dirigent), Orchester des Konzertvereins München, Oratorienverein Augsburg, Wiener A capella-Chor, Petri-Quartett, Wilh. Backhaus, Hoftheaterintendant Ferdinand Gregori, Tilly Cahnbley-Hinken, Mme. Charles Cahier, Jean Buysson, Alexander Heinemann.

5. August–4. September:

BEETHOVEN-BRAHMS-BRUCKNER-ZYKLUS

Zwölf symphonische Fest-konzerte in der Musikfesthalle
Dirigent: Ferdinand Löwe
Orchester des Konzert-Vereins München.

CHOR-KONZERTE

24. Mai:
Wiener A capella-Chor
Dirigent: Eugen Thomas
im Münchener Künstlertheater.

9. September:
Singverein der K. K. Gesellschaft der Musikfreunde Wien
Dirigent: Hofkapellmeister Franz Schalk
Beethoven: „Missa Solemnis"
in der Musikfesthalle

14. September:
Riedel-Verein Leipzig
Dirigent: Dr. Georg Göhler
Händel: „Deborah"
in der Musikfesthalle

23.–28. Juni:

RICHARD STRAUSS-WOCHE

Drei Fest-Vorstellungen
im Münchener Prinzregenten-Theater, veranstaltet von der Generalintendanz der K. Hoftheater, München:
Feuersnot — Salome — Elektra

Drei Fest-Konzerte
der Wiener Philharmoniker
(K. K. Hoforchester)
in der Musikfesthalle

Zwei Kammermusik- und Lieder-Matineen
im Münchener Künstlertheater
Mitwirkende:
Maud Fay, Zdenka Faßbender, Tilly Koenen, Margarete Preuse-Matzenauer, Lisbeth Ulbrig, Edyth Walker; Wilh. Backhaus, Paul Bender, Friedr. Buxbaum, Fritz Feinhals, Bapt. Hoffmann, Ernst Kraus, Arnold Rosé, Ant. ::: Ruzitska. :::
Fest-Dirigenten:
Felix Mottl - Rich. Strauß - E. v. Schuch

12. September:

GUSTAV MAHLER URAUFFÜHRUNG DER VIII. SYMPHONIE

in der Musikfesthalle
unter Leitung des Komponisten
Einzige Wiederholung: 13. Sept.
1000 Mitwirkende
Ausführende:
Singverein der K. K. Gesellschaft der Musikfreunde Wien — Riedel-Verein Leipzig — Knabenchor (München) — Verstärktes Orchester des Konzert-Vereins München — Acht hervorragende Solisten

Auskünfte, Prospekte, Billettbestellhefte
durch die Geschäftsstelle der Ausstellung (Musikfeste), München, Theatinerstraße 38, Reisebureau Schenker & Co., München, Promenadeplatz 16, Bayer. Landesverband für Fremdenverkehr, München-Hauptbahnhof, alle Reisebüros und Musikhandlungen.

Figure 1. Poster for the music festival at the Munich Exhibition 1910.

almost one thousand people. . . . There sits Hermann Bahr with Mildenburg, there Richard Strauss, there Reger. Writers and musicians from all milieus are absorbed into the masses in order to yield to the strength of one."[26] The Eighth Symphony, in sum, displayed the tension between perceiving the masses as a collection of individuals and as a single entity. Effect depended on the space and the crowd as well as on the scoring and the quality of performance.

For Mahler's contemporaries, the conductor and audience were as much part of the experience as was the sounding music. "One trusts him. One knows that he—the most able to form and to shape, among all conductors—understands how to deal with the masses," wrote the *Berliner Börsen-Courier*.[27] Gone was the idea of the symphony concert as a purely aesthetic experience, steeped in the nineteenth-century tradition of contemplation and edification. Bienenfeld, who had once mused over the philosophical nature of Mahler's earlier symphonies, now wished "to report on the impression and the manner of the performance," rather than describe "the essentials" of the symphony. "One feels oneself participating in a huge, shared enthusiasm, pulled along a course of gripping and shared emotions. It is a type of mass suggestion [*Massensuggestion*] such as may grip large groups of soldiers in battle—indeed as takes effect whenever masses of people grasp the same idea and are instinctively fired up at the same time."[28]

Some hoped to save the Eighth Symphony from the psychology of the masses. In a letter to the editor following an article on "musical gigantism" *(mammutismus)*, the cellist Hugo Schlemüller cited Mahler's Eighth as another example. He described the effect, in general, of large numbers in front of and behind the conductor's podium: "A mass in itself has an overwhelming effect. A mass of listeners produces a compelling effect, which is then transferred again to the podium. One calls this the 'contact' with the podium. Certainly, as well, in a gigantic space (as one knows from church concerts), sonority is freed of its gravity, so that tones seem to come from high in the open air and in greater vibrations." This new relationship between audience and performers, and perhaps also an anxiety in face of the masses, is hinted in one caricature in which Mahler's audience was depleted by the number of singers and musicians (Figure 2). The composer intended 1,500 performers, Schlemüller continued. The first to conduct the symphony since Mahler, Willem Mengelberg prepared for such a performance by building up the forces gradually. The initial performance included 500 musicians; he returned two months later, in February 1912, to the same city, Frankfurt, to conduct the symphony with 2,000 musicians. Then, Schlemüller explained, Mengelberg will amass "his Dutch troops from

Amsterdam and with 'the flying Dutchmen' go from land to land, his powerful choral symphony sounding before not a meager 2,000 but 20, 000 listeners." Schlemüller had grave reservations about mass concerts. During the initial Frankfurt performance, he recounted, "the thought tormented me: Is this smaller scoring really a sin against the composer's intentions or rather—what an impious thought—did the composer delude himself in the effects of a setting for the masses? Perhaps he overestimated rather than underestimated the mass."[29] After the second Frankfurt performance, Schlemüller discussed the misperceptions about mass concerts. With such numbers—2,000 performers and 15,000 listeners in the gigantic municipal festival hall—"one thinks of overwhelming and shattering effects. But it was not so. Only rarely did one have the impression of a mass effect." Instead, the music sounded distant, its shading and coherence difficult to perceive. As if to dispel the mythology surrounding the work itself, Schlemüller added that "Mahler's Eighth does not 'scream' in a mass realization or a monster performance. There are too many lyrical parts for that to occur."[30]

Public enthusiasm for the Eighth Symphony was attributed not just to the music but to a fascination with "mass" effects. August Spanuth, who had recently spent many years in Chicago, had a particular sensitivity to this phenomenon. In the journal he edited, *Signale für die*

Figure 2. Caricature of Mahler

musikalische Welt, he published four articles on the Eighth Symphony, in addition to those written by the correspondents in the respective cities where performances took place. "Whoever experienced the enthusiasm in Leipzig," he wrote of the first performance of the Eighth Symphony in that city, "must be convinced that the public has developed a very special receptivity to mass effects—that, for example, a mass chorus, through its unusual forces, through the visual appearance as well, has predisposed the ears."[31] The "current fashion, which at the moment is so favorably inclined toward the use of masses as expressive means," made judging the symphony impossible. The term *Massenkonzert* was so fashionable as to appear on concert tickets and in publicity.[32] Spanuth's correspondent for the Leipzig performance of the Eighth shared this interest in mass society: Max Steinitzer, who had written his dissertation on "the psychological effects of musical forms," admired Georg Göhler's "leadership," which was powerful and "penetrating" and "held the masses together tightly."[33]

There was concern that the power of the experience substituted for true emotional content. Oskar Bie described the radical contrast between Mahler as composer (in rural Toblach) and as conductor and public figure (at the urban premiere of the Eighth). "One month later I saw him embody his 'symphony' before a thousand performers. I remember vividly that this small person shaped the masses with such inconceivable plasticity—those performing and those receiving, including myself. I thought: what a feeling of control!" In this "great effect" was, however, "a betrayal of emotional integrity." Bie, who was himself Jewish, went on to associate such an approach with reading Hebrew texts from right to left, and therefore backward: "Thus it happens to us all, of every race, and especially this race. Including this author. I couldn't say it if I didn't include myself. Every day and every hour I am in danger of sacrificing feeling to effect because I am clever, because I have the means of doing so, and because I am cursed to think from backward to forward, so that the reader understands how I feel from forward to backward."[34]

What consequences did the amassing of performers have on the construction of the music? Did "mass" music have any distinguishing qualities, procedures and structures? Bienenfeld cited the "magnificent primitivism" of the two-part form in the Eighth Symphony.[35] Inherent in the idea of masses is to use the voices not as expressive individuals but as a component of an orchestral piece, as traditionally conceived. Unlike in Mahler's earlier symphonies, the individual had no place—whether the single instrumental line or the voice. Rudolf Louis, the influential right-wing critic, emphasized that in the Eighth Symphony the voices lose any human quality. And in this way, he felt that the work's designation as a "symphony" was correct.[36] Richard Robert, at least ten years older than Bienenfeld and Louis, held Mahler to the same standards as in his earlier symphonies. Robert criticized the composer for relegating the human voice to "mainly just coloristic purposes" and rejected the use of mass sonic devices: "It is doubtful whether the motto 'it can be achieved through a mass' [die Masse muss es bringen] has any artistic justification. The motifs of the two halves of the Eighth Symphony could serve as counterexample."[37]

In the bourgeois tradition, music was about control—the logic that governed thematic working, a control through the shaping of lines, even restrictions on what a symphony can mean. Robert, again, was one of the few who leveled the same critique as had prevailed in the reception of Mahler's Sixth Symphony, in 1906 and early 1907. "If only the depth and grandeur of the ideas" in the Eighth Symphony were in proportion to the exorbitant masses of the [orchestral and vocal] means employed, Mahler would be the greatest composer of all times, beside whom Beethoven, with his impoverished orchestra, would seem a village musician. But the composer has not demonstrated himself to be such a superman. What Mahler abandons, above all, is control over polyphony; if some voices are put on top of each other and crammed together for a few bars, that is not counterpoint."[38] With the Eighth Symphony, the locus of control shifted away from the composition itself—away from musical features—to the conductor. The very quality that made Mahler into "one of the great conductors"—namely, that "he could force the orchestra under his will"—determined the nature of his music, according to the musicologist and art historian Walter Riezler. "Mahler's music has far too much 'will'— not in the metaphysical sense of the world's will but in the sense of the individual. It is therefore truly objective and convincing where it is wholly subjective." Riezler had no specifically musical objections, but rather mused on the character of Mahler's music, as if repelled by the very idea that the Jewish composer had produced so important a composition. "Put metaphysically, every truly great artwork is preexistent; the artist, who has the talent of a visionary, looks into that world and gives humans access. His will must go completely into the will of the work. . . . With Mahler, it is *only* his will, which is lively, and his art has nothing in common with the Beyond."[39]

Sympathetic critics stressed the socially redemptive value of the Eighth Symphony. The vast choral passages could counteract the fin-de-siècle tendency to dwell on the pathologies of individualism. The symphony could also stake a claim to German identity. On the occasion of the symphony's premiere, Stefan extracted the introduction from his

Mahler book in which he refuted criticisms of the composer's "'contrived' naiveté, 'restlessness,' and 'brooding' or 'moody' quality as un-true and un-German." Such comments, Stefan maintained, were "misunderstood racial doctrine." He went so far as to claim that "anyone who has a look at Mahler's music, in particular his songs, will find that hardly any other artist has lived more in the German idea and the German ideal. And if 'German' means, since Wagner, to strive for something on its own terms, then certainly no one has been more German." Stefan's appeal also went beyond German nationality. "Mahler is our contemporary Christ."[40] Thomas Mann expressed similar awe after attending a performance of the Eighth Symphony, whereupon he sent Mahler his novel *Royal Highness,* with a disclaimer: "It is certainly a very poor return for what I received—a mere feather's weight in the hand of the man who, as I believe, expresses the art of our time in its profoundest and most sacred form."[41]

Mahler after World War I: A Political Aesthetic for a Mass Society

Mahler was the last composer "who has sought to endow the symphony with the power of social transformation," wrote Paul A. Pisk in 1925 in the Socialists' arts monthly, *Der Kampf.* As a composer and editor at the *Arbeiter-Zeitung,* Pisk took seriously the social responsibilities of the artist (see Figure 3). Mahler's materials, if often not their treatment, were typical of reformist aesthetic tropes for a mass culture. Pisk argued that Mahler inserted folk melodies into each symphony and chose philosophical problems accessible to everyone, such as universal love and life after death. "His art must be judged the final prewar effort to forge listeners into a community. The war has brought an end to these attempts for once and for all. Unforeseen by us, divisions and class conflicts have become deeper; in art, and especially in music, we see a creative individualism that does not take account of a social framework. Thus far we have failed to develop a proletarian music. . . . Only the future can tell whether we are generating a new music that can really express the feelings of the proletariat."[42] In the interwar period, the relationship of the artwork to the masses emerged as a central issue in musical thought. There were years when Webern conducted Mahler in the Workers' Symphony Concerts. The postwar reception of Mahler illuminates the more general problem, not only in Vienna but in interwar Central European society as a whole.

Figure 3. Paul A. Pisk, 1927.   Figure 4. David Josef Bach, 1927.

For all the power of the conductor, the socialist organizers of culture did not envisage the masses as a passive body but as one with creative impulses. David Josef Bach established the Socialist Art Office (*Kunststelle*) and championed musical progressivism as well as workers' concerts (Figure 4). Unrelenting in his advocacy of Mahler, he even claimed the authority of the Austrian Socialist Party patriarch, Viktor Adler. "Adler was always convinced of the significance of a Gustav Mahler, whom he knew already in his youth." The role that his music played first became clear to Bach in 1922, after a Mahler program of the Workers' Symphony Concerts: "Mahler's Third Symphony also has spoken to proletarian listeners, it has quite simply overwhelmed them. If Mahler had seen this! . . . In this work and on this night the unification of art and *Volk* has been consummated. . . . Mahler has become the property of the *Volk*."[43] Such rhetoric was common, as every facet of the city's cultural institutions was supposedly appropriated by the proletariat, including the *Ringstrasse* (Figure 5).

How extensively the *Volk* actually participated was contested. Bach and his colleagues emphasized that musical training was not required for the appreciation of symphonic music. As early as the premiere of the Eighth Symphony he had reported in the *Arbeiter-Zeitung*: Mahler "excites us and carries us with gripping force. Whoever feels the energy needs no interpretation from the learned in order to believe it and to

Figure 5. *The Ringstrasse of the Proletariat.* From the cover of the socialist journal, *Die Unzufriedene,* no. 35 (August 1930).

feel it for himself."[44] The concern developed that only a "very limited group" of workers really participated in the music program.[45] Bach replied that the Workers' Symphony Concerts drew its largest number of subscribers, 160, from the working-class district of Floridsdorf and that 95 percent were manual laborers.[46]

As Social Democratic musicians and political leaders looked back from the vantage of the 1920s, Mahler's affinity to their political and musical progressivism seemed self-evident. "There was a time when one's duty was to fight for Gustav Mahler as one of our greatest and most worthy German artists," Schrenk recalled after a Berlin performance of the Eighth Symphony in the late 1920s. "That was about fifteen or twenty years ago. . . . Much has changed since then; Mahler now stands firmly in the taste of the larger public as well."[47]

Perhaps for its curious mixture of traditional texts with modern forces, the Eighth Symphony loomed large, almost nostalgically, for critics during these years. Already in 1914 Mahler's biographer Paul Stefan had claimed, in an article on the composer's "belated triumph," that the Eighth Symphony was his only true success. Fifty performances within two years, was the number Stefan cited from the publisher.[48] In 1920, thinking back to the early performances, the composer James Simon remembered the Berlin premiere (1912) as "a celebrated and historic day." And in general, he insisted, the Eighth Symphony was the high point of Mahler's symphonic work.[49] Its importance extended well beyond Mahler's oeuvre: The Eighth Symphony "is intellectually as well as musically one of the greatest creative achievements of the last twenty years," Schrenk claimed in the late 1920s.[50]

Reviewers continued to be gripped by the display of power in the Eighth Symphony, long after the work's novelty had worn off. A Stuttgart critic recalled a performance conducted by Fritz Busch: "The masses flowed up to him, and we experienced something in Stuttgart that we never had before. . . . This striving for the idea to become flesh, this powerful ability, and the will to subject the high-flying imagination to form through *all* the modern expressive means, artistically intensified to the highest degree, and to create substance, are truly imposing. . . . He *controls* this gigantic apparatus of choruses and orchestra; he is the *leader* [Führer, given in italics]. . . . This performance had not only artistic meaning but social meaning."[51] The Eighth Symphony was cherished even once the idea of its masses was no longer novel. One Hamburg critic spoke out against its nickname, the Symphony of a Thousand. That "nasty Berlinification" (*Verberlinerung*), which commits a "sacrilege" against the music, should not turn listeners against the work itself.[52]

The "culmination of the cultural movement of Austromarxism," as Johann Wilhelm Seidl explains, was the April 1926 performance of the Eighth Symphony "by workers and workers' children, for an audience of workers," in the words of the *Arbeiter-Zeitung*. "The bold wager of marrying the highest, most sensitive kind of art—large symphonic music, which until now was the sole property of the bourgeoisie—to the true *Volk*, the workers, succeeded on the day that it was made. And today's concert is a symbol for how intimate the connection between art and the working class has become."[53] For David Josef Bach, the performance was "a triumph for the cause, a triumph of the public, a triumph for the work, a triumph of . . . the conductor Anton Webern, etc."[54] Reflecting back almost two decades later, Bach recalled, "The concerts were not a purpose unto themselves, but a means to an end. The aim was, then as now, the connection of art to the people, which must be achieved through the constant contact between the artist and the work and between the work and the public."[55]

In reflecting on the performance, Bach ceded that "Mahler always held himself aloof from political life and anything having to do with a party." Bach nonetheless upheld the composer as an advocate of socialism: "Everyone who came into contact with him knows that his politics were socialist. He showed it publicly."[56] In his article "Mahler for Everyone," Paul Stefan mused that if Mahler "could have participated in the three performances of the Eighth Symphony that Webern conducted in the Workers' Symphony Concerts, he would have taken particular pleasure in a public so large and new, so wholly unprejudiced." Stefan noted how much the Workers' Symphony Concerts had programmed Mahler and went so far as to claim that "Mahler dedicated his work to the entire *Volk*."[57] The Frankfurt critic and author Paul Bekker, who had no such clear affiliation with the workers' movement, championed the composer in his 1918 book on the symphony from Beethoven to Mahler for not dissimilar reasons. Concerned that art music was in jeopardy during and after World War I, Bekker wrote as a passionate advocate for a range of composers and genres, but above all for the genre of symphony, which unified the emotions and the intellect. Mahler "thereby eliminates the stratification that divides different circles of listeners according to their level of training, and makes symphonic art . . . accessible to *anyone* who is at all capable of participating in German cultural life today."[58]

It is not surprising that advocates for a socialist art turned to the symphony and to Mahler. The very qualities that critics at the fin de siècle had denigrated, in particular the immediacy of music, were those that appealed to musically untrained listeners. In a 1927 article on "mass culture" Else Reventlow, family member of the rightwing and anti-Semitic politician Ernst von Reventlow (1869–1943), noted that the traits of the masses were also found in children. In effect she made a plea for the Right to catch up with the socialists in capturing the childlike masses, with their "inactive intellect, strong instincts, predominance of drive and imagination, strong reactions to sensuous impressions, and asocial attitude toward the surrounding world." She believed that "current German socialist cultural politics can never lead to a mass culture, since its methods are uninformed by research into mass psychology." Reventlow hoped that politicians would turn to culture, since pressing economic and social problems had dominated the early years of the Social Democratic Republic. "The question of culture has developed into the question of mass culture," by virtue of the number of members, she argued. "The party has grown from thousands of members into tens of thousands, and from tens of thousands into hundreds of thousands."[59]

This emerging aesthetic of mass art extended well beyond traditional music. Physicality became the primary category in cultural and aesthetic thought. Articles in *Kunst und Volk* would address subjects normally excluded from a cultural journal. Coordinated mass gymnastics, or *Bewegungschöre* ("movement choruses") became a popular feature of politically sponsored rallies and mass recreation. They reflected the rediscovery of the human body as a positive element in culture and art, Ellinor Tordis maintained. Sports and art forms like *Bewegungschöre* promoted "the will to activity." "The masses who do gymnastics, swim, hike, and play sports *embody*—in the literal sense of the word—the transformation of the century." The goal was for "the whole body to express a life-feeling." In this art form, the legs execute the rhythm, while the face, hands, and upper body give shape to the melody and to emotions."[60] Gisa Geert, in an article on "the culture of the body and of festivals," saw the defining quality of mass culture as organized motion. The events she proposed would be accessible to all. "The ordered movement of many people, following formative ideas, contains such a compelling force! What a joyous feeling to move together in shared emotion, to feel together, and create together a unifying harmony of mass motion!" Through such events, individuals could "intensify the joys of life," she explained, but their ultimate purpose was to elevate the "the power of the totality."[61] Physicality also became the basis for musical interpretation. Egon Lustgarten's *Der Mensch ist unterwegs* deploys march material in "an unstoppable intensification," one socialist reporter noted. "A gripping musical image of the final victory of the people of the future, this work is one of the first artistically worthwhile attempts of a new workers' music."[62]

For the masses to participate actively in coordinated movement showed their advance over the passivity of anonymous bourgeois spectators and listeners. Bach quoted Victor Adler once again: "Music criticism . . . is an empty word for the worker today. The worker can't be brought to art through contemplation. . . . This monopoly of art must come to an end. It is possible to begin this work with music."[63] The space for the concert public was reconceived. Listeners became aware of their role as a single audience more than a collection of individuals, listening privately. Karl Laux observed the effect of the increased number of workers at concerts. They sat in rows rather than in individual subscription seats, "wishing to form a sense of community."[64] Rhythm had a role in politics, art and society in general, promising an aesthetic of vitalism rather than contemplation. The question, however, was which political groups would exploit this vitalism—and here there would be far more opportunistic parties on the Left and the Right.

By the end of the 1920s and in the 1930s, the political and cultural dangers of mass performance became clear. The search for mass participation brought left-wing commentators to the verge of simplistic proletcult—not surprisingly as the Communists, responding at least in part to Stalinist directives from Moscow, attacked reformist socialists after 1928 with increased harshness and accused the Arts Office of elitism. By the 1930s the aesthetics of the masses would be captured not by the reformists but by Communists on the Left as well as fascists on the Right. Their gymnastic shows, choruses, and simplified music would build on the elements of an aesthetic for the masses but turn them toward far more authoritarian goals. The fusion of movement, rhythm, and motion finally could not yet guarantee a program for democracy and emancipation.

Mahler's Eighth did not survive the National Socialists' coming to power, but not because the music itself lost its appeal. True, its ambitions had been superceded. "It no longer brings about its effects through mass (since the hypertrophic use of means that was needed to bring about an effect in late Romantic music is antithetical to contemporary attitudes and music theory)," explained Karl H. Ruppel, after a performance in Düsseldorf, 1929. Instead, he felt the effects come from "the expressive power and glow of its thematic material, the unshakable firmness of its tonal principle, and not least Mahler's enormous will-to-form, which in the first part makes the Baroque polyphony transparent and in the second part, alongside passages that are blurred and run together, shapes melodically the greatest inwardness and passion that late Romantic symphonic music (*Sinfonik*) has ever brought forth." Despite his own enthusiasm at the symphony's "glow and ecstasy" and the "extraordinary effect in the concert hall," Ruppel—who would thrive in Nazi Germany and passed even the most stringent tests of reliability from the Nazi propaganda ministry—felt compelled to allow for alternative, and perhaps anti-Semitic, viewpoints. "It is, however, still possible that reviewers can speak of 'Sunday afternoon entertainment' coming from an obviously highly bored composer who only wrote this score for marketing purposes."[65] The theme was not new ("There have been better symphonies that had less advertising," a Berlin critic once quipped),[66] but the peculiar attack on the composer as person became typical of the anti-Semitic press in the later 1920s and 30s.

* * * *

The Austrian Socialist appropriation of Mahler and the Eighth Symphony had implications far beyond their own movement. And herein lay some of its difficulties for Theodor Adorno—implicitly contemptuous of social democratic reformism. The social critic and philosopher identified the work as an exercise in collective ritual—the phenomenon that Émile Durkheim, a contemporary of Mahler, had analyzed—but claimed that as a product of advanced capitalism, its ritualistic content was spurious. It was a cultural product of what served as the ready Marxist explanation for inauthenticity, that is, "false consciousness." "Their Holy of Holies is empty."[67] Indeed, the Eighth Symphony, and the concept of the masses that it inscribed, was in line with the political vision of Europe's reform-minded socialists. For those further to the Left, from 1900 through mid-century—and they played a larger role in Germany proper than in German Austria—socialist reformism was itself mired in false consciousness. For Adorno, the Eighth Symphony began as, and remained, a deluded helpmate of capitalism, legitimating and prolonging the aesthetic and moral as well as the political and economic hegemony of the bourgeoisie.

Whether or not a listener shares Adorno's evaluation of the music, the left critique of Social Democratic reformism is certainly debatable. The contradictions inherent in its program of advancing workers' welfare in a regime of private property reflected not merely a lack of political resolution but the very real limits of its strength in an era when it confronted the voters of the countryside and the urban middle classes responsive to the appeals of mass nationalism, whether as Christian Socialism and pan-Germanism before 1914 or outright fascism from the late 1920s on. But the point is not to engage in a debate about the viability and virtues of Central European social democracy; historians will continue to differ on its role, just as music critics will differ on the virtues of the Eighth. Moreover, no significant artistic work, of course, is reducible only to politics, and few artists remain confined by a political program even if they reveal an ideological orientation. After the Eighth, Mahler turned to intensely "private" works, *Das Lied von der Erde*, the Ninth Symphony, and sketches for the Tenth.

When Mahler called upon the creator spiritus to ignite his heart and the heart of the masses, he could not have envisaged the political and aesthetic problematic arising a generation later. True, he had encountered some early warning signs in the political manipulation of anti-Semitism during his musical career. But he wrote the Eighth within a political and cultural context of hope. Did the composer divine, when he turned toward his deeply individual and more profound last works, that the Social Democratic resolution of individual and mass culture might be too facile and too optimistic a reading of history? There were, after all, other gods, simultaneously ancient and new, available for invocation in the coming years. Hofmannsthal and Strauss called upon Bacchus five years after Mahler bestowed his brilliant polyphony upon the creator spiritus ("Kommt der neue Gott gegangen / Hingegeben sind wir stumm") but to ignite the sphere of intimacy, not the wider world; eros not brotherhood. And in the first days of August 1914 Austria's greatest poet summoned the war god, who would fuse a hitherto disaggregated youth into a white-hot mass with a single iron heart. ("And us? Glowing, and forged, together into a whole, into a new creature animated by death.") Rilke's god did not tarry to melt down and reconstruct the masses. Mahler, even if he had understood that there would be a new music, was no longer around to learn there were also different gods and new masses.

At the end of the long century of the bourgeoisie, music could be a more egalitarian gathering of the masses than produced by other tools of social transformation. It generated energy between the performing body and the audience, which has its own amassed power. Mahler, of course, did not write music exclusively for a mass society. One can point to obvious ways in which the Eighth Symphony aspired to an intellectual discourse (the rigorous counterpoint) and a private spiritual state (the subjects of the texts as well as the general parallels with the Second Symphony's redemptive gesture). There was also the special relationship between the two parts of the symphony, which proved most problematic to scholars in the late twentieth century. One can, however, see the radical contrast as a massive structural replication of what Mahler's contemporary, Oskar Bie, described as the literary device of counterpoint in his review of the Eighth Symphony.[68] However much listeners are swept into the process of the individual movements, the residual effect of the composition, as a "symphony" in the nineteenth-century tradition, is that the two parts must form a single whole. In this sense the symphony taught a final lesson appropriate for the era of the masses: that coordinating such different components into a cohesive unit, societal or musical, meets considerable resistance and requires a relationship beyond mere control.

NOTES

Part of this paper was presented in a lecture for the conference *Music and the Aesthetics of Modernity,* in honor of Reinhold Brinkmann, at Harvard University, November 2001, and was inspired by his scholarship. I am grateful to Charles S. Maier for his generous help and Yael Braunschweig for her excellent research assistance; my thanks also to Paul De Angelis. The reviews of Mahler's Eighth used in this essay are located in the Vondenhoff collection of the Musiksammlung, Österreichische Nationalbibliothek, Vienna; the Bibliothèque Gustav Mahler, Paris; and the Steininger collection at the Geheimes Staatsarchiv, Preussische Kulturbesitz, Berlin.

1. Richard Specht, "Mahlers Weg," in *Der Merker: Österreichische Zeitschrift für Musik und Theater* 1, no. 23 (10 September 1910): 914.

2. Reinhardt was to send huge productions to London, St. Petersburg, and Moscow. See Charles S. Maier's essay in this volume.

3. Julius Braunthal, *In Search of the Millennium* (London, 1945), p. 59.

4. Roberto Michels, "Psychologie der antikapitalistischen Massenbewegungen," in *Grundriss der Sozialökonomik,* vol. 9, *Das soziale System des Kapitalismus,* part 1 (Tübingen, 1926), pp. 304, 349.

5. A number of relevant sources are translated in *Austro-Marxism,* ed. and trans. Tom Bottomore and Patrick Goode (Oxford, 1978), pp. 45–52, 57–68, 118–25. They include:

Otto Bauer, "Was ist Austro-Marxismus?" *Arbeiter-Zeitung*, 3 November 1927; *Die Nationalitätenfrage und die Sozialdemokratie* (Vienna, 1907), pp. 130–38; "Max Adler: Ein Beitrag zur Geschichte des Austro-Marxismus," *Der Kampf* (Neue Serie), iv (August 1937): 297–302; Max Adler, *Der soziologische Sinn der Lehre von Karl Marx* (Leipzig, 1914), pp. 11–18; and Karl Renner, *Marxismus, Krieg und Internationale: Kritische Studien über offene Probleme des wissenschaftlichen und des praktischen Sozialismus in und nach dem Weltkrieg* (Stuttgart, 1917), in an excerpt translated as "The Development of the National Idea."

6. Michels, "Psychologie der Massenbewegungen," p. 324.

7. Helmut Gruber, *Red Vienna: Experiment in Working-Class Culture, 1919–1934* (Oxford, 1991), p. 115.

8. Alma Mahler, *Gustav Mahler: Memories and Letters*, 2nd ed., ed. Donald Mitchell, trans. Basil Creighton (London, 1968), p. 181.

9. Mahler, undated letter, postmarked 18 [?] August 1906, to Mengelberg, in *Selected Letters of Gustav Mahler*, ed. Knud Martner, trans. Eithne Wilkins and Ernst Kaiser (New York, 1979), p. 294.

10. Mahler's conversation with Specht in Salzburg, August 1906, was reported in Richard Specht, *Tagespost*, Vienna, 14 June 1914; trans. adapted from Donald Mitchell, *Gustav Mahler*, vol. 3, *Songs and Symphonies of Life and Death: Interpretations and Annotations* (Berkeley and Los Angeles, 1985), p. 519.

11. Mahler, undated letters to Alma, 20–21 June 1910, in *Ein Glück ohne Ruh': Die Briefe Gustav Mahlers an Alma*, ed. Henry-Louis de La Grange and Günther Weiss (Berlin, 1995), pp. 431–32.

12. Paul Bekker, "Geistliches Musikfest in Frankfurt. Achte Symphonie von Gustav Mahler," *Frankfurter Zeitung*, 4 April 1912.

13. *Arbeiter-Zeitung*, 12 December 1905; from Johann Wilhelm Seidl, *Musik und Austromarxismus: Zur Musikrezeption der österreichischen Arbeiterbewegung im späten Kaiserreich und in der Ersten Republik* (Vienna, Cologne, and Graz, 1989), p. 121.

14. Specht, *Tagespost*, 14 June 1914; trans. adapted from Mitchell, *Mahler*, vol. 3, *Songs and Symphonies*, p. 519.

15. Elsa Bienenfeld, *Neues Wiener Journal*, 13 September 1910, review of the premiere of Mahler's Eighth Symphony in Munich.

16. Richard Specht, "Mahlers Weg": 919.

17. It seems all the more notable that a "people's newspaper" would allude to the ironic death of the French dramatist, who performed the role of the hypochondriac in *Le Malade imaginaire*, forced a laugh even toward the end of the comedy and died a few hours thereafter. *Sächsische Volkszeitung*, undated review of Mahler's Eighth Symphony with the Volkssingakademie under its director Kurt Striegler, at the Dresden Frauenkirche, April 1912 (review signed "Zck"); from the Steininger collection.

18. Richard Robert, review of Mahler's Eighth Symphony, the Philharmonic chorus and Vienna Singakademie, under Bruno Walter, on March 14–15, 1912; typescript from an unidentified Viennese newspaper, Vondenhoff collection. Robert (b. Vienna 1861), was one of the leading piano pedagogues in Vienna; his students included Rudolf Serkin, George Szell, and Vera Schapira (who later married Richard Specht). In 1885–91, Robert edited the *Musikalische Rundschau*; in 1909 he became director of the New Conservatory in Vienna and later the president of the Vienna Composers' Society. He published reviews in the *Wiener Sonn- und Montags-Zeitung* and the *Illustrirtes Wiener Extrablatt*.

19. Walter Schrenk, *Deutsche Allgemeine Zeitung*, undated review of a performance of Mahler's Eighth Symphony organized by the Gesellschaft der Musikfreunde, Berlin, and conducted by Heinz Unger; from the Steininger collection. Schrenk (b. Königsberg 1893, d. Berlin[?] 1932) studied art history, literature, and musicology in Königsberg,

where he accepted a post as critic of the *Königsberger Allgemeine Zeitung* in 1914. He moved to Berlin in 1919 and became critic of the *Deutsche Allgemeine Zeitung* in 1920. Schrenk's most influential publication was *Richard Strauss und die neue Musik* (Berlin, 1924), which was aimed at a broad audience.

20. For a sympathetic view of Mahler's socialist leanings, and an excellent overview of the May Day demonstration, see Henry-Louis de La Grange, *Gustav Mahler,* vol. 3, *Vienna: Triumph and Disillusion (1904–1907),* (Oxford, 1999), pp. 165–69.

21. "Eine Mahler-Anekdote," *Kunst und Volk: Mitteilungen des Vereines Sozialdemokratische Kunststelle* 3, no. 3 (Nov. 1928): 65. Alma Mahler was the sole witness of the episode. She apparently first reported on the events in 1920 in her *Ein Leben mit Mahler.* The version in her memoirs mentions only Pfitzner's agitation and his "rage against those 'proletarian faces.'" But she described Mahler's attitude in greater detail and even paraphrased his response to the workers: "They had all looked at him in such a brotherly fashion! They really *were* his brothers! These men were the future!" Mahler and Pfitzner, by her recollection, continued to argue for hours. Alma Mahler, *Gustav Mahler, Erinnerungen und Briefe* (Vienna, 1949), p. 106; trans. adapted from La Grange, *Mahler,* vol. 3, *Triumph and Disillusion,* pp. 166–67.

22. Carl Schmitt, *Politische Romantik* (Berlin, 1919), with multiple later editions.

23. Conversation of June 6, 1831, from Johann Peter Eckermann, *Gespräche mit Goethe in den letzten Jahren seines Lebens*, ed. Otto Schönberger (Stuttgart, 1998), p. 52. On Michael Steinberg's discussion of the particular appeal of Baroque Catholic themes for the Jewish converts in Austria, see his *The Meaning of the Salzburg Festival: Austria as Theater and Ideology, 1890–1938* (Ithaca, 1990), pp. 186–92.

24. Max Steinitzer, "Musikbrief aus Leipzig," *Signale für die musikalische Welt* 70, no. 11 (13 March 1912): 362, review of Mahler's Eighth Symphony, in Leipzig. Steinitzer (b. Innsbruck 1864; d. Leipzig 1936) was a critic at the *Mainzer Tagblatt* (1895–1897) and the important *Leipziger Neueste Nachrichten* (beginning in 1911). He also held posts as the conductor of various regional musical societies and as a teacher. His *Musikalische Strafpredigten* (1903) saw at least five editions before World War I. Other of his books that had appeared by the time of the Leipzig premiere were on human and animal psychology (1889), music history (1908), and a biography of Richard Strauss (1911).

25. August Spanuth, "Mahler's 'Achte' in Leipzig," *Signale für die musikalische Welt* 70, no. 10 (6 March 1912): 319, preview of the Leipzig performance of Mahler's Eighth Symphony.

26. *Berliner Börsen-Courier,* 14 September 1910, review of Mahler's Eighth Symphony, signed "B."

27. Ibid.

28. Elsa Bienenfeld, *Neues Wiener Journal,* 15 March 1912, review of Mahler's Eighth Symphony. She addressed the philosophical nature of his symphonies in a review of the Seventh Symphony, in the *Neues Wiener Journal,* 10 November 1909.

29. Hugo Schlemüller, *Signale für die musikalische Welt* 70, no. 9 (28 February 1912): 293, review of Mahler's Eighth Symphony. Schlemüller (b. Königsberg, 1872; d. Frankfurt-am-Main, 1918) was a respected cellist and chamber musician. He was a member of the Kaim Orchestra in Munich and the Winderstein Orchestra in Leipzig, as well as on the faculty of the Hochsche Konservatorium in Frankfurt. In 1910–1914, he edited the journal *Konzertprogramme der Gegenwart.*

30. Hugo Schlemüller, *Signale für die musikalische Welt* 70, no. 15 (10 April 1912): 506, review of Mahler's Eighth Symphony.

31. August Spanuth, "Mahler's 'Achte' in Leipzig": 318. On Spanuth's biography, see Zoë Lang's commentary in Part III of this book.

32. One later example is the Lenin Orchestra of Hamburg, which used the term "Massenkonzert" despite its modest resources as a group of fifty unemployed musicians. See the reproduction in Inge Lammel, *Arbeitermusikkultur in Deutschland, 1844–1945. Bilder und Dokumente* (Leipzig, 1984), p. 191.

33. Steinitzer, "Musikbrief aus Leipzig": 361.

34. Oskar Bie, "Mahlers Achte," *Die Neue Rundschau* 21, no. 4 (1910), typescript from the Vondenhoff collection.

35. Bienenfeld, *Neues Wiener Journal*, 14 March 1912, review of Mahler's Eighth Symphony.

36. Rudolf Louis, *Münchner Neueste Nachrichten*, 14 September 1910, review of Mahler's Eighth; cited from Christian Wildhagen, *Die Achte Symphonie von Gustav Mahler. Konzeption einer universalen Symphonik* (Frankfurt am Main, 2000), p. 144.

37. Robert, review of Mahler's Eighth Symphony, Vondenhoff collection.

38. Ibid.

39. Walther Riezler, "Rundschau. Gustav Mahlers Achte Symphonie," *Süddeutsche Monatshefte* 7, vol. 2 (November 1910): 605. Riezler (b. Munich 1878; d. Munich 1965) was a private tutor to Wilhelm Furtwängler (who was eight years his junior), when the latter's parents, upon noticing his exceptional talents, removed him from school; Riezler had worked with Furtwängler's father, a distinguished classical archaeologist. At the time of the review, Riezler was director of the municipal museum in Stettin [Szczecin, Poland]; he later taught musicology at the University of Munich.

40. Paul Stefan, "Zur Uraufführung der VIII. Symphonie von Gustav Mahler in München. Mahlers Erscheinung," *Neue Musik-Zeitung* 31, no. 24 (1910): 490. Stefan made the very same claim in a pocket book on the composer, written for a general audience: *Mahler für Jedermann* (Vienna and Leipzig, 1923), p. 22.

41. Thomas Mann, letter of September 1910 to Mahler, in Alma Mahler, *Gustav Mahler: Memories and Letters*, p. 342.

42. Paul A. Pisk, "Zur Soziologie der Musik," *Der Kampf: Sozialdemokratische Monatsschrift* 18, no. 5 (May 1925): 186–87. This quotation compresses text that originally appeared in two paragraphs.

43. David Josef Bach, *Arbeiter-Zeitung*, 9 June 1922, review of Mahler's Third Symphony.

44. David Josef Bach, *Arbeiter-Zeitung*, September 1910, review of the premiere of Mahler's Eighth Symphony in Munich, undated clipping from the Vondenhoff collection.

45. Oskar Pollak, "Warum haben wir keine sozialdemokratische Kunstpolitik?" *Der Kampf. Sozialdemokratische Monatsschrift* 22, no. 2 (February 1929): 83.

46. David Josef Bach, "Warum haben wir keine sozialdemokratische Kunstpolitik?" *Der Kampf: Sozialdemokratische Monatsschrift* 22, no. 3 (March 1929): 143.

47. Schrenk, *Deutsche Allgemeine Zeitung*, undated review of Mahler's Eighth; from the Steininger collection.

48. Paul Stefan, "Der späte Triumph Gustav Mahlers," *Vossische Zeitung*, 22 March 1914.

49. James Simon, "Gustav Mahler," *Signale für die musikalische Welt* 78, no. 17 (28 April 1920): 431–34, on the occasion of the Amsterdam festival. Simon (b. Berlin, 1880; d. Auschwitz, 1941) studied piano with Konrad Ansorge and composition with Max Bruch; he wrote a dissertation on Abbé Vogler. Apart from his book on Faust in music (1906), Simon was mainly active as a pianist and composer. In 1907–1919 he taught at the Klindworth-Scharwenka Conservatory in Berlin.

50. Walter Schrenk, *Deutsche Allgemeine Zeitung*, undated preview of the Berlin performance of Mahler's Eighth Symphony; from the Steininger collection, Geheimes Staatsarchiv.

51. Clipping of a review dated 2 December 1919, of the performance of Mahler's Eighth Symphony, signed "O. K.," likely from the *Schwäbische Merkur. Mit Schwäbischer Kronik und Handelszeitung*, Stuttgart from the Steininger collection.

52. *Hamburgischer Correspondent*, 13 December 1921, review of Mahler's Eighth Symphony, signed "H. F. Sch."

53. *Arbeiter-Zeitung*, 18 April 1926, review of Mahler's Eighth Symphony; quoted from Seidl, *Musik und Austromarxismus*, pp. 157–58, 159.

54. David Josef Bach, "Vierzig Jahre Arbeiter-Sinfoniekonzerte," *Arbeiter-Zeitung*, 30 December 1930.

55. David Josef Bach, interview by the Austrian service of the BBC, 28 December 1945; quoted from Henriette Kotlan-Werner, *Kunst und Volk: David Josef Bach, 1874–1947* (Vienna, 1977), pp. 49–50.

56. David Josef Bach, "Viktor Adler und Gustav Mahler," *Kunst und Volk: Mitteilungen des Vereines Sozialdemokratische Kunststelle* 1, no. 10 (November 1926): 6.

57. Paul Stefan, "Mahler für Jedermann," *Kunst und Volk: Mitteilungen des Vereines Sozialdemokratische Kunststelle* 4, no. 3 (November 1929): 82.

58. Paul Bekker, *Die Symphonie von Beethoven bis Mahler* (Berlin, 1918), p. 59; revised for *Neue Musik*, Gesammelte Schriften (Stuttgart and Berlin, 1923), p. 39.

59. Else Reventlow, "Massenkultur als Problem," *Kunst und Volk: Mitteilungen des Vereines Sozialdemokratische Kunststelle* 2, no. 3 (March 1927): 12–13. Reventlow edited three volumes of writings by the Countess Franziska Reventlow (1871–1918): an autobiography, the letters, and the complete works.

60. Ellinor Tordis, "Bewegungschöre," *Kunst und Volk: Mitteilungen des Vereines Sozialdemokratische Kunststelle* 3, no. 6 (February 1929): 178.

61. Gisa Geert, "Körperkultur und Festkultur," *Kunst und Volk: Mitteilungen des Vereines Sozialdemokratische Kunststelle* 4, no. 2 (October 1929): 76.

62. *Arbeiter-Zeitung*, 20 March 1929, review of Egon Lustgarten's "Der Mensch ist unterwegs" (text by Heinrich Lersch); quoted from Reinhard Kannonier, *Zwischen Beethoven und Eisler: Zur Arbeitermusikbewegung in Österreich* (Vienna, 1981), p. 111.

63. Victor Adler's letter is quoted in David Josef Bach, "Fünfundzwanzig Jahre Arbeiter-Sinfonie-Konzert," *Kunst und Volk: Mitteilungen des Vereines Sozialdemokratische Kunststelle* 4, no. 2 (October 1929): 41.

64. Karl Laux, "Die deutsche Kammermusik Baden-Baden 1929," *Zeitschrift für Musik* 96, no. 9 (September 1929): 539; translation from Stephen Hinton, *"Lehrstück:* An Aesthetics of Performance," in *Music and Performance during the Weimar Republic*, ed. Bryan Gilliam (Cambridge, Eng., 1994), p. 67. Laux (1896–1977) was a prolific critic and author, who remained active during the Third Reich and the German Democratic Republic.

65. Ruppel was permitted to continue in his post at the *Kölnische Zeitung* through the first purges in 1933 as well as the "Editor's law" later in the Third Reich; in 1950 he became the chief music critic of the *Süddeutsche Zeitung*, where he remained for over twenty-five years. His review of Mahler's Eighth Symphony, with Hans Weisbach conducting the Düsseldorf municipal musical society, appeared in the *Kölnische Zeitung*, 9 December 1929.

66. *Deutsche Zeitung*, 26 May 1912, review of Mahler's Eighth Symphony.

67. Theodor W. Adorno, *Mahler: A Musical Physiognomy*, trans. Edmund Jephcott (Chicago, 1992), pp. 138–39. There is a distinction to be emphasized: false consciousness—which Adorno ascribes to Wagner and Pfitzner and even some Schoenberg—is a mental confusion, a failure of insight into objective historical conditions, whereas inauthenticity results from a failure of artistic expressiveness.

68. Bie, *Die neue Rundschau* 21, no. 4 (1910), review of Mahler's Eighth Symphony.

PART II

ANALYSIS AND AESTHETICS

Musical Lyricism as Self-Exploration:

Reflections on Mahler's "Ich bin der Welt abhanden gekommen"

CAMILLA BORK

TRANSLATED BY IRENE ZEDLACHER

"You walk and walk, and you never get back home on time, because you are lost to time and it to you." Thus opens the last chapter of Thomas Mann's *The Magic Mountain*. The narrator has had the protagonist Hans Castorp return from the snow and now takes the reader for a long stroll by the shore, seeking to recreate the feeling of being lost within the "monotony of space" in which time "drowns."[1] Some time thereafter, Castorp, who was lost to himself, reveals the source of the quotation so cryptically introduced: "We have a folk-song that says," he tells Clavdia Chauchat, "'I am lost to the world.'"[2]

Thus Mahler's song, "Ich bin der Welt abhanden gekommen," became a signifier of a sensibility marked by capitulation to love and death, by eros, intoxication, and lassitude: the symbol of decadent modern existence. Mann's mention of the Mahler song is all the more striking since Mahler—aspiring director of the Vienna Court Opera and accustomed to success at the time of the song's composition, in the summer of 1901—had little in common with Castorp. Mahler represented the robust artist figure of the *Gründerzeit,* that period of rapid industrialization post 1871, rather than the morbid and decadent type. Mann's literary transformation nonetheless poignantly illustrates the coming to self-awareness of the subject in song.

"Ich bin der Welt abhanden gekommen" marks a profound artistic change in Mahler's song oeuvre. Together with the *Kindertotenlieder* nos. 1, 3, and 4, as well as "Blicke mir nicht in die Lieder," "Ich atmet' einen Lindenduft," and "Um Mitternacht," it signals an orientation away from the presubjective language of the *Wunderhorn* texts through an engagement with the poetry of Friedrich Rückert. "After *Des Knaben Wunderhorn* I could not compose anything but Rückert—that is, lyric poetry from the source, all else is lyric poetry of a derivative sort," Mahler wrote to Anton Webern.[3] Literary historians have found little to praise in Rückert's poetry, but its impact on the history of the lied is uncontestable. In Robert Schumann's words, the development of the genre "was spurred by a new school of poetry: Rückert and Eichendorff, although they had flourished earlier, became familiar to musicians; Uhland and Heine were very frequently set to music. Thus arose a more artistic and profound style of song which had been inconceivable for earlier composers; it was the new spirit of poetry reflected in music."[4]

While his *Wunderhorn* songs were often expansive compositions, in the Rückert lieder Mahler adopts an unmistakably chamberlike, reduced orchestral language. Moreover, "Ich bin der Welt abhanden gekommen" is, together with "Blicke mir nicht in die Lieder," his only composition with texts about artistic creation. As revealing as analytic and philosophical interpretations of the composition are, not least Stephen Hefling's seminal study, the text itself has rarely been examined.[5] Yet this musical work—whose linearity prefigures future compositional developments like almost no other song in Mahler's oeuvre—was created through a direct confrontation with Rückert's text. The poem asserts the subject's retreat into the world of art in a manner that cannot be reduced to the biographical.

Two questions provide the focus for this essay. In what ways does Mahler's compositional strategy respond to Rückert's poem? How does the musical composition imply a decontextualization and therefore novel interpretation of Rückert's poetry in the spirit of fin-de-siècle modernity? To answer these questions I will first analyze the poem's formal dimensions and then consider the structural importance of Rückert's poetry for Mahler's composition. And finally I will suggest how Mahler's music provides a new perspective on the substantive meaning of the poem.

"Ich bin der Welt abhanden gekommen" is part of a collection of three hundred mostly songlike poems written for private use but compiled in 1821 and published in 1834 under the title *A Spring of Love*, in the first volume of Rückert's collected poems. The poems were arranged in five sections, and in one section grouped into six "bouquets" with headings following the various stages of a love affair—awakened, separated, shunned, estranged, reclaimed, reunited—presented in all its ramifications through different lyrical genres (ghazal, sonnet, etc.).[6] Kurt Wölfel has called this collection a "lyrical diary" of Rückert's betrothal. It certainly is true that their writing in 1820–1821 coincided with his engagement to Luise Fischer-Wiethaus. However, Wölfel relies on an ideal construct of a poetry of experience and emotion—the very same way that Goethe's lyrical output was canonized, and a construct that has continued to dominate literary studies well into the twentieth century.[7]

Measured against this conception, Rückert's love lyrics seem light-weight and obsessed with form. They lack the expressive depth of true emotion and even seem derivative.[8] However, such judgments obscure the qualities of the poems that lie beyond the realm of poetry of experience. The biographical event—the engagement to the beloved—no doubt provided an impetus for the creation of the collection. But the extent to which the biographical circumstances—the identity of the beloved, for example—influenced the poetic representation remains open. It seems clear that Rückert made extensive use of poetic traditions in order to depict the character and appearance of the beloved. Her portrayal through a variety of petrarchian topoi transcends any specific individuality. The rich diversity of formal conventions that Rückert had at his disposal, some from his study of Asian cultures, played an important role. The poetic speech in *A Spring of Love* signifies an intellectual game with inherited forms and formulae.

"Ich bin der Welt abhanden gekommen" is from the fifth section, entitled "Reclaimed." It is embedded within a group of four poems dealing with the lyrical self's withdrawal into itself from the world. The resulting inwardness is dominated by love and art. Even the withdrawal from the world itself contributes to this idea. Love and art are considered one, as is evident in the conflation of kissing and writing (poem 27) and the idea that love might be the only possible subject of art (poem 28).[9] The central message remains constant, despite the shifts in emphasis: love and art are inseparably intertwined. Both can be realized only apart from the world and outside social reality. As if imitating a musical model, variation procedures run through the entire collection.

The gesture of circling in on oneself, so prominent in "Ich bin der Welt abhanden gekommen," is reflected in the formal structure of the three-stanza poem, reproduced below.

Ich bin der Welt abhanden gekommen,	I am lost to the world,
Mit der ich sonst viele Zeit verdorben.	Where once I wasted so much time.
Sie hat so lange von mir nichts vernommen,	It has heard nothing from me for so long,
Sie mag wohl glauben, ich sei gestorben.	It may well believe I am dead.

Es ist mir auch gar nichts daran gelegen,	To me it is of no consequence Whether the world thinks me
Ob sie mich für gestorben hält.	dead.
Ich kann auch gar nichts sagen dagegen,	Nor can I deny it, For truly, I am dead to the
Denn wirklich bin ich gestorben der Welt.	world.

Ich bin gestorben dem Weltgewimmel,	I am dead to the world's bustle
Und ruh' in einem stillen Gebiet.	And I rest in a tranquil realm.
Ich leb' in mir und meinem Himmel,	I live in me and in my heaven,
In meinem Lieben, in meinem Lied.	In my love, in my song.

Marked by repeating structural elements, the poem reveals a great propensity toward regularity. Alternating rhymes link the four lines of the individual stanzas, leading each stanza to become self-contained. Nonetheless, the anaphoric use of the pronoun *I* creates a web of manifold inner connections throughout the poem. The first lines of the outer stanzas create a frame through parallel images. The last line of the second stanza and the first line of the third are likewise closely connected. The end of the second line is repeated at the beginning of the third stanza through a chiastic construction. On the other hand, in the final two lines this syntactic linkage slowly comes apart in the sequence of associations of "in my heaven, in my life, in my song."

The unique formal position of the last stanza reflects its equally distinctive content. Beginning with the statement "I am lost to the world," the first two stanzas circle around the relationship between the self and the world. In contrast, the final stanza—particularly its last three lines—takes as its subject the condition of the lyrical self after its withdrawal from the world. An overarching duality is revealed. Although both spaces (the world and the realm of silence) lack detailed specificity, a conceptual arena is created around dual foci:

World	**Realm of silence**
time	silence
noise/sound	heaven
	life
world's hubbub	love
dying	song

Mahler sonically defines the difference between the two spheres by substituting Rückert's *Weltgewimmel* with *Weltgetümmel*. While the "realm of silence" is defined by the absence of sound, or solely through artistically formulated sound, *Weltgetümmel* suggests a loud and boisterous sonority.[10] And whereas the "world" points toward the idea of an infinite totality in which individuals can lose themselves, the "realm of silence" refers to a circumscribed space defined solely by its relationship to the lyrical subject.[11] The repeated use of possessive pronouns (my heaven, my love) makes this clear. What emerges does not represent a universal idea of paradise or an afterlife but rather is a function of the purely subjective imagination that stands in the tradition of a *hortus conclusus*—the garden of love as paradise on earth.[12]

The temporal structure of the poem derives from a circular pattern superimposed onto a linear sequence. The absence of any verbs of motion is striking. The first two stanzas illustrate an interior dialogue or reflective process that persistently revolves around the statement "I am dead to the world." Like an incantation, the pronoun *I* is repeated, but without permitting a concretization of the lyrical self. Every expression of the lyrical self appears only in relation to itself. It does not turn "out into the world." Even in its perception of the world, the self only turns back on itself. This fundamentally circular structure determines the overarching character of the poem in two ways. First, the parallel construction in the opening lines of the outer stanzas constitutes a frame. Second, by referring to the poem itself, the last word, *"Lied,"* creates an arch leading back to the beginning, so that the poem appears coherently closed into itself.

This arch is weighed down by a trajectory of development. In the first two stanzas the process of thought evolves with increasing confidence to form a transition from the potential to the indicative. Events are placed in a state of suspension, beginning with the euphemistic circumlocution "I am lost to the world" for "dying" and the use of verbs such as "may believe" and "thinks me dead." Only in the final line of the second stanza does the interior dialogue shift to the indicative— that is, from the hypothetical to the real: "For truly, I am dead to the world." In addition, a process of structuring or clarification emerges in the organization of vowels. The sequence of vowels at the end of lines— particularly exposed by the rhyme scheme—shows a gradual brightening in sound. The first stanza is dominated by dark o-sounds (*gekommen, verdorben, vernommen, gestorben*), the second stanza by the vowel "e" (*gelegen, dagegen, Welt*), and the conclusion of the poem by the vowel "i" (*Gebiet, Lieben, Lied*). This development is intensified by similar tendencies in the rhythmic and metrical structure. Lines consisting of eight, ten, and eleven syllables with four or five stresses alternate in the first two stanzas. In the last three lines this irregularity gives way to a series of regular nine-syllable lines with four stress points. The turning away from the disorder of the world toward art, music, and song is rendered explicit by the poem's sound character.

Three crucial aspects of Rückert's poetry influence Mahler's setting: the temporal structure, the construct of lyrical subjectivity from the interplay between vocal and instrumental lyricism, and the conception of the ending. Mahler follows the poem's binary temporal construction. He retains Rückert's verse form, producing the song as a double arch. But he then explodes this architectonic structure by deriving every musical event from one basic motive or chord. A remarkably effective thematic logic surrounds the work with a web of interrelationships. Like *Das Lied von der Erde* eight years later, the composition is based on a series of four notes (B♭, C, E♭, G) and their transformation through transposition, retrogression, and inversion.[13] For example, the main framing notes of the introductory motive expose the diastematic constellations that further determine the course of the music.[14] However, the use of developing variation serves less to guarantee an a priori meaning that might be jeopardized in the absence of a clear tonal center. Rather, developing variation becomes the compositional correlative to the insistent, pleading circling in on itself characteristic of the poem.

The contrast between opening and closing reveals clearly the linear progress of Rückert's poem. One can see its influence on the development within the song as well as the composition's overall concept. We first hear the contra B♭ of the harp that emerges barely noticeable out of silence (see Example 1). Then the English horn, hesitatingly and on a weak beat, enters, opening a space whose lower "boundary" disappears with the last note of the harp. Since the first beat of each measure is suppressed by ties, the lines of English horn and bassoon proceed in different directions almost without a sense of meter. Dark colors dominate the orchestration, with the bright timbre and higher registers of the piercing brass (trumpets, trombone) and flute excluded. The choice of the English horn as solo instrument is significant. In Berlioz's celebrated orchestration treatise, which Strauss would enlarge and revise in 1905, the English horn is admired as a sonority "less piercing, more veiled and heavy than that of the oboe." Moreover, it "does not lend itself too well to the gaiety of rustic melodies . . . . Its tones are melancholy, dreamy, noble, somewhat veiled—as if played in the distance."[15]

The harmony at the opening likewise remains suspended, diffuse, and ambiguous. While the sound of the harp may initially be inter-

Example 1. "Ich bin der Welt abhanden gekommen," mm. 1–5.

preted as a fifth (from the vantage point of the subsequent harmonic development), temporally it can hardly be considered as such. It is not the bass of a 6/4 chord. Rather, it provides the implication of a deep sonority above which a C-minor tonality is first generated, one that later turns toward E-flat major and then G minor. Only in m. 5 does the harmony stabilize into a B-flat-major sonority—still here weakened by the placement of the fifth in the bass.

The voice enters in m. 12, overlapping with the altered repetition of the introductory motive. "Calmly," Mahler instructs, the voice takes up the gesture of the prelude, although rhythmically slightly shifted in relation to the first violin. Theodor W. Adorno called this technique, which inscribes Romantic conventions into the aesthetics of the song, an "inauthentic unison."[16] Robert Schumann had used the strategy as a musical signifier of separation and loss of identity.[17] Mahler's connection to this Romantic convention suits the passage under discussion, for in both instances the text speaks of an estrangement from the world.

The repeat of the introduction at the beginning of the third stanza is similar in tone color, though some details are decisively altered. The spatial character of the beginning is absent, and one can discern a stabilization of meter, rhythm, and harmony. The accentuation of the bass line as well as the altered rhythm of the introductory motive create a fixed metric frame in which the volatile harmony of the beginning is replaced by a clear harmonization in the dominant. The opening melodic gesture of the English horn does not lead, as in the beginning, to a one-line B♭, but descends to a small B♭. The vocal line has a remarkable unison with the first violin. For the first time, the instrumental and vocal lines proceed in parallel fashion. The "breaking in two" of the beginning appears transcended.

There is a tendency for the vocal line and the instrumental lines to resemble each other in phrase structure. The harp accompaniment, with its triadic figurations, provides a continuous instrumental base. Above it there develops a close interaction between vocal and instrumental lines, resulting in an interaction of voices of identical weight. A transparent audibility of each voice is achieved through shared motivic material. The melismatic figure on *"gestorben"* first appears in the instrumental line of the preceding interlude. Instruments and voice often seem to exchange gestures. When the singer withdraws to assume the role of quasi narrator at the end of the second stanza, a melodic phrase develops in the first violin (Example 2). A similar pattern can be observed at the end of the last stanza. The oboe rises up into an espressivo line that is only belatedly joined by the singer (m. 54). As the embodiment of lyrical subjectivity, the voice recedes into the background, giving way to the

Example 2. "Ich bin der Welt abhanden gekommen," mm. 35–37.

supra-individual and nonlinguistic instrumental melody.

In the postlude, the English horn enters once again over a self-contained string sound, overlapping the voice with its phrase on the final syllable, "*Lied.*" Two interpretive perspectives emerge. On the one hand, there is a framing structure to the song: the rising second of the beginning is replaced with a descending one. On the other hand, the postlude can be understood as an instrumental variant of the final stanza, to which it is closely related motivically. The postlude finally returns to E-flat major without any dominant/tonic tension (Example 3). The violin motive soars above the subdominant (A-flat major), variously augmented and transfigured, nearly vanishing into nothingness. The bass meanwhile descends by a half step to G (m. 63). The resulting sound can be read in many ways. It anticipates E-flat major as a sixth chord with a suspended sixth and seventh. On the other hand, its G-minor coloring hints at the realm of the minor key from the song's beginning, until the phrase glides, with a drop of a third, into the closing sonority and thereby obliterates the boundary

Example 3. "Ich bin der Welt abhanden gekommen," mm. 57–67.

between sound and silence by its own slow dissolution. Although the harmony and the descending melodic line give the ending a sense of being self-contained, the closing melodic moment, with its descending line ending in a fifth and the final chord an open third, evokes the absence of closure through the sound itself. The sonic character as well as the performance instruction "transfigured" suggest one of those post-Wagnerian transfiguration endings that possess an aesthetic, quasi-religious significance, such as in Schoenberg's *Verklärte Nacht* and Strauss's *Tod und Verklärung*.[18]

Mahler's setting has obvious consequences for how we interpret Rückert. The poem placed in the context of the *Liebesfrühling* collection is without a doubt a love poem. But once removed from that collection, its meaning seems far less certain. The circumstances of love (if we consider the term "love" in the penultimate line emphatically) do not emerge conclusively from the text. Rather, in light of subsequent literary developments, the terms "heaven," "love," and "song" may be understood as "historically sequential objectifications of the self," for they express the apprehension of the self in God, in the moment of

Example 3 continued

intense emotion, and in art.[19] Hegel's definition of poetry may be applicable to Rückert's poem. "For the primary realization of the inner life is itself still inwardness, so that this emergence from self means only liberation from that immediate, dumb, void of ideas, concentration of the heart which now opens out to self-expression and therefore grasps and expresses in the form of self-conscious insights and ideas what formerly was only felt.—This in essence establishes the sphere and task of lyric poetry in distinction from epic and dramatic."[20]

The notion of poetry as a form of self-apprehension, as a "search for the self," was of particular relevance at the turn of the century. This becomes obvious when one considers the notion of the lyrical self as formulated by Margarete Susman in 1910. For her a poem is not the expression of personal feelings and experiences of the empirical self of a poet but the manifestation of a transcendental I. Only this lyrical self can convey the "truth of the person," independent from the personal fate of its author.[21] Viewed from this perspective, Rückert's text gains new meaning. The poem speaks precisely of the disconnect between self and reality implied by the lyrical self. This notion was repeatedly discussed by modernist intellectuals of fin-de-siècle Vienna, notably by Ernst Mach in his critique of language.[22] For Mach, the world consisted of relationships among experiences. The "ego" was dissolved in "combinations [of elements] of varying evanescence and permanence. . . . Since the apparent antithesis between real world and the world given through the senses lies entirely in our mode of view, and no actual gulf exists between them, a complicated and variously interconnected content of consciousness is no more difficult to understand than is the complicated interconnection of the world."[23] Although it is unknown whether Mahler, who maintained close contact with Viennese intellectuals, knew of Mach's ideas, one can find many similarities in their writings. In a letter to Alma Schindler, Mahler wrote: "You will feel that the only true reality on earth is our soul. For anyone who has once grasped this, what we call reality is no more than a formula, a shadow with no substance.—And you must not, please, take this for a poetical metaphor; it is a conviction which can hold its own at the bar of sober reason."[24] This insight is mirrored in Mahler's musical-lyrical work by its own turn inward, a turn described by Hugo von Hofmannsthal as one of the hallmarks of modernity: "Two things seem modern nowadays: the analysis of life, and the flight from life."[25] Mahler's fragile and artificial sound creation prefigures aspects of Webern's "absolute poetry," in Adorno's words.[26] Its sublime formal structure demonstrates that the inward turn cannot, as in Rückert, be considered a mere withdrawal into the private realm of love. It is rather the expression of a reflective shift toward the elevated sphere of art.

NOTES

The title of my essay is inspired by Gottfried Benn's statement, "A poem is always a self-exploration, and in the answer all sphinxes and images of Sais fuse into one," in his *Probleme der Lyrik* (Wiesbaden, 1951), in *Gottfried Benn: Sämtliche Werke*, vol. 6, ed. Gerhard Schuster (Stuttgart, 2001), p. 16.

1. Thomas Mann, *The Magic Mountain*, trans. John E. Woods (New York, 1995), pp. 536–37.

2. Thomas Mann, *The Magic Mountain*, trans. H. T. Lowe-Porter (London, 1960), p. 593.

3. Mahler's letter of 3 February 1905 to Webern, in Hans Moldenhauer and Rosaleen Moldenhauer, *Anton von Webern: A Chronicle of His Life and Work* (New York, 1979), p. 75.

4. Robert Schumann, *On Music and Musicians*, ed. Konrad Wolff, trans. Paul Rosenfeld (New York, 1946), pp. 241–42, translation modified.

5. Stephen E. Hefling, "The Composition of 'Ich bin der Welt abhanden gekommen,'" in *Gustav Mahler*, ed. Hermann Danuser (Darmstadt, 1999), pp. 96–158.

6. The German headings are "Erweckt," "Geschieden," "Gemieden," "Entfremdet," "Wiedergewonnen," and "Verbunden." The first independent edition of *Liebesfrühling* was published in 1844. It was followed by numerous editions, including the luxury editions of 1858 and 1872. It is not known which Rückert edition Mahler used. Zoltan Roman, "Revisionsbericht," in Gustav Mahler, *Lieder nach Texten von Friedrich Rückert, Sämtliche Werke*, vol. 14, no. 4 (Frankfurt am Main, 1984), p. vi.

7. Kurt Wölfel, "'Dichtergeist, entflammter Bräutigam!' Friedrich Rückerts 'Liebesfrühling'," *Rückert-Studien* 9 (1995): 33–48. The most influential proponent of the idea of poetry as a vehicle for communicating experience and emotion is Emil Staiger, *Grundbegriffe der Poetik* (Zurich and Freiburg im Breisgau, 1968), pp. 13–82.

8. Such claims run through the entire secondary literature. Annemarie Schimmel calls him a singer of "charming poems" and "delightful little songs," in her *Friedrich Rückert: Lebensbild und Einführung* (Freiburg im Breisgau, 1987), p. 15. See also Helmut Koopmann, "Rückerts lyrische Modernität im Zeitalter der Epigonen," in *Rückert-Studien* 5, (1990): 38–53.

9. The numbering of the poems comes from the posthumous edition, Friedrich Rückert, *Gesammelte poetische Werke*, vol. 1 (Frankfurt am Main, 1868).

10. Mahler adapts the text in other small but significant ways. There is the usual repetition of words, common at the end of a stanza: *gestorben* in the first stanza and *in meinem Lieben* in the third stanza. In line 3 of the first stanza, he changes the position of *"nichts"* (nothing), to be emphasized on the first beat of the measure. In line 3 of the final stanza, he simplifies and intensifies the original prose, "I live alone in my heaven" (*Ich leb' allein in meinem Himmel*).

11. Hans Heinrich Eggebrecht argues that for Mahler there was a duality between the world as reality of routine and appearance, and "another" world "whose presence alone achieves the feeling of inwardness and feeling." See the thorough study of Mahler's

concept of the world in his *Die Musik Gustav Mahlers* (Munich, 1982), pp. 255–82 (quotation on p. 257).

12. On the literary topos of the *hortus conclusus*, see Peter von Matt, "Versuch, den Himmel auf der Erde einzurichten: Der Absolutismus der Liebe in Goethes *Wahlverwandtschaften*," in *Über die Liebe,* ed. Heinrich Meier and Gerhard Neumann (Munich, 2001), pp. 263–304.

13. This analysis is based on the orchestral version transposed to E-flat major. Mahler himself transposed the song, presumably after the premiere. See Roman, "Revisionsbericht," p. xviii.

14. Stephen E. Hefling, "The Rückert Lieder," in *The Mahler Companion*, ed. Donald Mitchell and Andrew Nicholson (Oxford and New York, 1999), p. 356.

15. Hector Berlioz and Richard Strauss, *Treatise on Instrumentation,* trans. Theodore Front (1948; rpt. New York, 1991), p. 184. Berlioz's treatise was well-known before that point, having first been authoritatively translated into German by Alfred Dorffel in 1864, with six subsequent editions released through 1898.

16. Theodor W. Adorno, "Der getreue Korrepetitor," in *Gesammelte Schriften*, vol. 15 (*Musikalische Schriften,* vol. 5), ed. Rolf Tiedemann (Frankfurt am Main, 1976), p. 255.

17. For the inauthentic unison, see Reinhold Brinkmann, "Lied als individuelle Struktur. Ausgewählte Kommentare zu Schumanns 'Zwielicht,'" in *Analysen: Beiträge zu einer Problemgeschichte des Komponierens. Festschrift für Hans Heinrich Eggebrecht zum 65. Geburtstag,* ed. Werner Breig, Reinhold Brinkmann, and Elmar Budde (Stuttgart, 1984), p. 269.

18. See my "Death and Transfiguration: Isolde's *Liebestod* as a Model for Artistic Closure," in *Zukunftsbilder: Richard Wagners Revolution und ihre Folgen in Kunst und Politik,* ed. Hermann Danuser and Herfried Münkler (Schliengen, forthcoming in 2002).

19. Karl Pestalozzi, *Die Entstehung des lyrischen Ich* (Berlin, 1970), p. 350.

20. Georg Wilhelm Friedrich Hegel, *Aesthetics: Lectures on Fine Art,* trans. T. M. Knox, vol. 2 (Oxford, 1975), p. 1112. Reinhold Brinkmann uses Hegel's aesthetics of the lyric as a theoretical foundation for interpreting Schoenberg's songs and lyrical piano pieces from op. 6 to op. 15 as self-referential musical lyric, in his "The Lyric as Paradigm: Poetry and Foundation of Arnold Schoenberg's New Music," in *German Literature and Music: An Aesthetic Fusion, 1890–1989,* ed. Claus Reschke and Howard Pollack (Munich, 1992), pp. 95–129.

21. Margarete Susman, *Das Wesen der modernen deutschen Lyrik* (Stuttgart, 1910), pp. 5–20.

22. On points of contact between Mahler's musical thought and Mach's reflections, see Matthias Schmidt, "Komponierte Uneinholbarkeit. Anmerkungen zum 'Volkston' der *Wunderhorn*-Lieder," in *Gustav Mahler und das Lied,* ed. Bernd Sponheuer and Wolfram Steinbeck (Bonn, forthcoming).

23. Ernst Mach, *The Analysis of Sensations*, trans. C. M. Williams (Chicago and London, 1914), p. 22, 28.

24. Letter to Alma Schindler, 5 December 1901, in Alma Mahler, *Gustav Mahler: Memories and Letters,* ed. Donald Mitchell and Knud Martner, 3d ed. (London, 1975), p. 206.

25. Hugo von Hofmannsthal, "Gabriele d'Annunzio" (1893), in *Gesammelte Werke*, vol. 8, *Reden und Aufsätze* I, ed. Bernd Schoeller (Frankfurt am Main, 1986), p. 176.

26. Theodor W. Adorno, "Anton Webern: Zur Aufführung der Fünf Orchesterstücke, op. 10, in Zürich," in his *Gesammelte Schriften,* vol. 18 (*Musikalische Schriften,* vol. 5), ed. Rolf Tiedemann (Frankfurt am Main, 1984), p. 513.

"...the heart-wrenching sound

of farewell":

Mahler, Rückert, and the *Kindertotenlieder*

PETER REVERS
TRANSLATED BY IRENE ZEDLACHER

The death of children was one of the most tragic yet familiar facets of European everyday life in the nineteenth century. At the century's start, about half of all deaths were below the age of five; hardly a family was spared. Over the course of the century the rates of child mortality decreased only gradually. Mahler's early biography is paradigmatic. His mother buried eight of her fourteen children and survived to see a ninth die at an adult age. The death of siblings (only two of whom survived Mahler) was an experience he had to confront time and again from age six until his departure from Iglau in 1875 to study in Vienna.

After the turn of the century, advances in science and a general improvement in living conditions brought a marked decrease in child mortality. With new victories over disease and illness came a radical change in attitude. Before the late nineteenth century, many parents considered the fatal illnesses of infants and toddlers an inevitable part of life. But after 1900 parents responded to such loss with bitter sorrow rather than with Christian resignation or near indifference—all the more so because the number of children per household had decreased.[1] This was the case with Mahler, as early reviewers of his *Kindertotenlieder* would never forget, although they realized that the songs were composed prior to his own family tragedy, in June 1907. The death of his elder daughter Maria Anna from diphtheria and scarlet fever was especially traumatic since his younger daughter had recently survived a bout of scarlet fever. "Mahler loved this child devotedly; he hid himself in his room every day, taking leave of her in his heart," Alma recalled. "Weeping and sobbing, Mahler went again and again to the door of my bedroom, where she was; then fled away to be out of earshot of any sound. It was more than he could bear."[2] Born to an impoverished family of sixteen, Mahler, for all his financial and artistic success, was destined to head a family of three.

As a profound response to poetry from a century past, Mahler's *Kindertotenlieder* offers a rich resource for exploring how the emotional and intellectual processing of the painful loss of a child changed from the nineteenth century to the twentieth. What ideas and imaginative strategies were developed to overcome such tragic experiences? What consequences did they in turn have for the literary treatment of child mortality? No matter how familiar the emotional culture conveyed by the *Kindertotenlieder*, this work and the Rückert poetry it sets represent ways of thinking and experiencing whose intensity are emblematic of the nineteenth century. This historical residue affected Mahler's choice of song texts and their sequence as well as aspects of their compositional structure. The cyclical structure of the work in particular cannot be understood without taking this psychological and historical background into account. This background also sheds light on the distribution of tonalities, the phrase structure of vocal and instrumental voices, as well as the general dramaturgy of each individual song.

Mahler's reaction to the death of his child was similar to that of Friedrich Rückert when his two children, Luise and Ernst, died of scarlet fever in 1833 and 1834. Both men were gripped by the feeling of powerlessness in the face of the death of a child. Luise Rückert's account of her husband's response is harrowing: "One evening I held him [Ernst] in my arms and his father sat on the bed. Suddenly he became so weak that we—especially his father—thought he would pass away instantly. Once more I had to hear the sound, the heart-wrenching sound of farewell to this world. Then Rückert ran out into the open air and told any friends he encountered that the boy was dead. But not yet. The suffering would continue for eight more days."[3] She also reported on the death, salvaging the memory of the tragic experience from the anonymity of a simple family history. Her account and especially Rückert's 428 poems on the death of children became singular, almost manic documents of the psychological endeavor to cope with such loss. In ever new variations Rückert's poems attempt a poetic resuscitation of the children that is punctuated by anguished outbursts. But above all the poems show a quiet acquiescence to fate and to a peaceful world of solace.

Rückert's *Kindertotenlieder* were a private, almost obsessive testimony to the experience of pain, and were not intended for publication.[4] The topic was, however, common in poetry in the early nineteenth century. The *Deutsche Musenalmanach* published *Kindertoten* poems by Joseph von Eichendorff in 1834, Karl Barth in 1835, Rückert in 1838, and Hoffmann von Fallersleben in 1839.[5] The reasons for such a concentration are not merely sociohistorical. The child was the central ideal of Romantic and Biedermeier thought, and childhood was mythologized into a poetic stage of life. The idea of death also underwent fundamental changes in the early part of the nineteenth century. The emphasis lay on the reaction to the death of one's closest family and dear ones rather than on the fear of one's own death.[6] Death meant above all farewell and separation, although mitigated by the belief in an afterlife that would bring a reunion. There was a comforting notion of death as sleep. The conclusion of the poem for Mahler's *Kindertotenlieder* no. 5, the children "are sleeping as though in their mother's house," suggests an attempt to overcome the finality of death in intellectual and emotional terms. Sleep, especially in such familiar surroundings as a mother's house, suggests safety and a future. Sleep is followed by waking up. It is not—like death—an irrevocable caesura. Rest and sleep are among the oldest and most pervasive representations of an afterlife. They form part of a blissful paradise imagined by humans based on a worldly experience. The past (memory) and the present are transformed into an eternal future.

The belief in a future life and a reunion on the one hand, and the restoration of life through memory on the other, became the essential ways of psychologically coping with the death of a beloved person. The tension between the repressed fear of an irrevocable parting and the ultimate hope for a reunion plays a decisive role in the poem Mahler used in *Kindertotenlieder* no. 4, reproduced below. The poem expresses the constant and lingering fear of a loss that ultimately becomes a reality. This insecurity yields a multiplicity of responses. At first, a situation is recalled in which the speaker once again can hold on to hope, as if the children's death might still lie ahead. The memory of the living children initially can only be recapitulated ("*Often* I think"). The second half of the first stanza brings an allusion to the present ("The day *is* beautiful"), which wins out in the second stanza ("and will *now* return home"). However, the expression of fear and inner uncertainty is strengthened by the reversal of word order and the striking contrast between "beautiful" and "anxious" (compare the third line of the second stanza with that of the first stanza).

Certainty comes only in the third stanza, where the children's exit is irrevocable. In Rückert's original poem, the second line reads "und werden nicht hier nach Hause verlangen"—the children "won't be longing to return to this home." The house to which the children will return is therefore no longer of this world. If the events in this song up to this point could have been related to real life, Rückert's formulation now makes "house" clearly stand for the afterlife. This affects our understanding of the third stanza's final line. The "heights," which in the second stanza still evoked worldly intimacy, are now bathed in the light of transcendence. Those parted by death will be forever reunited. The text below is Rückert's *Kindertotenlieder* no. 4, as adapted by Mahler:

Oft denk ich, sie sind nur ausge-gangen!	Often I think they have merely gone out!
Bald werden sie wieder nach Hause gelangen!	Soon they will return home!
Der Tag ist schön! O sei nicht bang!	The day is beautiful! Oh, don't be anxious!
Sie machen nur einen weiten Gang.	They are only taking a long walk.
Jawohl, sie sind nur ausgegangen	Surely they have merely gone out
Und werden jetzt nach Hause gelangen!	And will now return home!
O, sei nicht bang, der Tag ist schön!	Oh, don't be anxious, the day is beautiful!
Sie machen nur den Gang zu jenen Höh'n!	They are only taking their walk to yonder heights!
Sie sind uns nur vorausgegangen	They have only gone on ahead of us
Und werden nicht wieder nach Hause verlangen!	And won't be longing for home any longer!
Wir holen sie ein auf jenen Höh'n im Sonnenschein!	We will overtake them on yonder height in the sunshine!
Der Tag ist schön auf jenen Höh'n!	The day is beautiful on yonder heights!

The closing image of sunshine brings the poem's first invocation of light and nature. In Rückert, light is not only a metaphor for good fortune and hope but also for the eternal light of a life after death. But eternity also means the suspension of time in a linear sense. Indeed, the temporal difference between past and future is eliminated throughout. The poem is a coming to terms with the death of children through a fusion of memory, the present time of the parents who remain behind, and the transfigured vision of a future reunion. The past, present, and future become an indissoluble unit that is paradigmatic of the process of mourning.

Mahler's setting of the poem treats the three stanzas like rungs on a ladder ascending toward the heights, as Reinhard Gerlach puts it. The song is, in effect, instrumental music that draws the words along with it.[7] In the piano version, the piano's upper voice is instructed to "continue the singing" at the end of both the first and second stanza. It is as if the meaning of the words is detached from the worldly sphere of human speech. Only in the third stanza is the songlike phrase returned from the piano to the realm of language. With the words "on yonder heights," the early Romantic metaphysics associated with instrumental music (so exquisitely formulated by Jean Paul, Tieck, and Wackenroder) becomes appropriated; the hope of the living assumes an immateriality unique to music more akin to transcendence.[8]

The image of sunshine, with its metaphorical meaning of eternal light, was introduced at the opening of the first song. Remarkably, Mahler composed a descending melodic line at "Now will the sun rise so brightly." This break with the tradition of illustrative sound symbolism—dawn as an ascending melodic progression—is significant. Set against this unchanging natural event, which is untouched by individual fate and has positive symbolic connotations, the human misfortune acquires a severe profile. The pointed contrast of an inherently peaceful image of nature with the self's desolate state is, of course, an important characteristic of literary Romanticism and decisive in the history of the art song, as Schubert's music reveals. The association of sunshine with the experience of pain is common in Mahler's lieder already in his earliest compositions. In "Im Lenz" (February 1880) the individual reacts to the question, "What is pain and regret if the sun shines on you?" with the impossibility that the positive nature image can be enjoyed in the face of loneliness and isolation. The same holds true for the *Lieder eines fahrenden Gesellen*. In "Ging heut' morgen übers Feld," nature is initially painted in glowing colors, but in the end this beautiful and safe world does not seem real. The individual cannot participate in such a carefree atmosphere. Nature seems to represent the individual's alter ego. It is the dreamlike vision of a joyous life set in sharp contrast to the individual's real feelings.

Time and again Mahler returns to this illusory world of happiness so remote from the individual subject. And it is through this polarization that the loss of security and the deep emotional confusion of the self is articulated. *Kindertotenlieder* no. 1 is paradigmatic in this way. The tragic distance from the usual sunshine is intensified musically, for the same melodic phrase, with only slight variation, is given to three different phrases, shown underlined or italicized in the poem below, *Kindertotenlieder* no. 1 (motivic repetition), mm. 13–15, 34–36, and

75–77. The last and brightest of these, in brutal irony, is to be performed "with anguish."

Nun will die Sonn' so hell aufgehn,	Now the sun will rise as brightly,
Als sei kein <u>Unglück die Nacht geschehn!</u>	As if no *misfortune had transpired in the night.*
Das Unglück geschah nur mir allein!	The misfortune has fallen on me alone.
Die Sonne, sie <u>scheinet allgemein!</u>	The sun—it *shines for everyone.*
Du mußt nicht die Nacht in dir verschränken,	You must not keep the night inside you;
Mußt sie ins ew'ge Licht versenken!	You must immerse it in eternal light!
Ein Lämplein verlosch in meinem Zelt!	A small lamp has been extinguished in my household;
<u>Heil sei dem Freudenlicht der Welt!</u>	*Light of joy in the world, be welcome.*

In the poem itself, the tragedy of human experience increases in nearly reverse proportion to the gradual intensification of the use of the metaphor of light. The light metaphor in the third couplet brings an expansion of the vocal range and an orchestral climax (mm. 59–63). This section begins with counterpoint between the voice and instrumental part, characteristic of the song's linearity. And in contrast to the first and second couplets, which here become absorbed into the counterpoint formed by the oboe, the vocal melody ascends. This, too, may be related to the text. While the suffering of the individual is at the center of the first two couplets, the third couplet aims toward the transcendental realm of light. The eternal light as symbol of immortality is emphasized by word repetition at the high point of an extensive melismatic arch. No less remarkable is the brightening of the key beginning at *"ew'ge Licht,"* which dims again to the darker minor key at the word *versenken.* For a brief moment, Mahler allows a glimmer of hope to shine and for consolation to appear, only to rob it of all illusion at the beginning of the final couplet.

The closed cyclical form is more pronounced in the *Kindertotenlieder* than in the *Lieder eines fahrenden Gesellen.* The configuration of key areas is only the most obvious element: D minor in the framing songs, C minor for songs 2 and 3, and to E-flat major for song 4. The vision of transcendence, which in the first song is still only an illusion unable to assuage the pain of loss, becomes reality in the final song, with the sense of fulfillment as the key area changes to the major mode. The tension at the opening of the cycle—the dialectics of undamaged nature and personal suffering—is resolved at its close. Initially, in the final song, the imagined tempestuous nature and the self's confused state correspond. The first three stanzas are governed by a taut, jagged melody with an almost obsessively descending movement, and are to be performed "with restless anguished expression." Yet finally the self is removed to a bright sound world distanced from all peril:

In diesem Wetter, in diesem Saus, in diesem Braus,	In this weather, in this storm, in this tumult
Sie ruh'n als wie in der Mutter Haus,	They are sleeping as if in their mother's house,
Von keinem Sturm erschrecket,	Frightened by no storm,
Von Gottes Hand bedecket.	Sheltered by God's hand.

A transfiguration of the key into D major, marking the close of the cycle, brings with it a substantial change in character. This final stanza is sung "slowly, like a lullaby." The vocal line, previously torn into short and breathless phrases, attains a songlike quality, a tranquility in which the despair over the death of the children is assuaged by the certainty of a home beyond time and space. The comfort bestowed by this certainty—the fact that the children will find eternal peace in a life removed from the grasp of harsh reality—is articulated by a brightening of the sonic character.

In the transition to the final stanza, the increased intensity and hectic quality, marked by dissonance and harsh coloration, give way to a bright, light sound, with the tripartite striking of A minor in the bells, the piccolo, and the harmonics of the cellos. Soon thereafter, a celesta enters together with the voice. There is no doubt that in Mahler's lieder this instrument signifies "eternity," as at the conclusion of *Lied von der Erde*. The very fact that the instrument was so new must have enhanced the association: patented in 1886, the celesta had been heard in Chausson's *La tempète* (1888), Tchaikovsky's *Nutcracker* (1892), as well as Charpentier's *Louise* (1900), which premiered in 1900 and was conducted by Mahler in 1903.

Mahler uses a variety of compositional strategies to resolve the tension between the individual and the course of events, first articulated at the opening of the *Kindertotenlieder*. The similarity between the outer songs turns on the depiction of nature and the human condition. The conflict between the positive image of sunshine and its contrast with a desperate inner reality (which remained unresolved in the first song) figures prominently in the last song. The dark and menacing colors of the storm image give way in the final stanza as the inner state of the human being triumphs over nature and the events of the world. With the recognition that the storm can no longer harm the children's eternal peace, the self finds emotional stability and the inner security first announced at the end of *Kindertotenlieder* no. 4, as the hope for a reunion in "yonder heights."

Kindertotenlieder nos. 2 through 4 express different temporal levels from the two framing songs, and therefore contrast with them in style, message, tonal character, and finally, orchestral color. In no. 2, the individual seems to revert to a time of remembrance in which the horrible events have not yet occurred. But the final lines leave no doubt that an inauspicious future lies ahead, making any sense of emotional security impossible:

Sieh' uns nur an, denn bald sind wir dir ferne!	Only look at us, for soon we will be far away from you!
Was dir nur Augen sind in diesen Tagen:	What to you are only eyes these days:
In künft'gen Nächten sind es dir nur Sterne.	Will for you be only stars in coming nights.

The harmony is fraught with suspensions, seventh chords, and especially ninth chords. The main theme, so clearly reminiscent of the theme from the Adagietto of the Fifth Symphony, evokes *Tristan und Isolde*. Despite the C-minor key signature, the tonality remains long undecided. The tonic chord is almost completely absent from the first thirteen measures, and even what follows may easily be interpreted as an evasion of the key. There are brief turns to C major (m. 15), D-flat minor (m. 25), D major (m. 41), and G minor (m. 49), but the tonal root remains essentially ambiguous until the final two measures. Harmonic tension and the nonarrival of the tonic—and therefore any reference point for the tonal development—become a compositional program that translates the openness and uncertainty conveyed by the text in exemplary ways.

The tonal relationships in *Kindertotenlieder* no. 3 are by comparison very secure. The basic key of C minor is never in question. Here the temporal sphere is that of memory, with the father of the deceased child recalling scenes from life: the mother enters by the door, her first glance falling upon the small daughter, or the child running to her room. Mahler's setting initially resembles a contrapuntal study in the style of Bach. A strictly diatonic counterpoint, progressing mainly in eighth notes, develops above the pizzicato bass of the cellos. During the summer of the song's composition, Mahler studied Bach intensively and was, as Natalie Bauer-Lechner reported, "deeply impressed by the composer."[9] As the image of the dead child emerges ("there, there, where your dear little face would be"), Mahler abruptly leaves the polyphonic mode, puncturing the music with chromaticisms and suspensions clearly linked to the main motive of the second song. The immersion into a transfigured world of remembrance cannot withstand the pain of the present moment, as the poignant closing line makes clear: "You, too quickly, too quickly extinguished gleam of joy in your father's cell." This phrase is performed "with an outpouring of sorrow," beginning on a high note f^1 and traversing two octaves lower (G) in the short span of eight measures. There is hardly a more powerful way to express the emotional drama of such an event. While *Kindertotenlieder* nos. 1 through 3 dealt with the merging of past and present (nos. 1 and 3) and of present and future (no. 2), in no. 4 all three temporal spheres coexist, with the future projecting into a transcendental afterlife. The division of temporal spheres is only obliterated in the final stanza of the last song, specifically through the consoling acceptance of the children's eternal rest.

The meaning of Rückert's moving and large-scale dirge cannot be reduced to a single message. Beneath the smooth and often quite virtuosic surface of the lyricism, he evokes a landscape of suffering, tragedy, and of a vulnerable childhood existence. The range of Rückert's confrontation with the death of children is expressed in the headings of the four major sections of the 1872 edition by Rückert's son Heinrich: "Song and Pain," "Sickness and Death," "Winter and Spring," and "Comfort and Transcendence." The character of Mahler's cycle is largely determined by his selection of texts from the last section, from which the texts for *Kindertotenlieder* nos. 1, 4, and 5 are taken. The two other texts (nos. 2 and 3) are from "Sickness and Death." But his choice of text, as well as the musical setting of the *Kindertotenlieder*, cannot finally be reduced either to a simple tragic and desperate examination of the experience of death, or to one that is comforting and transfiguring. Above all, it is the tension between both realms, the simultaneity of light and dark, that intensifies throughout the five poems and determines Mahler's cycle. Images of nature (such as the storm in song 5) become metaphors for deeply felt experiences. Even the abrupt disappearance of the storm—expressed by the sharp contrast of dark with high and light sonorities (m. 92, clarinet in low register, contrabassoon, horn in low register, timpani; and m. 93, piccolo, bells, harp, and cello harmonics)—refers to a symbolism of sound that in the ultimate vision of a music of angels reveals its distinctive characteristics.

The double meaning of "house" as the place of worldly, childlike comfort on the one hand (songs 3 and 4), and a transcendental, blissful existence (song 5) on the other, finds expression predominantly in the final section of song 5. The "lullaby," particularly beginning in m. 101, suggests security in a realm removed from all danger and threat. Since the eighteenth century, and especially in German-speaking areas, lullabies were written in the character of folk song. They were designed to be easy to comprehend, with regular (mostly eighth-note) phrase structures, simple vocal lines, and strophic form. It is therefore striking that Mahler's *Kindertotenlieder* only rarely uses symmetrical metric groups such as 4 + 4 meter. The closest he comes to such a grouping is in song 3, at the beginning, "When your dear mother comes in the door, and I turn my head, look at her," and at mm. 40–51, "When your dear mother comes in the door with her candle's glimmer, for me it is as always when you would enter with her, slip into the room behind her as usual!" Mahler quickly abandons such symmetry when the loss of the children turns into painful memory (mm. 23–33) and when he seeks to express psychological pain (mm. 55–64). "Folk song" thus becomes synonymous with a world of domestic comfort. That comfort is threatened at all times by impending loss. The "lullaby" at the closing of the cycle refers to the "homecoming into ultimate original trust"—as Hans Wollschläger has called it.[10]

A lullaby is invoked already in the third song, at the image of the paternal house. Once again, Mahler uses symmetrical phrase structures. Such balanced periodic structure (antecedent and consequent) is evident in particular at the lines, "Frightened by no storm, sheltered by God's hand, they are sleeping as though in their mother's house" (mm. 115–24), where it is further emphasized by the change in instrumentation. (The consequent lasts for altogether six measures, but its length is extended only by the repetition of the last line "wie in der Mutter Haus," mm. 123–124.)

The peaceful aura of the finality of heavenly comfort does not, however, go unchallenged. In the instrumental epilogue, the horn picks up the first phrase of the preceding vocal line (mm. 125–28). But Mahler proceeds to disrupt the metric equilibrium with the quintuple-meter consequent phrase (cello, mm. 129–33) and presents new thematic material. This section covertly refers to a brief instrumental interlude in song 3 (mm. 51–55, oboe and flute), which seemed to bridge the memory of the worldly sphere of idyllic family life—to be sung *innig* (with deep, genuine feeling)—with the articulation of the experienced pain at the irrevocable loss of a child.

Although the final song suggests a transcendent and comforting world of tranquility and heavenly peace, the musical structure of the epilogue makes clear the shadow of pain and loss that marks every measure of the *Kindertotenlieder* cycle. At the same time, however, Mahler refers to the first song by constructing the epilogue out of the quadruple- and quintuple-meter phrases that create yet another link (apart from the analogous tonal organization) between the framing songs of the cycle. Although the *Kindertotenlieder* cannot be reduced to the naïve perspective of a *per aspera ad astra,* they also are not without the prospect of what Kurt von Fischer has called an "open future."[11] In that future, pain and comfort are synthesized into a timeless existential experience shared by all human beings.

NOTES

1. Carlo A. Corsini and Pier Paolo Viazzo, *The Decline of Infant Mortality in Europe 1800–1950: Four National Case Studies* (Florence, 1993), p. 16.

2. Alma Mahler, *Gustav Mahler: Memories and Letters,* 4th ed., ed. Donald Mitchell and Knud Martner, trans. Basil Creighton (Seattle and London, 1990), p. 121.

3. Luise Rückert, "Aufzeichnungen zum Kindertod," in *Friedrich Rückert: Kindertotenlieder,* ed. Hans Wollschläger (Nördlingen, 1988), p. 571.

4. Rückert's son Heinrich published the *Kindertotenlieder* in 1872 but changed the author's sequence of the poems as well as details of orthography and punctation. The first complete critical edition was Hans Wollschläger's of 1988.

5. The *Deutsche Musenalmanach* was an annual anthology of mostly unpublished German lyric poems, founded in 1830 by Amadeus Wendt and edited from 1833 to 1839 by Gustav Schwab, Adalbert von Chamisso, and Franz von Gaudy. See Hans-Ulrich Wagner, "Klage, Trost und irre Lieder: Zur Poetik der Kindertotendichtung bei Friedrich Rückert und Joseph von Eichendorff," in *Gestörte Idylle,* ed. Max-Rainer Uhrig (Würzburg, 1995), pp. 21–22.

6. Philippe Ariès, *Geschichte des Todes* (Darmstadt, 1996), p. 785.

7. Reinhard Gerlach, *Strophen von Leben, Traum und Tod* (Wilhelmshaven, 1982), p. 84.

8. On the metaphysics of instrumental music, see Carl Dahlhaus, *The Idea of Absolute Music* (1978), trans. Roger Lustig (Chicago, 1991).

9. Conversation from summer 1901, in Natalie Bauer-Lechner, *Recollections of Gustav Mahler,* ed. and trans. Peter Franklin (Cambridge, Eng., 1980), p. 189.

10. Wollschläger, *Rückert: Kindertotenlieder,* p. 33.

11. Kurt von Fischer, *Bemerkungen zu Mahlers Liedern,* in *Gustav Mahler,* ed. Hermann Danuser, Wege der Forschung (Darmstadt, 1992), p. 81.

In Search of Lost Time:

Memory and Mahler's Broken Pastoral

Thomas Peattie

"My symphony will be something the world has never heard before! In it Nature herself acquires a voice and tells secrets so profound that they are perhaps glimpsed only in dreams!"[1] With this emphatic remark, Mahler demonstrated his attachment to the long-held idea of art as a mirror of Nature. In a letter written several months later to the Czech musicologist and critic Richard Batka, the breadth of this understanding is made clear. "I always feel it strange that when most people speak of 'Nature' what they mean is flowers, little birds, the scent of the pinewoods, etc. No one knows the god Dionysus, or Great Pan. Well: there you have a kind of program—i.e. a sample of how I compose. Always and everywhere it is the very sound of Nature (*Naturlaut*)!"[2]

Although both statements refer specifically to the Third Symphony, the view that they espouse has often been tied to Mahler's music in general. To be sure, the composer's scores contain numerous performance indications that refer not only to Nature in the broadest sense but as well to specific elements of the natural world.[3] But the musical content of the passages bearing these markings often brings into question the validity of Mahler's self-interpretation. The pastoral character that has been frequently identified by critics and audiences in connection with these and other passages is rarely presented as innocent and untroubled. These passages are generally fleeting, fragmentary, and in some cases seem to be disconnected entirely from the context in which they appear. Their instability is produced by interruption and the recollection of previously heard material in a compressed or distorted fashion, revealing a conception of the pastoral that is at its core fundamentally broken. The paradigmatic examples are the two posthorn episodes from the Scherzo of the Third Symphony. The musical processes that give rise to the sense of brokenness, in these passages as in much of Mahler's music, can be illuminated in relation to the concept of memory as a process of recollection.

Mahler's undermining of the pastoral is predicated on the existence of a clearly identifiable musical language. The musical language of the pastoral, which was already fully developed by the beginning of the seventeenth century, includes among its most prominent features the pedal point or drone supporting a simple melodic line.[4] Despite the relative stability of the pastoral as a musical *topos*, it was not always entirely innocent. In the eighteenth century its darker side is evident most notably in the music of Mozart.[5] In the nineteenth century an increased emphasis on the temporal dimension added a new layer of complexity. This is manifested most clearly in the works of Wagner, where repetition is employed as a means of suspending time. In the Prelude of *Das Rheingold* and the Forest Murmurs from Act II of *Siegfried* such suspension is employed to evoke specific aspects of the natural world.

While Mahler's music is clearly indebted to these varied conceptions of pastoral, by undermining a musical *topos* that had remained for centuries relatively stable he offers a critique of the pastoral's supposed innocence. This critical approach has an important historical precedent in the literary pastoral, which from its inception possessed an inherent critical tendency.[6] This is first manifested in the works of Theocritus (*Idylls*) and Virgil (*Eclogues*), where stylized language is employed to emphasize the artificial character of this early pastoral poetry. Although a critical element continued to play an important role in pastoral works, it is not until the nineteenth century that it receives its most powerful articulation in the antipastoral tradition. In the poetry of Matthew Arnold and William Blake the traditional idealization of nature is for the first time strongly undercut.[7]

Commentators have often ignored even the most striking moments where Mahler undercuts the traditional idealization of Nature. Many have heard the introduction to the First Symphony as an untroubled representation of Nature. On the surface the static character of this opening passage together with the marking "Like a sound of Nature (*Wie ein Naturlaut*) tends to support such an interpretation. Mahler himself was reported to have said that the curious sound created by the string harmonics evokes a nature image, the "shimmering and glimmering of the air."[8] And in a letter to the conductor Franz Schalk, Mahler stated unequivocally that this passage "is *not* music but the *sound of nature!*"[9] There is, however, good reason to question this interpretation.

As Mahler was generally meticulous about the accuracy of his annotations it is worth noting that in the published score the Naturlaut marking refers not to the introduction as a whole but rather to the descending fourths in the winds. The interval of a fourth, which generates both the exposition of the first movement and the opening of the second and third movements, is the fundamental building block of the symphony. In this understanding it seems entirely plausible that for Mahler these fourths represent the Naturlaut. If this is indeed the case the question that remains is how are the pedal point and in particular the harmonics to be interpreted? The most striking aspect of this pedal point is the sense of fragility created by the harmonics. Theodor W. Adorno describes the overall effect as "an unpleasant whistling sound like that emitted by old-fashioned steam engines." In Adorno's reading the concept of Naturlaut is brought into question by its opposite: the sound of the industrialized world.[10]

The relationship between the harmonics and the Naturlaut marking should be interpreted with care, not least because this marking was only added later. Almost a decade after the completion of the first version of the symphony in 1888, the marking first appears in the copyist's manuscript, used for the first published edition of the symphony.[11] This suggests that the term was most likely used for the first time in the Third Symphony, where it appears in the 1896 autograph at several points in the fourth movement: here, the piercing string harmonics enter *before* the Naturlaut marking, which refers only to the plaintive cry of the oboe. The separation of the harmonics from the Naturlaut brings them into sharp focus and presents them as a sonic opposite to the purity of the oboe's simple gesture. It is not coincidental that the text from Nietzsche's *Also sprach Zarathustra* (1883–1892), which Mahler set in this movement, refers not to untroubled Nature but rather to the sorrow of the world. In both cases the sound created by the harmonics sharply undercuts the idyllic character of these passages.

In Mahler's other symphonies the pastoral passages are more obviously undercut. The tranquility of the fleeting E major passage at the heart of the Scherzo in the Second Symphony (rehearsal numbers 40–43) never quite achieves the sense of repose toward which it seems to be striving. The relentless waves of sixteenth notes that dominate the Scherzo proper and define its *perpetuum mobile* character recede into the background in this passage, remaining a vague but nevertheless intrusive presence.[12] In the Sixth Symphony the fleeting pastoral passages are no longer restricted to a single movement. In the development section of the first movement (rehearsal numbers 21–25) and at several points in the finale (mm. 29–32, 237–48, 550–60 and 566–74) these passages are undercut by a distorted echo of the opening march that clouds their idyllic surface.

The most compelling example of Mahler's broken pastoral, however, can be found in the Scherzo of the Third Symphony. In the context of the movement as a whole the famous posthorn episodes are clearly set off as oases, and their fragmentary and transient nature is made clear at every turn. While their sense of detachment is, on the surface, a result of their contrast to the Scherzo material, this does not get to the core of their unusual temporal status. Even the elaborate transitional passages that join the Scherzo proper with the two posthorn episodes are unable to disguise these episodes, which when they arrive appear to be largely detached from the context in which they are found. In order to account for the unusual character of these episodes it is necessary to provide some context for their emergence.

Like many of Mahler's scherzos, the movement begins in a deceptively gentle and unassuming manner. The opening section is a relatively straightforward elaboration of one of his early *Wunderhorn* songs, "Ablösung im Sommer." This is followed by a newly composed section in $\frac{6}{8}$ meter, whose contrasting character intensifies the sense of perpetual motion already established at the beginning of the movement. After an extended reworking of the opening section, material from the contrasting $\frac{6}{8}$ section unsuccessfully attempts to reassert itself through a series of numbingly repetitive triplets in the timpani. This return is foiled when the triplet figure is reduced to a static pedal point and the sense of forward motion is brought to a halt. Then without warning a trumpet fanfare slices through the musical fabric (see Example 1a). The brightness of the sound makes it stand out in sharp relief against the fragmented orchestral texture. Shortly after the entrance of the fanfare

Example 1a. Third Symphony, Scherzo, mm. 225–54.

the triplet figure dissolves into a trill in the viola and clarinet, creating a hazy, unstable accompaniment over which it continues to sound.

When the fanfare enters a shudder runs through the music. Its opening gesture, comprising a dotted quarter note followed by two sixteenths, is jarring not only because of its timbre and its relationship to the established phrase structure, but also because it has no precedent in the movement. No sooner does the fanfare pierce the texture than it recedes into the background. Over the course of the next several measures a new figure attempts to rise (m. 230). Initially this figure remains buried and its struggle to emerge meets with little success. Gradually, however, the supporting orchestral texture in which it is embedded crumbles away and the trumpet emerges with increasing clarity. This is heightened by the development of this figure from a simple rhythmic gesture into a concise musical phrase. Despite the clear presentation of what is now a fully formed figure, there is a sense that the process set in motion by the fanfare remains incomplete. And then suddenly the posthorn enters, overlapping briefly with the trumpet and blurring the distinction between the transition and the passage that follows.

Shortly after the entrance of the posthorn, time seems to come to a standstill (Example 1b). The manner in which this is established, however, is decidedly ambiguous. When three measures after the entrance of the posthorn a sense of tranquility is attained, it is momentarily clouded by echoes of the fragmentary fanfarelike figures of the preceding transition as well as the emergence of a new such figure. It is out of these figures that a melodic line finally emerges at m. 263. At the moment this stylized and lilting melody arrives, the process set in motion by the original fanfare finally seems to have reached its goal. Through the combination of these two elements the tranquil and ultimately pastoral character of the episode is established.

Despite this elaborate transition, the first posthorn episode nevertheless seems out of place. Its radical sense of suspension and the stylized character of the posthorn itself impart a degree of unreality. In addition its temporary nature is emphasized by three interruptions of progressively greater intensity (at rehearsal numbers 15, 16, and 17). The latter two most forcefully shatter the static tranquility of this episode with a sudden return to the world of the Scherzo's *perpetuum mobile*. The intensity of this interruption is particularly pronounced at the close of the first episode. After the bass drum quietly recalls the funeral march from the first movement of the symphony, a trumpet fanfare shatters the calm and the music returns to the movement's opening tempo. This return to *Tempo I*, which at the opening is marked "without haste," is now marked "with mysterious haste!"

While the sense of detachment that characterizes this episode is achieved entirely through traditional compositional parameters, this is amplified in most modern performances by placing the posthorn offstage. It is, however, not at all clear that Mahler had such a placement in mind. In both the autograph and the published score Mahler distinguishes between the first episode, which is marked "as if from a far distance" (*Wie aus weiter Ferne*), and the second, which is marked "in the far distance" (*in weiter Entfernung* and *in weiter Ferne*). The sketch of the movement reveals that Mahler made this distinction at an early stage in the compositional process, most likely during the summer of 1895. Whereas the first episode bears no markings indicating distance, at the entrance of the fanfare that signals the transition to the second episode Mahler indicates that the trumpet should be placed offstage (*hinter der Szene*). (In the sketch the trumpet fanfare and what later became the posthorn have not yet been fully distinguished from each other.) Furthermore in the autograph Mahler makes a revealing correction. At m. 321 the marking "in the farthest distance" (*in weitester Ferne*) is

Example 1b. Third Symphony, Scherzo, first posthorn episode, mm. 255–67.

vigorously crossed out in blue pencil. That Mahler makes a distinction between these markings in the context of the Third Symphony is clear from the first movement where two prominent passages for full orchestra are marked "as if from a far distance" (rehearsal number 20) and "as if from the farthest distance" (rehearsal number 36 + 5 mm). Taken together, Mahler's subtle but clear distinctions and his correction in the autograph suggest that the composer intended only the second episode to be placed at a physical distance from the orchestra.

In addition to its general sense of detachment, the first episode is also distinguished by how the posthorn and the fanfare by which it is preceded emerges from, and then disappears into, the musical fabric. This suggests a connection with the process of recollection. One of the most important meditations on this topic can be found in the first volume of Marcel Proust's novel *In Search of Lost Time*. In *Swann's Way* (1913), Proust's narrator attempts to recall something from the past (his childhood in Combray) based on a vague sensation he feels upon tasting the crumbs of a petite madeleine soaked in tea.[13] What is significant about the passage is the elaborate process that the unexpected arrival of this sensation sets in motion.

When the narrator first tastes the spoonful of tea in which the crumbs of the petite madeleine have been soaked, he makes the following observation:

> No sooner had the warm liquid mixed with the crumbs touched my palate than a shiver ran through me and I stopped, intent upon the extraordinary thing that was happening to me. An exquisite pleasure had invaded my senses, something isolated, detached, with no suggestion of its origin.

Over the course of the next several paragraphs the narrator attempts to determine the source of this unexpected pleasure. He begins this process by taking a second and then a third mouthful of tea. Rather than bringing him closer to the source of the original sensation, this repeated action only serves to diminish its strength. He then begins to reflect more deeply on why these attempts do not meet with success.

> What an abyss of uncertainty, whenever the mind feels overtaken by itself; when it, the seeker, is at the same time the dark region through which it must go seeking and where all its equipment will avail it nothing. Seek? More than that: create. It is face to face with something which does not yet exist, which it alone can make actual, which it alone can bring into the light of day.

During the course of this self-examination, the narrator makes an important discovery. He realizes that the source of this sensation must not simply be sought after but rather that it must be created. With this newfound awareness he determines to achieve his aim in a careful and logical manner.

> And then for the second time I clear an empty space in front of it;
> I place in position before my mind's eye the still recent taste of that
> first mouthful, and I feel something start within me, something that
> leaves its resting-place and attempts to rise, something that has
> been anchored at a great depth; I do not know yet what it is, but
> I can feel it mounting slowly; I can measure the resistance, I can
> hear the echo of great spaces traversed.

The sudden awareness that something is trying to emerge is important for two reasons. First, it shows that the narrator's attempt to determine the source of this sensation is a gradual process that involves several well-defined stages, each involving a new discovery. And second, it undermines the narrator's own claim that these repeated attempts to discover the source of the original sensation serve only to diminish its strength. This awareness leads the narrator to another crucial discovery: "Undoubtedly what is thus palpitating in the depths of my being must be the image, the visual memory which, being linked to that taste, is trying to follow it into my conscious mind. But its struggles are too far off, too confused and chaotic." Indeed, this diminished sensation soon disappears entirely, forcing him to begin once again: "Ten times over I must essay the task, must lean down over the abyss." And then suddenly the memory returns. At the moment the narrator recognizes the taste as the crumbs of a petite madeleine soaked in lime-blossom tea served by his aunt Léonie, a vision of the Combray of his childhood rises up before him. What is striking about this vision is the way in which its artificial character and thus its status as a memory is emphasized. When the image of the gray house where as a child the narrator took his tea finally emerges, Proust describes it as rising up like a stage set (*vint comme un décor de théâtre*).

There are several points of intersection between the processes at work in Proust's madeleine episode and Mahler's first posthorn episode. Most important is that prior to the moment of recollection, a process is set in motion that is manifested as a struggle. In the madeleine episode a taste sensation creates a shiver in the narrator, compelling him to search for a memory obscured by time. At the beginning of the transition to the first posthorn episode the unexpected entrance of a trumpet fanfare creates a shudder in the music, which is followed by the gradual emergence of a fragmentary figure. What is particularly striking about this passage is that the figure is repeated several times as if an attempt were being made to reconstruct a lost melody. A further point of intersection occurs at the moment of recollection. When the past is recovered in the madeleine episode it is done so in a way that emphasizes the artificiality of its return. In the first posthorn episode the "memory," which can be understood in terms of both the episode's detached state and the stylized pastoral melody of the posthorn, possesses a similarly artificial character. In both cases the character of these moments seems to highlight their existence outside of the present.

The character of the first episode as well as the posthorn's stylized melody have a further analogue in *Swann's Way*. One of the novel's most important recurring motifs is a short phrase from a sonata for violin and piano by the composer Vinteuil. The phrase, which serves in the novel as a symbol of the love between Swann and Odette, is described by Proust with particular clarity in connection with a performance of the work by a pianist at the salon of the Verdurins.

> He would begin with the sustained tremolos of the violin part which for several bars were heard alone, filling the whole foreground; until suddenly they seemed to draw aside, and—as in those interiors by Pieter de Hooch which are deepened by the narrow frame of a half-opened door, in the far distance, of a different color, velvety with the radiance of some intervening light— the little phrase appeared, dancing, pastoral, interpolated, episodic, belonging to another world. It rippled past, simple and immortal, scattering on every side the bounties of its grace, with the same ineffable smile; but Swann thought that he could now discern in it some disenchantment. It seemed to be aware how vain, how hollow was the happiness to which it showed the way. In its airy grace there was the sense of something over and done with, like the mood of philosophic detachment which follows an outburst of vain regret.[14]

At the moment Vinteuil's "little phrase" appears, a distinct change occurs in the music. Like the first posthorn episode in Mahler's Third, an impression of distance is created without any spatial manipulation. Also of interest is the character of the phrase itself, which like the melody of the posthorn, is described as dancing and pastoral. In addition its otherworldly character closely resembles the sense of detached suspension possessed by the posthorn episode as a whole. The sense of disenchantment that Swann detects in Vinteuil's phrase is also significant. Its innocence and simplicity, which to Swann's ears rings false, is not unlike the banality that Adorno heard in the posthorn and that led him to dismiss it as kitsch.[15]

Mahler's posthorn may share the pastoral qualities and the philosophic detachment of Vinteuil's phrase, but from the perspective of musical process there is far more at stake. In addition to the detached quality of this fleeting and fragmentary episode, what ultimately distinguishes it from the context in which it is found is its retrospective cast. Although the question of whether music can evoke a sense of the past is itself vexing, it demands to be raised in this context. Carolyn Abbate has suggested that because music is, so to speak, tenseless, making claims for its ability to evoke the past is difficult.[16] As a result this ability has generally been acknowledged only in relation to quotations and certain forms of repetition. Yet as the first posthorn episode reveals, this potential seems to exist. What is significant about the way in which Mahler accomplishes this is that it has nothing to do with recollection in the traditional sense. When the posthorn first enters it simply echoes the fanfarelike figures from the preceding transitional passage. And when a melody finally emerges it does not appear to be a quotation either from earlier in the work or from an outside source. What creates the impression of a past moment is the arrival of a new state in which time comes to a standstill. Taken together with an understanding of this passage as a fleeting fragment that is detached from its original context, the first posthorn episode does not belong to the unfolding present but to another time: that of memory.

Of central importance in both the madeleine episode of Proust and the first posthorn episode of Mahler is the distinction that is made between the process by which a memory is recovered and the memory itself. One of the earliest theories of memory to make this distinction can be found in Aristotle's treatise *Parva Naturalia*. For Aristotle, memory (*mnemes*) is a state that belongs to the past while recollection (*anamensis*) is an active process that leads to this state. In relation to the latter, Aristotle suggests that "when a man is recollecting he infers that he has seen or heard or experienced something of the sort before, and the process is a kind of search."[17] In both Mahler and Proust a process is set in motion in which a struggle to recall something is made (recollection). And in both cases this leads in turn to the attainment of a new state (memory).

Although a sense of pastness is clearly evoked in the first posthorn episode it does not involve the recollection of previously heard material. It is not until the arrival of the second posthorn episode that such a return occurs. While the restatement of previously heard musical material is hardly a new idea, in the nineteenth century the manipulation of these returns gained increasing importance as a compositional strategy. The role that the concept of memory has to play in the analysis of such returns has been raised in connection with the music of Beethoven, Schubert, and Robert Schumann. Among the works in relation to which this question has been productively explored is Schumann's *Davidsbündlertänze,* op. 6 (1837). Toward the end of the eighth piece of Book Two, the Ländler from Book One makes an unexpected reappearance. Charles Rosen describes this moment as "a genuine return of the past—not a formal return, or a *da capo* or a recapitulation, but a memory."[18]

Although from a purely structural perspective the return of the Ländler is identical to its first appearance, there are a number of subtle changes. In addition to minor differences in phrasing, dynamics, and articulation, the tempo is marginally slower than the original (the quarter note equals 126, rather than 138, as before). If, as Rosen claims, this return can be understood as a memory, why does it differ from its original statement? Perhaps through these subtle changes Schumann is drawing attention to the fallibility of memory. Because a memory is only a recreation of something past, its accuracy is unavoidably affected by the context in which it is recalled. While the listener recognizes this moment as a return of the same music, Schumann nevertheless makes it clear that after a certain interval of time such a repetition cannot be identical.

In comparison with the return of the Ländler, the second posthorn episode represents a considerable distortion of the first. While the basic outline of this episode and the transition leading into it is similar to that of the first, it is radically truncated. The trumpet fanfare of the transition, which sent a shudder through the music, is here omitted entirely. Instead of emerging gradually from the musical fabric, the trumpet now completely dominates the shortened passage (see Example 2, mm. 466–83). The jarring insistence of its compressed repetitions, coupled with the dissonance of the supporting strings, seem to demand an immediate resolution. And then once again the posthorn enters. Like the return of the Ländler in Schumann's *Davidsbündlertänze,* the second posthorn episode is marked at a different tempo from the first. (The first episode is marked *Sehr gemächlich* and the second *Wieder sehr gemächlich, beinahe langsam.*) Despite the increase in tempo and the shorter length of this episode, it comes across as being more expansive than the first (see Example 2, mm. 482–93). This sense of expansiveness results from the deliberate drawing out of the posthorn melody and also because it is subject to only one real interruption. This general sense is further augmented by the placement of the posthorn at a physical distance from the rest of the orchestra. What in the first episode was only a general sense of disconnection becomes here a literal dislocation.

If these detached and fleeting episodes can be interpreted in connection with the concept of memory, the question that remains is what triggers these fragmentary associations. If, as in Adorno's interpretation, the *perpetuum mobile* of Mahler's scherzos are heard as an allegory of worldly bustle, it might be argued that it is this which triggers the fleeting pastoral escapes. While Mahler frequently expressed a general longing to withdraw from world he was also often specific in identifying the sources of his anxiety. One such source was the metropolis of which Mahler made clear his dislike. In a letter to Anna von Mildenberg, Mahler described a trip he made to a bell foundry on the outskirts of Berlin in the winter of 1895. "When I arrived in Zehlendorf (that is the name of the place) and tried to find the way amid pines and firs, all covered in snow, everything quite rural, with a pretty church gaily sparkling in the winter sun, I left my troubles behind, seeing how

Example 2. Third Symphony, Scherzo, second posthorn episode, mm. 466–93.

free and happy man becomes as soon as he leaves the unnatural, restless bustle of city life and returns to the tranquility of nature."[19]

Despite the enthusiastic tone of Mahler's letter, it also possesses an underlying note of melancholy. Writing from the perspective of the metropolis of Berlin, Mahler looks back on his journey to the bell foundry and reconstructs his experience as an idyllic escape. While Mahler often longed for such escapes, it is also clear that he craved metropolitan life. Like many of his contemporaries Mahler's attitude to the metropolis was an ambivalent one. If the broken pastoral does indeed reflect this ambivalence, the role that memory plays in its manifestation has much to offer further considerations of his music.

NOTES

I would like to thank the staff of the following libraries for their generous assistance: The Pierpont Morgan, New York; the New York Public Library for the Performing Arts; the music division of the Austrian National Library, Vienna, and the Beinecke Library, Yale University.

1. Mahler's letter of 18 July 1896, Steinbach am Attersee, to Anna von Mildenberg, in *Selected Letters of Gustav Mahler,* ed. Knud Martner, trans. Eithne Wilkins, Ernst Kaiser, and Bill Hopkins (London, 1979), p. 190. Herta Blaukopf suggests that the correct date of the letter may instead be June 29. See her edition, *Gustav Mahler Briefe* (Vienna, 1996), p. 188.

2. Mahler's letter of 18 [November] 1896, Hamburg, to Richard Batka. in *Selected Letters of Gustav Mahler,* pp. 197–98.

3. For example, in the introduction of the First Symphony the opening is marked "Like a sound of Nature," and the clarinet at m. 30 is marked "Imitating the sound of a cuckoo," and in the coda of the second movement from the Seventh Symphony the flute is marked "Like birdsong."

4. For a useful introduction to the basic elements of the musical pastoral, see Michael Beckerman, "Mozart's Pastoral," *Mozart-Jahrbuch* (1991): 93–102.

5. Peter Schleuning, *Die Sprache der Natur: Natur in der Musik des 18. Jahrhunderts* (Stuttgart, 1998), pp. 199–202.

6. Peter Marinelli, *Pastoral* (London, 1971), p. 12.

7. Terry Gifford, *Pastoral* (London, 1999), ch. 5, "The Anti-Pastoral Tradition," pp. 116–45.

8. Conversation from the 1900–1901 season, in Natalie Bauer-Lechner, *Recollections of Gustav Mahler,* ed. Peter Franklin, trans. Dika Newlin (Cambridge, Eng., 1980), p. 160.

9. Mahler's undated letter of February 1898 to Franz Schalk, in *Mahler's Unknown Letters,* ed. Herta Blaukopf, trans. Richard Stokes (Boston, 1987), p. 155.

10. Theodor W. Adorno, *Mahler: A Musical Physiognomy,* trans. Edmund Jephcott (Chicago, 1992), p. 4. For two readings that engage directly with Adorno's dialectical

interpretation of this passage, see Reinhold Brinkmann, "Vom Pfeifen und von alten Dampfmaschinen," in *Beiträge zur musikalischen Hermeneutik*, ed. Carl Dahlhaus (Regensburg, 1975), pp. 113–19, and Peter Franklin, "'. . . his fractures are the script of truth'—Adorno's Mahler," in *Mahler Studies*, ed. Stephen E. Hefling (Cambridge, Eng., 1997), pp. 271–94.

11. The copyist's manuscript (LI UE 375) is located in the Austrian National Library.

12. This contrast is brought out with particular clarity in Luciano Berio's reworking of this movement in his *Sinfonia* (1968).

13. The quotations that follow are from Marcel Proust, *Swann's Way*, trans. C. K. Scott Moncrieff and Terence Kilmartin, rev. D. J. Enright (New York, 1998), pp. 60–64.

14. Proust, *Swann's Way*, p. 308.

15. Adorno, *Mahler*, pp. 36–37.

16. Carolyn Abbate, *Unsung Voices: Opera and Musical Narrative in the Nineteenth Century* (Princeton, 1991), pp. 52–56.

17. In the section "On Memory and Recollection" from Aristotle's *Parva Naturalia*, trans. W. S. Hett, Loeb Classical Library 288 (Cambridge, Mass., 1936), p. 311.

18. Charles Rosen, *The Romantic Generation* (Cambridge, Mass., 1995), p. 233.

19. Mahler's letter of 8 December 1895 to Anna von Mildenberg, in *Selected Letters of Gustav Mahler*, pp. 170–71.

Aspects of Mahler's Late Style

STEPHEN E. HEFLING

Old age: the gradual withdrawal from appearance [*Erscheinung*].
—*Goethe*

. . . someone who says something familiar, but behind which his whole life stands, says something more and other than what he says.
—*Theodor W. Adorno*

"It is the grandest thing [*das Größte*] I have ever done" Mahler boasted to Willem Mengelberg about his Eighth Symphony, jubilantly comparing it to "the whole universe beginning to ring."[1] Yet within a year he would abandon such a grandiose manner of composition forever. His next completed work was heralded much more humbly: "I myself do not know how to express what the whole thing might be called. A beautiful time was granted me, and I believe it is the most personal thing [*das Persönlichste*] I have yet created." Thus he announced the completion of *Das Lied von der Erde* to Bruno Walter in September 1908.[2] With the abrupt turn from "the grandest" to "the most personal," Mahler established what has come to be regarded as his late style, at least since Paul Bekker's 1921 monograph on the Mahler symphonies.[3] His last compositions are "late works," as Adorno puts it, "in the most emphatic sense: they turn ascetic inwardness outwards."[4]

Mahler's creativity had long since become fused in a symbiotic union with his life. The late works are no exception; indeed, in the case of both *Das Lied von der Erde* and the incomplete Tenth, the personal "occasion" or "impulse" for composition (to use Mahler's terms) is more immediate and accessible than for either the Sixth or Seventh Symphonies. It is well known that the shattering personal events of 1907—the decision to leave the Vienna Opera for New York, death of a beloved child, and diagnosis of a heart-valve ailment—shook Mahler deeply; for the first time in a decade his summer holiday was unproductive. Although Alma Mahler's memoirs exaggerate the decline of Mahler's physical and mental health, recent efforts to correct the balance sometimes minimize the seriousness of his heart problem.[5] It had long been known that damaged heart valves were susceptible to malignant endocarditis—i. e., strings of microbes growing from the defective valves. This disease was invariably fatal prior to the discovery of antibiotics, as it proved to be for Mahler in the spring of 1911.[6]

Thus *Das Lied von der Erde*, in the words of Mahler's friend and long-time assistant conductor Bruno Walter, was a creation *sub specie mortis* (under the semblance of death): "death, toward whose mysteries his thought and perception had so often taken their flight, had suddenly come in sight."[7] Mahler was more aware than ever that the next work might well be his last. And he composed more rapidly than usual. No longer did he allow a work to occupy him for more than a single summer, as he had in writing his first seven symphonies. It now seems certain that *Das Lied von der Erde* and the Ninth Symphony were each the product of a single summer's work (1908 and 1909 respectively).[8] And the surviving materials for the incomplete Tenth Symphony suggest that, but for the crisis of Alma's affair with Walter Gropius plus the distractions of the Eighth Symphony premiere, Mahler might well have finished the Tenth in the summer of 1910. In short, if Mahler were to have a late style, the time for it was at hand, beginning in 1907.

Quite possibly Mahler himself recognized as much. He clearly envisioned his symphonies as an emerging, unified oeuvre, and his self-critical judgment was generally sound. Mahler was the first, for example, to recognize that his first four symphonies constitute a tetralogy, and that 1901 marked a crucial turning point in his creativity. In mid-July 1908, when he attempted to resume composing after the crises of the previous summer, Mahler had great difficulty getting down to work and made the poignant observation to Bruno Walter that "quite simply at a stroke I lost all the clarity and reassurance that I ever achieved; . . . I stood *vis-à-vis de rien* and now at the end of a life I must learn to walk and stand as a beginner."[9] This could almost be a paraphrase of Goethe, whose works Mahler read time and again: "To grow older means to enter upon a new occupation; all relationships change, and one must either entirely cease to act or consciously and deliberately take on a new role."[10]

Goethe was one of three artistic forebears Mahler revered most deeply who were also paragons of late style; Beethoven and Wagner were the other two. The late works of all three manifest an inward-looking maturity in an approach to art that seems at times mystical, occasionally outrageous, and sometimes sophisticatedly naïve, but always individualistic in ways that resonate with Goethe's maxim, "Old age: the gradual withdrawal from appearance."[11] It was just such a turning from appearance, through deafness, that Wagner had claimed to be an essential precondition for Beethoven's achievement of the sublime. And in his essay "Beethoven," which Mahler regarded as one the most profound writings on music, Wagner points specifically to the Quartet in C-sharp Minor, op. 131, as an analogy of a day in Beethoven's creative world. Mahler had become well versed in this music during his student days—he learned the sonatas through his own piano studies, and the quartets from the legendary performances by the Hellmesberger Quartet.[12] When Mahler first heard Wagner's last work, *Parsifal*, just months after the composer's death in 1883, he wrote his friend Fritz Löhr that he was "incapable of uttering a word. I knew that all that is greatest and most painful had dawned upon me, and that I would bear it within me, inviolate, throughout my life."[13] In the early twentieth century, the second part of Goethe's *Faust* had long been regarded as an icon of late style, the culmination of the poet's long career, and a focal point of European culture. Mahler had long wished to compose the final scene of *Faust*, yet only dared to do so in the conclusion of his Eighth Symphony. But the experiences of 1907 seemed to call for a new beginning.

Nor was this the first time that Mahler's compositional style was fundamentally transformed by intimations of death. In February 1901, after weeks of overwork, Mahler collapsed from a severe hemorrhoidal hemorrhage that made him believe his last hour had come. The following summer he marched his musical *Wunderhorn* persona to the gallows, as it were, in the song "Der Tamboursg'sell" and turned from the folkish, stereotypical poetic world of *Des Knaben Wunderhorn*, which had inspired both his songs and symphonies for over a decade, to the more intimate, introspective, individuated lyrics of Friedrich Rückert. Like "Der Tamboursg'sell," five of his Rückert lieder memorialize his near-brush with death: three of the *Kindertotenlieder*, "Um Mitternacht," and the most extraordinary song of the summer, "Ich bin der Welt abhanden gekommen," in which we find the strongest harbingers of Mahler's late style.[14]

Meditative withdrawal from the worldly tumult was a familiar theme to the orientalist Rückert, whose immersion in Eastern literature strongly influenced his own original poetry. For Mahler, however, it also resonated with the philosophy of Schopenhauer, which had deeply influenced him since his student days.[15] According to Schopenhauer it is essential to "still the wheel of Ixion," the perpetual cycle of striving and dissatisfaction that man brings upon himself through egocentric manifestation of the individual will. He acknowledges only two sources of relief from the vicious circle: the effect of grace occurring in Christian or Buddhist religion, and the temporary stilling of the will that comes about through dispassionate aesthetic contemplation of art. And in Schopenhauer's view, music is the highest of all arts because it "gives the innermost kernel of all form, or the heart of things."[16]

For his musical manifestation of being "lost to the world," Mahler drew upon the most common type of Eastern pentatonic scale (C-D-F-G-A plus permutations) both to blur the centrality and goal-orientation of traditional tonality and, somewhat paradoxically, to imbue the song with concentrated organic coherence such as he had previously achieved only in certain passages of the Fourth Symphony. The larger structure develops from a single motive—the pentatonic cell—in which is contained the germ of everything that is yet to be: this is a technique crucial to Mahler's late style, and one that anticipates the *Grundgestalten* (basic shapes) of Schoenberg's twelve-tone technique.[17] The subtle suppleness of line, delicacy of texture intermittently blurred by heterophony, orchestration bordering on chamber music, pentatonic exoticism, organic unification from cell to whole, and especially the very personal mode of utterance found in "Ich bin der Welt abhanden gekommen" become central aspects of *Das Lied von der Erde*, and of Mahler's late style overall.

Equally striking in "Ich bin der Welt" is Mahler's self-quotation of a particular musical topos that plays a significant role in his late style: music that is "dying away completely" (*gänzlich ersterbend*). The final stanza of the song draws directly upon the celestial close (rehearsal number 13, especially 13 mm. after it) of the slow movement in the Fourth Symphony—the ethereal passage that leads directly to the song-finale "Das himmlische Leben," the child's vision of paradise. In that slow movement (which both he and Richard Strauss regarded as the high point of the symphony),[18] Mahler achieves a new expressive intimacy by appropriating childhood memories of maternal love, death, and peaceful isolation. As his friend and confidante Natalie Bauer-Lechner reports his private commentary:

"A divinely serene and deeply sad melody runs throughout, at which you will both smile and weep."

He also said that it bore the countenance of St. Ursula (who is sung about in the "Heavenly Life" of the fourth movement). . .

At one point he also called the Andante the smile of St. Ursula, and said that in it there had hovered before him the face of his mother from childhood, with deep sadness, and as though smiling through tears; she suffered unendingly, yet always lovingly resolved and forgave everything.[19]

Mahler also likened the smile of the mother-saint to the expression of figures found on monuments in ancient churches: "they have the scarcely noticeable, peaceful smile of the slumbering, departed children of mankind."[20] He would later apply nearly the same imagery to "Ich bin der Welt abhanden gekommen," in which, according to Alma, Mahler had in mind "the monuments of the cardinals in Italy—where the bodies of the holy ones lie with folded hands in the churches."[21] The end of the Fourth's third movement is just such a moment, marked in the score "very sweetly and intimately," and notably, at the very end, "dying away completely."

Mahler had used the expression mark *gänzlich ersterbend* (dying away completely) only once before: at the close of "Urlicht," the *Wunderhorn* song immediately preceding the Last Judgment fresco of the Second Symphony's finale. He would use precisely that indication only once again: at the inconclusive ending of *Das Lied von der Erde*, after the singer has rapturously intoned "Ewig, ewig" (eternally) nine times. The dark counterpart to this moment of ecstatic dissolution, the conclusion of the Ninth Symphony, is marked "dying" twice on the last page of the score.[22] And the autograph orchestral draft of the Ninth's finale contains a number of private inscriptions that confirm his expressive intent: "O Beauty! Love!" *(O Schönheit! Liebe!,* m. 159), "Farewell" *(Lebt wol,* twice, mm. 162–67), "World!" *(Welt!,* m. 178), "Farewell!"*(Lebe wohl!,* mm. 180–82).[23]

Such moments of musical withdrawal may well reflect related experiences from his childhood, when Mahler would frequently remain motionless in one spot for hours on end, "lost to the world" in daydreaming, music, and later, literature. Both Bauer-Lechner and Alma relate his early memory of walking in the woods with his father; having forgotten something at home, the father told the boy to sit on a log until he returned. Gustav was completely forgotten until twilight, yet remained sitting motionless just as his father had ordered him, "his eyes peacefully lost in thought, without fear or astonishment," as Alma recalled. "And several hours had passed before evening fell."[24] While such dreaminess was one way of dodging childhood traumas, it also generated conflict—in reality, and probably in fantasy as well. Mahler told Bauer-Lechner that although he was tormented for his brooding and felt guilty about it, he later realized it had been essential to his spiritual development.[25] Psychoanalysts have suggested that such concentrated stillness as a way of avoiding conflict and fear of abandonment may provoke fantasies anticipating the stillness of death, and of return to the womb as the ultimate punishment; the flip side, however, is the craving to overcome fears of abandonment and death through womblike isolation that approaches claustrophilia, such as Mahler found in his secluded summer composing huts.[26] Alma Mahler, who learned *Das Lied von der Erde* from her husband at the keyboard, suggests that in it "with wondrous consequence his inner life returns to the visionary childhood scene in the woods. Is not his farewell [*Abschied*], the 'Song of the Earth,' the ripe fruit of that far-off melancholy contemplation, whose kernel may have come to life in the waiting boy?"[27]

The valedictory nature of *Das Lied von der Erde* is readily apparent, especially in its ending. And the earliest interpreters of Mahler's oeuvre were convinced that *Das Lied* also inspired the musical and spiritual world of his last completed work. According to Bruno Walter, "the title of the last song, "Der Abschied," could stand at the head of the Ninth."[28] Willem Mengelberg regarded the work as a "farewell from all that he loved—and from the world—! and from his art, his life, his music."[29] And Alban Berg, writing to his wife about the first movement, declared: "it is the expression of an unheard-of love for this earth, the longing to live in peace upon her, Nature, still to enjoy her utterly, even to her deepest depths—before Death comes. For it comes irresistibly. This entire movement is based upon a presentiment of death."[30] We also find hints of that presentiment in Mahler's letters and activities of 1909. "I am experiencing so infinitely much now (in the last eighteen months), I can hardly talk about it," he wrote to Bruno Walter about the period since the sorrowful summer of 1907: "How should I attempt to describe such a tremendous crisis? I see everything in such a new light—am so agitated; sometimes I wouldn't be surprised to find myself in a new body. (Like Faust in the last scene.) I am thirstier for life than ever, and find the 'habit of existence' sweeter than ever. These days of my life are in fact like the Sibylline Books."[31]

In the same letter, Mahler reveals "I cannot help thinking very often of Siegfried Lipiner," the poet-philosopher and influential mentor of his youth (whom Alma detested). "I would like to know whether he still thinks the same about death as he did 8 years ago, when he gave me the particulars of his so very remarkable views (at my somewhat importunate request—I was just convalescing from my hemorrhage)." The precise nature of Lipiner's views on mortality remain uncertain, but, as noted, the seeds of Mahler's late style were sown following his brush with death in 1901. Now in 1909, just months before he returned to Toblach to compose the symphony bearing the dreaded number 9 (the Ninth had been the last symphony for Beethoven, Bruckner and, it was then believed, Schubert), Mahler again wished to consult Lipiner.[32] Bruno Walter arranged the meeting, which took place shortly after Mahler's arrival in Austria in the spring of 1909.[33] That year Mahler also acquired a plot for a grave in the Grinzing cemetery, and in July the body of his elder daughter was transferred to the tomb that would ultimately be his as well.[34] Departure from life was clearly still in Mahler's thoughts as he approached the composition of the Ninth. Unlike *Das Lied von der Erde*, however, his last completed work does not dissolve in rapture, but simply stops on the threshold of being, "looking questioningly into uncertainty," as Adorno puts it,[35] *ersterbend*. The close of the Tenth Symphony also suggests departure without resolution, albeit in a very different mood.

*　*　*　*

Bringing symphonic works to quiet, slow, reflective, inconclusive endings entailed new approaches to overall structural planning and new treatments of basic musical language, especially time and tonality. Gone are the epic-heroic struggles that culminate in the affirmative breakthroughs and apotheosis-finales of the First, Second, Third, Fifth, and Eighth Symphonies; gone, too, is the Sixth's seemingly final shattering of heroic illusion. Each of the late symphonies embodies a constellation of movements different from any Mahler had previously undertaken, and the Adagio takes on extraordinary significance in all of them. All three close in slow tempo, and both the Ninth and the Tenth open with slow movements that are somewhat ambivalent in form and center upon a crisis that erupts approximately seven-tenths of the way through the movement (m. 314 in the Ninth, and m. 194 in the Tenth).

In *Das Lied von der Erde* Mahler inverts the Third Symphony's large binary scheme of one large and five shorter movements, the last of which he considered the "liberating resolution" of all the previous movements, which stills the Schopenhauerian wheel of Ixion.[36] He now positions the five shorter movements in the first *Abteilung*, making the slow finale—which lasts approximately as long as the first five movements combined—as it were, the liberating *dis*solution of the previous vignettes. The Third culminates in a broad, hymnic adagio that Mahler claimed could almost be entitled "What God tells me."[37] Yet whether the transition from this "Song of the Earth" is to eternal recurrence or a state of permanence, Mahler does not speculate. Spanning and transcending his unusual formal plan is an extraordinary fusion of two traditionally separate genres, song and symphony. Uniting them was a project that had occupied him intermittently since the time of the *Lieder eines fahrenden Gesellen* (*Songs of a Wayfarer*) and First Symphony (1885–1888), and it is arguable that the synthesis he achieved in *Das Lied* is his finest formal structure of any sort.

The Ninth Symphony, with its four-movement form, might on the surface seem the most traditional of the late works. Yet compared to Mahler's earlier symphonic worlds, each movement is relatively independent; no overarching symphonic drama compels the work to move through its cycle, very likely because the nature of the end is already known and not welcomed. Between its framing slow movements—a broad and nostalgic Andante comodo and a hymnic Adagio—are two extraordinary Mahlerian parodies, juxtaposed as never before in his oeuvre: the Ländler-waltz, and the virtuosically sarcastic Rondo-Burleske.

In the Tenth Symphony, the ordering of the five movements (which Mahler reconsidered more than once) is in certain respects closest to that of his Seventh. Cyclically related outer movements frame an interior arch structure in which the third movement is a shadowy, almost surrealistic piece *sui generis,* separating two other interludes that are broadly related. But here, too, the differences between the two symphonies are so marked as to suggest a conscious distortion. Whereas the cyclicism of the Seventh's outer movements is gratuitous to the point of irony, the return of the first-movement crisis in the finale of the Tenth is deadly serious; so, too, are the numerous recurrences of crucial phrases from its fleeting third-movement "Purgatorio" in both the fourth and fifth movements. And unlike the genial *Nachtmusik* movements of the Seventh, the second and fourth movements of the Tenth are both acridly parodistic—the first Scherzo comprising some of the most jagged, primitive-sounding music Mahler ever wrote, the second Scherzo a sardonic waltz inscribed by the composer: "The devil is dancing with me." Each of the formal plans Mahler adopted in his last three symphonic works is effective in its own context, yet each also presses the boundaries of the genre farther than anyone had previously.

Nearly the same may be said of tonal language in Mahler's late style. Tonality had always been the structural and symbolic manifestation of centrality for Mahler; so it remains in the late works, but that centrality is ever more frequently called into question. In *Das Lied von der Erde* a primary factor of tonal instability is of course the pentatonic scale formations that suffuse both melodies and harmonies in all movements of the work; whole-tone scales crop up as well. These exotic sounds magnify the quality of otherness in the poetry he selected, Hans Bethge's paraphrase-reworkings of translations of ancient Chinese poems. Mahler's pentatonicism not only diffuses tonal stability but also, as in "Ich bin der Welt abhanden gekommen," simultaneously manifests an underlying motivic coherence. In *Das Lied* this process reaches its apogee in the final "added sixth" sonority of "Der Abschied" (C-G-E-A), where for the first and final time Mahler does not resolve, but rather merges the tonal-poetic polarities of a symphonic world into its motivic substrate.

Strictly speaking, none of Mahler's music is atonal; triadic centers are always its structural pillars, and eventually the music resolves to one or another of them. But in his late works Mahler occasionally deploys pitch-class sets of the sort that would become standard vocabulary in the free atonal style of Schoenberg and his school. In an overall context of tonality, these expansions of traditional syntax typically yield a biting, anxious tone, as in several passages during the first movement of *Das Lied*, "Das Trinklied vom Jammer der Erde." Here an exceptionally cogent, perfectly balanced fusion of both sonata form and strophic procedure serves ironically as the highly rational framework for the bitter, half-drunken, nihilistic anxiety projected against it by the singer. Midway through the development section he rather wistfully observes that "The firmament is eternally blue, and the earth will long endure and blossom forth in spring" (rehearsal no. 31 +2mm). Then follows the acrid demand, "But you, O man, how long do you live?" In strophic manner, the musical gesture for these words is being heard for the third time in the song, and just as before, it culminates in pitch-class set 4Z-29—this time on the word *Du?* (rehearsal no. 35 +3mm).[38] What transpires next with the text—"Not a hundred years may you amuse yourself with all the rotten trash of this earth!" (rehearsal nos. 36–38)—is one of the two wildest passages of the movement, heavily laced with whole-tone and other sorts of atonal sonorities. In proper symphonic fashion the tonic of A minor returns at the recapitulation (rehearsal no. 39), but amidst screeching nonharmonic tones in the upper winds representing the howling of the monkey, a specter of death, on the gravestones. The perfunctory dominant preparation for this reprise is perhaps the shortest in all of symphonic literature: a single E, reinforced by the glockenspiel in the high register, brings the tonal focus back to its agitated A-minor centrality (rehearsal no. 39 -1m). Such music begins to approach the anguished utterances of Expressionism. To be sure, one could cite precedents: in the first two intertwined movements of the Fifth Symphony, music of shrieking intensity—"suddenly faster, passionately, wild" in the first movement (rehearsal no. 7) and "stormily agitated with greatest vehemence" in the opening of the second—is trapped between plodding refrains of a funeral march, calling to mind Karl Kraus's characterization of fin-de-siècle Vienna as "an isolation cell in which one was allowed to scream."[39] But neither in the Fifth nor elsewhere in earlier Mahler do we find the same degree of intensity in conjunction with the "inwardness turned outwards," to use Adorno's phrase, brought about by the musico-poetic situation allied with the immediate expressivity of the human voice.

In the fourth song of *Das Lied*, "Von der Schönheit," the idyllic commingling of tenderness, desire, and uncertainty in the character of the girl picking lotus blossoms is interrupted by the raw erotic power embodied in a band of lusty lads on horseback. The second orchestral interlude after their arrival (rehearsal no. 12 -3mm) projects the musical frenzy both linearly and vertically by a tonal mixture of A-flat and C minor that is virtually bitonal.[40] And in "Der Trunkene im Frühling," which closes the first *Abteilung* of *Das Lied*, the numerous lurching tonal shifts—especially A to B-flat in the "A" sections (e. g., mm. 1–5; rehearsal nos. 2–3; and from rehearsal no. 11 +2mm to rehearsal no. 12 +1m)—are used to evoke the reeling unsteadiness of drinking to the limits of endurance.

Tonality is pressed to extremes at various junctures in the Ninth and Tenth Symphonies as well. In the Ninth, for example, the penultimate gesture of collapse in the first movement (rehearsal no. 11) disintegrates into low-register sonorities that are genuinely atonal.[41] And the inner movements of the work are affectively linked by rising levels of ironic bitterness and distorted tonal syntax. In the second movement— a disorienting juxtaposition and parodying of a lumpish Ländler and a dapper waltz—the onset of the waltz "shocks through the reeling, overenergetic harmony of 'Der Trunkene im Frühling' and by its wild vulgarisms," in Adorno's words.[42] A passage such as mm. 96–102 (Example 1), although ultimately prolonging E major, seems inexplicable in conventional harmonic or contrapuntal terms.

Mahler's tour-de-force of syntactical stretching and contrapuntal complexity is the Ninth's Rondo-Burleske, the most riotously sardonic

Example 1. Ninth Symphony, second movement, mm. 96–102.

movement in all of his oeuvre: Mahler never ventured further into nihilism than here. The movement's underlying bitterness is clearly conveyed in its original dedication, subsequently suppressed: "To my brothers in Apollo."[43] As Christopher Lewis rightly observes, although the techniques Mahler deploys here are not altogether new, their intensification results in an extraordinary accumulation of surface dissonance, which contributes to the music's apparent modernity. Among Mahler's specific procedures are (1) superimposition of triads having different functions, and likewise of melodic strands implying different tonics; (2) the metric displacement of conventional harmonic and contrapuntal motions, which is related to the triadic and melodic superimposition just noted; (3) very fast changes of local triadic center; and (4) complex cross-relations.[44] As a result of such techniques, the clear articulations of tonal centricity marking the form of the movement function as framing devices—points of arrival and departure—that often exert only tangential influence upon what transpires between them.

Similar techniques are found in the sketches for the two Scherzos of the Tenth Symphony. The Tenth's opening Adagio is the most complete of the five movements, and its musical language prompts brief commentary here on two issues. The first is linearity. The linear dimension of music is crucial to late Mahler, and indeed sometimes gets the upper hand over harmonic functionality (as in the Rondo-Burleske). Through skillful voice leading Mahler is able to traverse extraordinary harmonic distances yet return quickly to the centerpoint—rather as though one's thoughts wandered into unforeseen reflections, only to revert to the present. Perhaps the most characteristic example of this is the main theme of the opening Adagio (mm. 16–24, and numerous recurrences),[45] which also exemplifies Mahler's penchant for wide-ranging melodies in the late works. During the course of the movement he varies almost endlessly the ways in which this rich music progresses linearly away from the tonic of F♯, only to return, and ultimately, to close there. (The essential technique is the same in the Ninth, both in the finale and, with significant modifications, in the first movement.)

The second issue raised by the Adagio is its shaping around the crisis point that erupts into the famous nine-note chord of mm. 204–208 (Example 2) which returns in the symphony's finale. The dissonant climax is a frequent feature in Mahler symphonies beginning with the "Todtenfeier" movement of the Second, but this is the least expected and most concentrated instance. Indeed, it is the most wrenchingly dissonant moment in all of Mahler. (Nor is that surprising, given this late Romantic's strong emotional investment in idealized love.) Yet characteristically, it is also based on impeccable musical logic. The principal

Example 2. Tenth Symphony, first movement, mm. 204–208.

tonal foci of both the first movement and the symphony as a whole are the third-related key centers of F-sharp (major) and B-flat (minor). The crisis chord consists of the dominant ninth of B-flat (f^2-a^2-c^3-$e\flat^3$-g^3) superimposed upon the (incomplete) dominant eleventh of F-sharp (C#-g#-b-d-f, plus doubling). The searing $a\natural^2$ that connects the repetitions of the chord can function linearly either as the leading tone to B-flat or as the lower neighbor to the third of F-sharp, the tonal center to which the heaped-up dissonances finally yield.[46]

Mahler's treatment of musical time in his late works is also novel. Perhaps most immediately apparent is his use of heterophony—dissynchronization of the music into blurred "indistinct unisons," already prominent in "Ich bin der Welt abhanden gekommen" of 1901—to impede the sense of traditional forward motion. This occurs topically in the first and second movements of *Das Lied*. And it becomes fundamental to the expressive import of "Der Abschied," where heterophony combines with a virtually endless recycling of ostinato-like foreground material and a general lack of tonal momentum to project the gradual yet inexorable dissolution of ordinary musical time and space. Nevertheless, "Der Abschied" remains focused in the immediate present, even as the present is slipping away. Elsewhere in *Das Lied*, and especially in the first movement of the Ninth, Mahler is able to evoke what Adorno so aptly terms "the splendor of immediate life reflected in the medium of memory."[47] The second song, "Der Einsame im Herbst," is based entirely on the fluid shifts of consciousness between the inexorable present course of autumn toward frozen winter, and recurring bittersweet recollections of a rich summer warmth never to be felt again. In the third and fourth songs the perspective shifts entirely to the past, in slightly wistful reminiscences of life stages gone by. Autumn is forgotten; these are songs of bright summer sunshine.

In the opening Andante of the Ninth Symphony, when the crisis arrives—a dissonant triple-forte transformation of the syncopated shards with which the movement hesitantly begins—it is as though the catastrophe "secretly . . . had always been known and nothing else were expected," to quote Adorno again.[48] Yet significantly, the high point occurs not, in classical fashion, at the moment of recapitulation, which would imply resolution of the conflict, but rather before it. The alternations between recollection and the present, passionate involvement and wistful detachment, culmination and collapse, determine the extraordinary formal and affective aspects of this movement, which although strongly shaped by the sonata principle, also manifests characteristics of double-variation and rondo formats. Mahler had experimented with formal hybridization in earlier first movements, but except for the first song of *Das Lied von der Erde*, never with the degree of outward impact through inward immediacy manifest in the Andante of the Ninth.

In addition to the bitterly ironic incongruities of "Der Trunkene im Frühling" and the Ninth's Rondo-Burleske, Mahler's late style manifests a milder, more subtle sort of irony that is nostalgic in nature, very much in contrast to the irony that pervades most of his other works.[49] The Andante of the Ninth frequently invokes it: how curious to ruminate with such intensity yet also tenderness upon what is already known from the outset. The gentle irony of conjuring up time past is also linked to the nature of the movement's thematic material. The main theme is heavily laden with reminiscences, as various writers have noted, to the "Lebewohl" Sonata of Beethoven, and to the closing of "Der Abschied" in *Das Lied von der Erde* ("Ewig, ewig" echoes in its emblematic $\hat{3}$–$\hat{2}$ gesture of stepwise descent). Moreover, this is a fairly old-fashioned theme for a symphonic work of 1909, and not far removed from nineteenth-century popular music in its simple shape and phrasing.[50] Indeed, in one of its numerous transformations it becomes a slow, four-beat paraphrase of a tune from Johann Strauss's waltz suite *Freuet Euch des Lebens* (Example 3), which Mahler probably

Example 3a. Johann Strauss (ii), *Freuet Euch des Lebens*, waltz 5, mm. 216–223, first violins.

Example 3b. Mahler, Ninth Symphony, first movement, mm. 148–51, first and second violins.

knew from his youth. It was composed for the inaugural ball on 15 January 1870 celebrating the new "Golden Hall" of the Gesellschaft der Musikfreunde in Vienna, to whom the waltz is dedicated.[51] The same building housed the Vienna Conservatory, where Mahler was a student in 1875–1878, and the Musikvereinsaal was where he had formerly conducted the Vienna Philharmonic, both as its titular head in 1898–1901, and in the special farewell performance of his Second Symphony that took place just before he left Vienna in 1907. At the second occurrence of this waltz variant (m. 269 ff.) Mahler marked in his draft score the private inscription "Oh days of youth! Vanished! Oh Love! Scattered!" (*O Jugendzeit! Entschwundene! O Liebe! Verwehte!*)[52] These are ironic moments, yet also poignant in their sweetness and intimacy; to my mind only Mahler, and in his late period, could deal effectively with such disparate polarities.

Another such instance occurs near the close of the finale of the Ninth. At the point where he writes "Lebt wol! Lebt wol!" in the draft score, Mahler incorporates into the music a slow-motion allusion to the fourth song of his *Kindertotenlieder*, "Oft denk' ich, sie sind nur ausgegangen" (Example 4). In the lied a feigned optimism would deny the tragedy of the children's death: "We'll go and fetch them up on the hills / In the sunshine! It's a beautiful day up on the hills!" But in the close of the Ninth, the meagerness of the quoted musical gesture and its gradual deterioration, underscored by a curious tonal instability, seem to tell a

Example 4a. *Kindertotenlieder*, "Oft denk' ich, sie sind nur ausgegangen," mm. 63–69.

Example 4b. Ninth Symphony, fourth movement, mm. 163–71.

different story: there is no further denial, and no further reminiscence.

In none of these late works does Mahler resolve such tensions and incongruities, as he would have done in earlier symphonies. Rather, just as in Friedrich Schlegel's incipient characterizations of irony, late Mahler tends to unfold thought and counterthought, self-creation and self-destruction—in short, dialectic, but without distinct teleology.[53]

And such is the case down to the last phrase of music in the Tenth Symphony. It is now widely known that, contrary to what she suggests in her memoirs, Alma did not break off her affair with Gropius and had no intention of doing so.[54] She continued her secret trysts with him even in Munich during September of 1910 while Mahler was rehearsing the premiere of his colossal Eighth Symphony, which bore the dedication "To my beloved wife Alma." The personal catastrophe surrounding the genesis of Mahler's last symphonic world became central to its nature. Not only do the agonizing inscriptions to Alma scattered in the manuscripts indicate this: the extant sketches contain strong hints that the first movement was originally conceived without its famous crisis passage.[55] In any case, this new symphony cannot have progressed very far during the period of approximately two weeks that Mahler had to work on it before he learned of Alma's liaison.[56] As so often in Mahler's oeuvre, personal experience once again became the impulse for composition.

Of the various sorts of ironic expression found in the Tenth, three instances involving self-quotation warrant special mention here. The second trio (mm. 165–245) of the rather gruff first Scherzo is a charming Ländler that directly recalls Mahler's 1892 *Wunderhorn* song, "Verlorene Müh," about a girl trying to win the affection of a lad. She offers a walk in the fields, a tasty snack, and finally her heart; and her line "Gelt ich soll—Gelt? Ich soll mein Herz dir schenke?" seems distinctly echoed in the Scherzo's trio. But he wants none of it and rejects her three times in a row. Ironically, of course, the tables had suddenly been turned on Mahler: he, a "lad" of fifty, was now being rejected.

That the brief perpetuum-mobile third movement, entitled "Purgatorio oder Inferno," grows out of another *Wunderhorn* song has long been recognized: "Das irdische Leben" is the tragic story of a hungry child begging its mother for bread. The child sings "Mother, ah, Mother, I'm hungry; give me bread or I'll die," to which she repeatedly answers "Just wait, just wait, my dear child," until at last the child is dead. As Freud made clear in their single four-hour consultation, Mahler's attachment to his mother had definitely come to rest upon Alma; in the "Purgatorio" movement, it would seem that she is the woman who refuses to nourish him.[57]

Two motives in the "Purgatorio" bear inscriptions, as shown in Example 5. The first is labeled "Tod! (Death!) and "Verk!," (now widely taken to be an abbreviation of *"Verkündigung"* or annunciation)—the annunciation of death, probably an allusion to the scene known as the *Todesverkündigung* in Wagner's *Die Walküre*.[58] The other, which occurs twice just a few bars after "Tod! Verk!" (Examples 5b and 5c), has two associated texts: *"Erbarmen!"* (Mercy! or Pity!), just below which Mahler writes "O Gott! O Gott! Warum hast du mich verlassen?" (O God, O God, why hast thou forsaken me? mm. 107–8), and "Dein Wille geschehe!" (Thy will be done! mm. 113–15).

The latter two inscriptions, of course, are phrases from the crucifixion and betrayal scenes in the New Testament, exactly as they read in Luther's German Bible.[59] Significantly, the "Tod! Verk!" and "Erbarmen! / Dein Wille geschehe!" motives influence a good deal of the thematic material in the following two movements of the Tenth, especially the finale, in contexts ranging from the pathetic to the parodic. But the larger irony concerns the addressee of these verbal and musical exclamations: Mahler was not formally religious or specifically Christian, particularly

Example 5a. Tenth Symphony, third movement (Purgatorio oder Inferno), mm. 92–95.

O Gott! O Gott! Warum hast du mich verlassen?

Example 5b. Tenth Symphony, third movement, mm. 107–109.

Example 5c. Tenth Symphony, third movement, mm. 113–115.

at this point in his life. Even more than divine mercy, he is invoking Alma's, just as he appeals to her at the very end of the Tenth.

"Für dich leben! Für dich sterben!/Almschi!" (To live for you! To die for you! / Almschi!) So reads the last page of the manuscript (see Figure 1):[60] "Whatever you do will be right," Alma reports Mahler's saying. "Make your decision."[61] She confessed to Gropius that "Gustav's love is so boundless—that my remaining with him—in spite of all that has happened—means life to him—and my leaving—will be death to him. . . . Gustav is like a sick, magnificent child."[62] The very last gesture of the Tenth, where Mahler wrote "Almschi!," is in fact a transformation of "Your will be done" from the "Purgatorio." But the passage just prior to that, inscribed "To live for you! To die for you!" harbors an extra-ordinary allusion (marked "[∗]" in Figure 1). This is one of the most immediate moments of the symphony, addressed directly to Alma. Yet like the close of the Ninth, with its clear and delicately ironic quotation from the *Kindertotenlieder*, the ending of the Tenth contains a bittersweet allusion to one of Mahler's earlier works: in key and melodic gesture (and in the Cooke performing version, also in instrumentation), it bears strong affinity to the conclusion of the second song in the *Lieder eines fahrenden Gesellen* (*Songs of a Wayfarer*), written after the breakup of Mahler's first serious love affair, twenty-five years before the Tenth Symphony (see Example 6). The singer poses the question: "Nun fängt auch mein Gluck wohl an?" (Now won't my happiness begin?) And then he answers it: "Nein, nein! Das, ich mein', mir nimmer, nimmer blühen kann!" (No, no! That, I believe, can never, never blossom for me!). Such invocation of memory in the immediacy of a most personal work is a hallmark of Mahler's late style. It is also his final gesture of musical irony, suggesting that, reluctantly, wistfully, Mahler had privately guessed how matters were likely to turn out with Alma.

Example 6. *Lieder eines fahrenden Gesellen*, no. 2. "Ging heut' morgens uber's Feld," mm. 114–127.

Example 6 continued

Example 6 continued

Figure 1. Mahler, Tenth Symphony, final page of manuscript.

NOTES

1. Letter of 15/16 August 1906, in *Selected Letters of Gustav Mahler*, ed. Knud Martner, trans. Eithne Wilkins, Ernst Kaiser, and Bill Hopkins (New York, 1979), p. 294, translation modified. The German texts of Mahler's letters will be found in *Gustav Mahler Briefe*, rev. and enl. ed., Herta Blaukopf (Vienna, 1982).

2. Ibid., p. 326, translation modified.

3. Paul Bekker, *Gustav Mahlers Sinfonien* (Berlin, 1921; rpt. Tutzing, 1969), pp. 315–16.

4. Theodor W. Adorno, *Mahler: A Musical Physiognomy*, trans. Edmund Jephcott (Chicago, 1992), p. 85. The epigraph to this essay is from p. 147.

5. See Henry-Louis de La Grange, *Gustav Mahler: Chronique d'une vie*, 3 vols. (Paris, 1979–84), vol. 3, pp. 80–90, 99–100, 478–79, 537–41, 754–63, *et passim*; for de La Grange's other writings related to this subject, see the bibliographies in his *Gustav Mahler*, vol. 1 (Garden City, 1973), and vols. 2 and 3 (Oxford, 1995–1999). Both Vera Micznik and Anthony Newcomb have subsequently claimed that Mahler's personal circumstances are not relevant to an interpretation of the Ninth Symphony; see Micznik, "The Farewell Story of Mahler's Ninth," *Nineteenth Century Music* 20 (1996): 144–66, and Newcomb, "Narrative Archetypes and Mahler's Ninth Symphony," in *Music and Text: Critical Inquiries*, ed. Steven Paul Scher (Cambridge, Eng., 1992), pp. 118–36, esp. p. 120.

6. For further information concerning Mahler's heart condition, see Hefling, *Gustav Mahler: Das Lied von der Erde* (Cambridge, Eng., 2000), pp. 29–31.

7. Bruno Walter, *Gustav Mahler* (Vienna, 1936), trans. James Galston (1941; rpt., New York, 1973), pp. 123 and 54.

8. On the chronology of these works see Hefling, *Gustav Mahler: Das Lied von der Erde*, pp. 31–32, 47, and "The Ninth Symphony," in *The Mahler Companion*, ed. Donald Mitchell and Andrew Nicholson (Oxford, 1999), p. 469. Another indication of Mahler's haste is that both the orchestral draft score and the autograph fair copy of the Ninth contain notably more revisions and corrections than comparable manuscripts for his earlier works. Mahler himself noted about the orchestral draft, "On account of the mad hurry and rush the score is quite mangled, and probably altogether illegible to unfamiliar eyes" (letter of August 1909 to Bruno Walter, in *Letters of Mahler*, ed. Martner, p. 341, translation modified).

9. Letter of 18 July 1908, in *Letters of Mahler*, ed. Martner, p. 324.

10. Johann Wolfgang von Goethe, "Maximen und Reflexionen," *Goethes Werke*, ed. Erich Trunz et al., vol. 12 (Hamburg, 1963), p. 542, no. 1328. For a useful overview of the notion of late style and its history, see Anthony Barone, "Richard Wagner's *Parsifal* and the Theory of Late Style," *Cambridge Opera Journal* 7 (1995): 55–72.

11. Goethe, "Maximen und Reflexionen," p. 470, no. 748.

12. See Guido Adler, *Gustav Mahler* (Vienna, 1916), trans. in Edward R. Reilly, *Gustav Mahler and Guido Adler: Records of a Friendship* (Cambridge, 1982), pp. 19 and 131, n. 7, as well as Fritz Löhr's annotations to Mahler's letters in *Letters of Mahler*, ed. Martner, pp. 392–93.

13. Letter of July 1883, in *Letters of Mahler*, ed. Martner, p. 73, translation modified.

14. Hefling, "The Rückert Lieder," in *The Mahler Companion*, pp. 338–64.

15. Alma Mahler reports that Mahler considered Schopenhauer and Wagner's "Beethoven" essay (derived from Schopenhauer) the most significant writings on the nature of music that he knew. *Letters of Mahler*, ed. Martner, p. 412, n.105.

16. Arthur Schopenhauer, *The World as Will and Representation*, 2 vols., trans. E. F. J. Payne (New York, 1966), vol. 1, p. 263.

17. Adorno, *Mahler*, p. 150. Schoenberg and his students were present for the first performances of Mahler's Rückert lieder in 1905, and after the second performance Mahler discussed the organic nature of the compositions with them; see Hans and Rosaleen Moldenhauer, *Anton von Webern: A Chronicle of His Life and Works* (New York, 1975), p. 75.

18. Conversation from 1901–1902 season, in Natalie Bauer-Lechner, *Recollections of Gustav Mahler*, trans. Dika Newlin, ed. Peter Franklin (Cambridge, Eng., 1980), p. 184.

19. Conversation from July 1900, in Bauer-Lechner, pp. 152–53, translation modified. The German text will be found in *Gustav Mahler in den Erinnerungen von Natalie Bauer-Lechner*, ed. Herbert Killian, with annotations by Knud Martner (Hamburg, 1984).

20. *Bruno Walter Briefe*, 1894–1962, ed. Lotte Walter Lindt (Frankfurt am Main, 1969), p. 52.

21. Alma Mahler, *Mein Leben* (Frankfurt am Main, 1960), p. 32.

22. While the Italian term *morendo* is common in his scores, Mahler uses the German *ersterbend* or *gänzlich ersterbend* only rarely, as also noted by Peter Andraschke, *Gustav Mahlers IX. Symphonie: Kompositionsprozeß und Analyse*, Beihefte zum Archiv für Musikwissenschaft, vol. 14 (Wiesbaden, 1981), p. 48.

23. Photofacsimiles of two of these pages are found in Donald Mitchell, ed., *Gustav Mahler: The World Listens* (Haarlem, 1995), pt. 4, p. 25. These exclamations of farewell distinctly echo the poetic line Mahler himself wrote for the rapturous midpoint climax of "Der Abschied": "O Beauty! O World drunken of eternal love-and-life!" *(O Schönheit, o ewigen Liebens, Lebens trunk'ne Welt!)*

24. Alma Mahler, *Gustav Mahler Briefe*, preface, trans. in *Selected Letters of Mahler*, ed. Martner, pp. 25–26. The reference to Bauer-Lechner is given in n. 25 below.

25. From the unpublished portion of Bauer-Lechner's diary housed at the Bibliothèque Gustav Mahler, Paris; cited in Henry-Louis de La Grange, *Mahler*, vol. 1 (Garden City, 1973), pp. 15–16.

26. Raymond Joly, "Gustav Mahler: Psychoanalytische Anmerkungen," in *Musik-Konzepte: Sonderband Gustav Mahler*, ed. Heinz-Klaus Metzger and Rainer Riehn (Munich, 1989), p. 200; Stuart Feder, "Gustav Mahler, Dying," *International Review of Psycho-Analysis* 5 (1978): 145.

27. Alma Mahler, preface to *Gustav Mahler Briefe*, in *Selected Letters of Mahler*, ed. Martner, p. 26, translation modified.

28. Walter, *Gustav Mahler*, trans. Galston, p. 124. See also Guido Adler, *Gustav Mahler*, trans. in Reilly, *Mahler and Adler*, p. 69.

29. These remarks from Mengelberg's conducting score are published in Andraschke, *Gustav Mahlers IX. Symphonie*, p. 81.

30. This letter has been dated autumn 1912 in Alban Berg, *Briefe an seine Frau*, ed. Franz Willnauer (Munich, 1965), p. 238, and *Letters to His Wife*, ed. and trans. Bernard Grun (New York, 1971), p. 147. But it appears to contain references to Mahler's orchestral draft score, the first three movements of which were given to Berg only in 1923. Constantin Floros, *Mahler: The Symphonies*, trans. Vernon Wicker (Portland, Ore., 1993), pp. 272, 274, and 341, n. 15; Erwin Ratz, preface to Mahler, *IX. Symphonie: Partiturentwurf der ersten drei Sätze, Faksimile nach der Handschrift* (Vienna, 1971), n.p.

31. Letter from the beginning of 1909 in *Selected Letters of Mahler*, ed. Martner, p. 329, translation modified. The Sibylline Books are the ancient Roman oracles consulted in time of crisis, which became more costly as their number decreased.

32. On Mahler's superstitious fear of composing a ninth symphony, see Alma Mahler, *Gustav Mahler: Memories and Letters*, trans. Basil Creighton, ed. Donald Mitchell and Knud Martner, 4th ed. (London, 1990), pp. 115, 139; Richard Specht, *Gustav Mahler* (Berlin, 1913), p. 355; Walter, *Gustav Mahler*, pp. 58–59; and William Ritter, "Le chant de la terre, de Gustave Mahler," *Gazette de Lausanne*, no. 326 (26 November 1911): 1ff.

33. Bruno Walter, *Theme and Variations: An Autobiography*, trans. James A. Galston (New York, 1946), p. 148; cf. also Mahler's letter to Alma of 13 June 1909, in her *Gustav Mahler: Memories and Letters*, p. 319.

34. Henry-Louis de La Grange, *Gustav Mahler: Chronique d'une vie*, vol. 3, pp. 83, 541.

35. Adorno, *Mahler*, p. 138.

36. Conversations from 4 July and early August 1896, in Bauer-Lechner, *Recollections*, pp. 64, 67; cf. Schopenhauer, *World as Will and Representation*, vol. 1, p. 196: "Thus the subject of willing is constantly lying on the revolving wheel of Ixion, is always drawing water in the sieve of the Danaids, and is the eternally thirsting Tantalus."

37. Letter of 1 July 1896, in *Selected Letters of Mahler*, ed. Martner, p. 188.

38. Pitch-class set 4Z-29 is one of two all-interval tetrachords; see Allen Forte, *The Structure of Atonal Music* (New Haven, 1973).

39. Cited in Alessandra Comini, *Gustav Klimt* (New York, 1975), p. 13.

40. There are related moments in Strauss's *Salome*, which Mahler had fought hard but unsuccessfully to premiere in Vienna; it is interesting to speculate whether Mahler's adoption of the technique may have been ironic.

41. Pitch-class sets 4–12 (m. 201) and 4–19 (m. 202).

42. Adorno, *Mahler*, p. 162.

43. Adler, *Gustav Mahler*, trans. in Reilly, *Mahler and Adler*, p. 54 (cf. also p. 59). The inscription is not found in any manuscript known today, but Adler's close acquaintance with Mahler and his circle plus his scrupulous attitude toward musical scholarship make it unlikely that the dedication is a fabrication.

44. Christopher Orlo Lewis, *Tonal Coherence in Mahler's Ninth Symphony* (Ann Arbor, 1984), ch. 4, esp. pp. 65–67; Hefling, "The Ninth Symphony," pp. 483–85.

45. Measure numbers are taken from Deryck Cooke et al., *Gustav Mahler: A Performing Version of the Draft for the Tenth Symphony*, 2d ed. (London, 1989).

46. Mahler originally drafted the conclusion of the Tenth in B-flat rather than F-sharp. Ibid., p. xxii.

47. Adorno, *Mahler*, p. 155.

48. Ibid., p. 160.

49. See *Gustav Mahler et l'ironie dans la culture viennoise au tournant du siècle: Actes du colloque de Montpellier 16–18 juillet 1996*, ed. André Castagné et al. (Castelnau-le-Lez: Climats, 2001), in particular Hefling, "Techniques of Irony in Mahler's Oeuvre," pp. 99–142.

50. Diether de la Motte, "Das komplizierte Einfache: Anmerkungen zum 1. Satz der 9. Sinfonie von Gustav Mahler," in *Gustav Mahler: Sinfonie und Wirklichkeit*, ed. Otto Kolleritsch (Graz, 1977), pp. 52–57.

51. Franz Grasberger and Lothar Knessl, *Hundert Jahre Goldener Saal: Das Haus der Gesellschaft der Musikfreunde am Karlsplatz* (Vienna, n. d.), pp. [14]–[17].

52. Mahler, *IX. Symphonie: Partiturentwurf*, p. I/29.

53. See the discussion in Ernst Behler, *Irony and the Discourse of Modernity* (Seattle, 1990), pp. 83–84.

54. Reginald Isaacs, *Gropius: An Illustrated Biography of the Creator of the Bauhaus* (Boston, 1991), pp. 33–37.

55. This point is also made by two essays in *The Mahler Companion*, Colin Matthews, "The Tenth Symphony," pp. 494–495, 503; and David Matthews, "Wagner, Lipiner, and the 'Purgatorio,'" pp. 512–514.

56. When he returned to Europe from New York that spring, Mahler was involved in the complex preparations for the premiere of the Eighth from the beginning of May through the end of June, and did not reach Toblach for his composing holiday until July 3. Meanwhile, since June 1 Alma had been taking a six-week cure at a spa where she met Gropius. July 7 was Mahler's fiftieth birthday, and innumerable congratulatory telegrams from notable people poured in, which he was obliged to answer; Alma, however, was not at home. Mahler's letters to her during this period suggest he did not get down to work until at least July 9. Alma returned to Toblach around July 15—we do not know exactly when because she destroyed much of their correspondence during this period. According to her account, about eight days later (i.e., ca. July 23) the famous love letter from Gropius "accidentally" addressed to Mahler arrived (see de La Grange, *Gustav Mahler: Chronique d'une vie*, vol. 3, ch. 57; Alma Mahler, *Gustav Mahler: Erinnerungen und Briefe* [Amsterdam, 1949], p. 215; and Henry-Louis de La Grange and Günther Weiss, eds., *Ein Gluck ohne Ruh': Die Briefe Gustav Mahlers an Alma* [Berlin, 1995], pp. 436–46). It is very unlikely that Mahler had done much, if any, preliminary work on the Tenth prior to July 1910: the finale of the Ninth Symphony is dated in the draft score 2 September 1909, and four days later Mahler ended his summer holiday and left Toblach for Vienna (see de La Grange and Weiss, eds., *Ein Gluck ohne Ruh'*, pp. 405–6).

57. De La Grange, "The Tenth Symphony: Purgatory or Catharsis?" in *Fragment or Completion? Proceedings of the Mahler X Symposium*, Utrecht 1986, ed. Paul Op de Coul (The Hague, 1991), pp. 162–63; and Eveline Nikkels, "Ist Mahlers Zehnte Symphonie ein Lied vom Tode?," ibid., pp. 168–71.

58. This reading was first suggested by the Viennese critic Julius Korngold following the first performance of the Adagio and *Purgatorio* in 1924; see de la Grange, *Gustav Mahler: Chronique d'une vie*, vol. 3, pp. 758, 761, n. 211, and 1238, as well as idem, "The Tenth Symphony," pp. 161–162, and David Matthews, "Wagner, Lipiner, and the 'Purgatorio,'" pp. 511–515. Other writers have suggested that "Tod! Verk!" is a reference to the Strauss tone poem *Tod und Verklärung* (*Death and Transfiguration*), but as de La Grange notes, Mahler was not fond of that work. He actually conducted it only twice (see Knud Martner, *Gustav Mahler im Konzertsaal* [Copenhagen, 1985], pp. 126 and 129).

59. Matthew 26:42, 27:46; Mark 15:34; Luke 22:42. There are hints of a certain messianic identification elsewhere in Mahler's comments about his own work, most notably regarding the Third Symphony. See Bauer-Lechner, *Recollections of Mahler*, pp. 61–62 [4 July 1896] as well as the passage entitled "Martyrdom," p. 54.

60. The inscriptions appear at the same points in the earlier B-flat major casting of the symphony's conclusion.

61. Alma Mahler, *Gustav Mahler: Memories and Letters*, p. 174.

62. Letter from Alma to Gropius (late July or August 1910), quoted in Isaacs, *Gropius*, p. 34.

PART III

MAHLER'S AMERICAN DEBUT

Mahler's American Debut:

The Reception of the Fourth and Fifth Symphonies,

1904–1906

Edited by Zoë Lang

Mahler was no stranger to American audiences when he accepted the conducting post at the Metropolitan Opera in 1907. His music had first been programmed three seasons earlier: the American premieres of the Fourth Symphony with the New York Symphony Orchestra under Walter Damrosch, and the Fifth Symphony with the Cincinnati Orchestra under Frank van der Stucken. The Boston Symphony Orchestra programmed the Fifth the following season, both at home and on its East Coast tour to Philadelphia and New York; the symphony was so well received that repeat performances were scheduled in Boston.

These early performances attracted considerable press coverage even beyond the daily newspapers. Lengthy preview articles discussed Mahler and the work that had been programmed; for example, Richard Aldrich's weekly article in the *New York Times Magazine* appeared on the day of the premiere of the Fourth Symphony. Mahler was also featured in the two main weekly periodicals: *Musical Courier,* which tended toward lengthy critical assessments of compositions, and *Musical America*, which provided an overview of concerts and soloists across the country. Mahler expressed great satisfaction at his early American reception. "The reviews have amazed me! . . . What a marvelous performance it must have been to make such a complicated structure clear to the audience, and to the inner self such demanding and unaccommodating patterns of sound."[1] Audiences and critics on the tour were not, however, as unanimously enthusiastic, and no other of his symphonies was performed until after the composer arrived in New York in December 1907. It is not surprising that Americans did not immediately import his difficult Sixth Symphony, which had mixed reports at its German premiere in May 1906, and the keen interest in new music may have discouraged performances of Mahler's earlier symphonies.

As a so-called modern composer, Mahler was often compared to Richard Strauss, who was well-known to American audiences. In 1885 the New York public had been introduced to Strauss through his Second Symphony.[2] In the season before the American premiere of Mahler's music, Strauss made his first trip to the United States, presenting festivals of his music in such cities as Philadelphia, Boston, and Washington, D.C. His seven-month tour began in New York with a concert of *Tod und Verklärung*, *Till Eulenspiegel*, *Also sprach Zarathustra*, *Don Quixote*, and *Ein Heldenleben*; the orchestral songs, sung by his wife Pauline de Ahna, were presented in another concert. The New York concerts included the American premiere of the *Symphonia domestica*, an event "so important that by comparison everything else pales into significance that has been done here in music since the first production of the Wagner 'Nibelungen' operas," the *Musical Courier* reported.[3] For American critics Strauss's visit proved that their own orchestras warranted the attention of leading composers. His impact was not soon forgotten, and contemporary music was scrutinized according to aesthetic criteria developed for his music—above all the categories of program music and absolute music.

Programs of Strauss and Mahler were but one facet of the broad German influence on American musical life in the late nineteenth and early twentieth centuries (and perhaps not the least part of German cultural imperialism).[4] Orchestra repertoire was mainly Austro-German, and German immigrants directed many of the leading performance institutions. The New York Symphony Society was founded in 1877 by Leopold Damrosch, a friend of Wagner and Liszt who had emigrated to the United States from Bremen in 1871. After his death in 1885, his son Walter (1862–1950) became music director. Walter Damrosch showed little interest in the orchestra until his ambitions to become the artistic director of the Metropolitan Opera and the music director of the New York Philharmonic failed in the spring of 1903. By this point, the New York Symphony Society had become a touring orchestra without an established series in New York. Damrosch renamed the organization the New York Symphony Orchestra and revived it, hiring fifty musicians for a subscription series of five concerts in 1903–1904, and instigating a successful series of Sunday afternoon concerts.[5] The Boston Symphony Orchestra also came under strong Austro-German influence. In the eyes of many critics at home, the orchestra became capable of playing challenging works only under the direction of the Austrian conductor Wilhelm Gericke (1845–1925). Health problems forced Gericke to resign in 1889, whereupon he returned to Vienna, but when the position reopened in 1898 he was reappointed director, and he remained with the orchestra until his retirement in 1906.

Unlike the Boston and New York orchestras, the Cincinnati Symphony Orchestra selected an American-born conductor as its first director, Frank van der Stucken (1858–1929). A Texan by birth, van der Stucken grew up in Antwerp beginning at age ten. Inspired by a visit to Bayreuth in 1876, he moved to Germany and studied with Grieg and others in Leipzig. His first post was at the municipal theater in Breslau in 1881. Liszt sponsored a concert of van der Stucken's music in Weimar in 1883. At age twenty-seven he returned to the United States as conductor of the Arion Society (a male chorus) in New York; he conducted the American premieres of Brahms's Third Symphony and Berlioz's *Les Troyens*. He also exported the music of American composers, such as Edward MacDowell and George Chadwick, to Europe. Van der Stucken was music director from the founding of the orchestra in 1895 until 1907, when difficulties with the musicians' union led to a two-year suspension of operations. He remained active in Cincinnati musical life, notably as the director of the May Festival in 1906–1912 and 1923–1927.[6]

The keen interest critics showed in Mahler's music may well have been heightened by rumors of his candidacy for directorship of the Boston Symphony Orchestra. At age thirty-three he had apparently been approached by Henry Higginson to succeed Arthur Nikisch at the end of his term (1889–1893), but had preferred to stay in Hamburg.[7] Now, on November 18, 1905, *Musical America* reported that Mahler was under consideration to lead the orchestra. It is unclear, however, whether this story was based on fact or was the product of a reporter's imagination. The speculation was not mentioned in the scholarly literature.

Mahler did not, however, conduct an American orchestra until after his appointment at the Metropolitan Opera, by which point his contract made such negotiations difficult. He ultimately secured permission to appear as a guest conductor of the New York Philharmonic Society and the New York Philharmonic.[8] Mahler was again formally contacted by Higginson in 1908. Though enthusiastic about the orchestra's playing, he declined and recommended his friend Willem Mengelberg.[9] The following selections reveal how Mahler was viewed in America prior to his acceptance of the position at the Metropolitan Opera.[10] Once he moved to New York, he was primarily considered a conductor; in these early reviews, however, we learn how critics viewed him as a composer.

Mahler's Fourth Symphony in New York

Walter Damrosch's New York Symphony Orchestra concerts often included works unknown to New Yorkers. His daring programs proved popular with audiences, and by the end of the decade Damrosch presented more concerts and won more critical acclaim than the rival New York Philharmonic. The November 6 opening of the 1904–1905 season well illustrates the bold programming. The concert began with a composition that had received its North American premiere the week before, in Chicago: Elgar's *In the South*. Three works from the standard repertoire followed: an aria from Gluck's *Alceste*, Liszt's *Hungarian Rhapsody* no. 4 in D, and Giovanni Battista Bassani's "Dormi bella" (an aria from the cantata *La Serenata*). The rest of the concert was devoted to the music of living composers: an unnamed work by Henri Duparc,[11] Strauss's *Cäcilie*, and the Fourth Symphony of a composer never before programmed in the United States, Gustav Mahler. Etta de Montjau was soloist.

Gustav Mahler—His Personality and His New Symphony

RICHARD ALDRICH

New York Times
November 6, 1904

Richard Aldrich (1863–1937) was one of the most celebrated American music critics of his generation. As an undergraduate at Harvard (class of 1885), he had reviewed concerts for *The Harvard Crimson*. Aldrich's first post as music critic was at the *Providence Journal*, during which time he also served as a private secretary to the United States Senator Nathan Dixon. Aldrich gave up his affiliation with politics to join the staff of the *New York Tribune* in 1891. From 1902 until his retirement in 1923 he was the lead critic at the *New York Times*, interrupted only by his service in the U.S. Army during the 1918–1919 concert season.[12] Aldrich assembled a significant book collection, later donated to his alma mater.

• • •

The name of Gustav Mahler is known on this side of the water chiefly as one of the most distinguished of the younger school of German conductors, as the present head of the Imperial Opera in Vienna. There he rules with an iron hand, bending prima donnas and first tenors to his will as though they were mere orchestral players; and there he has obtained some of the most remarkable results in performances which he has directed. Of recent years he has come to be seriously reckoned with as a composer, and some of his symphonies have made a striking impression where they have been performed. He is acclaimed in some quarters as the coming man, the one who is destined to work for the preservation of the older traditions against the movement that is all for "program" music, for symphonic pictures of persons, things, scenes, chapters of human life, and systems of philosophy. . . . None of his works has ever been performed in this country. At the first concert of the New York Orchestra, today, however, Mr. Walter Damrosch is to bring out Mahler's Fourth Symphony; it is a work that is likely to arouse great interest among music lovers, not only because of the singular reputation of its composer, but also because of its own qualities.

There are curious contradictions in Mahler's style as a composer. He is intimately familiar with all the modern resources of musical expression, with the refinements of orchestral technique as well as with the most daring of modern harmonic combinations and the manipulation of thematic material. With this goes an unmistakable predilection for the naive, the folk tune, the simplicity and sometimes the bareness of the archaic. This is in evidence in the much discussed Second Symphony; and it is still more so in the Fourth, to be played today, which is much more modest in its dimensions and in its style and content. Thus, for one thing, it has no part for trombones, though its scoring is extremely ingenious and goes into numberless subtleties of orchestral technique and unusual instrumental effects. The last movement is wholly given up to a soprano solo to the words of that old Bavarian folk song, "Der Himmel hängt voll Geigen"—"The heavens hang full of fiddles"—contained in the collection entitled *Des Knaben Wunderhorn*. For that collection, by the way, Mahler has shown a special fondness, and has written a large number of songs to verses derived from it. The naive and amusing little poem referred to tells of the joys of heaven, of its calm and quiet, and of the angelic life enjoyed there; of the dancing and singing that go on before the eyes of St. Peter; St. John leads the lamb to slaughter; St. Luke slaughters the ox; wine costs a penny, the angels bake the bread. Good vegetables and fruit are to be had for the asking; game runs through the streets. On fast days St. Peter, with his net, catches fish and St. Martha cooks. The music is far finer than any on earth, and 11,000 virgins dance, as St. Ursula smiles, and St. Cecilia and her companions are the court musicians.

There is a tune to which this ingenious piece of medieval imagining is traditionally sung, but Mahler has made no use of it in this symphony. Yet it seems clear that the whole work is, in a certain way, an expression of the time and place and atmosphere to which the verses take us back, although it is not in accordance with the composer's principles to set that forth as the raison d'être of this symphony. The first movement—marked in German "merrily, deliberate," and then "right leisurely"—has for its first theme a smoothly flowing, graceful, and ingratiating melody that might be Mozart's. The second theme does not depart far from the mood thus established, and is even simpler and more direct in its expression, having, in fact, all the character and the general feeling and outline of a German folk tune. It is also, curiously enough, reminiscent of a theme occurring in Beethoven's Italian *scena* "Ah Perfido" [op. 65], though the connection between that and a German folk tune is not close. Mahler's development of these themes, to which he has joined further brief bits of similar naive melody, is extremely ingenious, and is full of contrapuntal devices, employing the themes in fragments in which the different voices of the orchestra are treated with the utmost independence. The effect is of gaiety, often of boisterousness.

In the second movement, "in leisurely time," the character of folk music is kept up, though in quite a different mood, rather one of drastic—almost harsh—humor. Here Mahler has used a quite novel instrumental effect. There is a part for solo violin, tuned a tone higher than the normal violin, intended to gain a certain shrillness and penetrating quality; and to this instrument is allotted an angular and uncouth melody, which it is directed to play "wie ein Fidel" (like an old German fiddle), the primitive predecessor of the violin. It seems as if the composer, through his use of strange and uncomfortable intervals, wished in this to give the impression of some village fiddler monotonously sawing out of tune. Relief comes in the shape of a sweet and flowing melody with a charming lilt, decorated with little trills. This later takes on a form foreshadowing the theme to which, in the last movement, the solo soprano sings the verse of the poem, beginning "Angelic voices rejoice the senses."

The third movement, marked "quietly," is a set of variations on a broad and simple theme given out by the violas to the accompaniments of the cellos and double basses. The variations abound in new and unusual effects and surprises as well as in learned and adroit contrapuntal devices. A reminiscence of the Mozartish theme of the first movement is introduced.

In the last movement the soprano solo voice sings the delights of heaven in a long, free melody; drawn in broad lines, and following no regular formulas as to symmetry of structure, though certain of its melodic traits recur more than once. The orchestra has much more to do than to furnish an accompaniment to the voice in this movement. Its part is free and independent, sometimes like an improvisation. There are touches of realistic description, though scarcely more than touches, when the bleating of the lamb and the bellowing of the ox led forth to slaughter are suggested respectively in the oboes and contrabassoons.

For Mahler is no friend of the modern realistic conception of program music as it appears in the most extreme form in Strauss's later works. He has characterized his own idea of a program as diametrically opposed to that of Strauss; his music "comes to a program as to the ultimate ideal explanation of its meaning in language; with Strauss the program is a task set to be accomplished." He adds: "When I conceive a great musical picture I always arrive at the point where I must employ the "word" as the bearer of my musical idea . . . My experience with the last movement of my Second Symphony was such that I actually ransacked the literature of the world, up to the Bible, to find the expository 'word.'"

He has high appreciation of Strauss, his contemporary, one of those who generously called attention to his compositions when they were little known and little regarded. "Nobody should attribute to me the idea of considering myself his rival, as unfortunately has often happened," he writes. "Quite apart from the fact that if Strauss's success had not opened a path for me, I, with my works, would now be looked upon as a sort of monster. I consider it one of my greatest joys that I, with my colleagues, have found such a comrade in fighting and creating."

Even after he had demonstrated his talent Mahler arrived at recognition and success slowly. When Mr. Walter Damrosch was in Europe, in 1895, seeking opera singers for his company, he heard a performance of *Die Meistersinger* at the Hamburg Opera, conducted by Mahler. The orchestra was of very ordinary material, but the genius and force and temperament of the conductor resulted in a performance so fine that Mr. Damrosch on reaching his hotel sat down and penned Herr Mahler a note expressing his pleasure. Early the next morning came a reply by special messenger, in which Herr Mahler conveyed his appreciation of the visitor's praise, adding that it was the first time in his life that he had ever got a word of recognition from a colleague.

Yet Mahler was at that time thirty-five years old, and had been conductor at Hamburg for four years. He had previously occupied the same position at Pest, where he had infused a new life into the opera, and before that at Leipzig, where he was second in authority to Arthur Nikisch. In 1883 he was second conductor at Cassel, and in 1885 he worked with Angelo Neumann in Prague. He studied philosophy at the Vienna University and was a pupil, at the Conservatory, of Bruckner and Epstein. He reached the highest point in his career in 1897, when he succeeded Wilhelm Jahn as conductor of the Imperial Opera at Vienna and, for a time, was Hans Richter's successor at the head of the Vienna Philharmonic. Here his fame has blossomed and burgeoned, and here he has made himself felt as the autocratic and iron-handed conductor with whose will even the loftiest personages cannot interfere, as lofty personages connected with State-subventioned operas often try to do. As a man and as a conductor, though feared and in some quarters hated, Mahler is a strangely attractive personality. His achievements in composition are such that it is time his music was introduced to the attention of America's music lovers.

First Concert of Symphony Orchestra:
Elgar's New Overture and a Symphony by Mahler Heard

New York Times
November 7, 1904

The New York Symphony Orchestra, having met with success last season with a tentative series of Sunday afternoon concerts, begins this season another, in which half a dozen are announced. The first was given yesterday afternoon. These are not "popular" concerts in the ordinary sense. Mr. Damrosch, the conductor, apparently intends to give them a special interest for experienced listeners by bringing out in them new works of importance and old ones that are seldom heard. Yesterday he had two new works on the program—Sir Edward Elgar's new overture *In the South* and Gustav Mahler's Fourth Symphony—the latter being played for the first time in this country, being the first of any of the composer's works to be heard here, and the former following hard upon the first American production, which Mr. Thomas gave in Chicago on Saturday. There was also a new soprano, Mme. de Montjau, who made her debut.

Here was plenty of matter to engross the attention of the musical. The hall was fairly well filled. The orchestra has been considerably enlarged since last season, and there are many strange faces. It has apparently not quite "found itself" yet, and it must play with more smoothness, precision, and sonority. The strings seemed to lack solidity and brilliancy yesterday, and there was more or less vagueness as to the ensemble at times. All of which no doubt can be, and probably will be, remedied in the course of time. . . .

Mahler's symphony is a remarkably interesting composition, and clearly the work of a man of uncommon power, resource, and originality.

The ingenuous themes of the first two movements soon give place to a working out that is of the greatest subtlety and sophistication, and that sometimes almost reaches the bizarre. The orchestration is of extraordinary delicacy and finesse—trombones do not appear in the score—and abounds in effects that are ingenious and daring, sometimes charming, sometimes of a by no means obvious beauty. But through it all there is a singular persistence of the mood we have indicated.

All in all it is a work of power and mastery; but in one sense it is hard to take it seriously. It is "amusing," as painters sometimes speak of a dexterously and masterfully painted canvas as amusing. It is not easy to judge of the whole Mahler by this symphony, of the real artistic individuality of the man, because he so plainly set out to do something in a particular fashion, not entirely as an artistic expression of himself. Herr Mahler's bits of Mozart and of folk-song melody do not represent his own musical inspiration in any proper sense. But the symphony has an undeniable fascination, and prompts the desire to hear more of this man's music.

What Did It All Mean? The New York Symphony Presents Two Orchestral Novelties and Puzzles the Public

The Musical Courier
November 9, 1904

If the Elgar and Mahler works represent the best musical output of contemporary composers, then the output must be regarded as a sorry one indeed; and on the other hand, if aforesaid output is not the best, then why offer it to a sophisticated New York public, even on Sunday afternoons? The two works brought forward at the New York Symphony concert emphasized the remarkable melodic resource, the fertile imagination, and the transcendental genius in every direction of—Richard Strauss! The Mahler and Elgar works proved more potently than ever that the composer of *Ein Heldenleben* is in a class by himself, that he has dwarfed even the most serious of his musical contemporaries into relative insignificance, and that a single page of a Strauss score, yea, even a single measure from such a work as the *Symphonia domestica* or *Don Quixote* has in it more inspiration than the whole heap of Mahler and Elgar works piled lengthwise, with the five Mahler symphonies on top and Gerontius and The Apostles at the bottom . . .

It is not fair to the readers of *The Musical Courier* to take up their time with a detailed description of that musical monstrosity which masquerades under the title of Gustav Mahler's Fourth Symphony. There is nothing in the design, content, or execution of the work to impress the musician, except its grotesquerie; and there is not a moment in the whole score to save the lay listener from ineffable ennui. The only part of the symphony which is bearable is the soprano solo at the end, and that is not symphony. Beethoven also used a chorus in his Ninth, to be sure, but he has been sufficiently rebuked by the great composers who came after him. None of them employed the chorus except in "program" symphonies. And since we know the name of the poem which Beethoven used, the Ninth Symphony can be called "program" music by every law of logic and art. In the same manner Mahler's Fourth Symphony is "program" music, although he fights strenuously against the appellation. The following poem in the appended lumbering and amateurish translation was given the audience as a "program" for the symphony:

The Land of Cockaigne
(A Bavarian Folksong)

To us heav'n is yielding its pleasures:
Why heed then terrestrial treasures?
Earth's jars reach us never,
Contended forever
In quietude time passes by.
Our conduct, while truly seraphic,
With mirth holds voluminous traffic;
With singing and dancing
With skipping and prancing,
While Peter above lends an eye.

Turned loose by St. John the Lamb gambols
Naught dreaming of Herod's dark shambles
A spotless, an innocent
A guileless, an innocent
Creature we slew without dread.
For rue neither caring nor witting
St. Luke now the ox throat is slitting.
Our wines, which are many,
Cost never a penny,
And angels, sweet, bake all our bread.

Here practice we heavenly farming
Our harvests are almost alarming
Peas, pumpkins, potatoes

Beets, beans, and tomatoes—
Vast binfuls are lying in store.
Fine peaches, ripe plums and rare cherries,
Grapes, apples, sweet melons and berries.
Do rabbits or ven'son
Strike you as a ben'son?
They push through the kitchen's wide door.

Mayhap there's a day of strict fasting
O'er banquet and feast a pall casting
Then come the glad fishes
To fill the wide dishes
Which Peter so willingly sets.
Carps, herrings and eels without number
They crowd up the streams till they cumber
The heavenly fisherman's nets.

No music to mortal man given
Compares with that we have in heaven,
Cologne's maids are dancing
To measures entrancing,
St. Ursula beams with delight.
Caecilia and all her clansmen
Make excellent Royal Court Bandsmen,
At angelic voices
Our hearing rejoices;
They gladness unbounded invite.

The poem was translated by the music critic of the *New York Tribune*, and reflects neither the spirit nor the actual sense of the original. Has mortal man ever been offended by worse doggerel than

Our conduct, while truly seraphic,
With mirth holds voluminous traffic;

Or this classic line:

For rue neither caring nor witting
St. Luke now the ox-throat is slitting?

Why Mahler went to such poetical material for his inspiration will probably never be satisfactorily explained. Perhaps it was because Strauss set Nietzsche's *Zarathustra* in symphonic form. Mahler himself has said that he is the opposite of Richard Strauss. The proof could not have been better shown than in this Bavarian folk song symphony. It is very opposite indeed from anything and everything Strauss ever wrote, even when he sought inspiration in folklore, as in *Till Eulenspiegel* and *Feuersnot*. Of course Mahler orchestrates well, but so does every modern composer. Many of them have even been accused of orchestrating too well. The trick which Mahler uses in one episode, of tuning up the first violins in order to obtain a certain "color," has long ago been discounted by Strauss in *Heldenleben*, who tuned down his double basses below normal pitch. The inventor of the device was Paganini, who tuned up his violin in order to obtain brilliancy of pitch. No other remarkable "effect" was observed by the present reviewer in the Mahler orchestration, except a torturous and inexpressible tedium striving to make certain simple folk tunes serve as symphonic motives, and to wrest meanings from those monophonic lays which they never were meant to express and never could express.

A brochure written about Mahler by one of his friends calls the work "an inspired apotheosis of the folk tune symphonic form." The writer of the present review frankly admits that he does not know what to call the "Cockaigne" symphony. To him it was one hour or more of the most painful musical torture to which he has been compelled to submit in three years—in fact ever since he heard the same work in Berlin conducted by Richard Strauss. If Mahler sets to music "slit ox-throats," "ven'son," "ripe plums," "eels," "herrings" and other loathsome delicacies, what logical objection can anyone have to the Strauss plan of illustrating in symphonic form a day in his own household? At least he has seen his own household, while Mahler certainly has never seen heaven. If the "Cockaigne" symphony is really a truthful representation of that delectable place, then by all means give this scribe the other department. He likes Hubbard squash, oyster plant and chicken pot-pie, and they do not appear on Mahler's "Cockaigne" menu. . . . A large audience applauded the singer and the Liszt number but seemed pained at the rest of the program.

The American Premiere
of Mahler's Fifth Symphony

Frank van der Stucken decided to program Mahler's Fifth Symphony in the very same season of its world premiere, 1904–1905. It was a risky decision, but one characteristic of the music director at the Cincinnati Symphony Orchestra. The American premiere of Mahler's Fifth at the March 24–25 concerts would be preceded by Adolf Henselt's F Minor Concerto for Piano (with Madame Bloomfield Zeisler) and Wagner's *Kaisermarsch*.

The Fifth Symphony had also been heard in Prague (March 2) and several times in Germany (Dresden, January 27; Berlin, February 20; and Hamburg, March 13), but it was the Cologne premiere, on October 18, 1904, that caught the eye of the Cincinnati program-annotator. Perhaps not surprisingly, Emma L. Roedter painted a rosy picture of the public's response, while accurately reporting the critics' mixed reviews. She quoted at length one of the few entirely positive reports, that of the Munich critic, Rudolf Kastner. The concluding paragraph of his review, from which she paraphrased, discloses the purpose of the critic's defense: "I want to state emphatically that the public success of the symphony was very strong after the individual movements, and spontaneously exploded after the finale. There were lively ovations for Mahler; he had fired up the Gürzenich Orchestra, which was sublime beyond all praise. A few critical gentlemen used the attempts at hissing on the part of several vituperators to proclaim a half failure, but they were thoroughly disproved by the audience's breathless silence after the final sounds of the powerful second movement ended, proving better than could thundering applause that the masses understood genius instinctively, even if not consciously."[13]

It is hard to find corroboration for this report's claim that all movements were warmly received, even among local critics who were enthusiastic about the new symphony. Hermann Kipper witnessed "quite strong opposition" after the first two movements; and after the fourth, "the listeners were so surprised that they forgot themselves completely and applauded"; and "at the end, the success was undeniable."[14] Another critic likewise perceived a "somewhat cold" response to the first movements and "great approval" after the last two.[15] Paul Hiller, perhaps with his own biases, claimed that the entire symphony met a "merely weak applause, and not without opposition."[16]

Program Notes, Cincinnati Symphony Orchestra
Concert of March 24 & March 25, 1905

EMMA L. ROEDTER

Completed in the spring of 1903, this Symphony had its premiere at a Gürzenich concert in Cologne, October 18, 1904, under the direction of the composer. As to the merits of the work, opinions are widely divergent. The leading Frankfurt critic considers it "the most extreme music making" which moderns have been asked to listen to. The musical judge of Munich writes: "After the second movement, a few moments of almost breathless silence prevailed, which proved more potently than rousing applause, that the public instinctively felt the presence of genius." One critic made the few attempts at hissing the basis of his report of a fiasco, while another puts on record most emphatically that after the finale, Mahler was honored with a lively ovation. Thus, it will be observed, Mahler is meeting with the opposition which usually falls to the share of innovators.

Mahler allowed himself formerly to be misled by the attractions of program music and, it is said, composed his first four symphonies under this influence; yet, he has always shown himself to be a musician of glowing fantasy and dazzling intellect. His new work, the symphony at hand, is the expression of a powerful and rich temperament. In style and technique it is in the mode of absolute music and consists of five movements, divided into three parts, according to the logical sequence of ideas existing between the first and second and the fourth and fifth movements. Without constructing a "program" for the work, it may be regarded as (I) the plaint of one who has not realized his aspirations and in his disillusionment, stands at the verge of desperation; the harmless play and life of nature reconciles him to his lot (III–IV) and he returns to his life-work, which he resumes (V) with willingness, insight, and renewed strength, finally reaching heights before unattainable. Further than this, it would be useless to attempt to catalogue its meanings. . . . Mahler studied composition under the celebrated Anton Bruckner; his latest published work, the symphony just performed, proves him to be one of the most gifted of living musicians.

Boston Symphony Orchestra

Upon taking direction of the orchestra in 1884, Gericke initially met a negative public reaction to his programming. Audiences found the selections overbearing and "too heavy" in the preponderance of late nineteenth-century German repertoire like Brahms and Bruckner. Gericke persisted, and eventually the Boston audiences acquired a taste for lengthy and complicated symphonic music, including Mahler's. Indeed, when he resumed directorship of the orchestra in 1898, Gericke faced criticism for programming only familiar compositions. His decision to conduct the latest symphony of a fellow Viennese during his own final season reflects his broader orientation to new music by this point. At its premiere on February 2–3, 1906, Mahler's Fifth was preceded by Beethoven's *Egmont* Overture and Schumann's Piano Concerto (with Harold Bauer). The symphony was repeated on February 23 and 24. By the time he retired, Gericke had received wide recognition for programming modern music to great critical success.[17]

Gustav Mahler: The Composer Whom Boston First Hears This Week

AUGUST SPANUTH

Boston Evening Transcript
January 31, 1906

Trained as a pianist at the Frankfurt Conservatory, August Spanuth (1857–1920) moved to Chicago in 1886 to teach at a conservatory. Beginning in 1893 he also was a music critic for the German language *New Yorker Staats-Zeitung*. In 1906 Spanuth returned to Germany, where he held a professorship at the Stern Conservatory in Berlin and edited the weekly journal, *Die Signale für die musikalische Welt*. He also prepared piano arrangements and assembled biographical material for editions of music by Liszt and Adolf Jensen, a late Romantic composer who specialized in Lieder and piano works. In his review of Mahler's Fifth Symphony, Spanuth emphasized the integrity of formal structure over the originality of thematic material well before Paul Bekker made the very same argument in his 1921 book, *Mahlers Sinfonien* of 1921. Spanuth also predated Theodor Adorno's famous reference to the physiognomy of Mahler's music in this article.

• • •

At the age of forty-five and after a long period of strenuous activity as conductor and composer, Gustav Mahler has not yet been accorded a

definite valuation of his artistic merits on the part of the public and critics. While nobody dares speak slightingly of him, comparatively few are
ready to award him an exalted position among contemporary composers;
and many of those who are inclined to do so invite suspicion by their passionate zeal. They seem to be victims of one of the worst idiosyncrasies
of modern musical warfare, to extol their own idol by abusing those of
others. To see Mahler complacently sail his own steady course between
the turbulent waves of over- and underrating criticism is indeed a
remarkably interesting sight. It is also very creditable to the man.

Mahler seems almost immune to criticism. Even when abused he
refuses to enter a protest. He answers critics not by violent resentment
but by letting the plain facts speak for themselves. A few years ago he
produced Hugo Wolf's opera *Der Corregidor* at the Vienna Opera House,
in his own version, which in some respects differs considerably from the
original. Some of the Vienna critics were furious, and the consensus of
opinion seemed to be that the success would have been infinitely greater,
had the opera been produced as written by the composer. Thereupon
Mahler calmly rehearsed the original version, and after its first performance had the satisfaction that the critics admitted their mistake and
asked urgently for the restitution of the Mahler arrangement.

As a composer he affects a similar attitude. When asked, some time
ago, whether he would not like to come to America and conduct a sort
of Mahler festival, after the example of the Richard Strauss festival, he
replied: "Why should I? If I should absent myself from my post of duty
during the season, my singers would ask the same privilege, and that
I cannot grant. Furthermore, whenever one of my symphonies is played
before a new audience, failure is a foregone conclusion." And he said
this without any apparent bitterness. He seems to have inherited the
equanimity of Liszt, who used to appease the ardor of his propagan-
dists with the philosophical remark: "I can wait."[18]

In spite of Mahler's commanding position as director and conductor of the Vienna Imperial Opera House, his symphonies were ridiculed
by the critics and declined by the public when played for the first time
in the Austrian capital. But within the last few years the same symphonies have had the most flattering reception in the same concert hall
and from the same public. Mahler and his works were the same, but
the public had changed. Even some of the most conservative critics in
Austria and Germany now show hopeful signs of impartiality towards
the "crazy" Mahler and seem to be about to admit the honesty of his
artistic purpose. In New York, where new orchestral compositions as a
rule are played by one orchestra or the other almost instantly after they
have been published, Mahler the composer remained an unknown

quantity until Nov. 7, 1904, when Walter Damrosch conducted his Fourth Symphony at a Sunday afternoon concert of the New York Symphony Orchestra. Next Friday and Saturday, here in Boston, we shall hear a symphony by him for the first time.

It is difficult to define Mahler's position among the composers of our day, and all the more so because of the very nature of modern music in general. Although Mahler is an opera conductor par excellence, his creative ability does not gravitate towards theatrical composition, but towards orchestral music; hence the problem, or rather the problems, offered by Richard Wagner's music dramas do not concern us here, at least not directly. The concert room is Mahler's battlefield, and the question arises: Where does he stand in the contest of absolute music against program music? Some commentators have essayed to make him the very antithesis of Richard Strauss, but there is every reason to believe that the composer himself does not agree with this conception. It is true, Mahler does not write "symphonic poems," or "tone poems," but symphonies. It is also true that he has frequently refused to give detailed programs to his orchestral writings, though in this respect he has not been consistent. On the other hand the single movements of his symphonies seldom offer more than a faint and loose resemblance to the genuine symphonic forms, and their construction is in most cases dictated by an underlying, though not always definite program. There are instances where his poetic inspiration coincides with the traditional form, chiefly when he is bent on painting a mere mood picture. But he never seems to sacrifice a particle of his poetic imagination to the demands of musical formalism. Furthermore, he is by no means adverse to giving hints as to his programs in order to guide the receptive faculty of the hearer, but he frankly abominates the attempt to prescribe pedantically the route which the listener's fancy has to travel while listening to his compositions. He does not wish to preoccupy the hearer's mind with a detailed program. He prefers a naive public which he wants to convince through the power of his musical expression rather than through circumstantial explanation of what that music would convey. This does not imply that Mahler is satisfied to write music of less definite meaning than the adherents of the real program music, but the fact that he introduces human voices in some of his symphonies, in the form of choruses and soloists, leads one to believe that he cannot always find adequate musical expression in absolute music for his poetic inspiration.

If that is so, no lack of technical skill is the cause; in that respect Mahler is second to none. Whether he reaches in his fancy the boundaries of mere musical expression sooner than, for instance, does Strauss, is a very problematic question. At any rate, he does not seem to resort to the human voice because the source of his instrumental expression runs dry, but because he sees the chance of a climax in this very change and judges it to be entirely appropriate. It would be folly to assert that Mahler conceived this idea independently of Beethoven's example, for that would have been impossible; but his own explanations, in a letter to Dr. Arthur Seidl, clear him from the suspicion that he simply aped the earlier composer's Ninth Symphony. He writes: "You are right in saying that my music arrives at a program finally as a last ideal translation into words, while with Strauss the program is a given matter from the beginning. With this you touch the great riddle of our time and confront us with the 'aut-aut.' When I conceive a great tone picture I always arrive at the point where I need the 'word' to carry my musical idea. Beethoven in his Ninth must have had a similar experience, only that his time did not furnish him with adequate material, for, after all, Schiller's poem was not capable of embracing all the sublimity brooding in Beethoven's mind. Concerning my second symphony I had actually searched the literature of the world down to the Bible to find the releasing word. The way in which I received the inspiration is strongly significant of the nature of artistic impulses. For a long time I had contemplated letting the chorus take part in the last movement, but being afraid it would be taken for a superficial imitation of Beethoven I gave up the idea time and time again. Just then it happened that Bülow died, and I was present at the obsequies in Hamburg. Thinking constantly of the deceased, I was just in the mood of the composition I was to write. Suddenly the choir started singing Klopstock's choral, 'Aufersteh'n' (You Shall Rise Again). It struck me like lightning and everything was standing clear and distinct before my soul. It is this 'lightening' for which the creating artist waits—this is 'holy conception.' I had to translate into music what I had lived through in that moment. But how could I have had this experience, had the composition not been in my mind? Thousands of people sat around me in the church. And thus it is always with me. I compose only when I go through an experience of life and I am conscious of such experiences only when I compose."[19]

It is impossible to ignore another portion of the letter in which Mahler speaks of his gratitude for Richard Strauss: "I shall never forget how Strauss in a most generous way gave the impulse [for the first performance of a Mahler symphony]. Nobody can wish that I should consider myself his competitor, though unfortunately that has been done frequently of late. Aside from the fact that I should be looked upon as a monstrosity if the road had not been paved by the successes of Strauss, it is my greatest joy to have such a combatant and co-creator.

Schopenhauer speaks somewhere of two miners who enter the gorge from two different directions, but finally meet on their subterraneous ways. Thus my relation to Strauss is exactly characterized."[20]

As yet Mahler is much less known than Strauss, and he has to all appearances not yet reached a similarly high degree of development. He began later. He did not turn out well conceived and well modelled imitations of other masters at an early age. Consequently we must look for the bigger surprises from him in the future. Mahler, in contrast to Strauss, Weingartner and others, is largely self-taught, though he had excellent technical schooling from Bruckner, among others. But he preferred to live apart from the whirl of public musical doings when he was a student, and while he may have been deprived of many passing and some lasting impressions which fall to the lot of the regular musical student in big cities, he also escaped the danger of forming prejudices and misconceptions. When he began his career as a conductor he could not even boast of a theoretical routine. He was thrown upon his intuition entirely. He had to conduct operas which he had never heard before. Tradition did not exist for him. That he erred, goes without saying, but he nevertheless triumphed. Thus his independence grew constantly, until it reached a degree of inflexibility unheard of in one so young. At the age of thirty he had won considerable fame as an opera conductor, and the few really great opera houses in Germany and Austria began to look upon him as a highly desirable acquisition. After work at Budapest and Hamburg he became the successor to Hans Richter and Jahn at the Imperial Opera House in Vienna, and within a few years he had acquired an authority in that position of which his predecessors never would have dreamt. He exercises more autocratic power at that celebrated institution than the czar did in his empire before the reform movement. Mahler is the absolute despot at the Vienna Court Opera and there is no appeal against his rulings. He made many enemies among the singers, the orchestra and the public, and he was cursed by all those who had been used to the easy-going ways of Richter and Jahn. No wonder that everybody felt justified in prophesying an early end to his régime. But they had not taken into account his energy, his perseverance and his incredible capacity for work. He expected the utmost of every member of the company, be it a prima donna or a member of the orchestra, and when those people saw how he himself worked more indefatigably than anyone else, they could not resist the charm of the good example, and by and by hatred turned to respect and finally to honest sympathy. . . .

If Mahler could ever be convinced that this or that in his symphonies was bad or wrong, he would not hesitate to sacrifice it. He is not of the vain type of self-adoring weaklings, he has the making—as well as the looks—of an ascetic. It is apparently not from a silly love for every note he pens that some of his symphonies are interminably long. On the contrary he is fully convinced that such lengths are necessary to make his ideas understood. Perhaps he is right, and one should feel inclined to think so when one considers how the audiences in Vienna, in Berlin, and in Cologne, in Munich and other German cities are beginning to applaud the symphonies that a few years ago they found unbearable. To describe and analyze these symphonies or one of them would be a fruitless task and entirely against the ideas of the composer. "Listen to my symphonies, but do not analyze them," is his frequent and emphatic remonstrance to overzealous admirers. And it is well nigh impossible to remain indifferent to his compositions. If Mahler does not please you at least he stirs you. Sometimes, as in the first movement of the third symphony, when after a tremendously imposing and mysterious passage, a simple and gay march-melody, fit for an operetta, strikes the ear, one feels at the moment like striking the composer in return. But we must not forget that we needed many decades to get used to certain idiosyncrasies of Beethoven that originally produced a like effect. The celebrated place in the "Eroica" where the tonic and dominant are sounded simultaneously, which even a Richard Wagner "corrected" as a lapsus pennae, should serve as a warning.

Mahler is undoubtedly original in his thematic ideas and cannot easily be caught at reminiscences. His themes may not be of the deepest originality, but they are often bold and the architecture of his ideas has a physiognomy of its own. In the handling of his themes he is often extremely modern, varying them rather than developing them in symphonic style. More modern than his melodic invention is his harmonization, and in contrapuntal devices he is as prolific as any of the latter-day composers. His counterpoint, however, is of the reckless, modern kind, and much more so than that of his teacher Bruckner. Very remarkable is the different physiognomy he shows in the various symphonies of which he has written six in all. How far apart in contents, purpose and treatment are the Fourth and Fifth! The Fourth is the most naive of Mahler's larger compositions. It purports to illustrate a mediaeval poem, describing the joys of heaven. The Fifth Symphony, which we are to hear on Friday, knows nothing of heaven and nothing of mediaeval quaintness. It is filled with the most modern feeling, brimming over with emotionality. Funeral and carnival, death and love are pictured in its five movements, but there is no singing. The performance lasts nearly an hour and a half. Mahler has not confined himself to symphonies, and his songs, for instance, deserve commendation. But his real artistic physiognomy is shown only in the symphonic works.

Program Notes, Boston Symphony Orchestra
Concert of February 2, 1906

PHILIP HALE

After graduating from Yale in 1876, Philip Hale (1854–1934) studied music in Europe. Upon his return to the United States in 1889 he settled in Boston, where he worked as critic and editor for the *Boston Herald* and *Boston Post*. In 1892–1898 he was also the Boston correspondent for the *Musical Courier*. Hale is best remembered for his Boston Symphony Orchestra program notes, which he began for the 1901–1902 season. His predecessor, William F. Apthorp, provided pithy program notes with minimal guidance regarding the form of the music and a few sentences on the composer's life. Hale's contributions were far more extensive, with original reflections on the composer's biography. His writings became the model for the genre in the United States.

• • •

This symphony, known to some as "The Giant Symphony," was performed for the first time at a Gürzenich concert at Cologne, October 18, 1904.[21] The composer conducted. There was a difference of opinion concerning the merits of the work. A visiting critic from Munich stated that there was breathless silence after the first movement, "which proved more effectively than tremendous applause that the public was conscious of the presence of genius." It is stated that after the finale there was much applause, and that there was also hissing. . . .

Mahler conducted a performance of his Symphony in C Minor at a concert of the Munich Hugo Wolf Society. After the concert there was a supper, and in the course of the conversation someone mentioned program books. "Then was it as though lightning flashed in a joyous, sunny landscape. Mahler's eyes were more brilliant than ever, his forehead wrinkled, he sprang in excitement from the table and exclaimed in passionate tones: 'Away with program books, which breed false ideas! The audience should be left to its own thoughts over the work that is performing; it should not be forced to read during a performance; it should not be prejudiced in any manner. If a composer by his music forces on his hearers the sensations which streamed through his mind, then he reaches his goal. The speech of tones has then approached the language of words, but it is far more capable of expression and declaration.' And Mahler raised his glass and emptied it with 'Pereat den Programmen!'" . . . Let us respect the wishes of Mr. Mahler, even though we are all at this safe distance.

The symphony was completed in the spring in 1903. It is scored for four flutes (the third and fourth interchangeable with piccolo), three oboes, three clarinets (the third interchangeable with bass clarinet), two bassoons, one double-bassoon, six horns (in the third movement a horn obbligato), four trumpets, three trombones, one bass tuba, kettledrums, snare-drum, bass drum, cymbals, triangle, glockenspiel, gong, harp, and strings. . . .

Two or three of the earlier symphonies of Mahler may be justly characterized as program music, but it has been said that he is no friend of realism as it is understood by Richard Strauss. . . . Some invent a program for this Fifth Symphony. Thus the editor of the program books of the Cincinnati Orchestra wrote, when the work was produced in that city: "Without constructing a 'program' for the work, it may be regarded as (I.) the plaint of one who has not realized his aspirations, and in his disillusionment stands at the verge of desperation; the harmless play and life of nature reconcile him to his lot (III., IV.), and he returns to his life-work, which he resumes (V.) with willingness, insight, and renewed strength, finally reaching heights before unattainable." Further than this, it would be useless to attempt to catalogue its meanings. We do not know whether this argument is original with Miss Roedter, or whether she borrowed it from some German deep thinker.

It should be observed, however, that Mahler, who at first gave clues to his hearers by means of titles and mottos on the programs of two of his symphonies, published the same symphonies as purely absolute music. . . .

A Symphony by Mahler for the First Time

HENRY TAYLOR PARKER

Boston Evening Transcript
February 3, 1906

Bostonian and Harvard dropout Henry Taylor Parker (1867–1934) became the music and drama critic for the *Boston Evening Transcript* in 1905. He had little musical training and reviewed concerts mainly as a reporter. His articles were usually signed H.T.P., which some interpreted as "Hard to Please" or "Hell to Pay."[22] The allusions to Vincent d'Indy in the article below may have been provoked by the rumor that the French composer would succeed Gericke as the conductor of the Boston Symphony Orchestra. D'Indy had conducted the orchestra with a program of his Symphony in B-flat Major op. 57 and Ishtar Symphonic Variations (1–2 December 1905).

· · ·

The Mahler whom we in Boston heard yesterday in the first of his symphonies to be performed here seemed hardly the Mahler whose music has been so eagerly championed and so bitterly condemned these last eight years in Germany and in Austria. Audiences have hissed and squalled at one or another of his five symphonies—they can still on occasion take their music very demonstratively in Germany—and audiences have applauded and cheered them. Some reviewers have slighted them and scorned the composer. Others have extolled them rapturously, and placed Mahler himself almost side by side with Richard Strauss. There have been Mahler "banquets," where the chief course was vehement and laudatory speechmaking, and there have been angry protests to every conductor who has ventured, if only for curiosity's sake, to put a symphony by Mahler on his programs. As for the musical world outside of Germany and Austria, it has been told to weariness that these symphonies were of extraordinary length and that they required extraordinary forces to perform them. There are more important and interesting things about them. But the Fifth of Mahler's symphonies, that Mr. Gericke put on his program, hardly bore out even these premonitory warnings. Report had declared that to perform it required an hour and a half. In fact, it lasted fifty-five minutes, perhaps ten or fifteen minutes longer than does an ordinary symphony of large dimensions, but it held the interest of the audience to the end, with fewer desertions than are usual at the afternoon concerts and with no visible signs of weariness. The introductory pages of some of Mahler's earlier symphonies do ask an enormous and intricate orchestral and choral apparatus. In this Fifth he has been in contact with a full modern orchestra, ample in its woodwinds and horns and in its subordinate instruments. Perhaps the new version of the score which Mahler himself prepared only two months ago and which Mr. Gericke used accounts for these surprises.

Moreover, while the symphony was steadily interesting and now and then boldly individual and strikingly impressive, there was nothing portentous, so far as a single hearing might disclose, in its matter or its manner. In no sense did it seem "epoch-making," "revolutionary," "gigantic"—we are quoting assorted German epithets—or "impudent." Like most ultramodern and highly individual music, it will provoke very different opinions in different hearers, but it warrants very scantily either the ecstatic admiration or the savage attacks that it and Mahler's other symphonies have excited and maintained overseas. Perhaps from openness of mind, much hearing in sympathetic performances and from an even and discriminating musical temper, we at the Symphony concerts have come to take the ways of ultramodern music more or less for granted. Usually they interest us; sometimes they move us in their kind—yet they seem to madden some of our brethren—and no farther away than New York.

Mahler, for example, used the sanctified symphonic form very freely and loosely. He condenses or extends it; he modifies, varies and reshapes it according to his imaginative purpose, ideas and sensations and the musical expression that he would give them. But the Medean and Persian lawgivers did not fix the symphonic form unalterably. (A few hidebound pedants have done that in their stead.) And the beginning and the end of a form, in music or in any other art, is to give fullest and clearest expression to the individual ideas and imaginings behind. If the composer or the artist in general have them in him to express, he will shape the form to his needs, while the significance and the power of these ideas and the beauty and appeal of these imaginings will justify all his freedom. Contrast the eloquence and range of the later quartets of Beethoven, for example, with the ordered tinkle of Haydn's. Yet both are nominally of the same musical form. So Mahler, in this Fifth Symphony, has molded prescribed forms to his intellectual and emotional purpose. Sometimes he departs far and freely from them. Sometimes he follows them more or less closely. Do his ideas and imaginings and the expression of them justify the departure? The expression, as it seems to us, certainly does. It is something—nowadays, when we are all restless—to be musically interesting in any form for fifty-five consecutive minutes.

Mahler's themes in his Fifth Symphony and in his Fourth which was played in New York fifteen months ago, lack, like most themes in ultramodern music, frankly melodic character. They do not sing as Mozart's or Schubert's sing. They are the embodiment of thoughtfully evolved musical ideas rather than the impulsive upspringings of spontaneous musical temperament. They have not the splendid finality and inevitability of Beethoven's, for example. We moderns—and Mahler with the rest of us, hollow-eyed enthusiast though he is—do not affirm anything with such majestic surety. Mahler's themes, like Strauss's in his "tone poems" or d'Indy in his symphonies, are the fruit of intellectual process and selection for expressive ends. Strauss's are individually poignant and acrid; d'Indy's are individually fine and haunting; Mahler's, in this symphony have an individual bigness and breadth that promise large, fruitful and moving development and expression. They sound like the themes of no other composer.

Mahler, however, no more develops his themes in the old sense of enrichment, enlargement, and illustration than do Strauss, and especially d'Indy theirs. Rather, he varies them and reconstructs. He divides and subdivides them, so to say, and treats each fraction with ingenuity and imagination. Sometimes he seizes a suggestion buried in them; again he pursues some remote modulation; yet again—for the music is full of such contrasts—he is content with some almost obvious implication in theme. In this treatment of his themes he is masterful and fertile. His polyphony seemed hardly as intricate as Strauss's or as subtle as d'Indy's, but it is as firm and pliant of intellectual and technical grip and as unflagging in invention. Like them he catches and shapes new and strange harmonies—sometimes irresistibly. If the man were less sincere, he would seem now and then to pursue the bizarre for its own sake—to make the Philistines sit up champing, even as Strauss likes to make them. But Mahler is of another cast of mind. To himself—and to the world, if he chose—he can probably give a definite reason for his most daring and perplexing modulations. However much we that listen fail to grasp their purpose, that purpose was clearly in his mind.

Not from Mahler's themes or from his treatment of them, still less from his variations of established forms, spring what power and beauty there are in his music as this Fifth Symphony disclosed it. Their source, as it seemed equally in the immediate listening and in the subsequent reflection, is a command of instrumentation and an imagination in it that is unique and almost marvelous. Schubert's passion found voice in his melodies; Beethoven's in the magnificent march of his symphonic movements; Brahms's in austere contemplation; d'Indy's finds its voice in fine and disembodied subtleties of tone; Strauss's in the painting and the unrolling of superb musical canvases. There is passion in Mahler too, hot, deep, passion. There is intellectual force as well. His instrumentation is the voice of both. Thereby he is a twentieth-century Berlioz.

This instrumentation is not merely the technical mastery, the acquired suggestiveness of the practiced, meditative and watchful conductor. It seldom betrays the careful reflection behind and the ingenious calculation of the effect before as Strauss's often does. It is not, seemingly, the result of long striving and searching and polishing for the apt, the precise, the ultimate instrumental word as is d'Indy's and Debussy's. Doubtless all these processes have contributed to it, but Mahler does not often let our ears hear them. Rather in him is something very like a genius for instrumentation, for the power for it, for the beauty of it. Time and again, in the Fifth Symphony, he makes his instrumentation amazingly intricate, yet the euphony of it delights the ear. Equally he can give it a naive and lovely simplicity. He can make a single instrument or a group of instruments flash like tongues of fire. Some of his instrumental backgrounds are like tonal mosaics of very delicate and wholly harmonious colors and of perfect jointure. There are details in his instrumentation that sound almost as inspirations. He has a painter's sense of comparative instrumental "values." His themes and his treatment of them take significance to the mind, shape to the fancy and appeal to the emotions chiefly through the instrumental coloring of them. The rhythmic depth and force, "as of a funeral march" in the first movement of the symphony; the rhythmic charm and caress of the ländler that makes the third; the impetuous restlessness of the second; the lyric sweetness of the fourth; the exhilarating sweep of the last chiefly, as it seems to us, in the power and the beauty—almost the genius—of the instrumentation. By it, more than by any other capacity of music, he discloses ideas, imparts mood, compasses atmosphere, clothes his imaginings. What these would be naked the sympathetic listener neither knows nor cares. The instrumental investiture is enough. Often it is finely poignant or vividly pictorial. Almost always it is irresistibly sensuous. Of such instrumentation our conductor and our orchestra are past masters. They overcame the endless difficulties with which Mahler, who seems to write for an orchestra of Mahler's, achieves his end. Yet we that listened barely saw or felt them.

We have written of Mahler's symphony as of "absolute" music, because it is as such that most of those that listen to it are likely to hear it. "May programs perish from the earth" was his toast at a supper in his honor. Yet he made them, though without detail, or permitted others to make them, and with infinite detail, for some of his earlier symphonies. There is a little "programmatic" suggestion in the few directions to the conductor and band. . . that he prefixes to each movement of this Fifth Symphony. No doubt there was a program—or more properly a definite succession of poetic ideas—in his mind as he wrote. There is in the last analysis, as Mr. Newman was saying a few weeks ago in this column, behind all music that is emotionally potent. In his Fourth Symphony Mahler was indeed writing measurably delineative music. In the Fifth there is no hint of such purpose that the average imaginative listener can readily detect. No more is it music that would suggest the stress and strain and turnings and twistings of some intellectual conflict of ideas as does d'Indy's in the symphony that he conducted here. Mahler's is music of mood and passion. Often it summons the power and the beauty of ordered, imaginative and impassioned sound. Doing so, as often it kindles the mind and stirs the emotions. Thus it brings intense sensations. Within the limits palpably set by the composer, the listeners may give those sensations what color and significance they will.

During his reign as music director of the Boston Symphony Orchestra, Gericke oversaw changes that led to the full professionalization of the orchestra. Like its founder and principal supporter Henry Higginson, he felt that development of the ensemble would require an extension of the season; many players left Boston after the six-month season, which resulted in significant personnel changes each year. The example of the New York Philharmonic, which had recently begun to employ musicians year round, had shown "splendid results," according to the *Musical Courier*.[23] Gericke proposed an orchestra tour to extend the season. The first tour, which was mainly in New England (1885–1886), was not successful, but by the early 1900s the Boston Symphony Orchestra toured extensively within the United States and had developed into one of its leading orchestras. The tours included monthly concerts in Philadelphia.[24] The Philadelphia program of February 12 opened with Weber's Overture to *Der Freischütz* and Saint-Saëns's Cello Concerto no. 1 (with Elsa Ruegger) and concluded with Mahler's Fifth Symphony.

Mahler's Fifth Symphony the Feature of an Interesting Program

Philadelphia Evening Bulletin
February 13, 1906

Gustav Mahler, the Austrian composer, was a most venturesome musician to put forth such a stupendous work as his Symphony No. 5 in C-sharp Minor, without a definite program, and it is perhaps to this circumstance that his big symphony, played for the first time in this city by the Boston Orchestra, failed to make a worthy impression last night on the audience gathered in the Academy of Music.

Notwithstanding Richard Strauss and his *Symphonia domestica*, which was put forth without program or guide post that it might be judged purely as music, Mahler is not on such familiar ground as the family hearthstone, and cannot so surely trust to the imagination of his hearers. Strauss did not deny that his *Domestica* had a program—a very handsome and definite one—but he wished, it seemed, to outrage the critics who maintained that without a program his music was unintelligible. But he wavered at the last, and it was he himself who furnished a New York musical critic last winter with a more elaborate program than had been imagined by any of the uninformed gropers after his meaning.

But Mahler has out-Straussed Strauss. He would confuse critics and confound analysis, so that it becomes almost a duty to demand where such orchestral tomfoolery in the hazy realm of "absolute music" is leading us. Are these ultramodern composers emulating certain German philosophers of the last century of whom it was said "they dived deeper, staid down longer and came up muddier than any others?"

The symphony itself, which is cast in a mould all its own, with a bigness, a breadth, that is unsurpassed in modern music, is divided into three parts and five movements, and begins with "a dead march in measured step like a funeral train." Here is meaning and great rhythmic beauty. The next is a movement of stormy agitation where dissonance and discord have their wildest flight, with swarms of themes and counter themes mixed up in a make of weird instrumentation. Then comes a climax of cacophony, suggesting nothing short of a cataclysm. The third movement is a scherzo, the fourth a short adagietto and the fifth a rondo finale. Most haunting and poignant in feeling of all perhaps is the adagietto, full of passionate introspections "born of a joy that is passed."

Of large dimensions, enormously intricate in orchestration and rich in thematic material, there are yet few melodic or great moments in the entire work and as an entirety it fails on first hearing, at least, to be convincing, to give one a definite succession of poetic ideas, or even real emotions.

But when all is said this intensely modern symphony is one hardly made to Mr. Gericke's hand, well as his band of musicians did it—though played they never so well it would have failed to make its appeal on last night's audience, which seemed far better keyed to the pleasure to be found in Saint-Saëns's Concerto in A Minor.

A New Symphony by Gustav Mahler . . . His Works Have Made a Deep Impression Abroad, but Are Little Known Here

RICHARD ALDRICH

New York Times
February 11, 1906

One of the interesting and important incidents of the season will be the first performance in New York of Gustav Mahler's Fifth Symphony, which Mr. Gericke will give with the Boston Symphony Orchestra on Thursday evening. Only one other of Mahler's symphonies—of which he has written six, the last not yet having been publicly performed—has been heard in New York. That is the Fourth, which Walter Damrosch played last season with the New York Symphony Orchestra. The fact is noteworthy, since New York has generally heard most of the works of men of mark soon after they have been brought out in Europe. And Mahler is unquestionably a man of mark. He is one of the most distinguished of the younger school of German conductors, and is at present at the head of the Imperial Opera at Vienna, where he rules with an iron hand, bending prima donnas and first tenors to his will as though they were mere orchestral players, and brooking no interference with his policy by even the loftiest Court personages, who are prone in German Court theaters to attempt such meddling. There he has achieved results of the most remarkable sort, it is affirmed by competent witnesses, with means, at least so far as the leading singers are concerned, not of the best.

Of late years Mahler has come to be seriously reckoned with as a composer, and some of his symphonies—he has written nothing else of importance for orchestra—have made a deep impression and have summoned up a passionate propaganda for Mahler and his works, as well as a strong opposition to them. This militant championing of somebody with something new, or at least unusual, strange and to some repellent, to say in music, seems to be one of the intellectual necessities of modern Germany. It may take the shape of "Vereins," as the "Wolf Vereins" and even the "Ansorge Verein;" as once, with much better reason, it resulted in the formation of numerous Wagner Vereins, which now find their occupation gone. Or it may simply take the form of such pamphleteering as rages around Strauss and Reger, and, to a less extent, Mahler. . . .

Mahler occupies a curious and rather anomalous position in the field of modern orchestral music. He is no follower of the modern idea of "program music," as it is most characteristically embodied in the music of Richard Strauss. What he writes he calls symphonies, though they are symphonies often only in a loose acceptance of the term. They do not follow closely, sometimes they do not follow at all, the formal outlines of symphonic movements. He vehemently objects to having any "programs" laid down for his music, or even to permitting any thematic analyses to appear in the concert rooms where it is played, though a detailed thematic analysis of this Fifth Symphony has been published, apparently with his sanction. . . .

His style of writing, so far as we in New York know it through his Fourth Symphony, is individual. He has the modern's cheerful indifference in the face of dissonance and discord. He writes freely in that modern style of counterpoint that gets its themes and subjects and countersubjects together anyhow, whether euphoniously or not. He is by no means indifferent to effects, however, and his score swarms with the most minute directions as to tempo—changes, dynamic gradations, and all manner of points in expression. His themes are not only very numerous, but also often very extensive in compass. The analyst of this symphony points out that the opening theme of the funeral march is "only thirty-three measures long, that is, for Mahler, not a very long one." His predilection for melodies of a naive or folk-song character, which he indulged freely in his Fourth Symphony, comes to light in the scherzo of this one, which has the character of an Austrian Ländler; and the tendency to develop such themes with an almost fantastic elaboration goes with it.

Some have thought to find in this symphony a picture of life in Vienna; that the opening dead march was suggested by the military funerals in that capital, and that the Ländler is characteristically local in spirit. The editor of the program book of the Cincinnati Orchestra . . . found a more philosophical content in it. There were the plaint of one who has not realized his aspirations, and in his disillusionment stands at the verge of desperation; his reconciliation to his lot through the harmless play and life of nature; his return to his life work with willingness, insight, and renewed strength; finally reaching heights before unattainable. These two interpretations of the same thing seem to differ widely. There is not the slightest indication that the composer has ever given any sanction to either of them.

Fifth Symphony Played: A New and Difficult Work

New York Times
February 16, 1906

New York was the most common destination of the Boston Symphony Orchestra's tour. The format always remained the same: over two days the orchestra offered two programs in Carnegie Hall. Mahler's Fifth Symphony was played on February 15, 1906, in a concert that opened with Beethoven's *Egmont* Overture and Schumann's Piano Concerto (with Harold Bauer). This was the fourth New York trip during the 1905–06 season, following those in November, December, and January.

• • •

Mahler's symphony imposes by its length and breadth, the vast number and extent of its themes, the skillful handicraft with which they are put together, the bigness of the orchestral apparatus, the extraordinary skill with which it is managed. Yet it is a less unusual apparatus than that required by the less impressive Fourth Symphony, with its singing voice in the last movement, as it was heard here last season; and a much less elaborate machinery than is required for Mahler's Second Symphony, which has never been done in this country. This Fifth Symphony is a work that cannot be dismissed at one hearing as harsh, diffuse, lacking in distinction of theme and definiteness of purpose; although all these things appeared from time to time to be true of it, as it was unfolded before an uncommonly attentive and patient audience last evening.

That it is deeply felt and tremendously sincere music is continually borne in upon the listener; but that it is not the product of a strong and vigorous creative genius, an original force in music, is also evident. It seems that the composer is most strenuously seeking for self-expression; but though he is equipped with all that modern musical skill can give him in methods of treatment and resources of orchestration, his achievement seems continually to pant behind his ambition, rarely overtaking it.

There was discussion and explanation at length in the last Sunday's *Times* of Herr Mahler's work and his attitude toward the "program" and the explanation of music. This symphony has no suggestion of what it is; and the lack of one is inevitably felt as a bar to its understanding. For Herr Mahler plainly had some definite idea in his mind. We simply do not know what he was driving at; for it seems undeniable that many portions of his five movements are not intelligible simply as music—the treatment and the development seem unable to account for themselves purely as such.

The unusual division of the work was described the other day in the *Times*. The funeral march with which the symphony opens is highly effective—yet there are certainly commonplace passages in it that let down the "high erected thoughts" with jarring suddenness. The episode of wild and passionate outbursts in the midst of this march is seizing. The second movement carries on the feeling of the march, but is less tangible. In the Scherzo Herr Mahler has sought for a contrast with all this. Here is a "Ländler," a country waltz theme of naive tunefulness; but here, too, is the Mahler of the Fourth Symphony, who produces naive tunes only to toss them about and torment them with strange development and strained harmonies that leave little of their pretty and somewhat commonplace lustre.

There is here, and through the work, an ingenious and bold utilization of numerous themes in the crass kind of forced union that does
duty in these most modern days as counterpoint—a union that is
effected without regard to euphony. The adagietto has more ingratiating traits than any of the other movements; there is a poetical suggestion
in it that the others have not, yet even here there is a certain lack of
cogency and point; the movement seems to have little definite issue.
The last movement is a rondo-finale and still shows the lack of a clearly
discernible purpose. It has many interesting moments. There is a fugato
of considerable extent; there is a long climax in a sustained melody of
a choralelike character that is developed. There is also much that is dry
and harsh, as there is in every one of these movements.

The symphony arrests the attention of the listener for the hour of
its duration. Its vague and indeterminate bigness of conception and
elaborate dexterity of execution engage the interest of those who wish
to follow the technical methods of the composer. But of specific musical inspiration it seems, from the first hearing of the work, that the
composer has little. He appears, for instance, to stand considerably
below Strauss in originality. He is in many respects dramatically
opposed to Strauss; but he seems a lesser talent.

The performance of this symphony was an extraordinary achievement on the part of the orchestra and Mr. Gericke. He had devoted great
care to its preparation, and the perfection of its reproduction was the
result of much labor. It is said that Herr Mahler had sent Mr. Gericke
some revisions of the orchestration.[25] The audience listened to it with
close attention to the end but manifested little enthusiasm over it.

Variations

LEONARD LEIBLING

The Musical Courier
February 21, 1906

The popular response to the Scherzo, reported by Leonard
Leibling, is intriguing in view of how problematic this movement
was for German and Austrian contemporaries, who instead welcomed the powerful thrust of the Finale as a reward earned
through the suffering of the opening movements. It is not surprising that the Adagietto reminded Leibling of Charles Martin
Loeffler, whose music was frequently performed in the United

States. The fascination with orchestration and program music made Loeffler a "modern" composer in much the same way Mahler was perceived. The association with the Boston Symphony Orchestra was particularly strong, as Loeffler had three years prior retired from twenty-one years as second concertmaster. Loeffler emigrated from Berlin, via Paris, in 1881 and harbored intense anti-German sentiments.

• • •

The one number that stirred up the greatest interest at these two concerts—next to the unusually brilliant array of soloists—was Mahler's Fifth Symphony, which had been preceded here by bulletins of its fiasco d'estime abroad, and its unqualified acceptance in Boston, where they are said to be clamoring for an early repetition of the work. Other reports which helped to put our public in a state of unusual expectancy were to the effect that ten rehearsals had been found necessary to enable the Boston orchestra to master the "fabulous intricacies of the score," and that at a dinner given in Munich, when someone asked Mahler about his opinion of "programs" for symphonies, he "sprang in excitement from the table and exclaimed in passionate tones: 'Away with programs books, which breed false ideas! The audience should be left to its own thoughts over the work that is performing. Pereat den Programmen!'"

The advance excitement in our local musical circles was furthermore helped along by the remembrance of Mahler's Fourth Symphony—the one with the soprano solo—which caused so much futile discussion when it was produced here last season by Walter Damrosch. It was remembered that one camp had condemned Mahler as a pretentious charlatan, while another faction cried him out as a god and played him against Richard Strauss, as Hanslick pitted Brahms against Wagner. The dispassionate outsiders sat back and waited to see whether there would be any more performances of the work here. There were not. The present symphony, therefore, was expected to settle some of the disputes which arose after the production of the Fourth, and to enable the floundering critics and the puzzled public to give Mahler his proper place in the ranks of the symphonic composers. And has Mahler's measure now been taken, after the performance of last Thursday? Hardly. The abyss between his New York admirers and his detractors has grown wider than ever, and both sides are utterly at variance over even such a fundamental point as whether the work is an absolute or a program symphony. Mahler has been clever enough to call his first movement "Funeral March, C-sharp Minor, 2/2. With measured step. With marked precision. Like a funeral train." The second movement is labeled "A minor, 4/4. With stormy emotion. With the utmost vehemence." Those are "program" titles, of course, and might have ultimately given a clue to the real "story" of the work, had not the composer been sly enough to call the next three movements merely "scherzo," "adagietto," and "rondo-finale"—out and out "absolute" terms. And the whole work is divided into three parts (although there are five full stops) the two end parts containing two movements each and the middle part consisting solely of the "scherzo." No wonder Philip Hale in his Boston symphony annotations (usually so generous in explanation) dodges this symphonic salamagundi fairly and squarely and says with sly humility: "Let us respect the wishes of Mr. Mahler, even though we are all at this safe distance." The fertile Philip remains dumb after that Homeric utterance, and leaves the listener to wallow rudderless in a sea of sound and speculation. The conscientious Hale does not forget to mention, on the other hand, that Mahler studied in Iglau, and at various stages of his nefarious career conducted opera in Laibach, Olmütz and Cassel. We learn also from the annotation book that Mahler now is conductor and director of the Vienna Opera and "rules the opera house with an iron hand."

Fixing those elucidative facts firmly in our minds, let us proceed at once to a matter of fact explanation of the Fifth Symphony, since no one, not even the composer, seems inclined to give us any data on which to hang one of our favorite rhapsodical flights into the critical empyrean.

The first movement was evidently written with that iron hand which now rules the Vienna Opera, for it is somber, gruesome, heavy, reveling in the minor mode with all the fearful pleasure of absolute despair. As in all other funeral marches, there enters a second strain, scored higher in the staff, and, after being stated, it is swallowed by the first theme, only to be spewed forth again a little later, somewhat mangled, but still recognizable. There follow various reiterations of both themes, single, in shreds and in combination. The whole thing is unmistakably funereal, and must be acknowledged to possess a certain impressiveness, chiefly because of the rhythmic march syncopations in the bass and the dark colors in which the orchestration is seeped. However, fustian and bombast in the movement show forth plainly, and prevent any feeling of deeper emotion, such as is called forth, for instance, in Wagner's obsequial song over the death of Siegfried, Beethoven's mighty dirge in the "Eroica" and Tchaikowsky's threnetic ode at the close of his "Pathètique." The movement was liked by the audience and applauded warmly.

The section that followed baffles any clear description except the plain confession on the part of at least one listener, that to him the movement sounded quick, noisy, ugly, overscored, and much too long. The stopped horns, the characteristic use of the double bassoon and the episodical part writing for the strings brought forth strong suggestions of Strauss. However, if Mahler has caught some of great Richard's manner at moments, he is far behind him in the importance and suggestiveness of his thematic material. It is a matter of extreme difficulty to detect tangible themes in the second movement of the Mahler work, and it is an almost impossible task to follow them through the tortuous mazes of their formal and contrapuntal development. One has to cling by one's teeth, so to speak, to a shred of theme here and there, which appears for an occasional instant above the heaving masses of tone, only to be jumped upon immediately by the whole angry horde of instruments and stamped down into the very thick of the orchestral fray. The fighting grows so furious toward the finish that one is compelled to unclose one's teeth on the morsel of the theme, and lo and behold! it is seized upon, hurtled through the screaming and frenzied ranks of the combatants, and that is the last seen or heard of the poor little rag of a theme. It is imperative at this point of our analysis to become professional for a moment and to say, "All the resources of the modern orchestra, with its infinite capacity for climax, contrast, and color, are skillfully utilized by Mahler in the second movement, and indeed throughout the entire length (and it is long) of his Fifth Symphony." The second movement was not enjoyed by the audience, for it did not applaud.

The scherzo is easily disposed of, for it is mere music, pretty, in slow waltz rhythm, and decidedly Viennese in the charm and piquancy of its orchestration. A "program" touch is introduced, however, in the use of the glockenspiel and the xylophone. The musically wise scented a macabre allusion in that effect, and forthwith searched for apposite suggestion in Liszt's *Totentanz*, Berlioz's "Witches' Sabbath," Loeffler's "Dies Irae" paraphrase, and Saint-Saëns' optimistic *Dance of Death*. This movement was very well liked by the audience, for it applauded long and loudly.

The Adagietto moved in familiar territory so far as facture was concerned. There were two well contrasted subjects, treated as though Mahler liked them. The method was that of the conventional slow movement. The melodies were of grateful outline, even if not of surpassing beauty. When Mahler is content to "sing" he does it simply and well, and displays pure lyrical talent of no mean order. There ought to be a lesson in that circumstance, but where is the modern composer who cares to make mere melody when he can make mystery in his music instead? Strauss is always *hors de concours*, of course. The fourth movement was liked best of all by the audience, for it applauded louder and longer than after any of the other movements.

The finale, too, adhered to the safe and sane symphonic form of our forefathers. The leading motive was terse and tangible, and it made a subject for as finely wrought and spirited a fugato as it has been any composer's lot to weave this many a decade. The counterpoint was crystal clear in spite of its many voiced polyphony, and the fugued figures danced through the second theme, its development and all that followed, with an agility and grace that made the movement sparkle from its beginning to its coda, a full throated chorale intoned by all the band, in broad and cheerful major chords. Thus the work ends happily in spite of the funeral march with which it opens—another problem for commentators. It was hard to say whether the audience liked the last movement or not, for many of the listeners were putting on their street togs before the final chord, and forgot to applaud if they ever intended to do so. The symphony, in Gericke's version, takes just one hour to perform.

It will be observed in another column of *The Musical Courier* that some critics find in Mahler's Fifth Symphony resemblances to Brahms, Bruckner, Verdi, d'Indy, Strauss, and Wagner. The chronicler of the *Evening Sun* calls attention to Mahler's copying of Bach, Tchaikovsky, and Puccini. Harold Bauer says that the slow movement reminds him of Beethoven. The present writer set down his opinion above that the scherzo brought memories of Loeffler, Liszt, and Saint-Saëns. Is there no one to say that any part of the symphony sounds like Mahler? Criticism is so charitable.

NOTES

I would like to thank Mauro Calcagno, Richard Giarusso, and Gilbert Kaplan for assistance with this project, as well as Teri McKibben at the Cincinnati Symphony Orchestra. Capitalization and formatting in the documents have been standardized and typographical errors corrected. All endnotes are the editor's.

1. Mahler's letter of 28 February 1906 to Wilhelm Gericke, in Edward R. Reilly, "Gustav Mahler and Wilhelm Gericke," in *Mahler's Unknown Letters*, ed. Herta Blaukopf, trans. Richard Stokes (Boston, 1987), pp. 59–64. Elsa Bienenfeld reported on the Mahler/Gericke correspondence in the Viennese press, going so far as to claim that "from the moment" Gericke took over the Boston Symphony Orchestra, "it became one of the leading orchestras in the world." See her "Drei Briefe an Wilhelm Gericke, Dirigent des Bostoner Symphonie-orchesters. 1905-1906," *Neues Wiener Journal*, 11 April 1926.

2. Bryan Gilliam, *The Life of Richard Strauss* (Cambridge, Eng., 1999), p. 27.

3. *Musical Courier*, 23 March 1904. The February 27 program of orchestral poems was reviewed in *The Musical Courier*, 2 March 1904. See the summary of reviews from Strauss's first visit to America, from February to August 1904, in Robert Breuer's "Richard Strauss in Amerika," *Richard Strauss-Blätter*, no. 8 (1976): 1–17.

4. See the work of Jessica Gienow-Hecht, in particular "Music, Emotions and Politics in German-American Relations Since 1850: A Speculative Essay," *Journal of Social History* (forthcoming in March 2003).

5. George Martin, *The Damrosch Dynasty: America's First Family of Music* (Boston, 1983), pp. 185–200.

6. On the early years of the Cincinnati Symphony Orchestra, see Philip Hart's *Orpheus in the New World; The Symphony Orchestra as an American Cultural Institution* (New York, 1973), pp. 265–69.

7. Alma Mahler, *Gustav Mahler Briefe* (Vienna, 1924), pp. 130–31.

8. Edward R. Reilly, "Gustav Mahler and Walter Damrosch," in *Mahler's Unknown Letters*, ed. Blaukopf, pp. 35–45.

9. Letter to Mengelberg, in Alma Mahler, *Gustav Mahler Briefe*, pp. 402–404.

10. Zoltan Roman's *Gustav Mahler's American Years, 1907–1911: A Documentary History* (New York, 1919) provides further information about Mahler's reception in America.

11. Henri Duparc (1848–1933) was an intriguing choice for an orchestral program, all the more since there was so little available repertoire: the symphonic poem *Lénore*, which saw several performances in the period of its composition in 1875, and *Poème nocturne* (1874). An avid Wagnerian and early enthusiast of Tolstoy, this student of César Franck had suffered hyperaesthesia since 1885, at which point he abandoned composition.

12. Selections from Aldrich's reviews from the *New York Times* are reproduced in his *Concert Life in New York, 1902–1923* (New York, c. 1941).

13. Rudolf Kastner, *Münchener Neueste Nachrichten,* 23 October 1904.

14. Hermann Kipper, *Kölner Volkszeitung*, 19 October 1904.

15. *Rheinische Musik- und Theater-Zeitung* 5, no. 25 (29 October 1904).

16. Paul Hiller, *Die Musik* 4, no. 4 (November issue 2, 1904): 297.

17. Gericke's memoirs of his first few years with the Boston Symphony Orchestra are found in M.A. DeWolfe Howe and John N. Burk, *The Boston Symphony Orchestra, 1881–1931* (Boston, 1931), pp. 104–108.

18. The Liszt quotation is in Humphrey Searle, *The Music of Franz Liszt* (New York, 1966), p. 120.

19. Letter of 17 February 1897, in *Selected Letters of Gustav Mahler*, ed. Knud Martner, trans. Eithne Wilkins, Ernst Kaiser, and Bill Hopkins (London, 1979), p. 212.

20. Ibid., p. 213.

21. A shortened form appears in *Philip Hale's Boston Symphony Orchestra Program Notes*, ed. John N. Burk (Garden City, N.Y., 1935), 193–94.

22. Mark N. Grant, *Maestros of the Pen*, pp. 96–97. Taylor's works were collected in *Eighth Notes: Voices and Figures of Music and the Dance* (1922), rpt. (Freeport, NY, 1968).

23. *Musical Courier,* 31 March 1886.

24. Robert A. Gerson, *Music in Philadelphia* (Philadelphia, 1940), pp. 206–207.

25. Mahler's conducting score already included revisions for the premiere, in Cologne, so he felt it impossible to mark up the earlier published score (which appeared before the premiere) with the additional revisions for the Viennese premiere. He therefore sent Gericke his own copy of the revisions, in a letter postmarked only two days after the Viennese premiere of December 7, 1905. Reilly, "Mahler and Gericke," pp. 62–63.

PART IV

MAHLER'S
GERMAN-LANGUAGE CRITICS

Mahler's German-Language Critics

Edited and Translated by

Karen Painter and Bettina Varwig

"He who wants to become deeply immersed in Berlin music history must begin by understanding its music criticism. Sometimes it seems more important than music itself."[1] Adolf Weissmann's observation applies just as well to Vienna and other cities. The flowering of cultural journalism in Central Europe around 1900 had a more immediate impact on musical listening than on the reception of the other arts, not least because there was so little access to live performance. The turn of the century saw a broad range of papers and periodicals that devoted major resources to music reviews. Critics followed new compositions avidly and refrained from neither technical analysis nor interpretation. At this moment in music history, when orchestral color took on a novel but contested importance, aural impressions from concert listening became essential to the interpretation of a composition. The reviews by Mahler's contemporaries range in their judgments from ebullient praise to scathing criticism. Always, however, they give insight into his compositions as well as suggest ways of listening that have been lost to history. These writings offer a revealing glimpse into Mahler's musical world.

Concert reviews from the leading daily newspapers and artistic journals provide some of the most eloquent interpretations of music from the period. Still in its infancy, musicology often focused on the middle ages and Renaissance. Beyond their specific observations about the music, these commentaries reveal both the excitement and the contention that surrounded Mahler and his symphonies. Mahler was seen by some contemporaries as the only composer still writing symphonies. But he did so in ways that seemed jarring to many listeners. Mahler therefore became the locus of a contemporary debate over the value of tradition and the promise of innovation, a debate that had broad implications for the connections between music and society, politics, and culture.

Music history has largely focused on composers and performers, often losing track of the stories of individual critics. Yet this generation of music critics—a generation that would pass away with the disaster of 1933—had an important role in a wider, and widely known, history of emigration and persecution. Journalism was one area where Jews had a visible role, and the distribution of posts at major newspapers reflected the great influence of the Jewish intelligentsia in Vienna and Germany in the early twentieth century. This was, moreover, a period when, as the socialist critic David Josef Bach later recalled, in Vienna "the press still exerted great influence on the sector of society that controlled public and private practice of art."[2] Yet all but a few of the most important of music critics—measured by the standards of musicologists today—are omitted in the standard reference sources. Some have been utterly lost to history, signing their reviews through initials; others, however, can be reconstructed through contemporary sources, as is attempted here in the introductions to individual documents.

As a rule, music critics were among the intellectual and cultural elite in a society that cherished music as the quintessential German (and likewise Austro-German) art form. They often had rigorous practical training as well as a doctorate in music history or another field. Some worked full time as journalists, but most were also active as teachers, composers, and freelance writers. The particular training and other literary pursuits of a critic often influenced the nature of the music criticism: the many critics who began their formal training in the field of law tended to write with a remarkable rigor, while those trained in humanistic or literary fields generally veered toward broader cultural critique. The diverse biographical paths of these critics therefore carry interest in their own right. Berlin and Vienna of the years around 1900 represent a high point in the history of journalism; while no clear method of training existed for music critics, these were no inexperienced reporters. Those imparted with the power to judge musical culture had developed through a range of educational, literary, and musical activities. As Walter Schrenk wrote from the retrospective standpoint of 1929, music criticism "is not a profession in the bourgeois sense but rather depends on an entire orientation of the mind of a very personal nature. . . . A great critic is born for this profession, and no education can provide that for him. . . . He must be an intuitive person with every prophetic talent, as it were, to feel and interpret the organic power and future strength in an artwork."[3]

The reviews selected here—of the First, Fifth, and Seventh Symphonies and *Das Lied von der Erde*—not only deal with milestones in Mahler's creative career but represent as well turning points in the history of musical thought. The first symphony of a composer commanded particular attention in the press, especially at a time when the future of the genre seemed in jeopardy. Mahler's Fifth was significant as the composer's first symphony conceived without text or title. This work fascinated contemporaries, whether as a profound yet playful response to revered tradition, or as a tragic yet sensuous journey. The Seventh Symphony brought immediate and complete success at a critical point in Mahler's career—neither the radical innovations nor the gleaming irony that have sparked interest among today's musicologists were part of the world of Mahler's contemporaries. More general reflections on the conductor and composer, meanwhile, seemed particularly urgent upon Mahler's death. An outpouring of obituaries and retrospective assessments attempted to capture a world past as well as, at least among some earlier detractors, to assuage guilt for the composer's departure from Europe to settle in New York. The posthumous premiere of *Das Lied von der Erde* invited critics to again write analytically, now with greater distance, about the composer's development and achievements. At the celebrated 1920 Amsterdam Mahler festival, the composer's complete symphony cycle provided material for musical and historical reflection.

The documents are drawn from the leading critics of Mahler's generation. The composer had many detractors, some of whom are included here. Yet Mahler also enjoyed the support of several critics who had the courage, as Richard Specht put it, to respond positively to his music even before it became fashionable: "D. J. Bach, Dr. Elsa Bienenfeld, Paul Stefan, after some wavering, Julius Korngold," as well as Hermann Bahr.[4] A few others, who advocated for the composer almost to the complete exclusion of anyone else, remained on the margins of society. It remains to be explored whether these latter enthusiasts identified personally with the composer or his music. William Ritter is only the most famous case.[5] Ernst Otto Nodnagel, perhaps Mahler's most zealous supporter, died in a psychiatric ward at age thirty-nine, three years after his last known publication, which analyzed the Sixth Symphony. Richard Specht, Mahler's friend and first biographer—and a man whose alcohol and drug abuse did not go unmentioned in the press—was described in his obituary as "a hermit on the margins."[6]

As a whole, these documents expose some of the myths that have developed in the academic and popular literature. Mahler scholarship was long dominated by the question of whether or not his symphonies were programmatic—whether they conveyed particular images and narratives, or instead moved listeners through purely musical means.

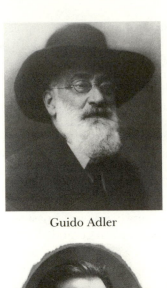

Guido Adler

Hermann Bahr

Paul Bekker

Elsa Bienenfeld

Max Graf

Eduard Hanslick

Robert Hirschfeld   Max Kalbeck

Julius Korngold   Ferdinand Pfohl   Gustav Schönaich

Richard Specht   Paul Stefan

The reviews translated here, however, suggest that the very question may be anachronistic: this generation did not distinguish between program music and "absolute" music as two separate genres. Mahler's symphonies could communicate novel and powerful experiences without sacrificing the criteria of the purely musical. Another myth that scholarship has perpetuated is that of Mahler as the underappreciated genius. While unequivocal proponents of his work were few, firm detractors were no more common. Mahler's music provoked serious reflection on the viability of the genre of symphony, the competence of the musical public, and the status of German music and culture. As a collective and strikingly large body of musical literature, the reviews of a century ago open up a cultural milieu in which it was taken for granted that music was a supremely important human endeavor. The deep engagement with Mahler's creations that these reviews manifest can refresh and intensify the music's importance for today's listeners as well.

Mahler as Conductor

Until the successful premiere of his *Kindertotenlieder* (January 29, 1905), Mahler was admired in Vienna more as a conductor than as a composer. (Anti-Semitic critics continued to speak of Mahler as a performer, rather than creator of music, through the scathing attacks issued upon him in Nazi Germany). As director of the Vienna Philharmonic (1898–1901), he introduced a number of new works into the orchestra's repertoire, including Bruckner's Fifth and Sixth Symphonies, Liszt's *Festklänge*, Berlioz's *Rob Roy* Overture, Franck's *Variations symphoniques* for piano and orchestra, Strauss's *Aus Italien*, as well as works by Smetana, Dvořák, Tchaikovsky, and Bizet. Mahler conducted his own First and Second Symphonies, a concert of his lieder, and, later as a guest conductor, his Fourth Symphony.

The intrigue and problems at the Court Opera held a great fascination in the press. Critics also lavished attention on Mahler's opera productions and his revisions to standard repertoire (above all the revisions to Beethoven's Ninth). But in reviews of symphony concerts, critics showed less interest in his conducting than in the music itself: such articles generally began with an extensive discussion of the program, in particular the new work, with only brief concluding remarks on the performance. The most vivid and detailed accounts of Mahler's conducting are therefore found in the obituaries sampled below (other obituaries can be found later in Part IV). Critics seized the historical moment and focused on his significance as an individual rather than on his music, which had established itself in the repertoire.

Gustav Mahler and the Vienna Court Opera

ELSA BIENENFELD

Neues Wiener Journal
May 19, 1911

Elsa Bienenfeld (b. Vienna, 1877; d. 1940) was the only female music critic at a major newspaper, and possibly the only woman reviewing concerts under her own by-line, until the work force opened up during World War I and in its aftermath. The newspaper that employed her, the *Neues Wiener Journal*, aimed at a female readership. Despite its emphasis on human interest (reports of crimes and violence, stories of sentimentality, fashion, and the private lives of celebrities), the *Neues Wiener Journal* displayed greater concern for aesthetic matters and generally had higher taste than, for example, the *Illustrirtes Wiener Extrablatt*. The newspaper claimed to have the highest circulation among Viennese newspapers (60,000 to 70,000) and even sent issues daily to South America. The *Neues Wiener Journal* was unique among major newspapers in not focusing on current events, and was thus an ideal tool of the cultural branch of the foreign ministry, which sought to influence German readers abroad by placing articles in its pages. Its musical coverage was extensive, including a "Viennese folk music" supplement with musical scores and texts.[7]

Bienenfeld had training in medicine and chemistry before studying music theory under Schoenberg and musicology under Guido Adler; her dissertation was on Wolfgang Schmeltzl and the sixteenth-century quodlibet. Schoenberg selected Bienenfeld and Alexander von Zemlinsky as his assistants in 1903–1905 when he taught at the academy of the great pedagogue Eugenie Schwarzwald, who knew Schoenberg through their mutual friend Adolf Loos. Initially a supporter, Bienenfeld became critical of his composing for an elite audience, in particular in the genre of chamber symphony, following the Viennese premieres of the First String Quartet and the First Chamber Symphony. Her reviews provoked several private responses on Schoenberg's part.[8] Bienenfeld continued in her post at the *Neues Wiener Journal* for decades and in this capacity figured prominently in Viennese musical life. She was one of the few women on the planning committee of the city's 1927 Beethoven festival. On the occasion of Adler's seventieth birthday, Bienenfeld published a lengthy essay on the musicologist in the Berlin journal *Die Musik*.[9] She is believed to have perished in a Nazi death camp.[10]

Beginning with her review of the Seventh Symphony (translated below), Bienenfeld covered the first Viennese performances of all Mahler's works. She published two obituaries, addressing different facets of Mahler's life; in addition to the article translated below, she wrote on "Gustav Mahler and Vienna" in the Berlin daily *Der Tag* (30 May 1911). In the 1920s she published an article on Mahler as conductor as well as reproduced previously unpublished letters of Mahler to Hans von Bülow and Wilhelm Gericke.

• • •

Gustav Mahler directed the Vienna Court Opera for ten years. This decade, 1897 to 1907, is already now recognized as one of the great eras of German opera—similar in historical significance to the activities of Carl Maria von Weber and Richard Wagner in Dresden and Liszt in Weimar. Mahler was thirty-seven when he left Hamburg and came to Vienna. He was announced as the court conductor, but secretly, already then, was the director of the Opera.

His miraculous accomplishments as director in Budapest and court conductor in Hamburg were intriguing to the musical world of Vienna. Within twenty months he had taken the Budapest opera so far from its then completely dilapidated state that Brahms declared its *Don Giovanni* superior to anything in Vienna. At the Hamburg opera no less a figure than Bülow was an ardent admirer of the gifted conductor. Mahler's first performance in Vienna, on May 11, after a single rehearsal, was *Lohengrin*; the magician instantly enchanted the Viennese public. He exerted an immediate and personal effect.

Mahler became Vienna's opera director officially only a half year later. He found an institution in which a lack of discipline prevailed. His task was to reform the Opera, and he took on that task with unmatched zeal and energy. It should not be forgotten that Mahler was primarily a creative artist. The earnestness with which he turned his operatic activity into his life's work is characteristic of his phenomenal strength and unusual sense of duty. Mahler not only restored artistic and administrative discipline throughout the opera house but also educated the whole ensemble, soloists, orchestra, choir, and even the public, to a degree of cultivation that had a decisive influence on everyone's development—without those involved even being aware of it. The effect went beyond anything personal. In Vienna, Mahler realized the idea of the Wagnerian Gesamtkunstwerk.

His first achievement was the unabridged performance of Wagner's operas. The absolute purity of the artwork became his highest principle. Operatic theater was elevated from the sphere of the merely social and virtuosic to the realm of the unconditionally artistic. There were some external factors: admission during the performance was forbidden, the hall was darkened, and the singers were not allowed to interrupt the performance with bowing or *da capos*. Once having directed Wagner's dramas, Mahler produced operas that had a spirituality and vitality to a degree never before imagined. Mahler was not only a musician but the finest and most ingenious director. For the first time on a stage that was not Bayreuth, the spirit of tragedy or comedy came straight from the music.

Frau Gutheil-Schoder once said, "Mahler never came to a rehearsal with a production that was completely finished." He planned a particular scene as the focus of an entire act and shaped the whole from the mood he wanted to capture, taking into account the individuality of the actor. His aim was not realistic representation. He showed us that every opera is a stylized artwork and that everything depends on the style of the music and poetry. Mahler often changed individual scenes twenty times, even in the final orchestral rehearsals. That something already "existed" did not stop him from making adjustments, even after the performance. Rehearsals were therefore all the more interesting. Normally the quality goes down after repetition; with Mahler, however, each performance improved. Nothing could enrage him more than an objection like "Herr Director, yesterday you requested it this way and today you want it different." He would answer: "Only just yesterday I convinced myself that it is not possible like this. You must follow me!" His suggestive force was incredible. He had only to strike a single chord to make everyone know how to sing and act the next.

One had to witness Mahler's rehearsals in order to understand the man as a teacher. He had the rare ability to clarify the most complicated matters in a single word. For even the most subtle shades in human and artistic relations he always had at hand, in absolute certainty, the appropriate expression creating new and yet immediately comprehensible formations with convincing plasticity. The knowledge of instrumental and vocal technique, which he had developed through his cultivated sense of sound was unquestionable, and his technical instructions therefore had authentic value. When he perceived intelligence and goodwill, Mahler was both charmed and charming. He never tired of making an idea musically and dramatically comprehensible to everyone in all its manifold meanings. He had a remarkable talent for clarifying the heroic with the same overwhelming force as a tender, spirited mood. Nothing was inconsequential for him; there was never a good-natured and sloppy *laisser aller*. His every nerve, his every muscle, was always tense. His slender figure was incomparably passionate, both absorbing and projecting back all the changing moods of the music. He was the will embodied. Most amazing in Mahler was his ability to feel so strongly and so unreservedly, and finally to exhaust himself so unconditionally, down to the last drop.

Gustav Mahler as Organizer

EMIL GUTMANN

Die Musik
June 1911

After moving to the United States, Mahler relied on the impresario Emil Gutmann (b. Vienna, 1877; d. Garmisch-Partenkirchen, 1920) to program his symphonies in Europe. Gutmann was proprietor of the Munich agency that produced performances of the Sixth Symphony (November 8, 1906) and the Seventh Symphony (October 27, 1908) and the premiere of the Eighth Symphony (September 12, 1910). That last collaboration is detailed in Mahler's ten letters to Gutmann, who was responsible for the work's nickname, "Symphony of a Thousand." Gutmann's model of art as "organization" may well have a practical basis in the complicated logistics required to bring off the premiere—indeed, he unsuccessfully tried to reduce Mahler's number of rehearsals. The impresario's fifty letters to the board of the Singverein of the Gesellschaft der Musikfreunde show the extent of the preparation, including ten orchestral rehearsals, two full rehearsals, and a two-part general rehearsal.[11]

The same year as the Mahler premiere, 1910, Gutmann organized a Robert Schumann memorial festival and corresponded with Schoenberg about programming his *Verklärte Nacht*, String Quartets opp. 7, 10, the Piano Pieces op. 11, and several songs. Schoenberg and Gutmann were again in touch late in 1913. Gutmann served in World War I, as a soldier stationed in Hungary. After spending some months in Munich following the war, in the fall of 1919 he moved to Davos—a town made famous for its sanitorium in Thomas Mann's *The Magic Mountain*. On July 1, 1920 he was admitted to the Eglfing hospital in Garmisch-Partenkirchen for nervous disorders.[12]

While music criticism in the early twentieth century tended to celebrate a conductor's total control, here, ironically, an impresario offers a more flexible and spiritual view on the relationship of the conductor to the work. It is also notable that Gutmann does not lament the onset of modernism. He rather celebrates the organicism in Mahler's achievements as a conductor (as well as composer) through an extended allegory of organization as *organ*-izing. The body, rather than nature in general, is the site of the metaphor. His argument has historical significance in connecting organicism (which had been popular in musical thought since the 1830s) to the newer model of energetics (popular among music theorists in the early twentieth century).[13] Gutmann's philosophizing touches on broader issues related to the choreography of mass politics, first in the organization of the workers before and after World War I, and later in the organization of the *Volk* as a whole in the 1930s.

· · ·

Gustav Mahler's power of suggestion, whether as creator or recreator, is best explained by the strength of his character. I mean "character" in Emerson's sense of a human genius who would rather become the scoundrel and fool of this world than sully his white hands through compromise. No other aspiring contemporary composer has had this musician's near prophetic determination and his magnificent sobriety, because none was artistically of such strong character (in the above sense) as Gustav Mahler.

It is not my task to demonstrate the great integrity of his character in his own creations. In that area, integrity is sensed and felt more than demonstrated. Even with the most self-conscious artists, the creative drive and process remain veiled in mystery. All the clearer, therefore, is the evidence in the other half of Mahler's sphere of influence, where his capacities to recreate prevail. They have always met uncontested admiration but have yet to benefit from analytic explication.

Mahler's power to recreate was not limited to mere conducting and staging. It was artistic activity of a higher order. Not only did he interpret each composition anew, he transformed performance from being a solely technical achievement into an event of great significance artistically and intellectually. The countless rehearsals demanded by Mahler had as their goal neither extreme discipline nor the complete domination of the material, nor a total subjugation of individual subjects under the will of the artwork alone. Mahler's work aimed at forming a homogeneity from the initially disparate materiality of the performing forces. ("Homogeneous material" was a favorite phrase of Mahler!) He fused singers, orchestra, and stage into a unified whole that represented nothing less than the characteristic *organism* of the artwork. In this sense, a symphony or opera was not merely translated from the score into sound and motion. Mahler gave to the artwork, which had been merely imagined but not yet created: the *body* in which it *lived* and in which it found *its* head, *its* feet, *its* heart, and *its* pulse. Mahler did not reproduce the work of art, he actualized its *organization*.

The uniquely divine nature of a true artist is most clearly demonstrated in this extraordinary understanding of the organic requirements and living conditions for the artwork. The artwork has its roots in the foundations of all becoming and perishing—foundations that resist any speculation. An understanding of the artwork is therefore wholly elemental. Mahler's divinatory instinct for the conditions of the artwork's viability also explains the severity and inflexibility with which this "tyrant" dealt with the carelessness of practitioners. Those who have the creative will to impart life cannot knowingly submit to the crippling or even murder of their creations.

The ability to refashion the disparate forces for re-creation into something homogeneous, into a unified artwork, and into the body of the artwork itself, is unique. Like Goethe's pantheism or Rodin's pleinairism, it must be valued as original artistic talent—as "genius."[14] This quality as well—rather, this quality alone—makes Mahler the unique phenomenon that he represents for our era. The proof of this talent lies alone in its activity (which is fully conscious on the part of the artist).

To explain this ability I will briefly discuss Mahler's performance of the Eighth Symphony. My choice of this work, rather than one of his productions of a music drama, is determined not merely by my limited insight into his activities in the area of opera (relative to my understanding of the organizational realization of this symphony, which I observed and collaborated in from start to finish). Instead, I chose it particularly because his special understanding of how to organize is most clearly explained with respect to self-understanding. Moreover, the corporeal realization of this work (which he repeatedly called his life's work) was the most complicated task Mahler ever set for himself. [Discussion of Mahler's care in selecting the performers.]

The initial rehearsals had to yield a complete technical mastery. In the full rehearsals he concentrated on expression; here, too, he worked with groups, never the whole ensemble. Every limb of the gigantic body received special instructions and explanations, colored in such a way that each group necessarily perceived its task as paramount and did not need to be concerned with what others played. (The arm doesn't care how the leg moves; it's only important that both move perfectly.) By requiring everyone to focus exclusively on their special task Mahler averted any distraction, failings, or mistakes on the musicians' part. In particular, he knew how to describe tangibly and clearly, in both words and gestures, what he wanted. A trumpeter may crack if he is aware of having to play a difficult high C. Yet once Mahler explained that what's at stake is not a C but a scream or a vital function of a musical organ, which is embodied in the trumpet, the player will certainly no longer crack.

For Mahler, organizing the artwork did not stop with the performers. He also provided it with the atmosphere in which to breathe. An artwork only lives once it is taken in and received. Mahler neglected nothing that he found essential to the listener's reception. The spatial arrangement of the masses was very important to him, so that the corporeal unity of this artwork was intelligible to the eye as well. Roller, ever loyal, knew to realize Mahler's intentions with an arrangement that was highly effective architecturally. Mahler also controlled the lighting and managed to have the streetcars that passed the concert hall drive slowly and not ring their bells during performances, in order to avoid these alien sounds!

Mahler prevented the sale of "guides," for what is reading and recognizing a theme compared with understanding and receiving the artwork as a living entity, such as he strived to have it! His concern for this unity of the organism and the unity in its reception even led him to abolish the program book, which in fact only contained the text (that is, the words that were sung), not even the names of the soloists and the choruses. For this same reason he refused any interpretation and superfluous addition. (One letter to me reads, "My Symphony is not called a Faust Symphony, it is no Faust Symphony, and I forbid any such label.") For Mahler, I think, there was no program music, because there was also no absolute music. He only knew one absolute art, which had to be embodied uniformly in each work of art. What was the result of this unified organization?

When Mahler stepped up to the podium in the partial darkness of the gigantic hall in which the black masses of listeners merged with the black and white masses of performers, everyone felt that a primeval being, viable and well organized, was about to receive its heart and that instantly the heart would begin to beat. At this moment there were no singers, no listeners, no instruments, nor resounding body; there was only a single body with a multitude of veins and nerves waiting for the blood and spirit of art to flow. No other conductor inspired in everyone such complete openness toward art, the artwork, and the reception of art. The name and purpose of this body became a concept: the community for art!

Mahler lowered the baton—and the vitalizing blood pounded rhythmically through the body. The mouth of all humanity that was gathered up on the holy mountain opened for the first time in the ardent outcry, "Veni creator spiritus!" Mahler never conducted anything that was not an invocation of creative deity. This, in the end, is what Mahler the organizer could impart to people who were willing to listen.[15]

Mahler as Director

HERMANN BAHR

Musikblätter des Anbruch
April 1920

Hermann Bahr (b. Linz, 1863; d. Munich, 1934) became a spokesman and critical theorist for the young generation of artists in the years around 1900, a group he sought to publicize as "Young Vienna." Bahr is best known for his keen portrayal of the components of literary impressionism so paradigmatic of the Austrian fin de siècle—heightened self-consciousness, feelings of ambivalence, and dark intimations about a civilization of excess. Bahr's artistic orientation, however, changed radically at several points. His early critical works sought to reconcile Naturalism with Romanticism ("On the Criticism of Modernity" and "Overcoming Naturalism," 1890–1891). He later fell under Maeterlinck's influence, championing mysticism and Symbolism. After the turn of the century Bahr's writings reflected the new interest in the social function of the arts ("Dialogue on Marsyas," 1904, and *Expressionism*, 1914). During World War I, Bahr returned to the Roman Catholic faith (in 1916) and wrote his novel *The Ascension*.

As a young man and into his thirties, Bahr worked as a journalist and critic in Berlin and Vienna. Mahler worked in two spheres, as both opera director and composer; Bahr, too, was involved with the theatrical world even as he produced a considerable literary oeuvre. In 1901 he and Felix Salten founded the Young Viennese Theater "Zum lieben Augustin" cabaret, with the idea of introducing the Gesamtkunstwerk into a new venue. In 1903 Bahr left journalism to become director of the Deutsches Theater in Berlin and, in 1918, was briefly the director of the prestigious Burgtheater in Vienna. Bahr was a passionate supporter of the Mahler and Alfred Roller collaborations at the Vienna Court Opera, as well as Hugo Wolf, and responded to music in various literary works such as his comedy *Das Konzert* (1909). That same year he married the soprano Anna von Mildenburg, who had been Mahler's great love from his Hamburg years. Bahr and Mildenburg co-authored *Bayreuth and Wagner's Theater* (1912). Bahr's move to Salzburg (where he penned the article below), was part of the postwar effort to reinvent the city as a new home for Central European culture, and then to Munich in 1922, where Mildenburg taught at the Academy of Music.

• • •

"In their most fortunate moments," Goethe said, "the best masters come close to the highest art, where individuality disappears and what is thoroughly right is produced."[16] Drama is an attempt for the common man to participate in these most fortunate moments of the best masters, transforming their own individual ecstasy into public celebration. This was the idea of Greek tragedy and the achievement of Baroque theater, which Wagner renewed in Bayreuth. To remove the common man's "individuality" and fill him with "what is thoroughly right," a master of magical power must supply and transfer to others what he himself experiences. This master, who can intoxicate all, is the actor. The experience of Baroque theater entailed deploying the combined energy of all supporting arts to elevate the actor to a divine bliss that ultimately passed from him through the *Volk* who were watching him. Watching becomes empathizing: nothing unique or individual in the spectator remains, nothing other than "what is thoroughly right." Those who even once had seen the light would reflect from the mere remembrance of it for the rest of their lives. Never again would they suffer total misfortune. It remains an incomprehensible mystery about the Germans that a people could experience this for one and a half centuries and then simply forget it. Wagner's unimaginable greatness was that he reinvented the Baroque theater for which Goethe yearned so much and which he grasped in a vision in the second *Faust*.[17] But to present this for ten years every day to the regulars at the opera house in Vienna—this was the foolhardy wager of Gustav Mahler.

When we experienced him as composer or director, Mahler seemed novel, without precedent. Now we realize that what he did was not so much to innovate as to fulfill. Along with Hugo Wolf and Anton Bruckner, he completed what Beethoven, Weber, and Schubert had begun. And he completed Wagner's goal at Bayreuth, the completion of the Baroque. He was the last German master.

Wagner lets the dramatist "speak from the actor's most individual nature" and sees in Shakespeare the "poetic actor."[18] Nietzsche recognizes in Wagner "the existence of an original histrionic talent" which "found its expedient and deliverance in drawing together all the arts into a great histrionic manifestation."[19] Wagner calls the actor "the element of our society that truly incites enthusiasm."[20] Mahler, then, forms the living sum of this: he was the mimic musician; enthusiasm was the impulse, content, and result of his staging.

In Mahler a Bohemian musician sat hand in hand with a young German craftsman and the demon of the metaphysician. He was a Baroque angel with a trumpet and a singer's mouth. Within him were both a devout believer and an actor of the most elemental kind. He was thus the true unification of the bourgeois: at the same time folklike, ghostly, and seraphic; mysteriously familiar with the dark forces of the abyss as well as the light ones of blessed heights, but foreign to the middle regions. In this Jewish Kapellmeister Kreisler, through whose facial expressions Goethe seemed to struggle with the devil, the genius of German music was among us for the last time—and, to complete the hellish joke of history, under Montenuovo's supervision.[21]

Amidst the usual sloth of the dilapidated German theater business, certain performances stand out as events, either as craftworks responsibly prepared and carefully executed or as improvisations aroused by fortunate inspiration and intensified at a favorable moment. The secret of Mahler's uniqueness was to combine craft with genius. As a result, performances of technical perfection and incomparable precision, as reliable as clockwork, became improvisations of breathless bliss under the intoxicating, igniting, and enrapturing force of his transfigured, inebriated look and his ever irresistible hand, now fiercely stirring, then tenderly appeasing. These improvisations came visibly into being before our eyes and overpowered singers, orchestra, and the demonic improviser himself, at the podium. Even those of us down in the audience were suddenly no longer there merely as spectators or listeners. We were no longer ourselves but were drawn into the drama, in its immense gravity. We lost ourselves only to find ourselves awakened, and from the empty phenomena of the day we passed to the fullness of eternal truth. Suddenly it was certain, in the most direct manner, that there is a realm of the beautiful, good, and true. We found our home.

That was Mahler's miracle, which he had us experience dithyrambically. He revived once again, at the Vienna Opera, our ancient Baroque theater. There was, to be sure, one small difference: Baroque theater reflected the truth of an immense living realm, Mahler's opera only the truth of a lonely dreaming artist. But it is the same truth.[22]

The First Symphony

Mahler conducted the premiere of his First Symphony (called a "Symphonisches Gedicht") in Budapest on November 20, 1889. He prepared a more elaborate literary program for its German premiere, in Hamburg (October 27, 1893), under the title "Titan," at the conclusion of a lengthy concert: Beethoven's *Egmont* Overture, two arias by Marschner and Adophe Adam, Mendelssohn's *Hebrides* Overture, and several lieder from his own *Des Knaben Wunderhorn*. Even in a venue favorably inclined to new music, the annual Composers' festival of the Pan-German Musical Society (Allgemeiner Deutscher Musikverein) in Weimar (June 3, 1894), the First Symphony proved taxing to listeners when it closed the first half of a program that extended over four hours. The concert opened with Liszt's *Weimar's Volkslied* for male chorus, Anton Rubinstein's Cello Concerto no. 1 in A minor, and Wagner's Wesendonck Lieder (orchestrated by Felix Mottl); the second half included von Bülow's orchestra ballad *Des Sängers Fluch*, Bernhard Stavenhagen's Piano Concerto in B minor, op. 4, Brünnhilde's Immolation Scene from Wagner's *Götterdämmerung*, and Wagner's *Kaisermarsch*. These early performances included the "Blumine" Andante movement, which Mahler removed in his revision of the Symphony.

Despite its mixed reception, the First Symphony saw many performances over the course of Mahler's life. Apart from one program of his own music (the first movement of the Second Symphony and the *Lieder eines fahrenden Gesellen)* which Mahler conducted on the occasion of the Berlin premiere (March 16, 1896), the First Symphony was often paired with Beethoven, whose music was important to his programming in general. At the Prague premiere (March 3, 1898), which Mahler conducted, the second half of the concert, with Franz Schalk conducting, included two movements from Berlioz's *La damnation de Faust* ("Menuet des follets" and "Ballet des sylphes," which was so warmly received that the movement was repeated), and Beethoven's *Leonore* Overture no. 3. The baritone Karl Scheidemantel sang Beethoven's "An die Hoffnung" (with orchestral accompaniment), Heinrich Hermann's "Drei Wanderer," Schumann's "Mit Myrthen und Rosen," Schubert's "Sei mir gegrüsst," as well as two encores, Jensen's "Magareth am Thore" and Beethoven's "Der Kuss" (with piano accompaniment). Likewise in Frankfurt am Main (March 8, 1899), Mahler conducted the First Symphony, and Ludwig Rottenberg, in turn, Beethoven's *Coriolan* Overture and Eighth Symphony as well as an aria from Haydn's *Creation*. At the first performance in Vienna (November 18, 1900), which the four reviews below covered, the First Symphony was preceded by Beethoven's

Prometheus Overture and Schumann's *Manfred* Overture. Many Viennese critics, including Eduard Hanslick and Theodor Helm below, may have been predisposed against the composer after their negative reviews of his arrangement for string orchestra of Beethoven's String Quartet in F minor op. 95, nearly two years before.[23]

Beethoven's *Leonore* Overture no. 3 was one of the works most frequently paired with Mahler's First Symphony—and as well the Seventh Symphony. (Defending one program that included the Seventh and a new work by Conrad Ansorge, Mahler's friend Max Marschalk noted wryly that the public, of course, would rather have heard yet another *Leonore* Overture no. 3.)[24] The overture was programmed with the First Symphony in Linz (January 20, 1907); Leopold Materna conducted the Beethoven and accompanied three Mahler songs on the piano ("Um Mitternacht," "Erinnerung," and "Aus! aus!)." The same pairing occurred in Wiesbaden in 1908, but with Mendelssohn's *Hebrides* Overture; Mahler conducted the entire concert. Some critics complained about the deleterious effect of hearing Beethoven after Mahler, as for example when Ferdinand Löwe conducted Mahler's First in Vienna followed by the *Emperor* Concerto (November 8, 1904).[25] Emerging gradually from silence, Mahler's First was effective at the start of a concert that concluded with Beethoven. Thus Richard Strauss, in a Berlin concert of 1909, programmed the First Symphony, Spohr's Notturno op. 34, for winds and Turkish band; Beethoven's Grosse Fuge op. 133 (arranged by Felix Weingartner for string orchestra), and the *Leonore* Overture no. 3.

A First Symphony

MAX GRAF

Wiener Rundschau
December 1, 1900

The son of a Viennese newspaper publisher, Max Graf (b. Vienna, 1873; d. Vienna, 1958) had the connections and the education to win himself an entrée into music criticism at an early age. Graf studied music theory with Bruckner and music history with Hanslick, writing a dissertation on women and music in the Renaissance (1896). After a brief stint in Paris, Graf returned to Vienna to join the staff of the progressive *Wiener Allgemeine Zeitung* in 1900 and work as a critic for the liberal *Neues Wiener Journal* in 1901–1906.

Graf organized the 1928 Vienna festival for the centenary of Schubert's death; until 1936 he also directed the annual Vienna May Music festivals, which developed from it.

Graf taught in a wide range of institutions in Vienna and the United States. In 1902, he was an instructor in musicology and musical aesthetics at the Conservatory of the Gesellschaft der Musikfreunde. When the institution renamed itself the Academy for Music and the Dramatic Arts in 1909, Graf became a professor in music at the Viennese State Academy. He was also a lecturer at the Austro-American Institute in Vienna (1930–1935). After the Anschluss, Graf fled to the United States, teaching at the New School of Social Research in New York City, and, as a visiting professor, at the Carnegie Institute and Temple University. Soon after the war, Graf returned to Vienna, where he taught a seminar on music criticism at the Academy for three years, by which point he was seventy-seven. He was also a visiting professor at the Mozarteum in Salzburg.

Graf was one of the first to relate Freud's psychoanalytic theory to music (in his *Wagner-Probleme, und andere Studien* of 1900, which he dedicated to Mahler). Applying the theory of a "Jewish psychologist" to "a great composer" brought him scorn in the Nazi catalogue of Jewish intellectuals. He was well-known for his promulgation of Freud's ideas, and his son Herbert Graf (1904–1973), who became a successful opera director and music administrator, was in 1909 one of Freud's important patients, "Little Hans."

Throughout his life Graf would champion talented, young composers. Mahler, however, was a special case. In the review below Graf, himself a mere twenty-seven, shows immense sympathy for the First Symphony Mahler completed at nearly the same age. The following year, upon joining the *Neues Wiener Journal*, Graf covered *Das klagende Lied* and wrote in *Die Wage* in support of Mahler as director. Graf's review of the Fourth Symphony from 1904, which was more critical, led to a famous clash with the composer. Plagued by guilt, Graf apologized to Mahler, citing his own moodiness; the gesture incensed the composer, who retorted that the critic understood his music as little when he praised it as when he did not. After this point, as Richard Specht reported it, Graf became an enemy of Mahler.[26] His later review of the Fifth Symphony had a peculiar format. In a tone of feigned neutrality, it presented a long series of quotations from philosophers, literary figures, and other authorities on culture, which pointed up the criteria unmet in Mahler's new work. In the end the review amounted to a devastating attack. After Mahler's daughter died, Graf sent a condolence letter that went unanswered. When they met on the Ringstrasse that summer, Mahler shook his hand and rushed away. Graf was unsure "whether it was the sudden memory of the sad event, which had brought us closer together, or whether it was a feeling of pain or disappointment, or the stirrings of anger after a moment of affability."[27] Graf later published an obituary of Mahler and an account of their interaction (14 August 1921), both in the *Neues Wiener Journal*.

. . .

[. . .] Gustav Mahler's First Symphony in D major provoked the worst kind of tactlessness from the Philharmonic audience. Like the *Symphonie fantastique,* this symphony arises from the storms, crises, and spiritual catastrophes of youth, and can count on being felt and understood by our younger generation. The composer knows that only this generation—thanks to their inner turbulence and their flexibility [*Bewegtheit und Beweglichkeit*]—can unite the work's crass mood swings between lyricism, parody, and pathos, and perceive the work as coherent despite its contrasts. Only this generation can feel the work's great emotional rapture, pleasure in intensely colored sound, and ecstasy of passion; only they can enjoy its parody and distortion of sacred emotion. I myself am far too close to this generation not to empathize with the work as if it were my own. Yet I can almost understand that an older generation finds it alien. Calmer, more solid, and less agile, they expect a certain uniformity in feeling and a wide distribution of inner force, regardless of any momentary richness in emotion. These individuals are masters of their passions (I have in mind the highest kind of person, not the everyday riffraff, who are entirely passionless), and they demand the taming, rather than the overflowing, of affect. They demand a certain chastity even in the strongest emotional expression, and they disdain all ostentation. They demand not a parody of feeling—which is always the result of a struggle between mind and heart—but the pure play of the mind (wit) or the pure play of the heart (humor). Perhaps I will feel the same about the work in a few years. All that matters is that every young generation will undoubtedly swear anew by this symphony of Gustav Mahler.

The symphony divides into two parts. The first projects images of peace, an idyllic and undesecrated nature, as well as the first joyous play of life's forces. The second shows a corrupted world stripped of peace which must struggle for redemption. Here, passions are stirred, and the grimaces of grotesque humor abound. While the first half reflects the world in a flat mirror, the second presents a fragmented and distorted image reflected from the broken pieces of a convex mirror. . . .

The structure of the symphony reminds one of a play in which the catastrophe takes place during the interlude between the second and third acts. The dramatic moment that causes the emotional denouement has been placed behind the scenes. The artist thus appeals to the listeners' imagination, allowing them to construct the bridge between the second and third acts of his tone-drama. And here, of course, is where the Philharmonic audience abandoned the artist: between the second and third movement of a symphony they usually think of dinner, not the emotional catastrophes of their days of youth and love. But perhaps this is too much to expect even from an audience that has a better artistic education than the Viennese: Mahler demands recourse to their imagination precisely at points where he himself did not know how to express the whole experience musically.

The two large main parts of the symphony, the lyrical-idyllic and the ironic-tragic, each comprise two movements. The first movement of the first part is filled with feelings of nature: bird songs and horns resound, and blaring trumpets are carried by the wind. The themes are tender and express pleasure, comfort, and cheerful devotion. They interweave freely, winding through and over each other only to slip away and rush back to the round dance. Listeners looking for a development in the old style will not find it here. Instead, in this attempt at a "Forest Murmurs" mood, a free interchange of motives runs through the whole movement: poetic meaning determines musical design.[28] The second movement, a scherzo, adapts this idyllic mood in a new form. The movement is forceful harmonically (though it remains in the same place for too long), causing one's very limbs to move. These are sounds of the same naïve world, only more energetic and lively. . . .

The opening movement of the second part is grotesquely humorous and suffused with a bizarre and grimacing spirit. I believe it to be the most peculiar movement of the work yet also emotionally deeper than one might think. . . . Certain excitable individuals who are deeply gripped by emotions can suppress them only by derision and distortion; they tear them into pieces and turn them into grimaces: they become comedians of their own pain. In this same way the composer frees himself from the tragedies that have caused emotional crises in his life—the memory of a beloved one who is now deceased, for example—by distorting his grief into a grimace and thereby deriding it. Within this caricature of a funeral march, the G-major passage is psychologically very refined: a true and pure feeling surfaces for a moment but soon gives way again to the grotesque happenings. Thus the third movement prepares the fourth, in which tragedy, despair, and suffering stormily break through, and redemption is finally fought out in the battle of the chorales. This movement, which harkens back to the first motivically, explodes with a vehemence that somehow is not able to wreak damage: the tense, naturalistic pathos constricts, rather than stimulates, the listener's imagination. An increase of force is impossible after the first measures, and without an increase (as Carl Maria von Weber once said), coldness always remains. With listeners as well, the iron must be cast while it is hot. In such an atmosphere the final triumph has the effect of sheer force: it shatters rather than elevates. . . . This, I think, is the emotional content of Gustav Mahler's First Symphony.

Theater and Art Reviews: Second Philharmonic Concert

EDUARD HANSLICK

Neue Freie Presse
November 20, 1900

At once the most powerful and most scorned critic of late nineteenth-century Vienna, Eduard Hanslick (b. Prague, 1825; d. Baden, near Vienna, 1904) developed a formalism that has been oversimplified in the annals of music history, especially in early twentieth-century perceptions. Authors of aesthetic treatises and interpretive writings on music at the turn of the century felt compelled to take up his 1854 treatise *On the Beautiful in Music* in the development of a new psychological aesthetic.[29] In his review of Mahler's First Symphony, below, Hanslick shows a different (and hardly formalist) face: here, as a professional music critic, he proposes that the incomprehensibility of the work in purely musical terms must mean that there is a secret program. Once famous for his sharp tongue, the august critic, at the age of seventy-five, published one of the more mild-manneredly skeptical reactions to the Viennese premiere, and even hoped to review the symphony at a future performance. He would not, however, live to hear the next performance in Vienna, which took place on November 8, 1904, at the Konzertverein under Ferdinand Löwe.

Hanslick was a brilliant stylist and an uncompromising critic. Perhaps more than any other individual, he was responsible for the prominence that music criticism won in the Viennese press, with reviews and music feuilletons often appearing on the front page. Though satirized relentlessly, Hanslick commanded an unmatched power and influence in his ability to promote musicians and place his protégés. His review of Mahler's First appeared in the leading Viennese newspaper, the *Neue Freie Presse*, established when a group of editors, including Hanslick, broke away from *Die Presse*. (When Mahler was in New York, he reported that "I learn about Vienna from random issues of the *Neue Freie Presse*—being used to deciphering the code between the lines of that newspaper.")[30]

Hanslick's review begins with a quotation now famous in the lore about Mahler's troubled reception among contemporaries: "One of us is crazy, and it is not I." Max Kalbeck, for example, picked up the thread the following season in a discussion of interpretive strategies.[31] Hanslick's quip is usually attributed to the critic himself, but the witty opening gambit is not, at least explicitly, his own judgment—a characteristically crafty rhetorical move from a master tactician.

· · ·

"One of us must be crazy, and it is not I!" This is how one of two stubborn scholars ended a long argument. It probably is I, I thought with genuine modesty, after recovering from the horrific Finale of Mahler's D Major Symphony. As a sincere admirer of the conductor Mahler, to whom the Opera and the Philharmonic Orchestra are so deeply indebted, I do not want to be hasty in my judgment of his strange symphony. On the other hand I owe sincerity to my readers and thus must sadly admit that the new symphony is the kind of music which for me is not music. Perhaps I would have developed a closer relationship (if hardly one of love) to the piece had its origin and meaning not remained secret. At its premiere in Weimar the symphony was called "Titan" and had a detailed program; critics found these "abstruse"; and, as a result, both were removed. Generally such poetic user manuals are partly annoying and partly suspect: our symphonic masters, from Haydn and Mozart to Brahms and Dvořák, have let us into their heaven without admission tickets. Mahler's symphony would hardly have pleased us more with a program than without. But we cannot remain indifferent to knowing what an ingenious man like Mahler had in mind with each of these movements and how he would have explained their puzzling coherence. Thus we lack a guide to show the correct path in the darkness. What does it mean when a cataclysmic Finale suddenly breaks forth, or when a Funeral March on the old student canon "Frère Jacques" is interrupted by a section entitled "parody"?

To be sure, the music itself would have neither gained nor lost anything with a program; still, the composer's intentions would have become clearer and the work therefore more comprehensible. Without such aid, we had to be satisfied with some witty details and stunningly brilliant orchestral technique. The execution of this outrageously difficult novelty was admirable, and the applause enthusiastic—at least from the younger audience. Crammed into the standing room and the gallery, they could not stop calling Mahler back onstage again and again. At a future performance of the symphony, I hope to be able to expand this brief review, which here is more confession than judgment. At present I lack a full appreciation of what at times this most intelligent composer also lacks: "the grace of God."

Viennese Musical Letter

THEODOR HELM

Pester Lloyd
November 27, 1900

Chronologically separated from Mahler by almost a generation, and aesthetically removed from him by an entire world, Theodor Helm (b. Vienna, 1843; d. Vienna, 1920) was a strong conservative voice in Vienna and one of the city's most respected critics. Orphaned at fifteen upon the death of his musical mother, a woman of noble lineage, Helm became a student of jurisprudence and entered into the civil service under the tutelage of his guardian, a general in the Hapsburg army. In a series of events that his followers would idealize, Helm became absorbed in the city's rich musical life; among his acquaintances were Brahms, Bruckner, and Hugo Wolf. Helm assisted his stepfather Carl Müller, who was music critic at the *Neues Fremdenblatt,* and upon his death in 1869, he assumed the position of music critic and married Müller's daughter. As one contemporary put it, Helm brushed up against tragedy early in his life. After the traumas of his own youth, his wife became deaf in their second year of marriage; five years later their firstborn died, whom Brahms believed to be a musical genius—or so Helm's admirers claimed.[32]

When the *Musikalisches Wochenblatt* was founded in 1870, Helm, twenty-seven, was recruited by Ernst Wilhelm Fritzsch to contribute articles. He wrote for the weekly until his death at seventy-seven;

from 1907 he served a term as editor-in-chief of this Leipzig conglomerate, which had been absorbed into the illustrious *Neue Zeitschrift für Musik*. After the *Neues Fremdenblatt* went under, Helm freelanced for the liberal Budapest *Pester Lloyd*, the *Wiener Salonblatt,* and the Leipzig *Tonhalle,* until 1884, when the nationalist Viennese *Deutsche Zeitung* was founded. He served as its music critic until 1901.

Helm contributed to Viennese musical culture in a range of venues. He had a long affiliation with Horak's Conservatory, first as a lecturer of aesthetics (from 1874) and music history (from 1882) and beginning in 1900 as a professor. He briefly edited the *Illustriertes Musik-, Theater- und Literatur-Journal* (1876–1878), and for over a quarter century, beginning in 1875, edited the *Kalender für die musikalische Welt,* which provided a list of the events of Viennese musical culture. Soon after the turning point in Bruckner reception, which contemporaries observed in 1900, Helm, who had known the composer, organized a three-year series of Bruckner evenings (Akademische Gesangverein), beginning in 1902, at which the symphonies were heard in four-hand piano arrangements, with explanatory lectures delivered.

Helm's most important publication was his analysis of Beethoven's string quartets, first published serially in the *Musikalisches Wochenblatt* (1873) and later in book form.[33] In that same journal, Helm reviewed Mahler's Symphonies nos. 1, 2, 4–7, and *Kindertotenlieder.* Helm met criticism for tailoring his reviews to specific audiences. There are marked differences between his writings for the *Musikalisches Wochenblatt* and *Deutsche Zeitung,* on the one hand, and his works for the liberal Hungarians who read *Pester Lloyd,* on the other; the latter paper ran the review translated below, revised from what had appeared in the *Deutsche Zeitung* one week earlier. Karl Kraus's *Die Fackel* poked fun at Helm for publishing contradictory reviews of a Karl Goldmark opera, calling him a "helmet without a head" and a critic whose inconsistent judgments arose from a "tragic conflict of professional duties."[34] His reminiscences of fifty years of Viennese musical life, first published in *Der Merker* in 1916, have been reproduced in book form.[35]

• • •

Gustav Mahler's First Symphony, heard at the last Philharmonic concert, was truly a bone of contention for the public as well as the critics. This is not to say that the piece wasn't superficially a success: a large majority of the audience applauded, and Mahler was repeatedly called out. But there were also startled faces all around, and some hissing was heard. When leaving the concert hall, on the stairs and in the coatroom, one couldn't have heard more contradictory comments about the new work. [Discussion of earlier reviews and the first version of the symphony.]

The work was first performed publicly under the direction of the composer in 1894 at the Composers' Festival of the Pan-German Musical Society in Weimar. At that time the symphony had an additional movement. The work was named *Titan*, from a novel by Jean Paul that has been mostly forgotten; with detailed titles throughout, it was program music through and through. [A list of the movement titles in the earlier version.] Since then Mahler has renounced this rather daring program. He removed all titles and explanatory remarks and now wants his First Symphony to be understood as absolute music. Indeed he went so far in denying what were ostensibly his own earlier artistic intentions as to forbid explicitly the customary technical analysis in the Philharmonic program book, according to a statement by the editor.

In my humble opinion the music of his First Symphony is not well served by this veil of mystery. With its entirely puzzling design, the symphony literally screams for an explanatory program. Without one, the listener cannot understand how the opening two movements, which are decisively pastoral, can be followed by a strangely parodic funeral march built upon the homey old student canon "Bruder Martin"—or, in another version, Frère Jaques. Nor can the listener grasp the relation between this piquant tragicomedy and the desperately furious orchestral storm of the Finale. In the light of such difficulties, it was cruel of the composer to deprive his unprepared Philharmonic audience of not only the program book but also any technical guide to this labyrinth of sound. [Discussion of the publisher Josef Weinberger, who provided the four-hand piano reduction.]

It seems strange that as the main theme of the first movement of his D Major Symphony Mahler takes the melody of the song "Ging heut Morgen über's Feld" from his own *Songs of a Wayfarer*. Even Max Kalbeck, who reviews Mahler's First favorably by interpreting it as a *Sinfonia ironica*, cannot appreciate this idea, which is more poetic than musical. The movement is otherwise without a program (though the idea of nature awakening would do much here to aid the listener's imagination). Judged by traditional symphonic standards, the movement lacks clarity and logic. How can one account for the presence of a cuckoo, continuously calling, in a work of absolute music?! N.B.: This cuckoo does not call on a minor third as it does in nature, or even—as in Beethoven's "Pastoral" Symphony or Humperdinck's *Hansel and Gretel*—on a major third, but rather issues provocatively abnormal calls on the descending fourth d to a! Perhaps Nietzsche, to whom we owe the term "superman," would have spoken here of a "supercuckoo," had he included animals in his poetic and symbolic philosophy of life. But to my knowledge Zarathustra did not speak of this.

The first movement is impressive mainly in its tone painting. In its more coherent passages, the movement resembles the work of a modern Haydn (introduction, $\frac{4}{4}$, D minor; Allegro, alla breve, D major). It is followed by a forceful, coarse peasant dance (slow waltz tempo, $\frac{3}{4}$, A major), which is musically the most amiable portion of the work, yet one that makes no attempt to hide its antecedents in Bruckner and even Weber (the "Freischütz" Waltz!) The sarcastic Funeral March brings out the melody of the canon "Frère Jacques" successively in low and high instruments, continuously supporting it with an ostinato bass of two notes (d and a): the whole thing seems like an old French carillon modeled after Bizet. A conspicuously Hungarian melody is used in the trio of the march, continuing the movement's drive toward the openly parodistic: the performance instruction "vulgar" appears over the section in the piano reduction. The Funeral March closes with the low basses playing D in triple piano; after this, the Finale opens like an outcry of horror in triple forte, in F minor—overly bold for a symphony in D major, especially entering immediately after D minor!—with a stormy pedal point on the dominant C. In the upper voices, the shrill piccolo whistles against a truly devastating cymbal clash.

The opening certainly must be downright "hellish" in a piece originally entitled "Dall' inferno al paradiso." The movement continues in this vein for some time. Only momentarily does a ray of light shine onto this dark night of despair: the beautiful D-flat melody. This melody shows what Mahler gained from studying with Anton Bruckner, but, unfortunately, it only appears occasionally. As one who studied the score can verify, the composer finally leads us into paradise with a combination of no fewer than four flutes, four oboes, four clarinets, seven horns (augmented), three trombones and a tuba; furthermore, the performance instructions stipulate literally, "Bells Up!—It is advisable to augment the horns until the end, when the hymnlike chorale that drowns everything else has reached the necessary sonority." Our horn players loyally submitted to Mahler's bidding, and thus the desired non plus ultra of sonority was reached—however with very mixed effects on the ears and nerves of the listeners. Only the composer could inform us whether the dynamic-acoustic outdoing of Berlioz which occurs at the end of this most peculiar symphony is also parodistic and satirical. No small number of visitors at the music festival in Weimar, 1894 assumed this; now many of the listeners in Vienna do as well. Yet this seems less than obvious to me: the colossal violence of the climaxes could also be the expression of a tremendous creative urge seeking recognition at all costs. [. . .]

Feuilleton: Philharmonic Concert

ROBERT HIRSCHFELD

Wiener Abendpost
November 20, 1900

Robert Hirschfeld (b. Gross Mesertsch, Moravia, 1858; d. Salzburg, 1914) was among Vienna's most eloquent advocates of an educated musical public and a repertoire dominated by the classical canon (including, above all, the works of Bruckner). *"Music for all*—the *highest* music for all—this was for him the fundamental goal of art. He was a true friend and supporter of the Workers' Symphony Concerts," David Josef Bach would recall years later.[36] Upon completing his doctorate under Hanslick in 1884, Hirschfeld taught aesthetics for fifteen years at the Vienna Conservatory. Outspoken from an early age, he denounced his former professor's lack of receptivity to Renaissance music in a pamphlet entitled *Das kritische Verfahren Hanslicks* (1885). Julius Korngold later recalled that Hirschfeld even trained his dog to growl and tear up a newspaper whenever instructed that it contained a review by Hanslick.[37] Hirschfeld's interest in early music extended well beyond his dissertation (on the fourteenth-century composer Johannes de Muris). Beginning in 1899, he organized concerts of early music, and in 1913 he assumed the directorship of the Mozarteum in Salzburg.

Hirschfeld promulgated traditional musical values in several practical venues. He wrote and edited program notes for the Vienna Philharmonic from 1892 until he left Vienna in 1913, and in 1896 became music critic for the *Wiener Zeitung*, publishing feuilletons in the evening edition, the *Wiener Abendpost*. Hirschfeld was known as an advocate of Bruckner and a detractor of Mahler, Hanslick, and Schoenberg—a critic, in other words, of the most important Jewish figures in Austro-German musical life. These critical positions—and the far-right supporters whom Hirschfeld won through his Bruckner advocacy—are one reason for his exclusion from Gerigk and Stengel's otherwise comprehensive *Lexikon der Juden in der Musik* (in which minor figures were identified through brief, neutral descriptions, and important musicians subjected to brutally anti-Semitic treatment).[38]

Hirschfeld was one of Mahler's three worst enemies in Vienna, according to Richard Specht—"the most hated and poisonous, branded with all the weapons of distortion, misinterpretation, and prejudice."[39] The sarcastic tone of Hirschfeld's review of the First Symphony, from 1900, throws into question the account given by his contemporary Paul Stefan. Stefan claimed that Hirschfeld responded positively to Mahler's work until autumn 1902, when, shortly after the premiere, Mahler canceled further performances of Mozart's Singpsiel *Zaide*—a production that Hirschfeld had arranged.[40] A friend recounted that Mahler once told him, "Hirschfeld's invective against me is so meaningless that it no longer interests me. I find even his tone unheard of. If one wants to criticize me, they should do so 'with one's hat in one's hand.' It doesn't enhance his reputation to treat me roughly. Moreover, he can do whatever he will but will not change the fact that I am continuing on my path, and nothing can lead me astray."[41]

In decrying modern artistic inclinations, Hirschfeld targeted the idea that music should reflect its cultural context. When repeated performances of Mahler symphonies indicated that the works were being admitted to the canon, rather than merely being introduced to the city, Hirschfeld responded more harshly. He lashed out at listeners who were "seduced by the clichés" that Mahler's music conveyed "'personality,' 'an expression of the times' and 'an element of culture.'" He went on to redefine what the "personality" of a symphony composer should be, drawing on a Brucknerian aesthetic: "We need only be certain that this personality possesses great inner strength and composure, follows a straight, linear course, and has the immense spiritual tranquility needed to shape a symphonic structure."[42] This review, from November 1909, would be Hirschfeld's last discussion of Mahler until the obituary. In effect, Hirschfeld developed a disgust for the culture in which he found himself, a musical world in which symphonies like Mahler's could continually find a venue, and wrote in a vein far removed from the pedantic wit he displays in the review of the First Symphony in 1900. Despite this antagonism, Hirschfeld continued to take seriously the job of a critic to report on what the new work sounded like and to explain its structure—the dual task that persists through his reviews of Symphonies 1–7 and assorted articles on Mahler's lieder and on other topics in the *Wiener Abendpost*, and freelancing for the *Österreichische Rundschau* and *Pester Lloyd*.

• • •

I understand: so capable an artist must simply have had the delightful idea of writing a satire of the symphony. Mahler's amusing parody of the symphonic spirit and form was performed at the second Philharmonic concert. "Venite pur avanti, vezzose mascherette!"[43] First one perceives a parody of invention. How hard some people must work in order to arrive at symphonic themes! Entire sketchbooks may be filled before a spark ignites. Mahler, however, shows that a wayfarer need only confer on the cello the melody of a pretty little song and a masked symphonic theme is ready! One adorns the usual scherzo formula with a few eighth notes, and the sharpened scherzo-motive looks like new. Assiduous, stalking reminiscence hunters are irritated at a few measures from the "Freischütz" Waltz, which require no great nose to find. In the trio of the Scherzo, the inventor's parody ironically pursues clever motivic development: a banal motive acquires its profile through octave leaps in the bass over empty fourths and fifths. In the third movement the parody on invention is elevated: the children's canon "Frère Jacques, dormez-vous?" becomes a funeral march that mourns, mockingly, the death of all independent thought. Here the habit of presuming a dead hero behind every symphonic funeral march is derided, and with good cause.

In the Finale Mahler's parody shows us a composer tirelessly attempting to shape a symphony's last movement from earlier motives. The "energetic" main theme of the movement becomes a warning sign: never use a very common phrase for a finale theme. Yet the parodying composer becomes disloyal to his pleasure in parody: the beautiful violin melody in D-flat major would be taken seriously in a different context, one that was indeed intended to be taken seriously. It is unfortunate that Mahler abandoned his role of the symphonic faun here. Or does even this melody, in its exclusively Brucknerian manner and feeling, ridicule those who so helplessly follow Bruckner? The work is otherwise for the perceptive listener a delightful and entirely successful parody of symphonic composers who borrow rather than create and who do not allow even one atom of their own selves to enter the symphonic form but instead draw together what their ears have taken in.

To me Mahler's parody of symphonic construction is even more successful. This parodistic symphony pokes fun at symphonists who only too willingly reject organic structure and who refuse to create their movements from a development of motives and fragments of ideas according to the laws of musical logic. The first movement mocks the lifeless juxtaposition in music. Themes are fragmented, undressed, shortened, and inverted; they are allowed to shine in new colors without ever achieving organic construction. Sections are strung together from sounds either very soft or very loud, either whispering or blaring; climaxes occur merely through the manipulation of dynamics and the multiplication of instruments, never organically compelled by interlocking motives. The movement is a continuous play of colors instead of a play of constructive forces. With this kind of shop window presentation (that is, the most effective arrangement possible), the Mahlerian parody is sharpened into *satire*. The counterpoint is entirely satirical in his parodistic D major symphony. With sumptuous examples Mahler castigates disgraceful counterpoint that, whatever the consequences may be, puts one voice *on top of* the other rather than *against* the other, *punctum* contra *punctum*. More effectively than a textbook example, this cheerful symphony turns against counterpoint that draws an irrelevant second voice from the first theme group instead of a developmental motive, i.e., a driving force. In his satirical mood, Mahler presents the most charming characteristics of this misjudgment: suddenly we come across contractions, inversions and similar such techniques, falling across the score like shooting stars without any sense of organic necessity.

Gustav Mahler's parody in this direction goes far beyond the symphonic realm and makes claims against all that is merely decorative in the modern arts. More recent masters, such as Johannes Brahms, tried to construct whole symphonic movements from a single motive. Mahler's parodistic symphony shows the listener how easily such a construction can be misunderstood or even turned into farce. The interval of the fourth appears at the beginning of his symphony; from then on, through the whole work, the artful satirist diligently employs this fourth leap like buttons on a Swabian coat. Wherever an empty space occurs, the fourth jumps in; all instruments, from the double bass to the piccolo, are anxious to sprinkle the score with fourths. [Discussion of the cuckoo.]

The parody is visible in the symphony's instrumentation, as well, expressing itself in the disproportion of the ideas to their orchestral clothing. [Description of the use of the brass in the Finale.] In this parodistic scoring, individual instruments are stripped of their natural sonorities through the unusual registration and manipulations of all kinds. The violins (*col legno*) must rattle, the trumpets sound like flutes; the horn may not sound like a horn, the cello not like a cello. A master in mixing sounds, Gustav Mahler fights the follies of our era of musical athletics with his satire of sound. What means, and what effect! With celli and basses divided threefold, the whole body of strings has to sustain a flageolet A over fifty measures, in all conceivable octaves, to achieve in the end the effect of a creaking door. The modern addiction to originality at all costs could not have been better ridiculed in Gustav Mahler's parodistic symphony.

Often enough, however, Mahler's serious art breaks through all jokes: looking into the eyes of a noble artist, we hear inspiring sounds and wondrous harmonies. But the symphony returns from such moments only too soon to its actual aim—the general exhibition of all sorts of orchestral effects. The trivial themes and crashing explosions in the orchestra certainly make for a trying listening experience. Nevertheless one appreciates the pedagogical intentions of this symphonic parody; its perhaps abhorrent example clarifies the relative importance of material stimuli and spiritual relations in art. As an energetic director of the Vienna opera, aspiring to the highest ideals, Mahler has often provided positive confirmation of this truth. The indirect, parodistic proof therefore had to be accepted without complaints at least as a curiosity, especially in the almost miraculous performance of the Philharmonic.

The Fifth Symphony

Mahler premiered his Fifth Symphony in Cologne (October 18, 1904) on a program including Schubert's "Ständchen," D 920, for women's chorus and solo alto, and three songs with piano accompaniment—"Bei dir allein," D 866/2, "Nacht und Träume," D 827, and "Das Lied im Grünen," D 917; "Heidenröslein," D 257, was an encore. The concert concluded with Beethoven's *Leonore* Overture no. 3, conducted by Fritz Steinbach. Early performances of the symphony often included vocal music, or music with other soloists, on the program. The length of the symphony, some critics complained, necessitated excerpting the other works on the program: the Dresden premiere (January 27, 1905), conducted by Ernst von Schuch, included two movements from Haydn's Cello Concerto in D. Arthur Nikisch conducted the Berlin premiere (February 20, 1905) with the symphony followed by a scene from Peter Cornelius's unfinished opera *Gunlöd* (orchestrated by Mottl) and the Prelude and Liebestod from Wagner's *Tristan und Isolde*. One of the most interesting programs was the first Viennese performance (December 7, 1905), covered in two of the documents translated below: Franz Schalk conducted Bach's motet "Singet dem Herrn ein neues Lied," BWV 225, followed by Mahler conducting the Fifth Symphony, a work that the composer felt had been profoundly affected by his study of Bach.

Programming the Fifth Symphony with the traditional symphonic repertoire often led to unfavorable comparisons in the press. One such example is the Hamburg premiere (March 13, 1905), which Mahler conducted, followed by Beethoven's Eighth Symphony under Max Fiedler; a review of this program is translated below. In Trieste (December 1, 1905), where even Mahler's conducting met some criticism, he programmed the Fifth Symphony with Mozart's "Jupiter" Symphony and Beethoven's *Coriolan* Overture. Again in the Vienna Philharmonic's memorial concert for Mahler (November 5, 1911), the Fifth Symphony was programmed with Mozart's "Jupiter." Another program that faced criticism, but mainly on account of its length, was at the first Alsace-Lorraine music festival, in Strasbourg (May 21, 1905). Following the Fifth Symphony, under Mahler's baton were Brahms's Alto Rhapsody for men's chorus and orchestra op. 53, under Ernst Münch (with such strong applause that the second half was repeated) and Mozart's Violin Concerto in G major, K. 216; as well as Strauss's *Sinfonia domestica,* under the composer.

Facing Mahler's innovative language for the first time without a program or vocal text, some contemporaries struggled in their attempt to understand the Fifth Symphony as absolute music—that is, as a traditional symphonic form. Others denied any distinction between a symphony that met the criterion of "absolute" music and one that conveyed a philosophical or emotional idea. This committed belief in the meaning of music, independent of any accompanying explanations, reflects Mahler's own thinking as it can be discerned from letters and reports of conversations. A further confirmation of this attitude on the part of the composer came from a local critic at the premiere of the Fifth Symphony, in Cologne. Hermann Kipper, who attended numerous rehearsals, maintained that, when "'asked whether there was an idea (*Idée*) underlying this symphony, Mahler answered: 'no, I wanted to compose only music.' But from the following brief remark that he told the orchestra about the first movement, entitled funeral march, we can presume that he had an idea afterwards: 'Think about someone who has had his ideas shattered.'"[44] As well, the critic Richard Batk claimed that Mahler challenged him in a conversation well before the premiere, "I want to see who can make a program for my Fifth."[45]

Gustav Mahler's Symphony No. 5

ERNST OTTO NODNAGEL

Allgemeine Musik-Zeitung
March 3, 1905

Ernst Otto Nodnagel (b. Dortmund, 1870; d. Berlin, 1909) was undoubtedly Mahler's most ardent advocate. He published "technical analyses" of the symphonies in the leading music journals—*Neue Musik-Zeitung* (First Symphony); *Musikalisches Wochenblatt* and *Heidelberger Zeitung* (Third Symphony); *Die Musik* (Second, Fifth, and Sixth Symphonies); and *Neue Zeitschrift für Musik* (Sixth Symphony). Several were reprinted and sold as pamphlets. Such analyses, along with four-hand piano arrangements, were often released prior to the premiere and helped to maintain the long bourgeois tradition of studying and playing a symphonic work before attending its performance. However, at the turn of the century, skepticism developed over the efficacy and risks of such analyses. Many individuals lacked the musical training that would allow these skeletal outlines to correlate closely with the aural experience of a vast and complex symphonic score. Moreover, the dissection of a score seemed antithetical to the metaphorical and expressive nature of music criticism as it had developed over the course of the nineteenth century. Richard Batka complained of Nodnagel and his Mahler analysis, "With the greatest of efforts, this cunning commentator avoids any mention of the mood and limits himself to formal analysis."[46]

It is not clear whether Mahler benefited from the efforts of this near-fanatical supporter, who was, the composer complained to his wife, "as enthusiastic as a young girl." Nor did Mahler himself appreciate the critic's efforts.[47] Nodnagel never secured a position at a prominent newspaper or conservatory. After studying law and music in Heidelberg and music at the conservatory in Berlin, he worked mainly as an independent writer and composer. Nodnagel held a brief appointment as a critic at a minor paper (*Ostpreussische Zeitung*) and as a conservatory teacher while living in Königsberg, 1899–1903. Nodnagel was the butt of jokes about Mahler's biased proponents; one Viennese critic, for example, found absurd Nodnagel's assertion of the composer's glory at Bruckner's expense: Mahler, according to Nodnagel, "enlivens and decorates the lines of his architecture with a fullness of secondary ideas and counterpoint. All this could only be possible because of the historical condition of Bruckner, whose own strength could not keep pace with his gigantic will—for whom the blocks of his own themes are too powerful, so that he was unable to tower the strong block-structure up to the greatest heights. Mahler, by contrast, not only climbs the highest ladder and framework of his gigantic structure but also handles even that which is most massive with such facility that he seems to be juggling."[48] In general, Nodnagel's analyses aimed to show that Mahler's symphonies were "absolute" music, explicable according to the rules of musical logic and convention. This conviction led to a public attack on Ludwig Schiedermair for interpreting Mahler's music as programmatic—perhaps one of the early signs of Nodnagel's fragile mental health.[49] He did not publish after 1906 and three years later died in a psychiatric hospital.

The one exception to Nodnagel's enthusiasm for Mahler's symphonies was the Adagietto of the Fifth. Even apart from its popular lyricism, the movement was embraced by other reviewers for its sonic beauty (alien to a formalist like Nodnagel) and for its expressive function, mediating between the extreme character contrasts in the first part of the symphony (the tragic opening movements), the second part (the sensuous Scherzo) and the final part: the Adagietto, it was felt, cleared the air for the crisp counterpoint of the Rondo-Finale. To be sure, other advocates of the composer, like Richard Strauss, found the seemingly feminine charm of the Adagietto incongruous with the heroism associated with the genre of symphony— antifeminine terms like "molly-coddled" were common among reviewers. But Nodnagel's sharp criticism of the sweet repetitions in the movement reveal some of the imbalance that came to pervade his writings.

· · ·

[. . .] *Gustav Mahler is not a programmatic composer and never has been.* His five symphonies (the Sixth I don't know yet) are *absolute music,* in a form that developed according to purely musical laws, and must be understood in that way. The endless requests for the "publication" of the "hidden" program misled Mahler into the inconsistent practice of adding programs to three of his symphonies, irrespective of his own intentions. In doing so, however, he only made it all the more *evident* to the sensible listener that he is *no* program musician. From that point on he quickly disposed of the pseudo-programs. In particular, the new symphony in D major contains nothing—nothing at all—that would justify any thought of program music. Not even the Funeral March

warrants a symbolic interpretation. Who would make the absurd declaration that the Eroica or the A-flat Major Sonata is "program music"?![50]
[Discussion of the formal structure of the symphony.]

Mahler's distinctive style is *especially prominent* in his *melodic invention*.
This remains true even despite those formulaic turns that sound like
"reminiscences" to the naïve listener (who, moreover, is grasping for support in what to focus upon). In nine of ten cases, "reminiscence" in music
is a mistake on the part of the listener, not the composer! This is as much
true for successions of pitches in Mahler's melodies as it is for their
rhythm (in the widest sense) and for their formal division. Especially in
the Fifth Symphony, a taut and sharply divided form with well-calculated
and proportioned climaxes is so prominent a characteristic of the style
that it seems to me wholly incomprehensible for a musically educated listener not to recognize it immediately, even after only a single hearing.
The "symphonic form" is not broken up, as many believe, but worked
out very clearly and precisely. Those who do not recognize it merely lack
the degree of understanding of the work that one is, after all, entitled to
expect from anyone discussing it publicly. No one would say in earnest
that the placement of a funeral march before the four traditionally
designed symphonic movements constitutes a "breaking up of form"?!

Felix Mendelssohn-Bartholdy and Robert Schumann had already
attempted a greater coherence of symphonic form through connecting
individual movements with shared themes. Anton Bruckner nurtured
these seeds into a higher development of form, and we find the same
organic coherence among individual parts in all five symphonies that
Mahler has published thus far. The Fifth goes the furthest in this regard.
The first two movements show the most intimate thematic connection.
The Adagietto, which makes its entrance as the fourth movement, takes
on a truly integral role in the fugue of the Finale: it returns several
times—nearly in its entirety—as the second theme. And finally, one of
the three fugue subjects is anticipated in the streaming brilliance of the
second movement's climax—that is, at the climax of the whole first main
part. This theme reappears in the form of a splendid chorale as the
highest pinnacle of the entire symphony, crowning the fugue itself. One
would think that these "signposts" alone, worked out with utmost clarity as they are, must warn against using the word *formless*, but they have
not even been noticed, at least nowhere have they been emphasized!

The first two movements are, incidentally, linked not only through
their unity of musical thought but also by their similarity in atmosphere: sorrow, anguished pain and silent lament. The Funeral March
has the simplest musical form, that of the three-part song. [Description
of the movement's structure.] The form of the second movement is so

regular that it originally contained a repeat sign—something never before seen in Mahler. The mood swings between grievous lamentation and resigned sorrow, here expressed with the very same theme that in the Funeral March was the musical carrier of the passionate outburst. [More discussion of the movement's structure.]

In its energy and untamed pathos, the Scherzo is similar to the Finale of the First Symphony. Wild effusions of Dionysian pleasure and orgiastic frenzy contrast ingeniously with moments of the most tender grace until, finally, all is whipped into a furious whirl of ecstasy. I can lay claim to the movement better than anyone else who has judged it for the public.[51] I know what I mean when I state not merely that "this is beautiful" but also declare that from Beethoven to Bruckner (or, to also include Symbolism, to *Till Eulenspiegel*) scherzi equal in artistic merit and technical perfection are few and far between.

The form of the Scherzo is clear and simple, though somewhat difficult to recognize owing to the movement's lusciously arabesque richness. [Description of the movement's structure.] Since each theme that determines the rich formal structure has its own counterpoint, this movement is especially difficult to grasp from the aural impressions it makes. This affects both the structural comprehension as well as the interplay of analysis and synthesis that constitutes the mental work of the listener (or should—if he would deign to do some mental work and to collaborate musically!) But to speak of the "formlessness" of this movement, especially in condescending or arrogant terms, is about as legitimate as talking of the haphazard disorder of the stars: the astronomer smiles. It is the highest triumph of Mahler's polyphony that even in the outrageous *embarras de richesse* of this movement's bold, reckless counterpoint, the essence—the melody—is always and with unfailing energy kept in the center of the sound image. He always treats the supporting materials with the right distance, maintaining the right proportions among them. Is the oak tree considered formless because its knotty branches carry twigs, upon which leaves grow? Does only the palm tree have a "form"?!

The Scherzo is thus not only the climax of Mahler's own creative work but in general a pinnacle of the symphonic world literature. However the Adagietto that follows it seems to me the weakest of anything Mahler has written and lacks any connection to the style of the symphony. It certainly sounds enchanting—indeed, it is five hundred times sweeter than sugar. But its invention is meager, truly banal, and not even deepened through elaboration. The very daring transition in the double basses does not fit the stylistic frame of the little movement and loses a considerable amount upon frequent repetition.[52] After the premiere of the symphony, I made no secret, around the composer, of my disparaging opinion of the sweet-sounding little piece. He asked if I advised cutting the movement; I answered that I would not take responsibility for such a decision. But now that I have heard it five times I would undoubtedly answer the same question affirmatively. For the public, however, this movement has become the highlight of the work. [Description of the restricted instrumentation, for strings and harp alone.]

The Rondo-Finale merges the form of a rondo with that of a triple fugue. The rondo theme itself always appears decorated with the most spirited counterpoint and with changing character. [Description of the movement's structure.] One of the many incomprehensible aspects of the reception of the symphony on the part of Berlin "critics" is the strange claim that the symphony was pervaded by "false pathos." Almost two-thirds of the work, namely the Scherzo and the Finale, seem to me to belong to the established genre of musical *humor*. [. . .]

Fourteenth Philharmonic Concert

Max Loewengard

Hamburgischer Correspondent
September 13, 1905

Unlike the many professional music critics with doctorates in the humanities or in law, Max Loewengard (b. Frankfurt-am-Main, 1860; d. Hamburg, 1915) had practical training and experience. He studied composition with Joachim Raff and was briefly employed as a conductor. His primary occupation was as a conservatory professor (in Wiesbaden, Berlin, and finally Hamburg), not as a university scholar. In contrast to the literary fantasies and aesthetic reflections typical of his Viennese colleagues, Loewengard's writings were clear and reasoned, rarely diverting from grounded musical discussion. It is not surprising that the politically cautious *Hamburgischer Correspondent* (which one contemporary quipped was the "grandmother" among Hamburg newspapers)[53] hired Loewengard in 1904 as its primary music critic. Loewengard was the author of a popular book on harmony (1892), reprinted numerous times, and one on counterpoint (1902), which gave authority to the observations on Mahler's harmonic writing and counterpoint in the review below. An acquaintance of Paul Bekker, Loewengard possibly influenced the younger critic's growing admiration for Mahler.[54]

• • •

[. . .] Some never forgave Mahler, master of great thematic integrity and master of the language of the orchestra, for making such utterly naïve music—without thematic integrity—and for remaining content with the most primitive means of expression. Others wanted to hold against him that someone who found pleasure in such naïve music came to them with profound problems, outbursts of strong passion, and a musical language that was not at all naïve. One wanted to believe in one or the other facet of this music; either of them had to be inauthentic— a calculated means to achieve strongly effective, external contrasts.

And yet Mahler's greatness is based on precisely this juxtaposition of fundamentally different methods of artistic expression. Those with the gift for easy invention and with a strong melodic inclination usually lack the higher ability; they keep their melodic instincts on the surface and do not let them dive to the deepest depths. Conversely, those who dig down to artistic foundations and build with only large boulders easily lose their sense for the lofty line of a melodic highrise, if indeed they ever had it. One therefore suspects inauthenticity in an art that appears simultaneously naïve and profound; one presumes affectation on one side or the other. One does not want to grant to Mahler that which one believed, though only once it was too late, Bruckner had. [Claims of the futility of searching for a specific program.]

Mahler's thematic invention has a rare sharpness of character. He certainly doesn't compose themes with an eye to workmanship and then, only on the side or afterward, shape them as melodically as is possible. Rather, he writes melodic impulses, each significant in itself yet capable of any degree of thematic deepening. Mahler's counterpoint is genuine, insofar as each independent voice—as many as there may be, and as recklessly as they hurry past each other—still follows its own logical law. With purposeful clarity, each voice heads for one and the same meeting point, striving toward coherence with the others and toward a clearly perceptible harmonic unity. The harmonic units, too, follow each other with compelling logic, never dictated by random coincidence.

What is best in Mahler's virtuosic treatment of the orchestra is that even where he achieves astounding sound effects, one senses the emotion that triggered them. They never seem assembled for mere effect.

It is unconventional to have a funeral march as the first movement of a symphony. But I know of no reason why the idea of the transience of all earthly things shouldn't be the content of a symphony's first movement. The Scherzo is born from the sedateness of the Viennese Ländler but grows into gigantic magnitude. It is a round dance in which mountain titans caper and worlds turn. This does not always happen smoothly—nor is it supposed to. The Adagietto is a delightful piece, full of charm in melody and sound, and completely harmonious. The dash of triviality added here and there to the melodic line in no way diminishes its value, for it always remains part of the character and never an unwanted melodic weakness. The Rondo-Finale, with its powerful fugue and its intoxicating stretti, is a worthy conclusion to the mighty work. [. . .]

Feuilleton: Gustav Mahler and His Symphony

MAX KALBECK

Neues Wiener Tagblatt
December 12, 1905

Max Kalbeck (b. Breslau [Wroclaw], 1850; d. Vienna, 1921) is best known for his friendship with Brahms, a relationship that produced several Brahms songs to Kalbeck's texts, as well as Kalbeck's four-volume study of the composer, which remains a standard in the literature. One of the leading music critics in Vienna, Kalbeck came from a literary background and remained active in that sphere. In his twenties and thirties he published several volumes of poetry, but by the last volume (*Aus alter und neuer Zeit*, 1890), Kalbeck's creative efforts had already turned to opera. He prepared German translations of Mozart's *Don Giovanni* (1886) and Gluck's *Orpheus* (1896) and over the years would translate many recent operas from French, Italian, Czech, Russian, and English.[55] In the 1890s Kalbeck wrote libretti for Johann Strauss's operetta *Jakuba*, Alexander von Fielitz's *Das stille Dorf* and Georg Henschel's *Nubia*. He also wrote the libretto for the Hungarian Ede Poldini's *Decius der Flötenspieler*, and Poldini adapted Kalbeck's *Märchenspiele für die Jugend* into three children's operas (composed in 1899 but first premiered in 1927 in Budapest).[56] As a novelist Kalbeck published three volumes of literary sketches noted for their shades of humor, from cozy fun to sarcasm and self-irony: *Capriccio* and *Humoresken und Phantasien* (1896), which over a half-century later colleagues still found engaging.[57]

Both his enemies and his friends were silent upon Kalbeck's death, according to David Josef Bach's obituary. One reason for this was the power he had exerted, Bach explained, which extended beyond that of any other critic, including Hanslick. Kalbeck was reputedly more hated as an enemy of Wagner than even Hanslick himself.[58] Having played Wagner's music as an orchestral violinist, Kalbeck published several parodistic and critical writings on the composer, including his very first books on music (*Nibelungen*, 1876; on the Bayreuth festival hall, 1877; and on *Parsifal*, 1883). Kalbeck's other books include three collections of his essays and biographies.

As a music critic, Kalbeck progressed rapidly through the ranks. After holding successive posts at the leading newspapers in his native Breslau, the *Schlesische Zeitung* and *Breslauer Zeitung*, Kalbeck moved to Vienna in 1880. Hanslick recommended his appointment to the staff of the *Wiener Allgemeine Zeitung* and, in 1883, Kalbeck became Hanslick's colleague at the *Neue Freie Presse*. His first permanent position was at the liberal *Neues Wiener Tagblatt* (which bore the subtitle "Demokratisches Organ"), where he was opera critic beginning in 1886; from 1895 on he was concert critic as well. Beginning in 1890 he also wrote for the *Wiener Montags-Revue*, a politically independent weekly. Kalbeck's opera reviews were reprinted in three volumes; two decades later, a colleague reported that these reviews "are still today the best and most incisive that have been written about dramatic music. He does not adopt fashionable stylistic gems, and these reviews exude such a healthful freshness in their portrayal that, once drawn in, one doesn't want to stop reading."[59]

Kalbeck reviewed all of the Viennese performances of Mahler's music despite the personal relationship that developed between them: the two men exchanged cordial letters, and Mahler had commissioned Kalbeck to prepare new German translations for *Don Giovanni* and *The Marriage of Figaro*. The sequence of his reviews and the extant correspondence is noteworthy.[60] On the night of his debut at the Vienna Court Opera (May 11, 1897), Mahler was eager, above all, to hear about the reactions of both Kalbeck and the critic at the *Neue Freie Presse*.[61] Kalbeck showed some hesitation over the First Symphony (November 1900); his subsequent review of *Das klagende Lied* was a full-fledged "essay on contemporary aesthetics" (23 February 1901). It is possible that Mahler's letters to Kalbeck opened the critic up to freer responses to music. Writing some four months after the review of *Das klagende Lied*, Mahler asked Kalbeck, "What is it that delights you, then, when you feel music: What makes you light-hearted and free?" Objecting to the critic's metaphors of energy, he continued,

"Transpose the problem to whatever plane you want; in the end, you will always reach that point, where 'your wisdom' begins to 'dream.'"[62] Kalbeck's review of the Fourth Symphony (1902) evoked one of Mahler's warmest letters. "On Sunday you acted as my 'audience.' Today it is my turn! And so you will have to put up with my *applause* and shouts of '*Bravo!*' I am constantly amazed at all sorts of things you say and am always wanting to ask how on earth do you know that? But I enjoy it." In the remainder of the letter, Mahler expresses his approval of Kalbeck's decision not to interpret the symphony as program music, and provides one of his most eloquent accounts of musical communication without programs.[63] From January 1904 to the fall of 1905, they exchanged friendly letters and collaborated on the new libretti. Kalbeck's enthusiastic response to the Fifth Symphony dismayed the young Max Graf, who poked fun at his older colleague (age fifty-five) for leaping "boldly over the whole development of modern music, with youthful vigor, to arrive at Mahler."[64] Kalbeck would also review the Sixth Symphony, just over a year later, in January 1907 and at the end of that year, was the only critic to receive a farewell letter from Mahler upon his departure for New York. "Our relationship is, alas, a fragment for which all the themes are doubtless extant, their 'development,' however, for many reasons, ever falling short of 'realization.' I sincerely hope this new shape my life will take will also draw you into the circle of all that is dear and precious to me, for I have long regarded you as a friend, with elective affinity. With kindest regards to yourself and to your good lady."[65]

• • •

Among the musical novelties lavished on us in recent weeks, Gustav Mahler's new symphony occupies the most distinguished place. The fifth in a row of sisters, it nonetheless seems in many respects the firstborn, first in both its external significance and its inner worth. It shows us that the composer, ever advancing on his own self-determined path, has reached a high point in this steep ascent. It deserves to be recognized as a milestone. As the probable turning point in Mahler's creativity, it opens up a most promising view of the future of art, both for him and for us.

Mahler's art, like any other, originates in the burning urge of a deep need to communicate. This need arises and develops most passionately in those lonely and introverted artists who listen more to the voices of their interior than to those of an alien and disparate reality. In Mahler's earlier works it was always the orchestra that decisively inspired his imagination—however, not the orchestra of the concert hall, which inspired the great masters of instrumental music, but rather that of the theater. [Discussion of the "emancipation" of the orchestra in recent opera composition.]

Opera and music drama not only colored Mahler's orchestra but also led him to deploy the human voice as a narrative instrument. So too did they invade the form of his symphonies, tearing it to pieces. Opera reformers transplanted the overloaded symphonic orchestra from the concert hall to the theater and turned it into the docile instrument of their poetic revelations. Mahler in turn led this opera orchestra from the theater to the concert hall, assigning it the mission of envoicing his musical intentions with unprecedented clarity.

But next to the symphonic musician spoke up a poet who was more lyric/epic than dramatic. Since both wanted to be heard at the same time, sometimes neither was; quarrels and misunderstandings ensued. Mahler-the-poet outlined a poetic text; Mahler-the-musician tore up the program after using it. This collaborator, whom Mahler-the-musician found deficient and irritating, was then to be appeased through a solo or choral song that called him back through the window after having thrown him out through the door. This is why Mahler's symphonies again and again traverse the boundary between the musical and the poetic. And why Mahler in turn endured constant questioning about this tendency of his compositions.

In his Fifth Symphony Mahler has now fully overcome this conflict and written a purely musical work. Though it cannot completely deny its connection to the composer's past, this symphony transcends all his earlier works in its rich, intriguing, and beautiful content, as well as its coherence of form. The declared or suppressed programs of his earlier works are replaced by a general idea—an idea of the kind music can express without relinquishing or denying its nature. In this work, the forces of life and death are opposed like two equally matched fighting giants who are then so closely reconciled that they forget their battle and embrace in brotherly love, whereupon they recognize their fate as inseparable twin brothers. The abstract generality of the idea gains concrete shape and individual character through the composer's personal history, which supplies his imagination with the memory of unforgettable moments.

The symphony consists of two large main parts, each of which is divided into two or three subsections.[66] The first two movements are dedicated to suffering; the last three, which are thematically connected with what has come before, are dedicated to the joys of life. Iris's consoling rainbow shines against that black wall of clouds from the thunderstorm of the first part, and, in the glory of the setting sun, the star of the following day glows. Trumpets, horns and trombones announce the final apotheosis. The first two movements are in minor. First, a funeral march passes by us in all the terrifying pomp of its measured steps; the mourner's heart is with the deceased, in the coffin. Yet strangely enough, this same cortège has a second observer, who is the mourner's critical *Doppelgänger*. His sharp eyes probe every detail of the grotesque and dark spectacle; sometimes the march provokes an ironic smile, sometimes an impatient sigh. While the other weeps during the violins' lamenting march melody in C-sharp minor, he thinks of a cheerful street song. [Description of the lyrics for such songs and the scoring for the brass.]

Mahler can't ever be happy or sad without resorting to wind instrumentation with three, four, or six to a part. And what other composers manage to express in eight measures he can barely exhaust in five times as many. The "unending" melody, the arioso, follows him from the orchestra of the music drama and casts contrapuntal shadows. Such "themes" are entire repositories of motivic material strung together, for which space needs to be created within the symphony.

The melodies that surge up and down seem to call for a poetic text, for they are far too long to be quickly grasped and retained, they are irregularly divided, and their style is more like that of a recitative rather than that of a song. The listener feels tempted to add words to them, like the recitatives in the Finale of the Ninth Symphony. Because we strongly wish it, we believe that at some point Mahler will do away entirely with such vestiges of that process of transformation and transplantation.

The second movement is thematically a continuation and development of the first and, like it, has an ending that fades away quietly. The first movement concludes with a fanfare from a half-suffocated trumpet, a ghostly, fluttering drum roll, and a final, muffled pizzicato from the lower strings.[67] In the second movement, after the fortissimo of the despair theme rears up again almost mechanistically, the conclusion brings sounds and images of night and morning woven together as in a dream, a play of light and sound waves, flashing sparks, ghostly figures rushing away, whispering breezes, jingling, whistling and humming sounds, the triangle quietly striking, harmonics briefly in the violins and violas in triplets, fleeting thirds in flutes and harps, creeping double basses, sustained sighing in individual solo instruments, and a final quiet timpani stroke. In these and other places Mahler proves himself a master of atmospheric enchantment, casting a shadow over the greatest virtuosi of orchestral sound. Yet the artist rises above the virtuoso at decisive points to bring about motivated changes of the most varied moods, always doing what is necessary, and surprising us without ever losing control over the form. Mahler has been compared to Max Klinger. But with regard to the enchanting power of his veiled orchestral colors I would rather compare him to Gustav Klimt. Nobody before Mahler has depicted in such gripping sounds the dreary emptiness of the house of sorrow that only reluctantly and hesitantly opens its curtained windows to the naked sunlight. These sounds do not merely touch on terror, they bravely grip it by the hair. Hardly anyone has dried the weeping eyes of pain so tenderly and gently as they stare into despairing nothingness. The voices of animated nature finally reach the ear of him who is bent by grief. Blinded by the light of the new day, intoxicated with the fresh air he has been lacking, he staggers out the door into a full life, greeted with joy.

After the Adagietto (a charming yet significant movement in F inserted between the Scherzo and the Finale), D major, the key of the naïve, joyous vitality, returns. An analytic discussion of the Scherzo and Finale would be nearly impossible and, moreover, would only confuse the reader more than the pieces themselves did in the concert hall. Mahler has made it easy for neither the audience nor himself. But the scenes of his narration—partly running parallel, partly crossing each other—are captivating throughout and greatly entertaining in a higher sense. One follows them with the feeling of being led by a guide whose steadfast hand smoothes a passage over critical and dangerous spots. The main section of the Scherzo alternates with two trios. It uses three themes, Viennese waltzes and Ländler, which in addition to their symphonic viability also impress through their contrapuntal presentation. Because of the accessibility of the main themes, they do not run the risk of not being heard or losing their red-cheeked nature. It is obvious that the Scherzo is not content with the banalities of a drinking bout. In the diligence of its artistic labor, and even more in its incorporation of unrestrained demonic elements, it points to the unrest and agitated will of a Faustian mind.

What sensual pleasure, symbolized in the dance, could not fulfill, love does. The little Adagio for strings accompanied by harp is dedicated to this love. Its sweet, unworldly sounds instill soothing balm into the hearts of the afflicted. How peacefully reconciled the charming piece sounds, bathed in harmony after the terrors of death and the wild storms of life! Its melody sings with such intimacy, almost as soothing, gentle, and persuasive, as the voice of a loving wife—and much more expressive through the polyphony in the quartet!

The instruction "*attacca* Rondo Finale" informs us that the Adagietto, inviting us into concentrated repose, is not merely a contrasting episode. Without this liberating and purifying experience the last movement would not be possible. It would have no deeper justification nor pronounce its truth so convincingly. The Finale, crown of the work, is also the most perfect of all of Mahler's symphonic movements. Breathing with new living force, the fresh themes are developed, repeated and intensified in freely fugal form until the shining trombones fulfill the promise of the first movement, and the coda, rejoicing to the heavens, concludes the whole.

This triumph promises new victories from the symphonist and brilliantly refutes any opposition.

Feuilleton: Mahler's "Fifth"

G U S T A V   S C H Ö N A I C H

Wiener Allgemeine Zeitung
December 13, 1905

Gustav Schönaich (b. Vienna, 1840; d. Vienna, 1906) grew up in an elite artistic and cultural environment. His mother hosted renowned salons for artists and musicians. Through his stepfather Joseph Standhartner, a close friend of Richard Wagner, Schönaich met the composer and became well known as a Wagner advocate. Wagner relied on Standhartner (a physician and director of the largest hospital in Vienna as well as a board member of the Gesellschaft der Musikfreunde) for help in establishing a place for his music in Vienna.

Following his study of law at the University of Vienna, Schönaich wrote for the *Wiener Tagblatt* and *Allgemeine Musik-Zeitung*, and then *Die Reichswehr* (a publication for officers in the imperial forces). His first permanent post was at the *Wiener Allgemeine Zeitung*, of which he became the editor in chief. Albeit stylistically bland and weaker in coverage than the *Neue Freie Presse* and *Neues Wiener Tagblatt*, the *Wiener Allgemeine Zeitung* played an important role in Vienna, advocating a federalist liberalism and policies designed to avert the national conflicts that wracked Habsburg politics.[68] Schönaich published in many other music and literary journals, including the *Neue Musikalische Presse, Die Musik*, and *Wiener Rundschau*. A rotund and eccentric man, he offered guidance to Hugo Wolf; the two men remained friends until Wolf, temperamental as always, abruptly broke off the relationship.

Schönaich's first reviews of Mahler as an opera conductor were in the *Neue Musikalische Presse* and the *Wiener Rundschau*. He wrote on the Second and Fourth Symphonies in *Die Reichswehr* (1900–1902). His ensuing reviews of the First and Third Symphonies were in *Die Musik* (1904–1905). Schönaich covered the Fifth Symphony in the review translated below, as well as Mahler's direction of Wagner's *Ring*, in his new paper, the *Wiener Allgemeine Zeitung*.

• • •

Writing about Mahler's newest symphony is no great pleasure. The effect of the work in today's milieu has already been determined. The symphony met enormous success, thanks to the strong support of out-siders whom Mahler knew to add to his usual musical congregation. Grown, albeit naïve, adults feel drawn in: they are attracted to Mahler's fascinating personality and they submit to the intoxicating colors of his orchestral effects. They are captivated by the secrecy of his intentions, which they cannot unveil. For them, music really only begins when Mahler appears. Inspired by this latest love, the deep thinkers among his admirers make the claim—belatedly, however—that the coming of the Messiah had been predicted by several predecessors with unmis-takable clarity, and this too could be perceived with a certain degree of

Figure 1. Otto Böhler, *Dancing Vienna*. From left to right: Gustav Mahler, Georg Reimers, Gustav Schönaich.

clarity; nowadays the public at large is entranced by the idea of musical progress. This phenomenon is no more pleasant than the reactionary obstinacy that dominated the second half of the past century, producing a narrow-minded and principle-bound criticism that only slowly admitted the value of truly innovative music. [Discussion of the reception of Liszt and Wagner, whose music was only gradually appreciated.]

[At the same time, however,] the public clings to what in a work is known and familiar to them. When in addition there happens to be something truly original in a piece, the public finds it a nuisance and a disruption of their enjoyment. Only slowly do they become aware of the rich expression to be discovered in a new melodic world. In Mahler, however, the audience suffered no such process. His contributions in the area of melodic originality are so sparse that Mahler's themes are grasped and understood even on a first hearing; they become second nature to the audience. Yet he presents them in the most modern attire, dressing them in a cloak dazzling with the newest orchestral effects. His themes thereby gain a somewhat foreign appearance, protecting the public from the embarrassment of having to greet them like old acquaintances on Unter den Linden.[69]

The inscrutable order of the movements and the wholly irrational structuring of the entire symphony give everyone the chance to wear a pensive expression and state as "self-evident" what is in fact totally incomprehensible. Everyone seemed to understand immediately why such a funeral march—one that, according to the instruction in the score, must sound "like a funeral procession [*Kondukt*]"—should serve as the introductory movement of a symphony. Until now, I've held the opinion that what is tragic or highly pathetic must have some kind of foundation—and should therefore be the result of a grand situation. The activities of undertakers (*Pompes funèbres*) have no profound effect on me. The Funeral March in the Eroica follows as compellingly from what preceded it, as Mahler's Funeral March appears arbitrary and inappropriate. Soon afterward, in the Scherzo, Mahler indulges in all sorts of Ländler and waltz motives: he puts on his jacket and climbs into his beloved's window. But he does not endure this comfortable mood for long. With his gauntlets, Mahler smashes the windows and the young girl escapes to the roof, screaming in fear (see Figure 2).[70] One is supposed to believe that everyone finds such rustic excursions as indigenous to Mahler as to Bruckner.

The "Adagietto" resembles the pretty images of saints that elegant abbots leave as visiting cards for their little countesses. Mahler has frequently trespassed in this way before. Yet he was never able to produce

Figure 2. Gustav Klimt's *Beethoven Frieze,* detail of the knight, with gauntlets. Klimt later pointed out the likeness to Mahler.

the desired magic that Schumann brings about with simple means in the brief Adagio of the C Major Symphony or in his piano work "Des Abends" [*Fantasiestücke* op. 12, no. 1]. I have nothing to criticize in the last movement. It is a perfectly shaped piece, with spirited and entertaining combinations and great orchestral witticism everywhere. The extraordinarily effective climaxes bring the unfortunate beginning of the symphony to a good end. Yet his art will always remain foreign to me. Everything in me resists its compulsive manner of self-expression, its exaggerated, flabby, and proclamatory thematicism, and its shapeless form. Certainly Mahler composes from his inner self, as he must. But then one shouldn't be very surprised if an alien visitor got the impression that someone intelligent has pulled off a huge practical joke.

The Seventh Symphony

Although the Seventh Symphony was composed in August 1905, it was not premiered until three years later, since Mahler needed to give attention to programming and overseeing the premiere of the Sixth. The premiere of the Seventh Symphony took place in Prague on September 19, 1908, with Mahler conducting; the work was programmed alone—although as the crowds departed from the concert hall a military band played Haydn's "Emperor's Hymn," which was interpreted as a sign of Mahler's victory. The concert was covered in Viennese, Berlin, and Munich publications, as well as by local Prague critics like Felix Adler and Richard Batka, whose reviews are translated below. Otto Klemperer and Alban Berg attended the performance, and the symphony won Schoenberg over to Mahler.

Five weeks later Mahler conducted the Seventh Symphony in Munich, on a program before the Prelude and *Liebestod* from Wagner's *Tristan und Isolde* and Beethoven's *Leonore* Overture no. 3. The following season, after spending the summer in Europe, Mahler conducted performances of the symphony in The Hague (October 2, 1909) and in Amsterdam (October 3 and 7). At the first two of these concerts, Mengelberg conducted Beethoven's Seventh. At the final concert, Mahler was to conduct Wagner's *Faust* Overture, *Siegfried Idyll*, and *Meistersinger* Overture, followed by his own Seventh Symphony; but the first two works preceding his symphony were dropped from the program.

The first performance under a conductor other than Mahler himself was the Viennese premiere, on November 3, 1909 under Ferdinand Löwe, where applause followed each of the five movements. The program opened with Beethoven's Second Symphony, a continuation of the Beethoven cycle at the Konzertverein. Two reviews of this concert, by Elsa Bienenfeld and Julius Korngold, are translated below. The Berlin premiere, and final performance of the work in Mahler's lifetime, took place in January 1911, under Oskar Fried; the program that followed the Mahler included the title role's aria from Charpentier's *Louise* and Mozart's Overture to *The Marriage of Figaro*—additions that some critics found superfluous.[71] The preceding season, Fried had included the fourth movement, Nachtmusik II, in a program following Haydn's "Le Midi" Symphony. The concert concluded with songs of Berlioz, Henri Duparc, and Liszt, and the Berlin premiere of Conrad Ansorge's *Aussöhnung,* for orchestra and tenor-chorus op. 25.[72]

Mahler's "Seventh Symphony"

FELIX ADLER

Bohemia
September 20, 1908

After training to become a conductor in Munich, Felix Adler (b. Vienna, 1876; d. Prague? 1928) moved to Dresden to begin a career in music criticism. One of his earliest articles, written for the Viennese *Montags-Revue*, was on Mahler. He also wrote on "the case of Mahler" for *Die Gesellschaft* (in its final year), an important journal edited by the enfant terrible Michael Georg Conrad, who advocated the literary movement of Naturalism. In 1906 Adler was hired by the leading newspaper in Prague, *Bohemia*. The following year, Adler was one of the few critics who showed some admiration for Schoenberg's String Quartet op. 7, performed at the annual festival of the Pan-German Musical Society. Though critical of the work's difficulty, he reported that it "contains lightning strokes of genius in the new harmonic and unharmonic combinations. One faces a new phenomenon that unwaveringly pursues its course."[73] Adler was less enthusiastic about Schoenberg's next quartet, which he likewise reviewed in *Bohemia*, 19 March 1912.

In his capacity as a critic for *Bohemia*, Adler remained a supporter of Mahler, reviewing the premieres of the late works, a 1914 performance of the Third Symphony, and the historic performances of the Sixth Symphony, which Zemlinsky conducted in Prague in 1923 and 1927. Adler's writings understand Mahler as an important cultural liaison between Bohemians and Germans, above all the essay in honor of the composer's fiftieth birthday that appeared in the journal *Deutsche Arbeit, für das geistige Leben der Deutschen in Böhmen*, published by the society for the support of German science, art, and literature in *Bohemia*.

• • •

A surprise: yesterday, after the final notes of his Seventh had faded, Gustav Mahler was celebrated with all imaginable signs of sincere, honest, and unfeigned admiration. Frankly, not even his greatest supporters and friends expected this. The history of Mahler premieres has a great abundance of failures and embarrassing errors; each symphony precipitated a "clash" between his advocates and his enemies. Anyone who understands the nature of Mahler's creative work cannot be surprised by this aspect of their reception: it lies in the nature of true novelty to evoke negative first impressions. Philistines are always offended by what they do not understand, and in this they are joined by Herr Marker (*Merker*), who immediately condemns anything that will not fit neatly into his head. No true artist has been unnerved by such failure; rather, it is cheap success that discredits.

One can rest assured that Mahler's success yesterday was in no way cheap. Nothing in the Seventh even approaches a concession to the crowds. There is no sign that the composer in any way became disloyal to himself. The saying "he proceeded firmly and unerringly" holds true for Mahler now more than ever. Yet at the same time all the *Sturm und Drang* in him has passed; what was before perceived as immoderate and excessive has given way to a compelling concentration. Idea and form are perfectly suited to each other. The further Mahler stretches, the bolder he strikes, and the greater the respect must be for the artistic personality whose will arrives at such convincing and impressive expression. It was this kind of respect that brought about the success of his Seventh yesterday.

The value and significance of this symphony lie in the purely musical. The work does not describe, narrate, or illustrate; nor is it written merely for the sake of combining sonorities. Rather, it harkens back to the original purpose of music—to express moods, feelings, and emotions for which there are no words. But these moods are very complicated and differentiated. Mysteriously dark, demonic forces and drives, of which we are not conscious but merely sense—the subcurrents of both nature and mankind—become musically alive. The composer's world of ideas is realized in themes that are outlined sharply and carved three-dimensionally. They are entirely diatonic and therefore accessible, even singable. The self-conscious popularity of these themes is of immense value in following the widely spread branches of a Mahlerian symphony movement. Already with the uncannily somber first theme in the tenor horn, what palpable conciseness lies in the Seventh Symphony. It almost bores into the ears and brain; one feels its emergence and growth viscerally.

In all its transformations, the theme never relinquishes its own presence. Its rhythm pulsates through the Allegro with vehement energy, propelled by an almost elemental force. In its logicality the development section is one of the boldest and most compelling Mahler has ever created. As elsewhere, he does not shy away from neighboring tonalities that seem diametrically opposed, but the courage to do so is born of inner necessity rather than mere exuberance. Suddenly the basic dark mood gives way, and a harp *glissando* sweeps the listeners into daylight. All the warmth and ardor the orchestra can express washes over us, as though the heavens want to open. But then, just as suddenly, we are torn from heaven; the dark forces again seize control. The somber accents of the introduction are heard again, stronger than before: herein lies a shattering force of titanic magnitude.

The three movements that follow are similar in character and together make up the second part of the symphony. These movements are the composer's impressions of night: with their eerie coloring, strange mood changes, and bizarre harmonic ideas, these pieces could easily be the work of E. T. A. Hoffmann's ingenious Kapellmeister Kreisler. One horn opens the march, followed by a second that calls from afar. The bizarre melody is picked up in the strings and interrupted by the haunting bustle of various goblins; a cymbal crash, a harp sound, a sustained trill in the violins—and suddenly this spectral moment is over. It is followed by the Scherzo, also a romantic night piece, but different in rhythm, sound, and color. The movement is very intimate and orchestrated with the most refined and intricate technique. It is a masterpiece of Mahler's pointillistic instrumentation and achieves true mastery in coherence of form. The ensuing serenade is very striking and has a wonderfully pensive mood. This is no mere chirping by a harmless Celadon to his lover but rather a piece of painfully restrained sadness.[74] The mood is strangely melancholic, bathed in moonlight and the pale glow of the stars. The violin sighs yearningly; the guitar and mandolin receive unexpected symphonic honors. The horn intones the wistfully simple melody that pervades this piece. The serenade fades as quietly as it started; with it passes a piece of poetry among the most beautiful any tone poet ever invented.

The Rondo-Finale that closes this broadly structured work provides a gripping contrast to what has come before. Here everything is cheerful, joyous, and life-affirming. The sun has risen, it has become *day*. The world is worth whatever it may cost! This is the mood of this movement, according to Mahler, this is what these sounds exclaim. The orchestra sings, finding joy in its own pleasure. A truly masterful happiness pervades this movement. But in its exuberance the movement confronts the most difficult compositional problems. Here Mahler plays catch with his motives, one of which is a genuine Carinthian Ländler, of the most jolly "one-step" gaiety.[75] The movement has an unprecedented dithyrambian energy. Mahler's counterpoint literally sparkles with new ideas. (The chromatically descending pedal point, in particular, should be mentioned in this regard.) Then, abruptly, the cheering stops. In the first movement, it suddenly became light and one could see the heavens open. In the Finale, the power of the demons momentarily returns in uncanny dissonances that refer back to the work's opening. But affirmation of life, joy, pleasure and exuberance again gain control, and with another colossal climax, the movement reaches its end. [. . .]

Gustav Mahler's "Seventh"

RICHARD BATKA

Prager Tagblatt
September 20, 1908

An advocate for "modern" music, Richard Batka (b. Prague, 1868; d. Vienna, 1922) was seen as a central proponent of the work of Bruckner, Mahler, and Hugo Wolf, at the same time as having deepened the public's understanding of Wagner's music. From his student years onward, 1896 to 1898, Batka edited the *Neue Musikalische Rundschau* in Prague with Hermann Teibler. When it was absorbed into Ferdinand Avenius's prestigious Munich arts journal *Der Kunstwart*, Batka continued as music editor. His first books dealt with German composers Schumann (1892), Bach (1892), Martin Plüddemann (1896)—and topics in early music (ancient Greece, 1900, and medieval polyphony, 1901). While still living in Prague, he published several collections of his reviews, which early on won an audience beyond Bohemia: *Aus der Musik und Theaterwelt*; *Musikalische Streifzüge*; *Kranz: Gesammelte Aufsätze über Musik*; *Aus der Opernwelt: Prager Kritiker und Skizzen*.[76] He was involved with various projects aimed at a broader public.[77]

During these years, Batka was a central figure in Czech musical and intellectual life. At age thirty-two, he became a contributor on music to a volume on German cultural work in Bohemia.[78] Batka subsequently published several books on music in Bohemia.[79] He also wrote more libretti for Czech composers than for composers of any other nationality.[80] His pride in Mahler's Bohemian heritage is clear in the review translated below.

In 1908, after losing his job at the leading Prague newspaper *Bohemia* and writing for the *Prager Tagblatt* for several months without securing a position as music critic, Batka accepted an offer with the *Wiener Fremdenblatt*. Just at this time Mahler's Seventh was premiered in Prague, and Batka published reviews in the *Fremdenblatt* and in revised form, in *Der Kunstwart* (as well as the review below). His most widely read book, a history of music, was published in three volumes (1909, 1911, and the third completed by Wilibald Nagel). Batka became well established in Vienna, editing *Der Merker* with Richard Specht from 1909 and teaching history at the Academy for Music and the Dramatic Arts. When the *Fremdenblatt* suspended publication in 1919 he was hired by the *Wiener Allgemeine Zeitung*.

Opera was of special interest to Batka as a writer,[81] but most of all as a librettist. He wrote a libretto for Lili Scheidl-Hutterstrasser (1882–1942), perhaps the only woman to have had an opera produced at the Vienna Volksoper: *Maria von Magdala* (1919), published under her pseudonym Lio Hans. Batka wrote numerous libretti for Hungarian, Austrian, and German composers and also translated many libretti into German.[82]

Mahler came into contact with Batka when replying to his questionnaire about the nature of artistic creativity, an attempt to determine whether artists share cultural aspirations. The composer, for his part, lamented the amount of discourse and reflection on creativity and hoped instead that his works would elude any translation into language.[83] Their exchange continued when Batka proposed writing a general article on Mahler and queried the composer on biographical matters as well as other issues, prompting the composer to a literary excursus on the nature of meaning in his music. Batka remained an enthusiast for Mahler's music, over and above his responsibility for covering performances in Prague (including a review of the Fifth Symphony for *Bohemia*). He was a correspondent for *Die Musik* (reviewing the First, Second, and Third Symphonies, and the *Kindertotenlieder*) and contributed several articles on Mahler to *Der Kunstwart*, including an obituary and a review of the Ninth Symphony.

The review below reveals Batka as one of Mahler's few contemporaries outside the anti-Semitic press to discuss Jewish identity. Two years later, spurred by Rudolf Louis's anti-Semitic treatment of Mahler in his book on "contemporary German music," he published an article on the "Jewish" qualities of Mahler's music, opening with the same paragraph on Arthur Schnitzler as in the following review. The article appeared in *Der Kunstwart*, and may have influenced Moritz Goldstein, a young editor at the Goldene Klassiker Bibliothek who sparked an important debate over Jewish-German identity the following year in the very same journal.[84]

• • •

Arthur Schnitzler apparently said in a recent private conversation that someone who didn't know that Richard Strauss is Aryan and Gustav Mahler of Jewish extraction would observe specifically Semitic characteristics in the composer of *Salome*: the luxuriant, erotic sensuality; the unbridled Oriental imagination; the proclivity toward outward effect; the talent for self-presentation, and in general the skill at the economic exploitation of his work. One would contrast him with Gustav Mahler, as a man of mystic rumination, one who climbs gigantic boulders, a chaste "Wunderhorn" singer who is able to render the "Wayfarer" music of the *Volk* into symphonic form, and an idealist—the paragon of the German artist. It is not my objective here to enter into the awkward question of the relationship between art and race. Rather, I touch on it only regarding the fact that in this exhibition concert, as well, Mahler was perceived and accepted as a representative of modern *German* art. As the best German musician from Bohemia and as someone whom expert judgment has long since led to be appointed the general music director of Austria, he makes a political statement without even wanting to do so. And yet the force of his personality is so compelling that it breaks down the great barriers between nations and finds followers in the Czech musical world. While before, Dvořák and Smetana represented music in Bohemia, the hero of this summer's concerts was undoubtedly our Mahler. This was the case simply because the others do not have anyone else amongst the living who would measure up to him.

The symphony has five movements, and already here I hesitate. [Explanation of the tradition of three- and four-movement symphonic forms.] I personally suspect that the future lies in the three-movement form, but we have a right to use any other number, so long as it comes across as plausible. To preclude a work falling from the symphonic realm down to the ground—to the suite—a spiritual bond must bind together the individual movements. Mahler unfortunately pays tribute to the principle of hidden programs, so we do not know why the marchlike Night Music (the second movement) is followed by a somber Scherzo-Capriccio, which is in turn succeeded by a Night Music resembling a serenade. We must guess why or mindlessly accept these facts. Likewise, we do not know why in the second and last movements cow bells suddenly ring. I understand that an artist like Mahler objects to the excessively literal use that the public often makes of detailed programs. But his opposition—avoiding even the briefest of hints that could point to the work's overall sense and coherence—only pushes us from an erroneous understanding into a complete lack thereof.

His aversion is doubly incomprehensible with a work, like the Seventh, that appears to be made up of impressions and musical reflex responses to external sensations and doesn't reveal much of the composer's inner life. Mahler's imagination is most inspired by events in everyday life—by parades, marches, and dances. Common experiences appeal to Mahler. He is not put off by their triviality. Popular *plein air* music is quite literally a specialty of his symphonic output.[85] It is a matter of taste whether a melody like the second movement's trio (led by the cello), pretty as it sounds, is suitable for the concert hall—whether it would not better be played in the open air, in the garden pavilion. Mahler loves such extreme affability, which contrasts starkly with his moments of remote and celestial ecstasy. *Les extrèmes se touchent.* Taken individually, not one of the motives is truly original. There are nowhere any musical ideas that are immediately understood to be those of a creative genius. But one of the strangest phenomena in the history of art is the manner in which Mahler's strong personality shapes these everyday motives and impresses a strong, individual stamp on them so that they are suddenly set into relief and acquire character. This process is no mere sham. It springs from an almost demonic will to impose one's own self onto things, perhaps from a disdain for the objectivity of the world—which for Mahler gains value and relevance only when it begins to live in his subjectivity.

Mahler presents us with a problem. He comes across as someone who conjoins the strongest, unbalanced spiritual contrasts, as both a strong-willed person [*Willensmensch*] and an effusive, enthusiastic nature lover, as both a most refined technician controlling all musical means and a naïve popular musician, and as a ruler over gigantic orchestral masses as well as the most delicate, pointillist instrumentation. He is a mystery we cannot solve, although we seem to experience almost corporeally the spiritual aura that emanates from him. [Description of the orchestra's unusual instrumental colors, including the guitar and mandolin.]

To me, the first movement is the most colossal, the second the most popular, the fourth a dainty morsel, and the fifth finally the most effective in general. They all are interesting, like their creator. This symphony is undoubtedly an important stage in his development. Mahler, whose enormous reach impressed even those who reject him as a composer, has entered his years of full artistic maturity and finally found his standard of measure within himself. The concentrated quality in his new creative period brings out all the more distinctly the coherence and logic of his formal design and musical language. [. . .]

Mahler's Seventh Symphony

ELSA BIENENFELD

Neues Wiener Journal
November 10, 1909

On Bienenfeld, see above.

• • •

Mahler is a composer of such significant individuality that a new work by him counts as a major musical event. There are few composers whose works excite their contemporaries to such a degree. Admittedly, Mahler does not compose works that have everyday relevance and whose value can be ascertained from the number of postpremiere performances. These works hardly matter to the cashier at the box-office window or the philistine seeking pleasant diversion after a fine dinner and a good cigar. But in art, many things lie between heaven and earth, and what matters is where one positions oneself in order to see them from the right perspective.[86] A young shoemaker's apprentice, for example, would consider it very funny if someone wanted to read Kant to him, and he would certainly find it most laughable that someone worries over the reality of things, since a boot, of course, really does exist. Things do indeed seem uncommonly funny when they exist at a totally different level from one's own thinking and life. [Explanation that truly original artists are limited, and that it is very difficult to actualize an idea in a composition.]

By this point Mahler has completed eight symphonies—eight works of the most enormous conception and design. This in itself is a life's work and demonstrates what ideas the composer possesses. Each of the symphonies aspires to what is immeasurable in the world—to the heights—and has gigantic arms extending into the distance, reaching toward the ultimate. Yet each work also has a special and peculiar character. It is not the task of criticism to explain whether the composer each time had a program in mind or to uncover what this program may have been. One could hardly state precisely what is meant in Beethoven's symphonies. Life and death, life on earth and life in heaven, mankind and nature, power and light—these are empty words for one person but the heart of the matter for another. It is Mahler's style to seek to express emotions in great expansion and serious pathos yet at the same time—in their opposites, in the bizarre play of satyrs, in tender and quiet moods. [Discussion of the expressive and formal variety in the other symphonies and Mahler's tendency toward expansion.]

In the Seventh Symphony, the most recent heard in Vienna, a tragic character dominates the first and last movements. Both movements are the high points of the symphony, with their heights reached through Dionysian passion. [A brief description of the three inner movements as a nature scene, another fantastical and eerie movement, and a third tender and rapturous.] An oppressive and brooding heaviness fell over the first movement like the weight of sinister air. The winds carry the themes and exchange them amongst one another, first stolid and husky, then, after the darkness rips open, like sharp lightning. The main theme is diatonic, constructed from a natural harmony, and in no way hides its affinity to Bruckner. But through the opening fourth interval, Mahler produces modulations that were previously alien to his own music. The shining light of B major fills the second group; extended transitional passages with marchlike rhythms bring back the main theme in numerous guises, interrupted by motives over chromatic and diminished harmonies. There are dense and ragged accumulations of sonorities, intensifications and explosions. But this first movement is more unified and polyphonic than usual in Mahler. However, it is still too broad and not tightly enough constructed to make every sound seem necessary, every connection organic, and every climax gripping—the way Beethoven and Brahms knew to hammer the content into the form. The Mahlerian form can hardly contain its content. The piece therefore stretches out to lengths and sounds that are oversized, as if a sublime word were overemphasized or recited with too grand a gesture.

I sense the same disproportion in the last movement, a rondo whose C major is frequently interrupted by episodes in four other major keys: A-flat, A, G-flat, and D. This orgiastic song of triumph springs from a very bold, powerful and life-affirming energy. Whoever wants to win over the world with such radiant and smiling exuberance must have had the strength to overcome the deep anguish and passions of that world. In this movement Mahler submits to a stricter form than before. But it is as though he cannot do enough to depict joy: as he places climax after climax, the piece founders in its sheer breadth. Still, Mahler's agile and imaginative mind transforms the themes in manifold and subtle ways. The strongest objection one could make against the movement is that he sometimes leads the themes into a paean of joy that is crude and unstylish.

Mahler is, however, an incomparable master in smaller forms and in the ambiguous moods suspended between light and dark. The second movement has the quite original title "Night Music." [An ornate description of the various instruments that enter successively.] Here one is reminded of the atmosphere in high mountains when night draws to an end but before dawn warms and colors the earth: mist covers the mountaintops, and everything shivers and appears gray in the cold, hazy light of the morning. Segantini's paintings often represent the cold, clear, and transparent air of the high mountains—air which gives them their sharp, pure, and peculiar shapes.[87] Something similar—something sounding like soft voices of nature, hardly perceptible to the ear—floats by in Mahler's Night Music. The stylization of timbre into mood makes this the most fascinating and imaginative music. (It is obvious that the somber cowbell here does not signify the presence of a herd but is instead blended in for its sonic effect).

The Scherzo evokes the mood of *A Midsummer Night's Dream* in a new guise. The movement flies past in scurrying triplets, with obstinate and menacing shouts mixing into its merry dances. A serenade follows, in which a languishing melody sways over the plucked sounds of a mandolin, soft and tender like a dear hand stroking the forehead. This F-Major piece is the spitting image of Mahler's reverence for Mozart. In hardly any of today's compositions is the style of a past era revived so vividly and peculiarly as in this delicate piece. Even Mahler can make music speak of the sweetest bliss.

This symphony displays Mahler's distinctive traits unmistakably. It also brings together the factors that determine his personality: a passionate *Sturm und Drang*, which always made him the foremost leader of the young; the subtle refinement of a highly cultivated style, a style as perceptive in differentiating moods as it is delicate and fussy in their rendering; and the rare naïveté of an unbridled impressionist fascinated by sounds and melodies. This last characteristic frequently misleads Mahler into using themes in a form that is not sufficiently stylized or polished. The second trait perhaps also misleads him into testing sounds and joining voices merely for the sake of diversity. And the first trait shows him building constructions whose gigantic outlines are too impetuous and insufficiently cemented. Thus one can rebuke, but it is the curmudgeons alone who continue doing so. We should not forget that these are only minor cavils: it is precisely the conjunction of those three predispositions—so bold, so witty and so genuine—that forms the personality of an artist who compels one to think his will and to feel his enthusiasm.

Feuilleton: Mahler's Seventh Symphony

JULIUS KORNGOLD

Neue Freie Presse
November 6, 1909

Among Mahler's most influential supporters was Julius Korngold (b. Brünn [Brno], 1860; d. Hollywood, 1945), music critic for the *Neue Freie Presse*. Korngold left Moravia to study law at the University of Vienna and music at the Vienna conservatory. His memoirs recall private meetings with Bruckner in a beer hall after class, where the professor would carry forth a monologue, often to his student's dismay. When Korngold defended Dvořák's instrumentation, Bruckner proclaimed, "Paint a pair of sausages green and blue if you like—isn't it still a pair of sausages?" (A more elegant version of this same bias against timbre is Mahler's comment, in a conversation with his brother, that Tchaikovsky's instrumentation in the *Pathétique* is no more substantial than a colored top that ceases to fascinate once it is no longer spinning.)[88] Returning to Moravia, Korngold practiced law and worked for the *Brünner Tagesbote*. As a young critic and admirer of Brahms, Korngold had attracted Hanslick's attention after defending a performance of the Fourth Symphony. Korngold befriended the critic and spent time with the composer during a visit to Vienna. Korngold's sympathies are yet another example of the false dichotomy history has drawn between Wagnerians and Brahmsians. As a youth Korngold met with friends each week to discuss and analyze Wagner, and his enthusiasm did not wane even as he discovered the music of Brahms. Brought onto the staff of the *Neue Freie Presse* by Hanslick, Korngold subsequently became the lead critic and remained in this post into the 1930s.

According to his memoirs, Korngold's move to Vienna was prompted by public ridicule after his critical review of an opera singer. The opportunity the move presented to promote his son's career in that musical capital must have been equally enticing; indeed, parallels were drawn between the young Erich Wolfgang Korngold (who became one of the leading Hollywood film score composers of his generation) and Mozart, promoted by his father. Cosmopolitan in taste, Korngold traveled to the Paris World Exposition of 1900 where he heard Debussy's *La Damoiselle élue*, and he claimed to have been the first critic to review Debussy for a German-language newspaper.[89] A few years later, however, Korngold became suspicious of new developments in music—above all, the work of Schoenberg. Korngold fled Austria in 1938 at the time of the Nazi Anschluss, emigrating to the United States.

Korngold developed cordial relations with Mahler following his favorable review of the Fifth Symphony. At a time when most critics viciously attacked the composer's Sixth Symphony, Korngold took its innovations and developments seriously. From that point on, the two had a friendly relationship, meeting regularly at a café or at Mahler's house. The Seventh Symphony, which had received a resounding endorsement in Prague from local critics as well as those traveling from Vienna, did not win such warm approval from Korngold. But neither did Korngold need to defend the work, as he had the Fifth and Sixth Symphonies; Mahler was by this point living in New York and did not require the support of the German-language press. When the Seventh Symphony was performed in Vienna in 1930, Korngold recast part of his original 1909 feuilleton into a more positive review, in part to uphold Mahler as a favorable alternative to the "radical experiments" of Schoenberg and Paul Dukas.[90]

• • •

Gustav Mahler says nothing about his work and even less about his working method. But if by chance he who is creating and those who are on holiday find themselves in the same area of the Dolomites where a symphony is being built, it might happen that something of his hammer strokes unintentionally penetrates into the neighbor's ear. One might note, in passing, that there is no more suitable environment for these giant symphonic children to be born than among the wild rocks; their bizarre peaks and jags seem to filter into the music. Close to the birthplace of these works, one is astounded at the almost superhuman energy of their creator. During long weeks he struggles without interruption or rest and in strict isolation, castigating himself like an Indian penitent and throwing the influx of ideas onto the paper in the utmost hurry, as though in a fever, and in a shorter span of time than a copyist would need for mechanical copying. If it should happen that the conversation suddenly turns to the subjects of analysis or program books, this new father, now agitated, may shoot out an objection: why would someone want to dismantle what the creator can hardly account for himself, having received it from mysterious forces? One really has to imagine Mahler in a state of trance, indeed obsessed, in the act of creation. He has visions and follows them relentlessly. Insofar as his spirit is awake and active he becomes the ally of disturbing forces. If the devil himself stepped into his study, Mahler would probably not throw his ink bottle at him but rather ensure his collaboration in a few pages of the score. . . .

The devil himself seems to have contributed to the first movement of the new symphony, although it becomes clear that he is indeed a fallen angel. Two of the inner movements bear the title "Night Music." Quite a few of Mahler's symphonic movements could be thus named. The first movement, in fact, could easily be called "Witches' Sabbath music," and the whole work "Night Symphony." It is almost self-evident that the jubilant Finale in C major leads from night to daylight. In no way do we wish to vouch for the composer consciously creating symphonic counterparts to, for example, Novalis's *Hymns to the Night*. He might instead have come to understand the finished work in this way only after realizing the connections to night and nocturnal things. The fact that Mahler wanted to omit from his compositions even explanatory programs of the emotional content proves unmistakably that no program guided him as he composed. Even less does Mahler depict objects: rather, he always only expresses himself and his emotional life. His strong and, unfortunately, also violent self barks at us in every measure. His symphonic music becomes a cinematograph[91] of the emotions of a complicated, nervous individual who listens to the demons in his heart and the sweet nocturnal ghosts inside him, then escapes longingly to the consoling arms of nature, and then again tries to relax with a song from the street. . . .

An artist such as Mahler will not change further; his faults, especially, will remain. We have repeatedly addressed the peculiarities of his style and technique—and have repeatedly called for tackling them. In the Seventh, as well, they create moments of appeal and repulsion alike. In this new work we encounter the same brutal accumulation of devices, immoderation in expression, boundless individualization and democratization of voices that are starkly juxtaposed and superimposed, lavish motivic and melodic play of transformation, insatiable developments, and sharp contrasts that grate on the nerves.[92] Again Mahler's glowing sonic imagination showers us with spirited combinations and sulphurous dissonances, here applying flaming colors "in stunning verve" with an enormous brush, there handling the silver pen with delightful delicacy.[93] Again new instruments are introduced: the romantic, languishing guitar and the chirping mandolin. The tenor horn advances, secures a soloistic role and produces prominent heroic sounds. From the Sixth Symphony the ringing of cow bells murmurs, further proving their purely coloristic, rather than programmatic, function. In the Finale, the ringing of bright, high bells casts rays of sunlight over the festive exultation. In its five-movement form the Seventh recalls the Fifth. Here, however, the two outer movements are more concentrated; in any case Mahler has organically consolidated his unique style, especially in the first movement. The two outer movements frame the middle three— the first Night Music, the Scherzo and the second Night Music—so that the whole work could be described as a symphony with a three-movement serenade at its center.

Mahler, like every late-born, is no cogent inventor. But he still is one of the few modern musicians to whom things significant and attractive occur. Objections against the invention in his symphonies are particularly insupportable—this old cannon, always aimed at his themes and melodies, should finally be abandoned. Mahler seeks his thematic material mainly in the diatonic realm, where it is certainly no longer easy to find wholly new basic ideas (*Grundgedanken*). There is no dearth of voices already now proclaiming an exhaustion of melodic reserves. Indeed, an interesting article entitled "The End of Song" has announced a bleak future for this sweetest of musical wonders.[94] We are less pessimistic, however, and still believe in unlimited possibilities. [Discussion of the "modern" approach to harmony and melody.]

In general, in works of the Moderns we encounter either "old melody" struggling with the classical and romantic model, beside the most advanced harmony, or we encounter an inorganic conjunction of the two. This happens most often, for example, in Strauss, when he wants to be outright lyrical, whereas otherwise his themes are made of wide leaps drawn from the suspensions and alterations of contemporary harmony. Certainly—and this is what the author of "The End of Song" emphasizes, new melodies will more often be those that one cannot inwardly *sing* or carry in one's head. Mahler's melodic writing presents another point of contention. He is inclined to successions of notes that sound too affable and too popular, possessing little in the way of noble character. These he dresses up minimally or not at all; rather, with an often conscious tendency toward realism, he squeezes them into the symphony, wearing their street or working clothes. This does not always work; at times, it provokes or seems out of context.

Nevertheless, we repeat, Mahler has to be counted as a musician who succeeds with melodies of expressive value and charm and melodies that are genuine and thought through to the end.

The themes should not be underestimated, even in the first movement. As if running its head against the wall, the first main theme in E minor immediately sounds dissonant against the accompanying chords in the strings, which march along, rattling their weapons. Coherent and sculpturesque in its working out, the theme has truly symphonic contours and character. A new, fruitful idea with the wide intervals of the "new melody" follows it effortlessly—now noble and proud, now plunging into wild and despairing rebellion. This is followed by the second main theme, singing and widely arched, initially in C major; in the Mahlerian manner, this theme experiences the most surprising transformations without ever becoming distorted. One of these transformations opens the windows of the music onto a radiant B major, admitting light and beauty into the steamy atmosphere of struggle. In his musician's novel *Love among the Artists*, George Bernard Shaw ridicules those who in an original work search for the individual themes, "their working out, and the rest of the childishness that could be taught to a poodle."[95] Despite all his originality Mahler is well suited for this search for "childish tricks" in symphonic construction. We are surprised by the slow introduction that reappears before the recapitulation, anticipating the main ideas of the first movement, like ghosts shaking their limbs. As a whole the movement is filled with truly Mahlerian gestures of invocation and conquest, passing like a terrible but purifying nocturnal thunderstorm. . . .

After this movement, which stands above the rest of the symphony in its pathetic—or perhaps rather demonic—character, let us single out the one most prominent in the graceful idiom: the second *Notturno*, in F major. With its delicate Eichendorff atmosphere this movement is perhaps the most uplifting, amiable music Mahler has ever written. The witty aspect of gracefulness here recedes in favor of a pure, romantically pensive feeling. Yearning melodies alternate with tender sounds, drifting along in sweet harmony. In all this richness of colors and shapes nothing is emphasized, nothing underlined. Between the other two middle movements, we prefer the Scherzo to such a degree that we can leave out the first Night Music entirely. There the major and minor modes march through dark forests at night for too long, in expanses too wide and spacious; such ideas have no place in a symphony. The Scherzo, however, is a coherent movement, worked out finely and moderately, a Hoffmannesque waltz of ghosts in which Doctor Miracle actually dances through, shaking his bottles. In the Finale, which is a rondo, the scene changes completely. Here we have come to a single ecstasy of joy, a *Meistersinger* festival atmosphere, a burst of exultation and festive jubilation. The movement displays a great deal of solid contrapuntal work and diligent detail; the main theme returns again and again, admirably fulfilling its rondo function, releasing new surges of joy. The whole, however, roars too much, and runs the risk of fading out. [Discussion of the difficulties of evaluating "modern" music and the future success of Mahler's work.]

Even the most enthusiastic contemporary approval cannot give any indication of immortality. But undoubtedly these judgments determine what is valuable for our era. The nervous art of Strauss and Mahler pronounces the era's concerns, disclosing the futile yearnings that make up its desires. More graspable than these, however, are those sources of inspiration and motivation that enrich music through the discovery of new expressive and emotional realms, the unexpected extension of the world of instrumental sounds and the penetration of new formal ideas. We think it dishonorable to attack those dark and somber productions that struggle for new forms by insistently opposing them to the completed high developments of the past. Already Brahms spoke disdainfully of those who "absolutely want to see the top of the finished cathedral of music."[96] No, fortunately this cathedral is completed neither in the interior nor on the outside, and it will never be. But we want to pray also at those altars that rise up, as we hope for something new, for something beautiful if ever so dissimilar to the old.

Das Lied von der Erde

Mahler's protégé Bruno Walter conducted the premiere of *Das Lied von der Erde* in a commemorative concert for the composer on November 20, 1911, in Munich. In a highly unusual pairing, the work was followed by the Second Symphony. The alto for *Das Lied* was Madame Charles Cahier, a celebrated performer of Mahler lieder, and the tenor was William Miller. The two documents that follow, by Richard Specht and Rudolf Louis, show the range of responses to this performance. Performances followed that same season in Zurich, Leipzig, Frankfurt, Graz, and Mannheim.

Feuilleton: *Das Lied von der Erde*

R I C H A R D S P E C H T

Neue Freie Presse
December 4, 1911

More than with any other of his contemporaries, the career and publications of Richard Specht (b. Vienna, 1870; d. Vienna, 1932) exemplify the range of genres and methods by which the musical public was educated. Born with considerable musical talent into a wealthy Jewish industrial family, Specht received excellent training, studying music theory with Alexander von Zemlinsky and Franz Schreker and composition under the guidance of Brahms and Karl Goldmark. In his twenties Specht wrote poetry and published a book on the Burgtheater (1899). Even after he turned to music criticism in 1901, Specht remained active in the literary world with a wide range of publications. He wrote libretti, published a set of *Jugendstil*-illustrated poems on Mozart (c.1910), edited the writings of Johann Peter Hebbel, and published books on Schnitzler (1922) and Alma Mahler's third husband, Franz Werfel (1926). Among his several wives was the concert pianist Vera Schapira (1891–1930).

Specht freelanced for several newspapers. He began as an assistant to Richard Wallaschek at *Die Zeit*, where he served as music critic in 1904–1908. In 1909, he founded *Der Merker*, the Austrian biweekly for music and theater, with Richard Batka and the composer Julius Bittner, and remained editor until October 1919. During those same years, 1912–1920, he was also a music critic at the *Illustrirtes Wiener Extrablatt*. Thereafter, as his colleague Ernst Decsey wrote in an obituary, "Specht found no place at a Viennese newspaper. . . . His personal manner of presentation, the 'Specht style,' which enriched the art of writing on music, was not suitable for newspapers. He wrote in Ciceronian phrases; sentences of Baroque splendor, sentences that breathe deeply and slowly; snakelike long sentences that attacked, defended, surrounded and expanded; that inflamed and dampened; and through 'although's' and 'indeed's' sought to protect his enthusiasm from any misunderstanding."[97] No doubt his lifestyle also contributed to this instability. Reports abounded about Specht's drinking and the deep furrows allegedly brought on by morphine abuse.

Unable to secure a permanent appointment as a critic, Specht was forced to write books, Decsey explained. Throughout these years Specht also contributed to the literature for concert audiences, writing program books for the Vienna May festival and the Society for the Friends of Music. He was appointed professor at the Academy of Music and the Dramatic Arts. Active as a lecturer, especially in Germany, he gained international stature and was admitted into the Academie Française in 1926.

While his books ranged far afield in musical taste, Specht never abandoned a format and approach that would remain accessible to a concert audience. After World War I he published a book on the Vienna opera house, a wistful look back at the start of an era. His other books were all biographies: Johann Strauss (1909, with a second edition in 1922), Richard Strauss (1921), Julius Bittner (1921), Furtwängler as conductor and composer (1922), the Austrian composer and conductor Emil Nikolaus von Reznicek (Leipzig, 1923), Brahms (1928), Beethoven (1930), and Puccini (1931). Although they brought him recognition in Europe and the United States, Specht lived under financial strain, for it was possible "to breakfast, but not live, off writing music books."[98]

Mahler and Specht met for the first time in 1895, and the critic remained a loyal advocate for years. In 1905 he published one of the earliest Mahler biographies; the composer's minor objections were miscommunicated by Bruno Walter, leading to friction between Mahler and Specht. It was only after the composer's death that Specht published another, longer biography of Mahler. In addition to his reviews of Viennese performances, Specht wrote thematic guides for individual symphonies and other essays on the composer, such as "Mahler's Victory" (1920) and "Mahler's Enemies" (1921).

· · ·

In the six symphonic movements with voice that are joined into a "Symphony for tenor and alto with orchestra" under the title *Das Lied von der Erde*, Mahler has composed six "serious songs." It is perhaps his greatest work ever, certainly his most personal. Brahms, in those other *Serious Songs*, overcame the shudder from a premonition of death, his resolute heart strengthened through life and through love. In Mahler's work, as well, there is a mood of farewell from earthly things, but more removed, resigned, and idealized. An almost unbearably quiet grieving is expressed in a voice of serene and gentle renunciation, utterly calm and entirely without pathos or grand gestures. It is the tranquil voice of a knowing subject in whom all the suffering of life still resonates but who has already been liberated from, and transported beyond, any feeling of pain. It is the voice of one who, having known the world, turns back to it once more, to all the beautiful, colorful, and foolish delights of existence. The work is a great farewell to youth, beauty, and friendship. It moves one so deeply at a personal level through its aura of a "last" work. Mahler composed *Das Lied von der Erde* at a difficult time. Now, after the death of his beloved child, he was disturbed by dark premonitions of his own death. He truly believed that after *Das Lied von der Erde* he would put away his pen, never to compose another work. He was mistaken: he would still complete his Ninth Symphony. But this mood prevailed, and the sonorities are incredibly poignant in their unsentimental and unearthly grieving—so much that the work seems to be a self-portrait from Mahler's last period. *The Song of the Earth* became *The Song of Gustav Mahler.*

Mahler shaped these six pieces using ancient Chinese poetry. [Discussion of the appeal of the poetry, compared to that of *Des Knaben Wunderhorn*.] The opening of the first, "Das Trinklied vom Jammer der Erde," is glowing and orgiastic yet also steeped in melancholy. A most remarkable emotion, unsettling but still almost exuberant, enters in the first measures with great determination and power, drunk with pain: "The song of trouble should resound, laughing in the soul." There is a widely arched melody of immense energy—defiantly effervescent yet at the same time seeming to release a paroxysm of suffering. It then calms down to the refrain *[Abgesang]*, sinking into a quiet shudder, "Life is dark, death is dark." After another surge and decline, it reaches a mystic inwardness, "the earth will endure long and laugh in the spring, but you humans, how long can you live?" There follows a turn to the fiercely grotesque, presented in terrible irony, "Look down there! In the moonlight on the graves a wild ghostly form is squatting. It's an ape! Do you hear how his howls scream out into the sweet fragrance of life?" And now the song struggles to its feet, with the superior, invulnerable feeling of one who has all knowledge of the world, "Now take the wine! Now it is time, comrades. Empty your golden cups to the lees! Life is dark, death is dark!"

It is marvelous how Mahler arranged the poetry, almost shaping it into symphonic form. This first song, like the last one, is a perfect symphonic movement, with the most rigorous structure. To be sure, the structure is very concise, with the most slender build, but formally the song is entirely "unobjectionable" (not that this really matters). Perhaps on first hearing this structure doesn't even show, for the whole flows with such complete freedom and the musical arch stretches from beginning to end. Perhaps, as well, this form is overlooked for a reason quite opposite to what has usually provoked misunderstanding of Mahler's works. In his eight symphonies, the immense dimensions of the movements and even the individual themes made it difficult to achieve a complete overview of each work; here, however, the almost epigrammatically concentrated form, which avoids anything hypertrophic, obstructs its recognition. But this work is no less structured than his symphonies.

It should be mentioned that the objections Mahler's enemies repeatedly raise against his symphonic music do not hold for this work. *Das Lied von der Erde* has none of the "immoderation" in architecture, the "shrill" contrasts, and especially the "triviality" so often ridiculed in the master's first seven symphonies, where they formed his stylistic principles. Nor are there the gigantic symphonic structure and the imposing thematic viaducts that united each of those works into a single colossal organism. Here one finds the greatest mastery in concentration: no measure contains too much, and the highest degree of expression and form is achieved without excess or seeming boundlessness. There is also nothing of Mahler's earlier woodcutter's humor, which enjoyed juxtaposing bizarre, quaint worlds (an enthusiasm for folk song) with the pathos of grand tragedy (bold march rhythms). Here the melodic writing has become so personal, so compellingly mature, and so "finished," that the language cannot be mistaken for any other. Individual movements exude a gentle happiness as never before in his earlier works, like a peaceful sunset glowing on placid water. This work is also quieter, more wistful, inward, and transcendent.

Mahler's humor in the early symphonies was bizarre as with Callot, Goya or Hoffmann, or even the Kapellmeister Kreisler.[99] More than anything else, the humor in those works was contentious and, with its unrestrained ferocity, sought to conquer the burlesque of existence as an analgesic for suffering. In his last works, however, the humor has become more deliberate, more conscious of pain and how to overcome it. *Das Lied von der Erde* in particular has a wholly transcendent composure and grace. These songs are full of loving and blissful contemplation.

Most beautiful in this regard are the third, fourth and fifth movements of the symphony. They are prepared by the second movement, "Der Einsame im Herbst," with its unspeakably mild, tender, and fatigued evocation of the past. The song drifts by like a breath of wind, a pantheistic withering without spite or grief. ("My heart is weary" and "Give me rest, I need refreshment! I weep much in my loneliness. The autumn in my heart persists too long.") A touching melody in the woodwinds rises like a sad and gentle breeze above the flowing but monochrome voice.

This voice is nothing but a sound of nature—falling leaves and rippling brooks. In sum, an autumnal landscape in tones.

The three ensuing movements are animated by an enchanting radiance but, of course, the radiance of a parting day, which brings melancholy. Each is a self-contained image with extraordinary color and clarity in contour. The songs are symbols of farewell to youth ("Von der Jugend"), to beauty ("Von der Schönheit")—thus the songs are titled—and to spring, in the song "Der Trunkene im Frühling." The scherzo "Von der Jugend" is an irresistible piece. It is the only one whose style has some of the erotic nature of Chinese paintings—the scent and mellowness of their porcelain colors—together with a vibrant grace that fills the poetry. [Quotations, from lines of verse.] It is delightful how light-footed "Von der Jugend" proceeds and how gracefully the poetic and musical arabesques unite in a neat and comfortably flowing $\frac{4}{4}$ beat, forming a most charming, transparent image. This is an image of youth in which everything is reflected upside down. Two wonderfully beautiful tone paintings follow: girls beside the water watch as slender young men pass by on horse. Glowing sonorities are shot through with mysterious sounds, as if Klinger's *Fantasies* had become music.[100] . . . Mahler's polyphony has reached its consummation: no harshness or rough collisions, but everywhere pure sonority and a myriad of singing and luxuriating voices that unify into one immense song.

And then the drunkard in spring, who tosses off all troubles and worries to find brief contentment in drunkenness and sleep. Not for long: parting is in store. I know of very few pieces of music that speak a language similar to this last song. A mood of renunciation, parting with sweet existence, and turning inward, is so utterly restrained and calm, so completely without strong accents or anything declamatory, that one is shaken to the core—so agonizing is this music. What is more, if by chance one compares the original poetry and the composition, one discovers how many seemingly insignificant phrases and verses Mahler added. Not only such characteristic ones as "From the deepest contemplation, I suddenly listened" (in "Der Trunkene im Frühling"), which almost give a summary of his own nature, but also those that reveal his feelings of utter loneliness and despair: "My heart is still and awaits its hour" (in "Der Abschied"). With a simplicity shunning all pathos, this phrase is whispered without tones—an impact from which no one can escape. In the floating transparency of these immaterial and wholly spiritual sounds, in their most intense tenderness and sensitivity, the music has a force to which even those who miss the human element in this overwhelming confiteor must submit. They must feel the eternal tragedy of the artist, shaped with incredible purity. [. . .]

Gustav Mahler: *Das Lied von der Erde*

RUDOLF LOUIS

Rheinische Musik- und Theaterzeitung
December 2, 1911

Rudolf Louis (b. Schwetzingen, 1870; d. Munich, 1914) was a leading conservative and anti-Semitic music critic in the early twentieth century. Both his training and his writing epitomize the close connection between philosophy, aesthetics, and ideology that characterize the period. Louis studied philosophy in Geneva and Vienna, receiving a doctorate with a dissertation on conflict in music (1893); his next two books were on Wagner (Wagner as an aesthetician of music, 1897, and his Weltanschauung, 1898). Louis studied composition with Bruckner's student Friedrich Klose, a right-wing nationalist, and prepared the piano arrangement for the latter's *Ilsebill,* a folk opera that came to serve as a paradigm for conservative aesthetic and ideological musical concepts over the ensuing decades.

Louis worked as a music critic in Munich from age twenty-seven and within three years secured a post at the leading Bavarian newspaper, the *Münchener Neueste Nachrichten*. He was a prolific writer, authoring several monographs on Liszt, Berlioz, Bruckner, and general musical topics. His book *Die deutsche Musik der Gegenwart* (1909), one of the first general discussions of German music of the turn of the century, became widely popular and influenced the next generation of German nationalist writers, such as Karl Storck and Hans Joachim Moser. Louis also composed, and possibly his failure to develop and sustain a reputation during the very years that Mahler gained recognition contributed to his antipathy to the Jewish composers of his own generation. Arnold Schoenberg, for example, was absent from the book's index and was omitted from the book altogether. Louis's most well-received composition was the symphonic poem *Proteus* (1903), a theme harkening back to his writing on conflict and struggle in music, performed at the 1903 Pan-German Musical Society (three years before Mahler's own Sixth Symphony was premiered in the same festival).

Louis showed the same partisanship across his writings, consistently favoring Bruckner and Strauss over Mahler and Schoenberg. However, the nature and extent of his anti-Semitism differed from venue to venue. When writing for the main newspaper in Munich, which had a readership extending beyond any single party or political orientation, he took seriously the critic's job of reporting on the music as heard, along with judging the composition by his own criteria. While never writing positively on Mahler's music, he gave detailed attention to performances of the Second, Fourth, Seventh, and Eighth Symphonies as well as *Das Lied von der Erde*. Yet within the covers of his own books, whose readers knew, or could know, the orientation of the author, Louis wrote scathingly about Mahler as a Jewish conductor who merited no consideration as a composer. This was true of his Bruckner book (1905) as well as *Die deutsche Musik der Gegenwart*. More suggestive than the specific diatribes in the latter was the very framework of the book, which despite its title "contemporary German music," was devoted to tracing an unbroken line of development from the nineteenth century through to the living composers he deemed significant. Likewise, Louis's harmony textbook (1907), written in collaboration with the influential composer Ludwig Thuille, promoted a specific repertoire, which included composers up through Richard Strauss but banished Mahler and other so-called modernists.

[. . .] So dangerous was Louis—"as clever as he is questionable"—that Specht refused to include him in an article on Mahler's enemies. He was the "Meister Eckhart" of music—a pun capturing both the depth and the danger of the music critic by referring simultaneously to the famous fourteenth-century scholastic and mystic, Meister Eckhart, and to the virulent anti-Semite Dietrich Eckart, who patronized Hitler as he built the Munich base of the National Socialist Party. Specht demurred that Louis possessed "a racial feeling that is alien to art," and, in an hapless attempt to protect music from ideology claimed that Louis rejected music as Jewish when he found it inaccessible.[101] It is not surprising that Louis reviewed *Das Lied von der Erde* for the *Rheinische Musik- und Theater-Zeitung*. Since 1906, the editor-in-chief was Gerhard Tischer (1877–1959), a publisher (Tischer & Jagenberg) and lecturer in musicology who became an early proponent of National Socialism in the pages of his journal.

• • •

[. . .] Mahler used as his text Chinese poetry from Hans Bethge's collection *Die chinesische Flöte* (Leipzig, 1907). From a purely literary perspective, the composer made a truly marvelous choice with these poems. They are as strange as they are poetically worthy. In part *because* they are so outstanding poetically, and therefore extremely difficult to be set to music, even someone of much stronger creativity than Mahler would have failed. With *Das Lied von der Erde* as much as all of Mahler's other compositions, there can be no doubt that his ambitious artistic desire does not have any significant creative capacity at its disposal. The composer dares to approach the most sublime things with a naïve, childlike self-confidence and a technical ability that is more orchestral than compositional. In this work, too, Mahler's music is fundamentally impotent. Its invention is not his own; material borrowed from others supplies the actual musical substance. The only noticeable difference from his earlier works is that over time Mahler's eclecticism has progressed. If before Beethoven, Schubert, Wagner, Bruckner and Viennese folk music were Mahler's main sources of inspiration, now we occasionally see him taking loans from pieces by Richard Strauss or contemporary French and Italian composers. Even certain exotic influences, derived from the texts, arise here and there (though rarely). It should not be denied that Mahler knows how to weld together these heterogeneous ingredients with immense energy, fashioning something that in its outer language appears quite original. Yet the essence, insofar as it has one at all, can always be proven to be borrowed, or at least hopelessly imitated.

The Tenth Symphony does not show Mahler's creativity from a significantly new perspective. Still there is something to be said in praise of this posthumous work that in my view elevates it above most if not all of the earlier symphonies. That which often outright repels and sickens one with Mahler's music, namely the trivial and banal, the greasy sweet and the disgustingly sentimental, is found far less often here than elsewhere. *Das Lied von der Erde* is through and through musically more serious and nobler in its emotional expression than one is accustomed to in Mahler. However, also partly because of this, it probably does not belong to those Mahler works that impress the general crowd, like the Second or Eighth Symphony. The composer here avoids, rather than searches for, outward effects (insofar as that was even possible for him). It gives an overall impression of something artistically "respectable," an impression otherwise rare with Mahler.

Of the six songs that constitute the whole, the first and fifth are most similar (a similarity already determined by their texts). "Das Trinklied vom Jammer der Erde" and "Der Trunkene im Frühling" are both vivacious and brisk in their composition, though here the musician owes much to the poet, who is especially ingenious in the first poem. I find the greatest congruence between poetry and music in the deeply melancholy second movement, "Der Einsame im Herbst." But it must buy the privilege of a misty, gray atmosphere of gloom, sustained with relent-less consistency, at the cost of a certain monotony. This is even more the case in the final piece, "Der Abschied," where monotony rises to a marked boredom. Its resolution to C major (which is, moreover, woe-ful in the bad sense) comes too late at the end to save anything. The two middle movements, "Von der Jugend" and "Von der Schönheit," are character pieces that are by no means weighty but very pretty and, especially in their sonorities, unusually attractive. [. . .]

Fourth Philharmonic Concert: *Das Lied von der Erde*

FERDINAND PFOHL

Hamburger Nachrichten

A Bohemian living in Hamburg, like Mahler himself, Ferdinand Pfohl (b. Elbogen [Cheb], Bohemia, 1863; d. Hamburg, 1949) became a friend and supporter of the composer. Pfohl helped pre-pare the literary program for the First Symphony at its performance in Hamburg, with its references to Jean-Paul's *Titan* and *Siebenkäs* and E. T. A. Hoffmann's *Fantasiestücke in Callots Manier*. He reviewed performances of Mahler's music from 1893 to 1930, including the First Symphony through the Fifth, the Ninth, Tenth, *Kindertotenlieder,* and *Das Lied von der Erde*. It is strik-ing that Pfohl's two autobiographical sketches, from 1932 and 1942, do not even mention Mahler's name. To do so in a positive vein would have had political repercussions by the time he pub-lished the second autobiographical sketch, in the Third Reich. Furthermore, the journal in which both appeared, the *Zeitschrift für Musik*, had changed its orientation after 1929 and supported pro-Nazi causes well before 1933.[102] In writing his first autobio-graphical sketch, Pfohl may have decided to focus his memoirs on his Leipzig years, before he knew Mahler, precisely in order to obscure his connection to the Jewish composer.[103]

After studying law in Prague and later music and philosophy in Leipzig, Pfohl began writing for the *Leipziger Tageblatt* and *Leipziger Nachrichten*, then moved to Hamburg in 1892 as music critic at the prestigious *Hamburger Nachrichten,* a position he held for thirty years. With the largest circulation of any north German newspaper outside Berlin, the *Hamburger Nachrichten* also had a readership in the business communities in England and North

America. Pfohl was affiliated with the Vogt'sche Conservatory in Hamburg, first as an instructor of music theory and history and from 1908 as a co-director. During his years in Hamburg, he published books on "modern opera" (1895), Arthur Nikisch (1900), and Beethoven (1922). Wagner was a particular interest; Pfohl published *Die Bayreuther Fanfaren* (1891), *Die Nibelungen in Bayreuth* (1897), and a biography of Wagner (1911) as well as co-authored a book with Hans Merian on Wagner's musical dramas (1909). He also wrote opera guides to *Der fliegende Holländer, Lohengrin, Tannhäuser, Tristan und Isolde, Die Meistersinger,* and *Parsifal* (as well as *Fidelio*). Pfohl was a composer of works of note, including his symphonic fantasy *Das Meer*; a song cycle *Mondrondels*, on the Albert Giraud poems that Schoenberg used for *Pierrot lunaire*; and several piano pieces.[104]

• • •

Gustav Mahler's symphony *Das Lied von der Erde* sprang from the same metaphysical urge, nostalgia for life, yearning for eternity as all the other music that the artist composed before this strange work. He calls it a symphony and with this title wants to hint at the universality of the symphonic form as a cyclic-symbolic form of the entire world and cosmos. This form lies close to all secrets of being, to life and death, and to the great unfathomable—the mystery of the world, which causes Gustav Mahler's soul to experience pain as had no musician before him. It becomes his soul's "painfully wonderful" content. In reality Mahler's symphony, in its alternation between songs for a tenor and an alto voice, is nothing but a song cycle on the basis of an orchestral accompaniment that blossoms forth in the richest symphonism (*Symphonik*) and proceeds by shimmering in colors of unspeakable appeal. The accompaniment paints continuously, listens and learns the most delicate stimuli from the poetry, plunges into the infinities of feeling, and reaches out to the afterworld with a mystic sense of nature and a foreboding of distant eternities.

The orchestral writing is almost always a lucid translation of the word into music. It becomes a parable for everything beyond language, extremely flexible and finely balanced in expression, with a subtle mix of colors. Upon closer examination, the orchestral accompaniment is a completely self-contained organism into which the vocal line grows like a pulsing lifeline. It occasionally expands into long, purely instrumental episodes, where the voice falls silent and the orchestra becomes immersed in visions or has the poetically prepared moods swing freely in full pendulum. At other times it builds bridges to close or distant shores, bridges to the mystical, spanning the gap between earth and the unearthly. Mahler's *Lied von der Erde* is a song of yearning that, with its peculiar sounds, revives the ancient lament of the fate of the beautiful that must vanish. It is a song that, just as Friedrich Nietzsche extols Dionysian bliss and Hafiz extols intoxication, finally falters, defeated by the desire for sleep and rest.[105] [Discussion of the poetry Mahler used.]

Fortunately Mahler's work was inspired only by the exquisiteness of the Chinese poetry, not by the exotic peculiarity of Chinese music. It was simply a requirement of good taste that he refrain from a distinctive Chinese flavor and avoid climbing around on the Chinese scale, which surely is no Jacob's ladder and does not lead to heaven. His music remains genuine Mahler throughout, even where it cultivates disharmonious sounds or makes concessions to the old (and therefore very modern) whole-tone scale or to a daring harmonic idiom. It always remains aesthetically satisfying and resolves its tensions spiritually. Its motives are short, sometimes deformed, but almost always stubbornly ornate. They move in agitated figures and hail down onto the earth like arrows of a peculiarly fierce and grim humor. In the first movement, "Das Trinklied vom Jammer der Erde," sounds and sonorities pour forth like the howling of the ghostly ape who sits on the graves in the moonlight. All the sibilanting and sighing of grief—indeed all the wailing of the world—howl and screech in this strange drinking piece, which is not beautiful but rather creatively grotesque. It depicts drunkenness even in its motives and rhythms. A very wistful song, "Der Einsame im Herbst," portrays the autumnal mists silently rising and all the melancholic withering of heart weariness and lonesome bitterness. It is a poetry of lost sonorities.

The bucolic yet epicurean nature of the composer, whose pathos and Hamletian or Faustian tragic character so often only serve to hide blatant inability, reveals itself most charmingly in the two cheerful middle movements. They tell of youth and beauty in delightful sounds. Certainly one already knows this string of Mahler's harp from earlier works, especially from his "Himmlisches Leben." Even though it does not sound new, this music is still of enchanting amiability, charming chatter, and capricious grace, all bathed in harmonious sound. It is, moreover, a showpiece in the art of instrumentation, with light agility and porcelain grace. Another drinking song, "Der Trunkene im Frühling," elevates drunkenness to a philosophy and captures its exterior image with staggering, tottering figures and rhythmic realism. The finale "Der Abschied" follows, despondently spun out, perhaps even overstretched and overextended. It opens with menacing, horrible sounds of nature and flies out into the infinities of the universe with an anxious, uneasy question. The middle part of the piece is taken up by a purely orchestral interlude whipped up to a cry of despair. This, finally, is a terrible march over all the misery of life. [. . .]

Obituaries

In the wake of Mahler's death some of even his fiercest opponents reflected on his contributions, expressed regret over his passing, and deployed neutral terms in attempting to understand his importance, at least as a conductor, if not as a composer. Robert Hirschfeld's obituary is among the most remarkable of contributions from this camp. Unlike his reviews, which appeared in the evening edition, the obituary was published in the main morning edition of the *Wiener Zeitung*.

The remaining obituaries translated here show the responses of the next generation of critics, writing on the phenomenon Mahler represented at the very start of their career. All three writers would later develop a very different attitude to Mahler in the intensified polemical debate during and after World War I and leading up to the Third Reich.

Gustav Mahler

ROBERT HIRSCHFELD

Wiener Zeitung
May 20, 1911

On Hirschfeld, see above.

• • •

[. . .] It is certainly true that Mahler resisted the calm and soft nature of the Viennese and that his energy often discharged like a hostile force. Yet the intensive involvement in Viennese society, whether in an official position or pursuing his ideas independently, never left him. Our admiration was, admittedly, directed less at his creative spirit itself than at the frequently strange form of its utterances or at the changes in terms and nature of his professional duties. Gustav Mahler's manner of setting everything into motion was attractive even when, stubborn and inflexible, he missed the mark. The dynamism of his nature brought him supporters even when his individualistic and almost peculiar impulses made him appear lonesome. Mahler's capacity to isolate himself in thought and deed and to withdraw from tradition as well as from the general public has led many to think of him as a genius. Yet Mahler showed only the attitude and behavior of a genius in his technique, energy and dynamism. The imperative conditions of genius—creativity, naïveté and patience—were lacking. His invention was derivative; emotion emanated from his consciousness, which was brainy and externally illuminated. In Mahler's songs and symphonies, naïveté was not the source but rather the desire of his art. The more he directed his unusual energy toward the semblance of naïveté— that is, the more he attempted to enter the naïve aura through the "Knaben Wunderhorn," angels, popular saints, animal voices, cowbells, sounds of nature, ordinary marching rhythms and simple folk tones—the clearer it became that his path lay along the border between the unconscious and the conscious.

The fact that he was the leading Mozart conductor did not arise from an inner kinship with the composer. His art sprang from a different source. But when conducting Mozart, he suppressed through sheer will power the demon that raged in his heart. His will released him from those elements that were contrary to Mozart and banished his own flickering restlessness, so that he could put himself in a frame of mind for Mozart. Always accustomed to retreating into his subjectivity— rather than the instinctive, uncalculated devotion and selflessness of Hans Richter—Mahler did not approach Beethoven directly. Rather, he kept a certain distance from the great man, which allowed him to prepare Beethoven scores from his own perspective. In the process he was swept into such stormy and boundless excitement that the dynamism of his Beethoven performances catapulted the poor souls out of their bourgeois routine with raging force.

Gustav Mahler also lacked the great, all-encompassing human love that resides in true genius. He detested the general public even as he ardently sought its approval. He desired the favor of people whom he made feel far beneath him. This was the terrible conflict in Mahler as a person: he could never be at peace in his relationship to the world. The deep roots of Mahler's conflicted nature often led him to thrust together happiness and pain in his symphonies, to render the brightest joy ironic, and to parody suffering through intentionally trivialized funeral marches. He did not seek faith through love. Rather, with all the energy of a fighter he sought to gain it through struggle. His achievements came through fighting.

As a stage director he gladly avoided artists who were popular, talented, and amiable. He tended to gather around him groups of artists with whom he had to work laboriously to conquer the public anew every time. He was most satisfied when he won success in an area that was alien or barely accessible to the artists. What they achieved there was, then, always the result of his efforts, always his personal success. Willpower, and the ability to transfer this energy to others, was so strongly developed in Mahler that he seemed to envoice the dumb and bestow talent upon those ungifted. He moved his baton like the commanding scepter of a ruler, stirring everyone and igniting even the smallest artistic spark. Under his baton the inept became skillful, the dull sharp, and the fatigued vitalized. But this impact always required his personal presence: the example offered by this teacher—Mahler's school, as it were—did not suffice. Imitators and emulators easily became caricatures, because the unusual degree of energy that Mahler summoned up could only be realized by his personality and by an artist of his caliber. Not only his mind but the whole mechanism of his body had to be engaged. His glance was needed to tap into the springs of the artistic deed; his word was needed to vitalize the people around him, holding them in suspense; and finally his own action was needed to fire up the musicians, breaking the barriers of complacency and self-satisfaction.

We cheered on Mahler as he drove through reforms at the Vienna Court Opera and as he, himself a model of indefatigable work, compelled the public through draconian regulations into a serious experience of art as rigorous mental work. We cheered when he touched every nerve of his artists, filled every corner of the Opera with life, and bestowed upon Mozart and Richard Wagner their full rights (before they were distorted by Roller). And we cheered when the insignificant in musical comedies became meaningful, lit up in Mahler's mind, and when the most extreme statements of modernity, to which he imparted an inwardness, excited even the most reserved.

But then, with a rashness typical of all of Mahler's resolutions, he ceased drawing any deep pleasure from mastering the artists, satisfying their ambitions, appointing new members, and communicating the art of others to the people. With the same energy as he earlier brought to opera's salvation, Mahler increased his production of grandly designed works. He piled up symphonies in uncanny haste. He could quickly shift, at any free moment, from his duties as director to his creative activity. (It is simply wrong to assert that Mahler only worked on the symphonies in the summer, on vacation from his opera duties.) He subjugated the technique of orchestration through a wondrous force and mastery. The individual instrument seemed to provide him with the mood. If the idea was not original, its novel and unusual sound was nevertheless captivating. If the theme itself was insignificant, the dazzling light was nevertheless gripping. Violent turns in rhythmic pulse, new combinations of instrumental groups, extensions of the conventional, but also remarkably taut structures, and an inconceivable abundance of sparking details, compensated for everything that a great and sublime symphony should evoke.

Like his method of artistic direction, Mahler's symphonies require his presence as a person and conductor, as one who arranges and who spurs on others. Much, and perhaps even most of his oeuvre was explicable and tolerable only when Gustav Mahler communicated it as a conductor, a conductor of the public. The energy of his fascinating movements on the podium as well as the striking and characteristic phenomenon of his conducting surely enhanced the success of his works. This was the tragic fate of the artistic life of this extraordinary man. The more often Mahler had to take responsibility for his symphonic works in Vienna and abroad through his personal presence, the more he was alienated from the Opera and the public. He became indifferent or even averse to the theater business. This feeling provoked a deplorable crisis that robbed the Opera of its once incomparable vitality.

Death took Gustav Mahler from the world at an age and time when, having strengthened and clarified his demonic nature, and freed himself from burdens and duties, he hoped to contribute to the dissemination of his works and to produce new ones. We are filled with deep, painful sorrow about this bitter stroke of fate. It is not enough to praise Mahler only as the complete representative of contemporary artistic life. His significance is not limited to the realm of the aesthetic. The energy that his aspirations represented both physically and mentally belongs to the energetic worldview of modern philosophy. Contemporary beauty in art is not oriented toward aesthetics but toward the energy of artistic action and creativity. From this perspective of energism, Mahler will always be remembered with the highest esteem, regardless of how one views what he gave and achieved.

Gustav Mahler†

PAUL BEKKER

Frankfurter Zeitung
May 1911

One of the most influential advocates for progressive composers—Mahler, Schoenberg, Schreker, Krenek, Delius, Busoni and Debussy were among his favorites—Paul Bekker (b. Berlin, 1882; d. New York, 1937) was, however, a professional music critic in Germany for less than two decades. His first post, at age twenty-four, was at the

Berliner Neueste Nachrichten, which he soon left after the newspaper underwent significant changes and reemerged as the *Berliner Allgemeine Zeitung* in 1908. In 1911, Bekker became critic at one of the leading German newspapers, the *Frankfurter Zeitung,* where he remained the chief critic until the early 1920s. Long aspiring to a career in opera direction, at age forty-three Bekker took over the state theater in Kassel (where Krenek was his assistant and where Mahler had once conducted); two years later, in 1927, he assumed the directorship of the theater in Wiesbaden, where he remained until the Nazis came to power. In 1933 he emigrated to the United States, working in New York for the Parisian emigré press.

It is not surprising that Bekker's obituary focuses on Mahler as a conductor and opera director. Trained as a conductor, Bekker published his first book on a conductor, Oskar Fried (1907). His next two, from 1909, were on the opera (and operetta) composer Jacques Offenbach and on music drama (*Das Musikdrama der Gegenwart*). Following these, in 1911, was what has become his most important work for English-language readers, a book on Beethoven that appeared in numerous editions. Prior to the Mahler obituary, Bekker had written articles on Mahler as a conductor and on the *Kindertotenlieder* for the *Norddeutsche Allgemeine Zeitung,* the *Grazer Tagespost,* and the *Allgemeine Musik-Zeitung;* an essay on the Third Symphony appeared in the 1906–1907 program book of the Berlin Philharmonic.[106]

The obituary translated below reveals an attitude far removed from the one Bekker would adopt toward Mahler a decade later, in his first extended analytic study of the composer's works. In this 1921 book, *Gustav Mahlers Sinfonien,* Bekker argued vehemently against the critical commonplaces he had espoused in the obituary, such as the lack of connection between "form and content" in Mahler's music. By then, he was ready to attribute to Mahler's own music the power that he had in 1911 reserved for his conducting.[107]

• • •

One of the most significant contemporary figures in music, and one of the strangest and most contested artistic personalities of our day, has forever left the stage. At the height of his life, the indefatigable Gustav Mahler had to abandon his work long before he could bring his thoughts to a conclusion. [Presentation of the standard biographical information.]

While evaluation of Mahler's compositional activity is highly controversial still today, there have never been serious doubts about his merits as a conductor. Among modern masters of the baton he was perhaps one of the most deeply serious, strict, and ruthless toward both himself and others. For musicians the name Mahler was inseparably linked to the idea of a despot. Not merely a teacher, he could also be called a master disciplinarian. He knew no such thing as fun, relief, or relaxation. The greatest challenges were not enough for him, and he worked through them with unrelenting determination. "This is very difficult," the musicians complained. "But wherefore are we artists?" he retorted—a true and beautiful artistic statement. Everything he said revealed a personality that approached its task with complete earnestness. He was not only strict with others but apparently strict and even harsh with himself. Looking into his face, one knew that this individual must have worked and fought to extremes; he must have struggled with all his force. He must already have conquered himself in order to gain demonic power over others. It was not a pleasure to obey and follow Mahler, but one simply had to. There was something dictatorial in his conducting style. It seemed that he struggled almost continuously with the will of the masses, resistant though it was: he paralyzed them and forced them to act according to his commands. While conducting he had no need to extend himself or use any superfluous movements, for he knew: I am the master, you must obey me, willing or not.

In performance Mahler directed his whole consciousness, through the immense energy of his will, to what had been said in the rehearsals. His mere glances sufficed to make musicians automatically execute his thoughts. None of our other conductors had so clear an awareness of power. No one else had therefore to fight clandestine, or sometimes even open, resistance. It was probably just this awareness of his ability to reduce the orchestra to slavish dependency that produced Mahler's vast contempt for the masses, expressed in his bitter and malicious irony. In Bülow it was witty sarcasm, in Nikisch amiable mockery, in Strauss more or less good humor—in Mahler it was fierce, caustic scorn.

His discipline, strict as it was, had a positive effect on artistic achievement. Bülow alone, perhaps, rivals Mahler as an educator of musicians. Among the living no one can even remotely be compared to him. Upon examining his scores or orchestral parts, one is amazed to discover such an incredible number of performance instructions. To him nothing was superfluous: each marking had to be observed, even if he had to sing the phrase in question a hundred times and have it played back just as often. He was most enraged when staccato markings were overlooked. "In music, just as in the Bible, the least should be the largest. There is no musical performance without observing the dots."[108]

Seeing Mahler conduct for the first time, one was always astonished at the imposing calm of his motions. If there was a strong gesture during a performance, one could be assured it was in response to a mistake. It was very different in rehearsals. To see Mahler rehearse was one of the most peculiar and instructive spectacles for a musician. A small, unremarkable, beardless man with a peculiarly deep voice—was this the feared representative of our modern musical absolutism? Nervous energy literally sparked from his fingertips; it was also expressed in his loud manner of speech. Mahler always sounded irritated and fierce. His most polite speech was still curt and harsh. Whether he was correcting a female vocal soloist or the percussionist playing the bass drum didn't matter—so strong was his sense of objectivity. His fine and differentiating ear could hardly be surpassed. More than once he discovered a mistake in some hidden secondary voice; at first the musician concerned would deny it, but after playing it again his mistake would come to the fore and prove Mahler right.

While Mahler's unrivaled orchestral pedagogy rapidly secured him universal recognition as a conductor, the verdict on his compositions is as yet undecided. Because he did not give his symphonies any programs, one saw in him a representative of absolute music, the antipode to the programmatic musician Strauss. Mahler, however, belongs to that class of composers who lack a language of their own and therefore speak in many.[109] His agility and technical mastery are so significant that the inner lack of independence of his protean nature is almost forgotten. At times he is folklike, at times extremely modern. He copies Papa Haydn's endearingly cheerful dialect of the delicately ornate, grandfatherly style of the eighteenth century just as deceptively as he adopts the powerful grandeur of his teacher Bruckner and the impressionistic manner of expression of the most modern. But that which is essential to each of these contrasting styles—the necessary inner coherence of form and content—is mostly missing in Mahler.

Mostly, but not always. Mahler has moments when he reaches up to the stars, moments when his great mental ability, which made him one of the most ingenious of performing artists, rises to unexpected heights with enormous strength. Then he finds sounds that pour out directly from his inner self, sounds that immediately build a magical bridge to the listeners' hearts and allow them to forget the peculiarities of this complicated artistic figure. Thus the entry of the chorus in the last part of his C Minor Symphony. This movement, "the Great Call," begins with fanfares sounding from the different ends of the world—a reveille for the dead. The last call has died away—and then the chorus starts in ghostly pianissimo: "Aufersteh'n—ja, Aufersteh'n." This isolated choral entry is one of the most gripping moments not only in more recent music but in the entire span of musical literature. One finds oneself involuntarily under the spell of an artistic revelation. But the sanctified atmosphere does not prevail. The composer lacks the power to sustain the phenomenon he so magically achieved. What was a deeply inward experience sinks into an elegantly developed but merely outward intensification.

Another trait of Mahler as a composer reveals his perhaps most original side: his humor. It is a rustic and burlesque kind of humor; refined wit and irony recede into populist coarseness. Paradoxical though it sounds, it may not be wrong to say that in Mahler an operetta composer was lost.

Time will be the judge. Mahler's artistic legacy is rich enough to make such judgment possible in the future. There are eight symphonies (among them several that fill an evening), a great number of songs, and several choral pieces, along with a few dramatic youthful works. Even those who cannot feel unconditional sympathy for this imposing legacy of works are still impelled to deep respect at the immense mental labor behind these works. There are few artists to whom the saying "To be human means to be a fighter" applies as much as to Gustav Mahler.[110]

Gustav Mahler

ADOLF WEISSMANN

Leonards Illustrierte Musikzeitung
May 1911

"Since Eduard Hanslick," reported an obituary of Adolf Weissmann (b. Rosenberg, Upper Silesia, 1873; d. Haifa, 1929), "we have had no music critic who stood at the center of musical life" as much as Weissmann, "someone who, among musicians as well as in public, hurled himself for and against, just like someone possessed."[111] Weissmann was perhaps Berlin's most influential music critic, and his books commanded one of the widest readerships among German writers on music. He held positions at two of the major daily newspapers, the liberal *Berliner Tageblatt* (1900–1905), which aimed at the new middle class, and the *BZ am Mittag* (from 1916), the first German-language tabloid and a *Boulevardzeitung* designed for mass street sales and accessible reportage for the harried urban reader.[112] Beginning in 1904, Weissmann also wrote for two weeklies: *Roland von Berlin* and *Montagszeitung*. He contributed to *Die Musik* for two decades.

No major critic was so drawn to Berlin as Weissmann. He published books on the history of musical life in Berlin from 1740 to his day and on Arthur Nikisch's reign at the Berlin Philharmonic. Conductors held a special interest for the critic, with essays in *Die Musik* on Toscanini (1920) and Klemperer (1921) as well as a book on "the conductor in the twentieth century" (a presumptuous title, given that the book appeared in 1925). Fascinated by the culture of music, Weissmann published books on the virtuoso (1918), the prima donna (1920), the erotic in music (1920), and the desacralization of music (1928), as well as an article in *Die Musik* on "Humans and Machines" (1920).

Through his weekly radio program on new music and as a founding member of the International Society for Contemporary Music, Weissmann was considered a spokesman for modern music.[113] In fact, he harbored grave reservations about contemporary composers, in particular Schoenberg, Debussy, Puccini, and Richard Strauss. Weissmann's enthusiasm was confined to the neoclassical developments in the work of Krenek and Hindemith (who, at age twenty-two, was featured by Weissmann in *Die Musik*). A general skepticism of contemporary German music, along with its cultural and ideological claims, pervades Weissmann's most widely read book, his 1922 study of music and the "world crisis" (*Die Musik in der Weltkrise*, translated rather tamely into English in 1925 as *The Problems of Modern Music*). Given his cultural critique of Bruckner and Pfitzner, skepticism of Mahler, and outright rejection of Schoenberg, it is not surprising that Weissmann's books on composers were not devoted to German music. Weissmann published on the French composers Bizet (1907) and Chopin (1912) and on Italian composers Puccini (1922) and Verdi (1922). The latter work was, according to Edward J. Dent, his most influential book. Dent's obituary recalled that after Germany had been cut off from foreign music during the Great War, Weissmann "encouraged all that was new, whatever its country of origin; Stravinsky's immense popularity in Germany may be said to have been Weissmann's creation."[114]

Weissmann examined the nature of Jewish identity in music, and the problematic history of German-Jewish identity, over the course of several publications, including the Mahler chapter in *Die Musik in der Weltkrise*. In an essay on "race and nationality in music," published in Universal Edition's 1926 volume on new music, edited by Paul Stefan, Weissmann hoped that the tired term "race" would disappear from European thought, partly as a result of the mixture of qualities from different races, such as he perceived in the work of Mahler and Schoenberg.[115]

. . .

Mahler has made it both easy and difficult for those writing his obituary. Easy, because his tragic struggle, against an overpowering enemy, continued for days and weeks, so this sad ending did not come unexpectedly. Difficult, because his complex personality, with all its contradictions, does not allow for an obituary in the usual sense. He is not one of those artists who can be dealt with in a few phrases. But neither is he one who caused a revolution of the mind. Immortality is difficult to achieve in music in general. This art of tones gains in intensity of effect what it loses because it is the most mortal of all the arts. Have Mahler's great creative deeds pointed to new objectives for such a decidedly mortal art? Has he secured a certain degree of immortality for his name? Mahler's works have made the strongest impressions on important literary figures. Yet expert musicians, when asked, have a thousand "ifs" and "buts." The very fact that so many outside music have spoken in favor of this man proves the strong expressive force of his personality—especially as Mahler finally did not write literary music.

Among modern composers, he was a truly naïve musician. But Mahler also lived under the spell of his times. This led him to heighten the means of expression to an extreme and entrust all his thinking and feeling to the language of sonority. It is of no importance whether or not he had a program in mind. His music combined naïveté and speculation. Upon hearing his symphonies, with all their instrumental pomp, one could easily think that the composer chiefly strived for the most outward effects. The naïveté not only resided in the invention itself, which was undeniably Austrian and lightweight, but was also manifest in how the composer took up alien materials without hesitation. In utter contrast to this, however, were the magnitude of design and the ingenuity of its disposition.

But the composer, inspiring as he was, did injustice to Mahler as an artist and person. The latter was at heart an idealist who summoned up all his strength to create the great artwork; the composer Mahler, however, was unable to achieve a balance between basic musicianship and modern thought. Despite all the beauty of detail, there existed a deep rupture between purely musical potency—which always pointed to a much narrower realm than that of the symphony itself—and the immense form such potency was made to fill. The idealist who was unable to reach the peak became an advocate for outwardness. It was the fault and merit of the conductor's mighty personality that true musicianship was pushed off its path. Nothing is more interesting to observe than the strong influence the conductor nowadays has on the composer. Who could escape it completely? The orchestra conquers those who submit entirely.

In Mahler, the conductor outweighed everything else. No conductor since Bülow has been such a tyrant as Mahler; nor has any conductor realized the score's demands with such ruthlessness. Any remaining doubt over this would be dispelled by witnessing the immense energy he expended in the rehearsals. In performances, however, the conductor was exemplary in the calmness of his motions. Only his eyes betrayed the tension in his nervous system. Riven with discord as both human being and creator, Mahler nevertheless produced something whole, great and ingenious when he stood in the service of a greater aim. For ten years the Viennese had the good fortune to see Richard Wagner and Mozart recreated from a single idea. Did they appreciate it? He who pursues his path relentlessly offends more easily in this milieu than in any other. Controversy about Mahler broke out. Embittered, he could not resist the lure of the America that would discharge him as a man on his deathbed. Now the Viennese mourn him—the city to which he yearned to return. We also mourn him as an artist whose idealism knew no concessions, whose energy seemed inexhaustible, and whose personality as a whole was overpowering.

Gustav Mahler

PAUL ZSCHORLICH

Die Hilfe
May 25, 1911

Paul Zschorlich (b. Frankfurt am Main, 1876; d. after 1941) may be the most extreme case among the music critics who changed their outlook between the years around 1900 and the Nazi era. Henry-Louis de La Grange lavishes praise on Zschorlich, citing foresight, courage, "eloquence and discernment" in his review of the Third Symphony in Leipzig, November 1904, a city where Mahler was roundly criticized by colleagues.[116] Even in that review, however, Zschorlich deployed anti-Semitic rhetoric, finding Mahler's manner to be "repellent." Upon Mahler's death, he wrote on the conductor for a Strasbourg newspaper, reminiscing fondly about the rehearsals and performance of the Third Symphony in Leipzig in 1904; another article by Zschorlich on Mahler as conductor appeared in *Das Theater* in 1911. The Mahler obituary translated below appeared in the journal Friedrich Naumann founded in 1895 as a party organ of the Progressive Party (a left-liberal group that periodically split and reorganized itself and remained open, as exemplified in Naumann's case, to nationalist and imperialist currents); *Die Hilfe*, however, quickly developed a readership beyond its original political affiliation.[117]

Trained in Leipzig, Zschorlich apparently moved to Berlin in 1902, where he freelanced for various newspapers and continued to compose. He wrote on a range of topics for the yearbook on politics and the arts, *Patria*, which Naumann edited in 1901–1913 for the series "Books for Culture and Freedom" at the same publisher as that of *Die Hilfe*. Zschorlich wrote on Shakespeare as a philosopher of music (1903), d'Albert's operas (1904), and "modern music" (1909). Zschorlich also wrote a book on the theatrical works of the "folk poet" Ludwig Anzengruber (1922) reflecting *völkisch* enthusiasm for *Blut und Boden* of the 1920s.

Zschorlich's final post as a music critic was at the *Deutsche Zeitung*, which had a nationalist and anti-Semitic orientation. He initially claimed objectivity in his treatment of Mahler (e.g., "The 'clumsy' Bruckner and Mahler's Mockery: A Factual Answer to a Naïve Question," 1927) but later developed an openly aggressive stance. Most striking are his articles for the 1927 centennial commemorations of Beethoven's death and the attacks on Schoenberg and Hindemith in the early 1930s. Zschorlich may well have been responsible for the press's turn against Hindemith (in part because his wife was Jewish), which eventually contributed to the composer's decision to emigrate from Germany.[118]

Though openly anti-Semitic and nationalist, Zschorlich gave up music criticism in 1936, three years into the Third Reich. By this point, as his colleague Walter Abendroth explained, stringent advocates were no longer necessary; later that year came the ban on arts criticism (Kunstkritik), contributing to a milieu in which as fiercely independent a critic as Zschorlich might, ironically, have felt uncomfortable. Zschorlich moved to Bavaria and devoted his attention to composing.[119]

• • •

Anyone who had seen Mahler in action faced a terrible and cruel mystery upon hearing the news of his death. Everything in that gaunt, vibrant, and mercurial body was vitality, motion, energy, and restlessness. His ascetic figure seemed to be literally charged with nervous tension that demanded release. He was an accumulator with unpredictable energy and a flow of enthusiasm that was unfailingly communicated to those in his sphere. As a person Mahler had golden character traits, but he withheld them in an almost calculated manner from all but those closest to him. Others who came into contact with him found him prickly and brusque. In a semiconscious state, as death approached, he remained true to himself, merely reacting and giving laconic answers. People with such an intensive inner life close up as soon as they sense a cold response. [Description of Mahler's manner of rehearsing, conducting and organizing.]

It is difficult to predict how long his reputation as a productive artist will last. In the wake of his death all the laughter and sneering at his music suddenly fell silent. The same critics who until recently had cast a sarcastic eye on Mahler's work now wistfully revealed to the public the perspectives that they themselves had missed before. It is indeed very difficult to come to terms with Mahler as a composer, because he combines the most heterogeneous elements. One finds the most grotesque melodic leaps and the most tricky harmonic turns juxtaposed with what is populist, healthy, and naïve. Alongside passages of intoxicating orchestral splendor and rich melodies are instrumental effects apparently concocted purely for the sake of experiment. Mahler approaches Berlioz in his rather cool, crafty manner of construction, which often enough substitutes calculation for inner necessity. Both, in a sense, are engineers of music. Certainly there is no lack of warm and deep passages (as in the solo sections in the Third Symphony and the religious passages in the Eighth), but one has to become fully absorbed in order to savor them. They have nothing breathtaking or ardent in them. As much as the creative Mahler may have achieved in details, his death had no significance of any kind in the context of contemporary music history (as will, however, be the case with Strauss and Humperdinck).

Mahler's compositional creativity has in fact always played a secondary role. He was far too eclectic to create his own compositional values, although of course some personal manner of expression cannot be denied entirely. But with all due respect to his strong imagination and virtuosic talent, one cannot seriously imagine that his oeuvre will have a life span of even half a century. The pious disposition of the symphony we will surely experience in the next season [the Eighth] cannot alter this impression. Economic considerations also play a role in this. Thus even if we see a Mahler wave approaching, we must not conclude that the initial onrush will last. His greatness does not reside in compositional creativity, and perhaps not even in his wholly distinctive and irreplicable ability as a conductor. No. His greatest success lay where, as an individual, he suggested a multiplicity. He formed a reservoir of power and of possibilities for achievement from which thousands could be fed. Those remaining deaf to his influence and education would have been condemned.

He was a standard of measure for true artistry—an unfailingly competent judge of the true and the fabricated in art. Dilettantes and brawlers were smashed by the purity of his personality: a single look from his sharp eyes made them blush. With a personality so sharply profiled and opposed to cliques, he followed his own path, refusing to rely on anyone but himself. Charged with energy and devoted entirely to art, never to the people, he did not make the slightest concession, even in the midst of all the barking and shabby intrigues. He was willing to sacrifice himself rather than the work he served. It is this truly rare and precious character that has so forcefully captivated and enchanted us as contemporary witnesses. Where shall we find his equal? Gustav Mahler, at fifty-one, could have gone much further had he better handled the fuss of the press and the tricks of personal interaction. It was in his nature to care little about himself. Because his sincere life was marked by hardship and ingratitude, his death affects our hearts deeply—as if we were partly guilty for his sudden departure.

The Mahler Amsterdam Festival, 1920

World War I brought a level of politicization of music and musical thought not seen since the Napoleonic Wars. Artists and intellectuals throughout Europe and the United States took strong positions during the war, whether inspired or repelled by it. In either case, artists and intellectuals found their emotional resources depleted after the armistice. Writers theorized that, as the most abstract of the arts, music could play a special role in the rebuilding of Germany and Austria. Adolf Weissmann, a vocal pacifist, wrote only months into the war that "Even if this world war eventually releases us as victors, it brings the total suffering of a half-mature people. It can, perhaps belatedly, bear fruit, sour but ripe, because music will be its final bloom."[120]

In the wake of the war and in line with efforts to reconstruct a sense of European unity through culture, Willem Mengelberg, director of the Concertgebouw Orchestra, programmed all of Mahler's symphonies and song cycles over the course of nearly two weeks (May 6–19) in what became a historic festival. Germans and Austrians alike felt a sense of national humiliation after the close of the war; musicians hoped that music could create a more genuine peace and reconstitution. Symphonic music performed at a site that had remained neutral, offered a chance for reintegration the very year after the signing of the Versailles Treaty in 1919.[121] Many musicians were in attendance. The International Society for Contemporary Music was founded in the same spirit three years later by Rudolf Réti, with help from Paul Stefan, Egon Wellesz, and other Viennese.

Amsterdam was the ideal location for what contemporaries dubbed a Mahler "peace conference." Mengelberg had frequently programmed Mahler's symphonies, with the composer usually conducting the first performances. In October 1903, Mahler conducted his First Symphony and two performances of the Third Symphony in its Amsterdam premiere. The following October, 1904, he returned to the city to present his Fourth Symphony, heard twice in the same concert, and Second Symphony a few days later. In 1906, Mahler conducted the first Amsterdam performance of the Fifth Symphony, together with the *Kindertotenlieder* and "Ich bin der Welt abhanden gekommen." The composer's final appearance in Amsterdam was in October 1909, when he conducted his Seventh Symphony in two concerts. Mengelberg programmed many subsequent performances of these works—for example, the Fourth Symphony in 1905, the First Symphony in 1907, and in 1910 the Fourth Symphony and two performances of the Seventh. During Mahler's lifetime there were twenty-six performances of his works in Amsterdam and, in the eight seasons up to the 1920 festival, 106 concerts included music by the composer.[122]

The Mahler Festival in Amsterdam

Oskar Bie

Neue Rundschau
April 1920

A prolific and widely read author on music and the arts, Oskar Bie (b. Breslau, 1864; d. Berlin, 1938) was an important figure in cultural journalism. By age thirty he was an editor at the influential Berlin journal, the *Neue deutsche Rundschau*, whose progressive orientation could be discerned from its previous incarnations, first as the *Freie Bühne für modernes Leben*, when it was founded in 1890 by Otto Brahms, and then as the *Freie Bühne für den Entwicklungskampf der Zeit* (1892–1893). The journal changed title once again in 1904 to the *Neue Rundschau*, under which it still appears to this day, in order to distinguish it from Julius Rodenberg's national-liberal *Deutsche Rundschau* (which supported a union that included Austria). The journal reached a high point in Weimar Germany under Bie's term as editor in chief, a position he held until 1922.[123]

Bie was a writer of broad interests. His doctoral thesis and first four books, written when he was a lecturer in art history at the Technische Hochschule in Berlin, were on ancient Greek and Roman art. He subsequently turned to music, writing on piano music (1898), dance music (1900), and chamber music (*Intime Musik*, 1904). Over the next years Bie published many books on music, dance, and art history.[124] His wide-ranging interests notwithstanding, Bie remained closely involved with music throughout his life. He was an avid composer, particularly of arrangements for the harmonium, and for years served as opera and music critic at the *Berliner Börsen Courier*.

An article Bie wrote on Mahler for the *Neue deutsche Rundschau* in March 1895, at a time when the composer had received little recognition (and certainly none in Berlin publications), spurred Mahler to write a letter in gratitude.[125] That December, Mahler wrote warmly to another Berlin critic, Max Marschalk, about the impact that his and Bie's support would have on his own compositional development.[126]

• • •

[. . .] The entire world should know that the first celebration of peace will take place in May in Amsterdam at an international music festival built upon German art. For the first time, the peoples of different lands will gather neither to kill one another nor to discuss the consequences of the killings. They will gather instead to enjoy the very art that during the war proved to be exceptionally valuable for those more humane, across various ethnicities during the war—this art brings consolation, reconciliation, solidarity, culture, and true good for the future. In Amsterdam, Mahler's complete oeuvre will be performed over several weeks under Mengelberg's direction. It is generally known what Mengelberg means for Mahler, Mahler for the Netherlands, the Netherlands for the world. There are no coincidences here. There will be delegates from all nations. They will shake hands. For the first time the angel's song will sound with the innocence of paradise, the last movement of Mahler's symphonies.

The undertaking is marvelously well prepared. [List of the supporters and committee members.] Excellent soloists have been engaged. The festival will be one of the most enormous musical events ever, especially the performance of the Eighth—not only in size but especially in terms of content, the emphasis on serious ideals, and the significance for the future. [List of concurrent events.]

With this festival, Willem Mengelberg—the great conductor of probably the best European orchestra—celebrates his twenty-five years in the profession. As we have no idea, here, of what he achieved for Mahler in the Netherlands, let me present some astonishing statistics. Since 1903, when Mahler conducted his First Symphony, which Mengelberg prepared in rehearsals, the work has been performed by Mengelberg twenty-three times. [List of the number of performances for each Mahler symphony and of other composers whose works Mengelberg had recently conducted, including Strauss and Debussy.]

Mahler was attached to the Netherlands and this orchestra like a child to its mother. Under Mengelberg the extreme individualization of the players became the special quality of the orchestra, and I suspect that Mahler was directly inspired by this orchestra and even thought of its sonority at certain points in his compositions. It is a strange and wonderful fact that this complicated artist found satisfaction and redemption in the serious and massive art of the Netherlands. Now, after all the suffering in world history, we see his broad path to an international future. In the Netherlands they call Mahler the Beethoven of our time—profound, explosive and direct, he had inner strength and longed for freedom. Yet typical of our era, Mahler's character was more complicated than Beethoven's: his sensibilities could turn to divine irony and deploy technical means to spiritualize the modernity, in its enormous mechical facets. Mahler's suffering—the suffering of modern humanity—wants to sneak past the ghosts of death and find expression in a childlike yearning for folk songs, soldiers' marches, the legends of saints, wayfarers' adventures, nature, and spring—sing away! Sing about death, drink from the spring! Enter, intoxicated by the tears of peace, into heaven, where in the old paintings angels turn pain into sweetness. . . . Make music! Be a musician, play from the joy of music. Play, exorcising a thousand troubles from the heart, each with its own voice and instrument, running side by side, independent, without ties to convention, without dull, embarrassing filler material, without ruptures in harmony or clouds of chords! The last polyphony and counterpoint, the music of man's soul, without conventional filling. Mahler was ever thus, and thus will he remain. He connects old and new, and in this way he connects all of us. The young look up to him. When his entire oeuvre finally resounds in Amsterdam, we will all enjoy it, but the best of us will understand it as a document of our time. [. . .][127]

A Musician's Journey to Holland:
The Mahler Festival in Amsterdam

PAUL STEFAN

Neues Wiener Tagblatt
May 27, 1920

Paul Stefan (b. Brünn [Brno], 1879; d. New York, 1943) was a prolific author of books on music and the arts. He was trained in art history, philosophy, and law, receiving his doctorate in the last field. Stefan remained involved in the visual arts, writing the introduction to Kokoschka's *Dramen und Bilder* (1913) and contributing to the catalogue for the 1913 International Black/White Exhibition in Vienna. Stefan was catholic in his musical taste and, above all, a strong advocate for new music. He studied with Schoenberg and figured prominently in the founding of the Ansorge Society in 1903, a group devoted to new music. In 1921, he founded *Musikblätter des Anbruch*, the organ for Universal Edition of Vienna, which published the music of Schoenberg and the Second Viennese School. Stefan edited the journal from 1923 until 1938, the year of the Nazi Anschluss. He fled Austria and eventually settled in the United States, where he wrote for the *Neue Zürcher Zeitung* and *Musical America*.

Stefan published in a number of papers but without any ongoing affiliation as critic or correspondent. His Mahler reviews appeared in journals like *Erdgeist* (Seventh Symphony) and *Die Musik* (Eighth Symphony) as well as daily newspapers, from the local *Badische Landes-Zeitung* (*Das Lied von der Erde*) to the important Berlin *Vossische Zeitung* and Viennese *Neues Wiener Tagblatt*. In addition to the standard literature cited, Stefan also published a "sociological and psychological analysis" of Wagner's enemies (1918) and a study of Smetana's *Bartered Bride* (1937). Following his 1912 book on Oscar Fried, Stefan's two remaining studies of conductors appeared at strategic historical moments: in 1935 he published a book on Toscanini, a declared opponent of Mussolini, and in 1936 he completed a book on Bruno Walter, who had been deprived of his podium in Leipzig and was unable to conduct in Germany after the Nazi rise to power.

Throughout his life Stefan remained committed to Viennese subjects, which he treated with a certain sentimentality. One book chronicled Viennese life from 1903 to 1911, concluding with

Mahler's funeral, under the ironic title *The Grave in Vienna*. In the wake of World War I, when Austria consolidated its cultural identity as a replacement for its former political power, Stefan published two histories of the Court Opera (1919 and 1934), a book on Max Reinhardt subtitled *An Artist's Path Home to Vienna* (1923), another on Schubert (1928), the quintessential Viennese composer, and in 1924 perhaps his most important book, on Schoenberg. Well into the rule of Austria's authoritarian and fascist-influenced regime, Stefan published two books on Mozart operas, a topic that the most conservative branches of Austrian politics sought to appropriate, conveying as it did both traditionalism and an Austrian identity separate from that of Germany.

Most of Stefan's writings on Mahler appeared after his review of the Seventh Symphony, translated below. In addition to this review, which appeared in the *Neues Wiener Tagblatt*, he covered the work for the weekly *Erdgeist*. His discussion of the Eighth Symphony appeared in *Die Musik*, and *Das Lied von der Erde* in the *Neue Badische Landes-Zeitung*. Upon Mahler's departure from the Court Opera for New York, Stefan published a book on his operatic legacy. His main study of Mahler, with the subtitle "Personality and his Works," appeared in 1910; enlarged editions appeared in both 1911 and 1912. Stefan also edited a festschrift for Mahler (1910), to which Auguste Rodin, Guido Adler, Conrad Ansorge, Gerhard Hauptmann, Hugo von Hofmannsthal, Oskar Bie, Alfred Roller, Stefan Zweig, Romain Rolland, Richard Strauss, Arthur Schnitzler, Max Reger, Bruno Walter, Gustav Klimt, and many others contributed.

• • •

[. . .] I arrived in the afternoon and had seen nothing of the town, but that same evening attended the dress rehearsal for the first event, Gustav Mahler's *Das klagende Lied* and First Symphony. The dress rehearsal was inexpensive and open to the public, with special seats for festival guests. The spacious and elegant hall was sold out. There was no public: only listeners. Listeners at dress rehearsals are, of course, often better than those at concerts. There were many old acquaintances, as at music festivals before, in times of peace. Even for those who knew the orchestra it was quite an experience. The truly incredible concert-master L[ouis] Zimmermann led the strings, with their almost legendarily refined manner. What our Vienna Philharmonic offers in luster is here achieved through the most diligent work: no experiments with "individuality" in bowing or fingering. It is rewarding to study individual orchestral parts. The amount that has been written in, corrected, and written again, almost exceeds the printed text. The cellos can play a melody marked piano without a false "feeling." There are an astonishing number of five-stringed basses. The woodwinds are wonderful, and the oboes have an unmistakably French sound. However, the French horns are fuller in Vienna. The trumpets, especially the first trumpet, are unsurpassable. The trombones are trained to play pianissimo. The tuba, timpani, and percussion are first class, the piccolo timpani of a special construction. Four harps play together, even when the score calls for only one harp—an enchanting effect. [Discussion of assistant conductor Cornelisz Dopper as well as the rehearsal and concert schedule.]

Mengelberg is the soul of all who make and live music here. As a genuine leader (and not merely the conductor) of this wonderful orchestra and as an artist, he shapes the face of a nation whose old musical glory he has splendidly renewed. It has been his orchestra for twenty-five years, and with the most beautiful results. The orchestra is an instrument put together laboriously and splendidly, upon which the master plays. He plays it truly as a master, in fact, one whose mastery reminds one of Mahler in so many ways. Mahler was indeed Mengelberg's most valued master, and Mengelberg in turn was admired and loved by him (rare for Mahler). In a particularly Mahlerian manner, there is still room for improvisation in the concert, even after the infinitely painstaking and wonderfully precise work in the rehearsal. Everything can grow anew, as if presented by a single and powerful virtuoso like Liszt. Nothing sounds fatigued or overrehearsed. It is this ability, veneration, and devotion in playing that make these days in Amsterdam unforgettable. (The devotion holds especially for Mahler, whose music every child here knows and about whom everyone is aware.) [Description of the uniqueness of the occasion, Mengelberg's fame, and the circumstances surrounding the celebrations.]

The applause before and after the concerts is overwhelming. The stage is decorated with palm leaves and red flowers. In the front there is a copy of the Mahler bust by Rodin. *Das klagende Lied* became a new work for me in this performance. Its artistic perfection commands a special place in the series of Mahler's grand statements. [Discussion of the soprano Gertrud Foerstel.] The First Symphony, which followed, clearly shows the theoretical and biographical connections between his youthful works; the following day the concert itself only strengthened this impression. One saw—for the first time since the war!—festively dressed and adorned listeners from all countries and an exhibition of Dutch wealth and taste. There were deep emotions, without any disruption of applause between movements. [Discussion of individual performers.] The chorus combines southern fullness of sound with Nordic precision and work ethic; it will be hard to surpass. [Report on the high quality of the children's choir and the orchestral playing, as well as the chamber music concerts and lectures.]

We came to a Mahler festival. We forget the Netherlands, its cities and its wonders, even the paintings in the museums, as we sit in Mengelberg's rehearsals from nine to twelve or even one o'clock, and on days with no concerts, even on into the evening. We—Schoenberg with his students, Gustav Mahler's daughter, Mengelberg's German relatives, and the conductor Alfred Herz from San Francisco, along with Dutch, German, and Austrian musicians—were invited by Mengelberg and his orchestra. Even though almost everything is already rehearsed, Mengelberg spends his nights immersed in the familiar scores, studying every detail, clarifying everything again and conjuring up in his memory everything he ever said—he calls this his "system." Again and again he interrupts to ask and finally plead for the musicians to play "systematically." One day there was a morning rehearsal, chamber music in the afternoon, and a rehearsal in the evening. Mengelberg jumps from the melancholy first movement of Mahler's Ninth Symphony to the exuberant Finale of the Fifth. Then a coffee break. Meanwhile the choir rehearsed the Eighth next door. Mengelberg continues this rehearsal while Herr Dopper works on the Adagietto of the Fifth with the orchestra. Finish at eleven o'clock at night. The next morning the Adagietto is rehearsed through six times! This certainly explains a lot, if not everything.

The Mahler Festival in Amsterdam

GUIDO ADLER

Zeitschrift für Musikwissenschaft
July 1920

The single most important individual in the establishment of modern musicology, Guido Adler (b. Eibenschütz [Ivancice], Moravia, 1855; d. Vienna, 1941) grew up in Iglau, like Mahler, whom he befriended at the Vienna Conservatory. They remained in regular but occasional contact (Adler's relationship to Alma Mahler being tense) until the composer's death. Adler helped Mahler secure his position in Budapest in 1888 and within a year of each other (1897–98) they took on, respectively, the leading academic position in music in Austro-Hungary—formerly held by Eduard Hanslick—and the leading conducting post, at the Vienna Court Opera, which Adler helped Mahler secure.[128]

Although he did not review concerts, Adler published numerous articles for the *Neue Freie Presse*, in which he addressed music's role in the cultural and national agenda. "Austria is thus not merely a conglomerate of nations protected and secured by a military," he argued; "it is also an artistic manifestation with a distinct physiognomy. One recognizes its features most clearly in the works of that art that are bound to no specific language. Thus, just as the customs of the Austrian peoples are interwoven in the works of the classical composers of music, and as the motivic material is taken from the national legacies, which the artists develop into classical structures, so may a superior statecraft join the particularities of the various peoples into a higher unity."[129] In an article on problems in contemporary musical culture, Adler cited Mahler as offering a solution to the alleged conflict between program music and absolute music, since his works had the communicative power expected of program music and yet followed the formal requirements of absolute music.[130] In the same newspaper, he published an article commemorating Mahler's fiftieth birthday (7 July 1910). Adler's 1916 book on the composer (which has been re-published with the correspondence of the two men)[131] holds a special place in his publications; Mahler was the only composer to whom Adler devoted an entire book.

• • •

At the Mahler festival in Amsterdam, the nine symphonies, *Das klagende Lied, Kindertotenlieder, Das Lied von der Erde,* and the composer's other orchestral songs were performed over nine concerts. Willem Mengelberg, artistic director of the Concertgebouw, selected and arranged the programs on the occasion of his twenty-fifth anniversary at this institution. The event thereby became a double celebration, manifest, for example, in a commemorative coin with the image of Mahler on the front and Mengelberg on the back [see Figure 3]. Mengelberg has penetrated deeply into the essence of Mahler's art. Through many years of practice and repeated performances of Mahler's works, his highly disciplined, expanded orchestra [Description of the instrumentation.] and the equally well assembled chorus, drawn together from the best local choral societies. [List of the societies and number of members.] 853 participants in total were so well prepared for the great, difficult task that the results were virtually perfect. [List of the soloists.] There were

sold-out halls, devout and enthusiastic audiences from the educated circles of the art-loving city, guests from all musically cultured countries.
It was a union of believers in art that revealed the solidarity of the like-
minded from nations that had been feuding for so long, as well as from
the fortunate, neutral ones. Already in this respect it was a highly significant event, promising much for the future development of normalized
international relations. For the first time the whole of Mahler's oeuvre
could be experienced live, and his artistic personality was revealed in its
unity. The whole event was made possible only through the laudable dedication and unique productive enthusiasm of all participants. All
performed their best, spurred on by the director who, in a consistent,
almost systematic way, carried out everything he regarded as essential
and absolutely imperative for the realization. [Discussion of the special
effort made by all the performers.] The effect of the cycle was one of
intensification, reaching its high point in the Ninth and its conclusion
in the Eighth. [. . .][132]

Figure 3. Mahler/Mengelberg Coin, 1920.

A Second Letter from Amsterdam

O S K A R   B I E

Dresdner Neueste Nachrichten
May 25, 1920

On Bie, see above.

* * *

When the great Mahler festival came to an end, we sat around a small table—writers and artists from all countries. We cordially discussed a memorandum that would combine an expression of gratitude for our enjoyment with our wish to repeat such an international musical assembly, which finally brought nations closer together, at least through art. *One* signed from *each* country—Germany, France, England, America, Italy, Russia, Belgium, Denmark, the Netherlands, etc. We shook hands and complained about the effects of the war, asking: Why couldn't politicians have sat down at a table like this, peacefully and reasonably, before it was too late? Later the American Cesar Saerchinger read the document before the full assembly and expressed the hope that *this peace treaty was better* than *the one of Versailles. Immense applause* proved his point.[133]

At this moment I had the feeling of something coming to an end that had engaged me for a long time. If I had to sum up my stay in Amsterdam, I would describe it as closure to what for years has been interrupted and stagnant within us. As I have said, I had difficulty separating the material pleasures from the spiritual ones. I took a trip on a steam ship far out into the Zuider See [Ijsselmeer] by invitation of the city of Amsterdam. I saw the distant horizon on the water and breathed deeply. In the afternoon I went out to Zandvoort and threw myself down into the sand at the shore of the shimmering North Sea for an hour, forever forgetting what now lies at its bottom.[134] I lived again as a European, and also as a material being. I compared this perfection, derived from an old culture, with the perfection of the music I had heard the evening before, which likewise rested upon the old discipline and practice exercised by the conductor over his musicians. In all this I felt complete closure—an aspiration toward the ultimate possibilities, a sense of advancing toward a bright, shining, glorious point that seemed to us to lie in the infinite distance and not in the enchantingly near finitude. We were intoxicated. Was this still the same bloodstained world? At some point we will all return to our homes, yet we will not forget this moment. When we speak about the war, we who were once enemies experience the same scornful twitch in face and hands. But when we think back to the moment of Amsterdam, our eyes light up with that glowing expression through which we understand and unite. [Description of the chamber music concerts.]

Now to turn to Mahler. Hearing all of Mahler's works in succession produces the image not of a coherent personality but rather of one who straddles two eras and struggles with himself—someone who experiences the tragedy of all great conflicts. The most profound mysticism vies with a popularity touching on the banal. Endlessly intricate polyphony is intertwined with yearning for the most eloquent melody. The most genuine emotion is mixed with a drive to the grandest means and unrestrained excess, as well as to hidden theatricality and masks. The maturest knowledge of form is deconstructed into an unending breath of cyclical series. Innovations in instrumentation—which produced a completely new orchestral language important especially for its use of the woodwinds—achieve the most profound spiritual expression, entering a contest with the human voice. A large part of Mahler's energy is depleted in this double engagement. These conflicts are closely juxtaposed up through the Fourth Symphony. The middle symphonies struggle with absolute music in a new way. The Eighth expresses the whole complex in a form that I do not consider the final solution. It is stronger in effect than in significance, and purer in its voices than in emotion. The Ninth is the most perfect solution of his absolute orchestral art—grand, strong, strange and of the most tender profundity. *Das Lied von der Erde* is the most successful of his song cycles—the genre that was for him perhaps the most risky. As I sat listening, there came before my eyes the image of modern humans who make their way between emotion and creation, knowledge and ability; as each movement of each symphony passed, I recognized and tested it as a stage on this path of suffering. If I wrote a book on Mahler, it would be an analysis of contemporary human suffering, movement by movement, voice by voice. I sat and heard *the suffering of time*, whose infinity is its finitude.

But even in Amsterdam this infinity gained closure.[135] Even here there was an ending. Here Mahler is seen as someone who completes, as the greatest and as the only future. Mengelberg's perfect execution is the bible of this salvation. The missionary celebrates himself with his mission. Grand speeches filled the hall at the end of the festival. Medals of Mahler and Mengelberg were placed on the wall. The president honored Mengelberg in the name of a grateful nation. A Mahler society will be founded with him as chairman. He rises, speaks, and expresses his thanks, always smiling. The audience breaks into a storm. The atmosphere dissolves in a cry of joy shouted out from so many nations as they finally experience the quiet hope of their hearts.[136]

NOTES

We are grateful to Reinhold Brinkmann and Christopher Gibbs for their generous help with the scholarly apparatus. Leon Botstein shared his extensive knowledge of the Viennese intellectual milieu. This project benefited from the research assistance of Christina Linklater, Yael Braunschweig, and Gabrielle Clark and the astute editorial hand of Andrew Lynn, which left its mark on every page, and Paul De Angelis. Many of these documents were drawn from the Eleonore Vondenhoff collection at the Musiksammlung, Österreichische Nationalbibliothek, Vienna; the Bibliothèque Gustav Mahler, Paris; and the Steininger collection at the Geheimes Staatsarchiv, Preussischer Kulturbesitz, Berlin. Thanks to the kind help of Suzanne Eggleston Lovejoy at the Yale Music Library, Christa Traunsteiner at the Austrian National Library, Timothy Day from the British Library, and Therese Muxeneder at the Arnold Schönberg Center, Vienna.

All ellipses, except those indicated by brackets or bracketed comments, are in the original documents. Some paragraph breaks have been added, and other brief paragraphs joined together. All endnotes are the editors'. Secondary sources beyond the *New Grove Dictionary of Music and Musicians*, Hugo Riemann's *Musik-Lexikon* (various editions), and other biographical dictionaries are listed within individual citations. A good English-language source on Viennese newspapers and critics is Sandra McColl, *Music Criticism in Vienna, 1896–1897: Critically Moving Forms* (Oxford, 1996).

1. Adolf Weissmann, "Die Musik der Weltstadt," *Die Musik* 10, no. 13 (April issue no. 1, 1911): 3; quoted in Eberhard Preussner, "Adolf Weissmann," *Die Musik* 21, no. 2 (June 1929): 660.

2. David Josef Bach, "Max Kalbeck zur Erinnerung," *Der Merker* 12, no. 10 (15 May 1921): 228.

3. Walter Schrenk, "Adolf Weissmann," *Die Musik* 16, no. 7 (April 1924): 480.

4. Richard Specht, "Mahlers Feinde," *Musikblätter des Anbruch* 3, no. 13/14 (September 1921): 279.

5. Ritter is a source of considerable fascination in Henry-Louis de La Grange's *Gustav Mahler*, vol. 3, *Vienna: Triumph and Disillusion (1904–1907)* (Oxford, 1999), pp. 509–21.

6. Ernst Decsey, "Andante funèbre für Richard Specht," *Die Musik* 24/2, no. 8 (May issue no. 2, 1932): 595.

7. Kurt Paupié, *Handbuch der österreichischen Pressegeschichte 1848–1959* (Vienna, 1960), 1:154–56.

8. Schoenberg's unpublished essay "Die kernige Elsa" (in response to her review of 8 May 1927) and his annotated copy of another review (5 June 1918) are located in the Arnold Schönberg Center.

9. Elsa Bienenfeld, "Guido Adler," *Die Musik* 18, no. 1 (November issue no. 2, 1925): 113–24.

10. This biographical overview draws from Henry-Louis de La Grange, *Gustav Mahler,* vol. 2, *Vienna: The Years of Challenge, 1897–1904* (Oxford, 1995), p. 686, n. 128.

11. Peter Altmann, "Zur Uraufführung der achten Symphonie," *Nachrichten zur Mahler-Forschung* 16 (1986): 3–5.

12. Peter Revers, "Gustav Mahler and Emil Gutmann," in *Mahler's Unknown Letters,* ed. Herta Blaukopf, trans. Richard Stokes (Boston, 1987), pp. 66–67.

13. Lee Rothfarb, "Energetics," in *Cambridge History of Music Theory*, ed. Thomas Christensen (Cambridge, Eng., 2002), pp. 928–55.

14. Gutmann in effect links Mahler's organicism to two well-known and respected aesthetics of nature, of Goethe (whose pantheism was deeply connected to nature), and Rodin, with his production of statues for the outdoors. In a source often cited in the early twentieth century, Goethe wrote: "In science we strive to be pantheists, in poetry polytheists, and in ethics monotheists." "Maximen und Reflexionen über Literatur und Ethik: Aus dem Nachlass," in *Goethes Werke: Weimarer Ausgabe,* part I, vol. 42/2 (Weimar, 1907), p. 211. The comparison with Rodin was fitting, since Mahler's father-in-law had commissioned a sculpture from Rodin, for which the composer sat twice in 1909; Rodin also took Mahler's death mask. The first reproduction of the death mask is in Hermann Danuser, *Gustav Mahler und seine Zeit* (Laaber, 1991), p. 351.

15. Emil Gutmann, "Gustav Mahler als Organisator," *Die Musik* 10, no. 18 (June issue no. 2, 1911, entitled *Gustav Mahler*): 364–68. This translation shares isolated phrases with the elegant but freer and unannotated translation in Revers, "Mahler and Gutmann," pp. 84–88.

16. Bahr misinterprets Goethe's statement as a Nietzschean loss of individuality through experiencing art. The original passage, in a letter of 6 August 1804 to Johann Christian von Manlich, seems to involve the individual's absorption in the act of viewing a painting. "An artist does not in fact create a painting such that it should be placed in a gallery; he paints it for an altar—for the wall of a hall or a room—and considers it an isolated but always closed whole. Nothing is more desirable than to see it in a quiet room, hanging alone. In large houses, however, an enormous space would be necessary. Thus it is entirely fitting that one brings together paintings that are excellent, since the best masters come close to the highest art, where individuality disappears and what is thoroughly right is produced. Such an arrangement prepares the amateur for a great pleasure and gives the connoisseur occasion for the most interesting comparisons." *Goethes Werke: Weimarer Ausgabe,* part IV, vol. 17 (Weimar, 1895), p. 183.

17. The lineage proposed is intriguing in light of Arthur Groos's examination of Wagner's *Tristan und Isolde* as a case of Harold Bloom's "anxiety of influence" with respect to Goethe's *Faust*. Arthur Groos, "Appropriation in Wagner's *Tristan* Libretto," *Reading Opera*, ed. Groos and Roger Parker (Princeton, 1988), pp. 26–33.

18. The original passages, from Wagner's "Über die Bestimmung der Oper" (1871), read: "To explain the nature of drama, we must look to the *dramatist,* not the poet; the dramatist stands no nearer to the poet proper than to the *actor* himself, from whose most heart of hearts he must issue if, as poet, he means to "hold up his mirror to life. . . . Whereas no poet of any artistic epoch can be likened to Beethoven, Shakespeare alone strikes us as comparable in the very fact that the latter, as poet, would forever remain a problem for us could we not detect in him before all else the poet-*actor*." *Richard Wagner's Prose Works,* ed. and trans. W. A. Ellis, vol. 5 (London, 1892–99), pp. 143, 148.

19. The quotation is from Nietzsche's "Richard Wagner in Bayreuth," *Unzeitgemässe Betrachtungen,* iv (1876); trans. R. J. Hollingdale as *Untimely Meditations,* ed. Daniel Breazeale, Cambridge Texts in the History of Philosophy (Cambridge, Eng., 1997), pp. 223–24.

20. Wagner addresses these themes in several publications, including *Oper und Drama* (1851) and "Über Schauspieler und Sänger" (1872), in Ellis, *Wagner's Prose Works,* ed. and trans. Ellis, vols. 2 and 5:157–228.

21. Kreisler was a character in E. T. A. Hoffmann's novels. Prince Alfred Montenuovo was the administrator at the Viennese Court to whom Mahler reported as director of the Court Opera.

22. Hermann Bahr, "Mahler als Direktor," *Musikblätter des Anbruch* 2, no. 7/8 (April 1920): 275–76.

23. Reviews of Mahler's arrangement of Beethoven's String Quartet in F minor op. 95 appeared in the *Neue Freie Presse,* 17 January 1899 (Hanslick) and *Deutsche Zeitung* (Helm). For summaries, see de La Grange, *Gustav Mahler,* vol. 2, *Years of Challenge,* pp. 136–38.

24. Max Marschalk, *Vossische Zeitung,* 19 January 1910.

25. Maximilian Muntz, *Deutsche Zeitung,* 12 November 1904, review of Mahler's First Symphony and Beethoven's *Emperor* Concerto.

26. Specht, "Mahlers Feinde": 282–83.

27. Max Graf, *Die Wiener Oper* (Vienna, 1955), p. 92; translation adapted from de La Grange, *Gustav Mahler,* vol. 3, *Triumph and Disillusion,* p. 698.

28. The "Forest Murmurs" (Waldweben) scene in Wagner's *Siegfried,* act II, scene ii, had iconic status as an invocation of undisturbed nature: tonally closed in G major, it was a shimmering plane of sound and pure figuration. "Waldweben," literally a weaving in the forest, forms a pun with Graf's description of Mahler's "free interweaving" of motifs.

29. Karl Grunsky, for example, wrote "That music is an expression of mental life is today admitted, defended, and demanded from nearly all sides, because we barely pay attention to Hanslick any longer," in his *Musikästhetik* (Leipzig, 1907), p. 22. Otto Neitzel, in the preface to his book interpreting Beethoven's symphonies "according to their emotional content," reported that Hanslick "could even say: 'The form of music is thus its content.'" Otto Neitzel, *Beethovens Symphonien nach ihrem Stimmungsgehalt erläutert* (Cologne, 1912), n.p.

30. Mahler, undated letter of February 1909 to Alfred Roller, in *Selected Letters of Mahler,* ed. Martner, p. 331.

31. Max Kalbeck, *Neues Wiener Tagblatt,* 16 January 1902, review of Mahler's Fourth Symphony; quoted in Sandra McColl, "Max Kalbeck and Gustav Mahler," *Nineteenth Century Music* 20, no. 2 (1996): 173–74.

32. This biographical introduction draws on Max Unger, "Zwei Jubilare: Theodor Helm und Max Kalbeck," *Neue Zeitschrift für Musik* 87, no. 1/2 (15 January 1920): 3.

33. Theodor Helm, *Beethovens Streichquartette: Versuch einer technischen Analyse dieser Werke im Zusammenhang mit ihrem geistigen Gehalt* (Leipzig, 1885), with subsequent editions in 1910 and 1921. He had previously written on Beethoven's last quartets in the first volume of the short-lived Leipzig journal *Tonhalle* (1868).

34. Karl Kraus, "Antworten des Herausgebers," *Die Fackel* 4, no. 123 (December 1902): 26–27. Margaret Notley, "Musical Culture in Vienna at the Turn of the Twentieth Century," in *Schoenberg, Berg, and Webern: A Companion to the Second Viennese School,* ed. Bryan R. Simms (Westport, 1999), p. 46.

35. Theodor Helm, *Fünfzig Jahre Wiener Musikleben, 1866–1916: Erinnerungen eines Musikkritikers,* ed. Max Schönherr (Vienna, 1977).

36. David Josef Bach, "Fünfundzwanzig Jahre Arbeiter-Sinfonie-Konzert," *Kunst und Volk: Mitteilungen des Vereines Sozialdemokratische Kunststelle* 4, no. 2 (October 1929): 42.

37. John H. Youell, "From the Memoirs of Doctor Julius Korngold," *Jahrbuch für Opernforschung* (1990): 88.

38. Herbert Gerigk and Theo Stengel, *Lexikon der Juden in der Musik* (Berlin, 1940); rpt. in Eva Weissweiler, *Ausgemerzt! Das Lexikon der Juden in der Musik und seine mörderischen Folgen* (Cologne, 1999).

39. Specht, "Mahlers Feinde": 284.

40. Paul Stefan, *Gustav Mahlers Erbe: Ein Beitrag zur neuesten Geschichte der deutschen Bühne und des Herrn Felix von Weingartner* (Munich, 1908), p. 23.

41. Ludwig Karpath, *Begegnung mit dem Genius* (Vienna, 1934), p. 138. Karpath, who was a friend of Mahler, likewise disagreed with Stefan's interpretation.

42. Robert Hirschfeld, *Wiener Abendpost*, 5 November 1909; review of Mahler's Third and Seventh Symphonies; from Karen Painter, "The Sensuality of Timbre: Responses to Mahler and Modernity at the *Fin de siècle,*" *Nineteenth-Century Music* 18, no. 3 (1995): 248, translation adapted.

43. With this line, "Now come forward, charming masqueraders!" Leporello welcomes Don Ottavio, Donna Anna, and Donna Elvira into Don Giovanni's ball.

44. Hermann Kipper, *Kölner Volkszeitung*, 19 October 1904. See also the summary of his review in La Grange, *Mahler,* vol. 3, *Triumph and Disillusion,* p. 30.

45. According to Batka, the discussion took place a year before he reported it in his review of the Fifth Symphony (*Bohemia*, 4 March 1905).

46. Batka, *Bohemia*, 4 March 1905, review of the Fifth Symphony.

47. Mahler's letter to Alma, 2 February 1904, in *Ein Glück ohne Ruh': Die Briefe Gustav Mahlers an Alma*, ed. Henry-Louis de La Grange and Günther Weiss (Berlin, 1995), p. 185.

48. The passage was quoted by the *Reichspost* (7 November 1911) when the symphony was next performed in Vienna. Ernst Otto Nodnagel, "Gustav Mahlers fünfte Symphonie in Cis-Moll: Technicalische Analyse," *Die Musik* 4, no. 4 (issue no. 2 of November 1904): 245.

49. Ernst Otto Nodnagel, "Offener Brief an Herrn Dr. Ludwig Schiedermair," *Allgemeine Musik-Zeitung* 29, no. 34/35 (22/29 August 1902): 570–72.

50. Beethoven was inevitably the reference point in discussions about the narrative capacity of absolute music. Nodnagel refers to the funeral marches in the "Eroica" Symphony and the Piano Sonata in A-flat op. 26.

51. Nodnagel had written an analysis of the symphony that was often cited by earlier reviewers: "Mahlers Fünfte. Technicalische Analyse," in *Die Musik* 4, no. 4 (issue no. 2, November 1904): 243–44; no. 5 (issue no. 1, December 1904): 314–23.

52. These observations about the effect of repeated hearings suggest one reason why the Adagietto could be heard as almost the only non-diegetic (background) music in Visconti's *Death in Venice* (1974), where it is heard some eight times throughout the film.

53. Theodor Mügge, the founder of the Berlin *National-Zeitung*; cited in Ernst Baasch, *Geschichte des Hamburgischen Zeitungswesens von den Anfängen bis 1914* (Hamburg, 1930), p. 42.

54. See Loewengard's unpublished letters, for example that of 19 December 1907, to Bekker in Paul Bekker Collection, housed at the music library of Yale University.

55. Kalbeck's translations include *Pique-Dame*; *Otello* and *Falstaff; Tosca;* Smetana's *Bartered Bride* and *The Secret*; Giordano Umberto's *Andrea Chénier*; and Ermanno Wolf-Ferrari's *Il segreto di Susanna* (premiered in 1909 in German).

56. Kalbeck also published three collections of his essays (1885–1896) and wrote biographies of the important eighteenth-century poet Johann Christian Günther (1879) —who, like Kalbeck, was from Silesia—and the great Viennese satirist and friend of Brahms,

Daniel Spitzer (1894). Together with Otto Erich Deutsch, Kalbeck later published an edition of Spitzer's *Wiener Spaziergänge* as well as his collected writings (1912).

57. Anton Würz, "Max Kalbeck. Eine Würdigung," *Zeitschrift für Musik* 111, no. 2 (February 1950): 95.

58. Bach, "Kalbeck," 228.

59. Unger, "Zwei Jubilare: Helm und Kalbeck": 3.

60. Handwritten copies of other unpublished letters to Kalbeck from the same period as those which appear in the standard letter collections are in the Bibliothèque Gustav Mahler, Paris. De La Grange, *Mahler*, vol. 3, *Triumph and Disillusion*, p. 238.

61. De La Grange, *Mahler*, vol. 2, *Years of Challenge*, p. 27.

62. Mahler, 22 June 1901 letter to Kalbeck, in *Selected Letters of Gustav Mahler*, ed. Knud Martner (New York, 1979), pp. 251–52, translation adapted.

63. Mahler, undated letter of January 1902 to Kalbeck, in *Selected Letters of Mahler*, ed. Martner, p. 262.

64. Max Graf, *Neues Wiener Journal*, 15 December 1905, review of Mahler's Fifth Symphony.

65. Mahler's undated letter of December 1907, to Kalbeck, in *Selected Letters of Mahler*, ed. Martner, p. 302. On Mahler's departure, see de La Grange, *Mahler*, vol. 3, *Triumph and Disillusion*, p. 789.

66. Although the score groups the five movements into three parts, Mahler's contemporaries (like Kalbeck here) took liberty in the terms for movements and the large-scale structure. One critic, for example, spoke of the "introduction" when discussing the first movement, and another referred to the symphony as having three "movements." See the review of the Berlin Philharmonic performance of 20 February 1905 under Arthur Nikisch in the *Norddeutsche Allgemeine Zeitung* [signed R.F.].

67. This description supports Gilbert Kaplan's observation that the *sforzando* marking at the end of the movement should *not* entail a general increase in dynamics, as has been common practice. See his "In One Note of Mahler, a World of Meaning," *New York Times*, 17 March 2002.

68. Paupié, *Österreichische Pressegeschichte*, 1:158.

69. The Viennese critic's reference to the the main avenue in Berlin, Unter den Linden, may be part of the common critique of Mahler as an urban, modern artist, exploiting techniques without natural invention, and therefore also an allusion to the tension between Vienna and Berlin as cultural centers.

70. The image of Mahler in armor (*eiserne Handschuhe*) may have been a reference to his representation as a knight in Klimt's *Beethoven Frieze* in the Viennese Secession building, which opened in 1902. Klimt presented a photograph of the knight as his contribution to Paul Stefan's volume of tributes, *Gustav Mahler; ein Bild seiner Persönlichkeit in Widmungen* (Munich, 1910). The knight could be taken as Mahler, a soldier in the fight against philistinism.

71. Hugo Leichtentritt, *Signale für die musikalische Welt* 69, no. 4 (25 January 1911): 135, review of the Berlin premiere of Mahler's Seventh Symphony.

72 According to Bruno Vondenhoff, Fried conducted both Nachtmusik movements. However Wilhelm Altmann twice reported that the fourth movement was programmed alone. See his reviews in *Die Musik* 9, no. 11 (March issue 1, 1910): 190–91, and *Die Musik* 10, no. 10 (Feb. issue 2, 1911): 248–49. Bruno Vondenhoff, *Gustav Mahler Dokumentation, Sammlung Elenore Vondenhoff: Materialen zu Leben und Werk* (Tutzing, 1978), p. 387.

73. Felix Adler, *Bohemia*, 1 July 1907; from the Arnold Schönberg Center, review of Schoenberg's First String Quartet op. 7.

74. Celadon, the lover of Astrée in Honoré d'Urfé's extended tale of shepherds and shepherdesses, *L'Astrée* (1627), was better known through Dryden's witty *Secret Love, or the Maiden Queen* (1667), and almost a century later, in Kleist's pastoral poem "Das Gespenst."

75. Carinthia (Kärnten) is a province near the southern border of Austria, west of Vienna. Adler probably placed "one-step" (*schieberischer*) in quotations to emphasize the double meaning of *Schieber* as a profiteer as well as a dance form.

76. Batka's 1899 collection perhaps inspired the title of the Berlioz collection *Musikalische Streifzüge: Studien, Vergötterungen, Ausfälle und Kritiken*, trans. Elly Elles (Leipzig, 1912). Berlioz's original French title was *À travers chants*, a pun on "À travers champs."

77. Batka edited a collection of "cheery" works for students, *Bunte Bühne: Fröhliche Tonkunst*, 2 vols. (Munich, 1902); Bach's keyboard works for Anna Magdalena Bach (1904); a volume of Mozart's poetry (1906); and an assortment of house music (1907).

78. *Deutsche Arbeit in Böhmen: Kulturbilder*, ed. Hermann Bachmann (Berlin, 1900; rpt. Munich, 1969).

79. Batka's writings on Bohemian topics include a more academic text of 1902, a historical book (Prague, 1906), and a more general book for Richard Strauss's popular Berlin series *Die Musik* (1906). With Paul Runge he also prepared an edition of the fourteenth-century composer Mülich von Prag (1905).

80. While still living in Prague, Batka wrote the libretti for Karel Weis's *Der polnische Jude* (with Victor Leon, 1901) and Anselm Goetzel's *Zierpuppen* (1905). After settling in Vienna, Batka produced libretti for K. Bastl's *Der Abmarsch* (1911), Weis's *Der Sturm auf die Mühle* (1911), and Theodor Veidl's *Ländlische Liebesorakel* (1913).

81. Most of Batka's articles were on opera: Friedrich Konrad Griepenkerl's reworking of Beethoven's incidental music for the *Ruins of Athens* (in the 1909 festschrift for Riemann), the Austrian impresario Angelo Neumann (1910), and "Wagner from a domestic perspective" (1914). The last two articles appeared in *Der Merker*. Batka's book on Wagner (1912) saw two subsequent editions (1919 and 1924); he also published a book on the traditional Italian opera aria (1912).

82. Batka prepared libretti for the Hungarian Gyula Major's *Mila* (with M. Wassermann, 1913), and the French/Swede Henri Marteau's *Meister Schwalbe* (1921). Three libretti were for Austrian colleagues, Wilhelm Kienzl's *Der Kuhreigen* (1911); Oskar Straus's *Die himmelblaue Zeit* (with P. Wertheimer, 1914); and Richard Stöhr's fantastical *Ilse*. He also wrote several libretti for two German colleagues: Eugen d'Albert's *Die verschenkte Frau* (with R. Lothar, 1912) and *Der Stier von Olivera* (1918); and Leo Blech's *Das war ich* (1902), *Alpenkönig und Menschenfeind* (1903), which Batka and the composer revised as *Rappelkopf* for the Berlin 1917 production, and *Versiegelt* (1908). He translated several libretti into German, including Dvořák's *Kate and the Devil* (published in Prague, 1908) and two operas by Ermanno Wolf-Ferrari which had their premieres in Germany: *Le Donne curiose* (1903) and *L'Amore medico* (1913).

83. See Mahler's undated letter to Batka, Hamburg 1896[?], in *Selected Letters of Mahler*, ed. Martner, p. 176.

84. Richard Bakta, "Das Jüdische bei Gustav Mahler," *Kunstwart* 23, no. 20 (July issue 2, 1910): 97–98; Moritz Goldstein, "Deutsch-jüdischer Parnaß," *Kunstwart* 25, no. 11 (March issue 1, 1912): 281–94. On Goldstein and the wider debate following his article, see Hans Puttnies and Gary Smith, *Benjaminiana* (Giessen, 1991), pp. 41–54.

85. Batka's comparison of Mahler's music to *plein air* painting is an apt one. His composing hut on the Wörthersee was so cramped as to serve merely as an interface to the surrounding natural world. Moreover, the intensity of expression and purity of color, characteristic of Monet, Pisarro, and Renoir in their *plein air* painting, formed a parallel, noted by Mahler's contemporaries, to the composer's fascination with timbre.

86. Bienenfeld probably alludes to *Hamlet*, "There are more things in heaven and earth, Horatio, / Than are dreamt of in your philosophy" (act I, scene 5).

87. Giovanni Segantini (1858–99) was the only Italian artist of his generation to enjoy a strong reputation in Germany as well as Austria; he had ties to Klimt in Vienna. Segantini's technique of divisionism and his careful distribution of light sources might be compared to Mahler's exploration of timbral colors.

88. Conversation from the 1900/01 concert season, in Natalie Bauer-Lechner, *Recollections of Gustav Mahler*, ed. Peter Franklin, trans. Dika Newlin (Cambridge, Eng., 1980), p. 166.

89. Youell, "From the Memoirs of Korngold," 92. See also Korngold's memoirs as gathered under the title *Die Korngolds in Wien: Der Musikkritiker und das Wunderkind, Aufzeichnungen von Julius Korngold* (Zurich, 1991).

90. Julius Korngold, *Neue Freie Presse*, 16 December 1930, review of Mahler's Seventh Symphony.

91. Predecessor to cinema, a cinematograph allowed a series of photographs of moving objects, taken in rapid succession and projected on a screen, to produce the illusion of a single, moving scene. The technique was often discussed in the period 1896–1902. Thereafter, metaphoric uses prevailed, such as Korngold's and "Handwriting was a cinematograph of the heart" (Oxford English Dictionary, 2d., s.v. cinematograph).

92. In the 1930 review this passage was revised, its cultural and political associations outmoded by this point. He carefully rewrote terms like an "immoderation" in expression as well as politically charged terms like "boundless individualization and democratization of voices."

93. The phrase in quotations, "in bestürzender Verve," could be a play on Mahler's notoriously detailed and expressive performance indications. As Hirschfeld once put it, "If absolutely no symphonic themes flow from a composer and yet he feels compelled to write symphonies, he must somehow avail himself. With Mahler, countless performance indications impart the unique features—which make the score swell into a thick novel." *Wiener Abendpost*, 10 January 1907, review of Mahler's Sixth Symphony. We have not found "in bestürzender Verve," in any of Mahler's symphony scores, at least not in the reliable *Gesamtausgabe* edition. "Verve" was included in the category "meager terms of praise" in Goethe's list of the "terms of judgment used by French critics." See his "Über Kunst und Alterthum" (1816–22), in *Goethes Werke: Weimarer Ausgabe*, part I, vol. 41, section 1 (Weimar, 1902), p. 124.

94. Heinrich Löwy, "Das Ende vom Lied. Eine musikalische Untersuchung," *Annalen der Naturphilosophie* 8 (25 March 1909): 153–74. The article is dated "Munich 1908."

95. The full passage in Shaw reads: "They are showing one another why [my music] ought not to have been written—hunting out my consecutive fifths and sevenths, and my false relations—looking for my first subject, my second subject, my working out, and the rest of the childishness that could be taught to a poodle. Don't they wish they may find them?" George Bernard Shaw, *Love among the Artists*, Collected Works of Bernard Shaw, novels, vol. 3 (New York, 1930), p. 143.

96. The citation is from a letter of 11 October 1857, which Brahms wrote Clara Schumann about Carl Debrois von Bruyck (1828–1902), a friend of Robert Schumann and critic for the Viennese *Deutsche Musikzeitung*. "The most stupid part of it is that this little fellow Debrois insists on regarding himself as the apex of the musical world. Who today can ever be in a position to say that anything has reached its limit when it can never have any limit at all!" *Letters of Clara Schumann and Johannes Brahms, 1853–1896*, ed. Berthold Litzmann (New York, 1971), 1:79.

97. Decsey, "Andante funèbre für Specht," 595.

98. Ibid.

99. Jacques Callot (1592/93–1635) and Francisco de Goya (1746–1828) were important in the history of caricature and the grotesque in the visual arts. Callot was also significant as one of the first great artists to work exclusively within the graphic arts. Goya's satirical brush drawings invoke folk sayings as universal themes more than as mere comedy. The program for the Hamburg premiere of the First Symphony alluded to E. T. A. Hoffmann's *Fantasiestücke in Callots Manier* (1814–15) in the subtitle, "A Funeral March in Callot's Manner." On Hoffmann's Kreisler, see n. 21.

100. Specht refers to the five works in Max Klinger's 1894 Brahms Fantasy cycle, which deploy etching, engraving, aquatint and mezzotint.

101. When Specht published his essay on Mahler's enemies, Eckart was a figure much discussed in the wake of the anti-Semitic journal he had founded, *Auf Gut Deutsch: Wochenschrift für Ordnung und Recht*, and the serial article, "Das Judentum in und ausser uns," he published in its inaugural volume in 1919: no. 2 (10 January): 28–31; no. 3 (17 January): 45–48; no. 4 (24 January): 61–64; (31 January): 79–80; no. 6 (7 February): 95–96, no. 7 (14 February): 109–12. The entire Specht quotation reads, "On account of a racial feeling that is alien to art, the Munich Rudolf Louis, just as clever as questionable, found no access to Mahler's music. . . . This Meister Eckhart of music, who rejected alien things as 'Jewish' . . . is not to be discussed here." Specht, "Mahlers Feinde": 287.

102. In 1929, Fritz Stege (later a fanatical Nazi, who had been musical advisor to the Deutschvölkische Freiheitsbewegung, a political organization that later fed into the Nazi Party) joined the staff of *Die Zeitschrift für Musik*. On the ideological orientation of the journal, see Erik Levi, *Music in the Third Reich* (New York, 1994), pp. 11–12.

103. Ferdinand Pfohl, "Mein Leipziger Lebensabschnitt: Wie ich Musikkritiker wurde," *Zeitschrift für Musik* 99, no. 11 (November 1932): 959–61, and "Leben und Schaffen," *Zeitschrift für Musik* 109, no. 10 (October 1942): 445–50.

104. Knud Martner, introduction to Ferdinand Pfohl, *Gustav Mahler: Eindrücke und Erinnerungen aus den Hamburger Jahren* (Hamburg, 1973), pp. 7–9.

105. "Hafiz" was a title of respect which referred to a Muslim who knew the Koran from memory.

106. Paul Bekker, *Norddeutsche Allgemeine Zeitung* (1905), cited from Otto Keller (Munich), "Gustav Mahler-Literatur," *Die Musik* 10, no. 18 (June issue no. 2, 1911): 371; "Meister des Taktstocks III. Gustav Mahler," *Allgemeine Musik-Zeitung* 32, no. 23 (9 June 1905): 412–15. Bekker's review of *Kindertotenlieder* appeared in *Allgemeine Musik-Zeitung* 34, no. 8 (22 February 1907): 143–44.

107. Bekker published another entirely different Mahler obituary, which was reprinted as "Mahler (1911)," in *Klang und Eros: Gesammelte Schriften*, vol. 2 (Stuttgart and Berlin, 1922), pp. 220–27. Two other obituaries by Bekker on Mahler appeared in *Musikpädagogische Blätter* 34, no. 11 (1 June 1911): 248–50—according to Arthur Seidl, "Gustav Mahler-Literatur," *Die Musik* 10, no. 21 (August issue no. 1, 1911): 155—and the Berlin *National-Zeitung*, cited from Vondenhoff, *Mahler Dokumentation*, p. 156.

108. Mahler would have been paraphrasing from Luke 9:47–49, "Then he said to them, 'Whoever welcomes this little child in my name welcomes me; and whoever welcomes me welcomes the one who sent me. For he who is least among you all—he is the greatest.'"

109. This passage could have been interpreted as an allusion to Wagner's famous anti-Semitic diatribe and, from only two years before his own Mahler obituary, Rudolf Louis's brutal anti-Semitic attack: "If Mahler's music would *speak* Jewish, it would perhaps simply be incomprehensible to me. But it is so horribly disgusting because it *jewifies* [jüdelt]. That is, it speaks musical German, if I may say, but with an accent, with a tone, and above all with

the *gestures* of the East, the all-too Eastern Jews." Rudolf Louis, *Die deutsche Musik der Gegenwart* (Munich and Leipzig, 1909), p. 181.

110. The quotation is from Goethe's *West-östlicher Divan:* "Denn ich bin ein Mensch gewesen / Und das heisst ein Kämpfer sein" (Buch des Paradieses, Einlass, 15–16). Goethe's irony is lost when quoted by Bekker as well as by Hugo Fleischer in an essay on the aesthetics and cultural ideology of the symphony, "Der symbolische Gehalt der symphonischen Formen," *Der Merker* 4, no. 15 (1 August 1913): 566. Paul Bekker, "Feuilleton, Gustav Mahler," *Dresdner Anzeiger*, 20 May 1911; from the Steininger Sammlung, Geheimes Staatsarchiv, Berlin.

111. Preussner, "Weissmann": 660.

112. Koszyk, *Deutsche Pressse*, 2:289–90.

113. Weissmann would, however, later be attacked as one of the "prominent early campaigners for musical bolshevism," in the catalogue of the Nazis' Degenerate Music exhibition. Hans Severus Ziegler, ed., *Entartete Musik: Eine Abrechnung*, 2d (Düsseldorf, 1939), pp. 14–16; cited in Pamela M. Potter, *Most German of the Arts: Musicology and Society from the Weimar Republic to the End of Hitler's Reich* (New Haven, 1998), p. 18.

114. Edward J. Dent, "Adolf Weissmann: 1873–1929," *Monthly Musical Record* 29, no. 102 (1 June 1929): 167.

115. Adolf Weissmann, "Rasse und Nation in der Musik," in *25 Jahre Neue Musik. Jahrbuch 1926 der Universal-Edition*, ed. Hans Heinsheimer and Paul Stefan (Vienna, 1926), p. 104.

116. De La Grange discusses a review by Zschorlich in the *Leipziger Tageblatt* but does not give a citation; he also quotes from Zschorlich's Mahler obituary, which is translated below. De La Grange, *Mahler*, vol. 3 *Triumph and Disillusion*, p. 352.

117. Paupié, *Österreichische Pressegeschichte*, 1:153–54.

118. See Paul Zschorlich, "Furtwängler und Hindemith. Eine Uraufführung im 9. Philharmonischen Konzert," *Deutsche Zeitung*, 13 March 1934, review of the *Mathis der Mahler* Symphony; and Zschorlich, "Der internationale Hindemith," *Deutsche Zeitung*, 17 March 1934; cited from Karen Painter, "Symphonic Ambitions, Operatic Redemption: *Mathis der Maler* and *Palestrina* in the Third Reich," *Musical Quarterly* 85, no. 1 (2001): 131.

119. Walter Abendroth, "Paul Zschorlich," *Zeitschrift für Musik* 103, no. 5 (May 1936): 590.

120. Adolf Weissmann, "Musik und Krieg," *Die Musik* 14, no. 3 (November 1914): 106. This passage was quoted in his obituary: Preussner, "Weissmann," 661.

121. The theme of peace is taken up in Oskar Bie's review, translated below, and in Olga Samaroff-Stokowski's *An American Musician's Story* (New York, 1939), ch. 9, "Peace Conference of Amsterdam: Holland Honors Mahler and Mengelberg," pp. 157–69. Samaroff was a piano professor at Juilliard and the first woman to write under her own name for a major American newspaper, the *New York Post* (1926-28); she helped Leopold Stokowski secure his position as conductor with the Cincinnati Symphony Orchestra in 1909 and later married him.

122. Johan Giskes, ed. *Mahler in Amsterdam; van Mengelberg tot Chailly* (Bussum 1995), p. 38.

123. Koszyk, *Deutsche Pressse*, 2: 298.

124. Bie mainly wrote for the art series Bard, Marquardt: Topics included drawings of the old masters (1904); the artistic treatment of walls (1904); ballet (1905); dance (1906); modern drawing (1906); modern art (1906); "modern music and Strauss" (1906, with subsequent editions under other titles); the piano, organ, and harmonium (1910); opera (1913); and Dutch drawing (1911). He also published an essay on modern dance

in the 1920 inaugural volume of the *Sang und Klang Almanach*, which Adolf Weissmann edited.

125. Mahler's letter of 3 April 1895 to Bie, in *Selected Letters of Mahler,* ed. Martner, p. 160.

126. Mahler, letter of 17 December 1895 to Max Marschalk. In the summer of 1896, Mahler wrote to Marschalk, asking why he had heard nothing from Bie. *Selected Letters of Mahler*, ed. Martner, pp. 173, 192.

127. Oskar Bie, *Die neue Rundschau* 31, no. 4 (April 1920): 483–85.

128. Edward R. Reilly, *Gustav Mahler and Guido Adler: Records of a Friendship* (Cambridge, 1982), pp. 18, 23.

129. Adler, *Neue Freie Presse*, 27 January 1906, "The Significance of the Academic Mozart Festival"; from Notley, "Vienna at the Turn of the Twentieth Century," p. 52, translation adapted.

130. Guido Adler, "Problems of Musical Culture in Our Time," *Neue Freie Presse*, 17 December 1906; from Leon Botstein, "Strauss and the Viennese Critics," in *Richard Strauss and His World*, ed. Bryan Gilliam (Princeton, 1992), p. 327.

131. Edward R. Reilly, *Gustav Mahler and Guido Adler: Records of a Friendship* (Cambridge, 1982).

132. Guido Adler, "Mahler-Fest in Amsterdam," *Zeitschrift für Musikwissenschaft* 2 (July 1920): 607–08.

133. Cesar Saerchinger (1889–1971) continued as a pacifist into World War II. His book *The Way Out of War* (1940) was followed by a compilation of translated interviews of Fritz Thyssen (*I Paid Hitler,* 1941), the sole pacifist in the Reichstag, but whose account would be discredited after 1945. Saerchinger translated Artur Schnabel's University of Manchester lecture, "Reflections on Music" (1933) and published a biography of the pianist (1957). He was also the translator of Alfred Einstein's *Greatness in Music* (1941).

134. The remains from the Battle of Jutland, resting on the seabed, must have been stupendous. It was history's largest naval battle until the Second World War. Together, the British and Germans lost 8,819 officers and men, thirteen destroyers, nine cruisers, and one battleship.

135. Here, as well as in the previous and the next sentences, Bie plays off the pun of perfection/completion: *Nichtvollendung, Vollendung, vollenden,* and *vollendet.*

136. Oskar Bie. "Ein zweiter Amsterdamer Brief," *Dresdner Neueste Nachrichten,* 25 May 1920.

INDEX AND CONTRIBUTORS

Index

Notes on the Contributors

Talia Pecker Berio teaches music history and philology at the University of Siena. Her research covers nineteenth- and early twentieth-century music with a focus on Schubert and Mahler. Her *Dire la musica: Saggi di ermeneutica musicale* (Siena, 2000) explores musical hermeneutics in relation to Jewish thought. Her forthcoming projects include the critical edition of Schubert's symphonic fragments (*Neue Schubert-Ausgabe*) and the edition of her husband Luciano Berio's writings.

Camilla Bork is a lecturer in the musicology department of Humboldt University Berlin. She is completing a book on Hindemith's early works and Frankfurt Expressionism. Her recent publications include "Death and Transfiguration: Isolde's *Liebestod* as a model for artistic closure," in *Zukunftsbilder: Richard Wagners Revolution und ihre Folgen in Kunst und Politik*, ed. Hermann Danuser and Herfried Münkler (Schliengen, forthcoming in 2002).

Leon Botstein is President and Leon Levy Professor in the Arts and Humanities at Bard College. He is the author of *Judentum und Modernität* (Vienna, 1991) and *Jefferson's Children: Education and the Promise of American Culture* (New York, 1997). He is also the editor of *The Compleat Brahms* (New York, 1999) and *The Musical Quarterly*, as well as music director of the American Symphony Orchestra. He has recorded works by, among others, Szymanowski, Hartmann, Bruch, Dohnányi, Bruckner, Richard Strauss, and Mendelssohn for Telarc, CRI, Koch, Arabesque, and New World Records.

Peter Franklin is Reader in Music at the University of Oxford, where he is a Fellow of St Catherine's College. His recent work includes a biography of Mahler (1997) and the Mahler entry for the *Revised New Grove Dictionary of Music and Musicians*. He also writes on early twenty-century opera and Hollywood film music.

Stephen E. Hefling, Professor of Music at Case Western Reserve University, is the author of *Gustav Mahler: Das Lied von der Erde* (Cambridge

Music Handbooks, 2000), and edited the autograph piano version of that work for the Mahler Kritische Gesamtausgabe (Vienna, 1989). He is also editor of *Mahler Studies* (Cambridge, 1997) and *Nineteenth-Century Chamber Music* (New York, 1998), and has contributed articles and chapters on Mahler to many books and journals. Also a specialist in baroque performance practice, Hefling has performed widely with early music ensembles in the northeastern US, and his book *Rhythmic Alteration in Seventeenth- and Eighteenth-Century Music* (New York, 1994) is widely regarded as a standard reference on that topic.

Zoë Lang, a graduate student at Harvard University, is writing a dissertation on the waltz in fin-de-siècle Vienna, including its compositional reception in the music of Schoenberg, Mahler, and Richard Strauss.

Charles S. Maier is Krupp Foundation Professor of European Studies at Harvard University. His most recent works include *Dissolution: The Crisis of Communism and the End of East Germany* (1997) and "City, Empire, and Imperial Aftermath: Contending Contexts for the Urban Vision," in *Shaping the Great City, Modern Architecture in Central Europe 1890–1937*, ed. Eve Blau and Monika Platzer (1999). He is currently writing a history of the rise and decline of territorial space as a principle of political organization.

Karen Painter, associate professor of music at Harvard University, specializes in nineteenth- and twentieth-century music in relation to aesthetics, ideology, and musical thought. She has recently published articles on configurations of works by Schoenberg, Mahler, and Richard Strauss (*Archiv für Musikwissenschaft*), and by Hindemith and Pfitzner (*Musical Quarterly*), and is completing a book entitled *Symphonic Aspirations: German Ideology and Musical Listening, 1900–45*, for Harvard University Press.

Thomas Peattie is completing his dissertation, *The Fin-de-siècle Metropolis: Time, Memory and the Music of Gustav Mahler* at Harvard University. His other research areas include Schoenberg, Debussy, and Ives.

Peter Revers is professor of music history at the University of Music and the Dramatic Arts in Graz and is the president of the Austrian Musicological Society. He is currently writing a book on Mahler's symphonies (Munich: Beck) and working on the critical edition of works by Jean Sibelius. His publications include *Gustav Mahler: Untersuchungen zu den späten Sinfonien* (Hamburg, 1985) and *Mahlers Lieder* (Munich, 2000).

Bettina Varwig, a German native, studied musicology at King's College London and bassoon performance at the Royal Academy of Music. She is completing her doctoral work in musicology at Harvard University. Her research interests include the music and culture of the German and French Baroque as well as reception history and criticism. Recent projects have focused on Bach's Orchestral Suites and the ideology of dance music in German bourgeois culture.